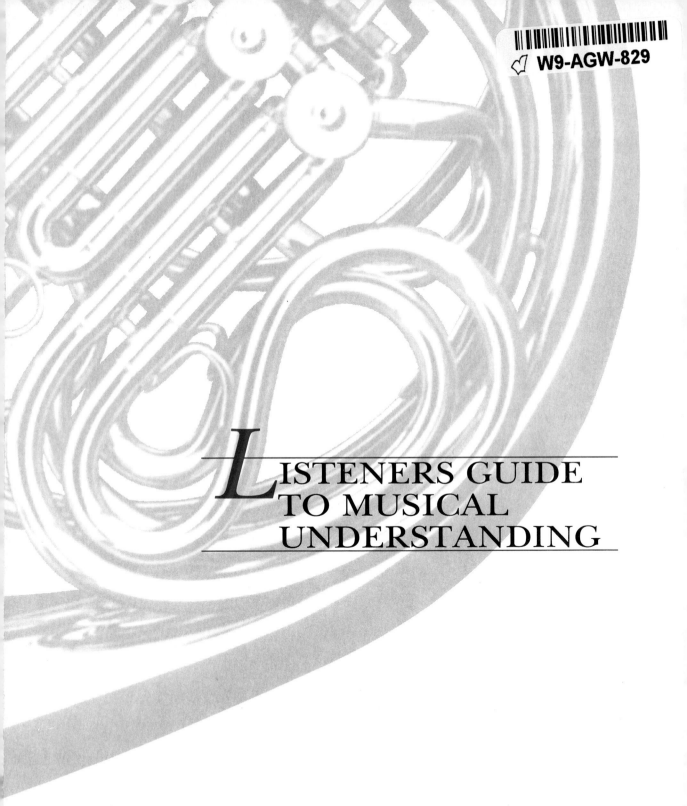

*L*ISTENERS GUIDE TO MUSICAL UNDERSTANDING

EIGHTH EDITION

*L*ISTENERS GUIDE TO MUSICAL UNDERSTANDING

LEON DALLIN

EMERITUS

CALIFORNIA STATE UNIVERSITY, LONG BEACH

WCB Brown & Benchmark
PUBLISHERS

Madison, Wisconsin • Dubuque, Iowa

Book Team

Developmental Editor *Deborah Daniel Reinbold*
Production Editor *Connie Balius-Haakinson*
Designer *Lu Ann Schrandt*
Art Editor *Kathleen Huinker-Timp*
Permissions Coordinator *Vicki Krug*
Visuals/Design Developmental Consultant *Marilyn A. Phelps*
Visuals/Design Freelance Specialist *Mary L. Christianson*
Publishing Services Specialist *Sherry Padden*
Advertising Manager *Nancy Milling*

Brown &
Benchmark

A Division of Wm. C. Brown Communications, Inc.

Executive Vice President/General Manager *Thomas E. Doran*
Vice President/Editor in Chief *Edgar J. Laube*
Vice President/Sales and Marketing *Eric Ziegler*
Director of Production *Vickie Putman Caughron*
Director of Custom and Electronic Publishing *Chris Rogers*

Wm. C. Brown Communications, Inc.

President and Chief Executive Officer *G. Franklin Lewis*
Corporate Senior Vice President and Chief Financial Officer *Robert Chesterman*
Corporate Senior Vice President and President of Manufacturing *Roger Meyer*

Cover image: Orazio Gentileschi, THE LUTE PLAYER, Alisa Mellon
Bruce Fund, © 1993 National Gallery of Art, Washington, 1610,
canvas, 1.435 × 1.288 (56½ × 50⅝ in.).
Background image: Conn French horn photo courtesy of United
Musical Instruments U.S.A. Inc.

Copyedited by Joan Torkildson

Consulting Editor Frederick W. Westphal

The credits section for this book begins on page 345 and is
considered an extension of the copyright page.

Copyright © 1959, 1968, 1972, 1977, 1982, 1986, 1990, 1994 by
Wm. C. Brown Communications, Inc. All rights reserved

A Times Mirror Company

Library of Congress Catalog Card Number: 93–71215

ISBN 0–697–12509–2

No part of this publication may be reproduced, stored in a retrieval
system, or transmitted, in any form or by any means, electronic,
mechanical, photocopying, recording, or otherwise, without the
prior written permission of the publisher.

Printed in the United States of America by Wm. C. Brown Communications, Inc.,
2460 Kerper Boulevard, Dubuque, IA 52001

10 9 8 7 6 5 4 3 2 1

TO LYNN

*Who did much
more than
"only stand and
wait"*

CONTENTS

COLORPLATES

ix

PREFACE

Listeners Guide to Musical Understanding is a textbook designed for use in introductory music courses for general college students. Its purpose is to increase students' enjoyment and knowledge of music and to cultivate the art of intelligent, perceptive listening. No prior training or experience in music is assumed or needed. Technical terminology is kept to a minimum while a working vocabulary of common and essential terms is developed. The various aspects of music are discussed objectively for the ultimate purpose of enhancing the subjective responses of individual listeners.

A distinctive feature of the text is that it guides the listening experiences of readers without reference to musical notation. A survey conducted on representative campuses revealed that a high percentage of students enrolled in music appreciation classes lacked a functional knowledge of notation and that even those who played an instrument could not readily comprehend abstract examples of printed music. The results of this survey were confirmed by a National Assessment of Educational Progress study which found in a random sampling of the U.S. population that fewer than 15 percent could read even the simplest line of music. In view of this evidence and the importance of developing music listening skills rather than music reading skills, notated music examples are not used in the body of the text. An appendix of music examples is provided for the convenience of teachers and those students and general readers who find it helpful, but the ability to read music is not essential for complete comprehension of the text or for listening pleasure.

The listening experiences suggested for the sequential units of study are planned to acquaint students by the end of the course with the principal materials, elements, mediums, forms, genres, periods, styles, and composers of music. In selecting the examples, four criteria were considered: musical value, appeal, suitability, and availability. The specified listening examples or equivalents can be found in most college and university collections of recordings. Except as noted, the composers and works are listed in the current Schwann *Opus* or *Spectrum* catalogs or are included in the *Listeners Guide* recordings, a set of four compact discs or cassettes, available from the publisher. The eighty-five recorded selections in the *Listeners Guide* collection are keyed to the text, and many of them appear more than once to encourage repeated hearings with attention focused on different aspects of the works. Throughout the text, dates are given for composers and works to place them in the proper time frame and historical context. When the exact date is unknown or disputed, an authoritative approximation is given.

The amount and kind of listening can be adapted to the available time, resources, and facilities. Listening can be done in or out of the classroom, individually or in groups, and from the *Listeners Guide* recordings, commercial recordings, or specially prepared tapes. More listening examples are listed than can ordinarily be heard in a typical course for the following reasons: (1) to suggest a wide range of listening experiences, (2) to provide alternate selections when all are not available, (3) to allow latitude for individual preferences, (4) to include adequate material for more comprehensive courses, and (5) to provide multiple examples for teachers who prefer to use excerpts. Performance times are given as an aid in planning classroom listening and outside assignments. Elapsed time is also used as an aid in the perception of musical form.

The organization of the book, starting with the materials and elements of music (Part One), makes it possible to begin the course with music that is immediately appealing to students and for them to focus their attention initially on aspects of music which they can perceive without difficulty. In Part Two the forms and genres of music are discussed, and descriptive outlines provided for the listening examples enable students to follow the various plans of musical organization without recourse to notation. The periods and styles of music are introduced chronologically in Part Three, but the preceding sections contain extensive background information pertaining to style. Chapter 5, Elements of Music, is particularly rich in references to style. The relative emphasis on each area of study and the order of presentation can be adjusted to individual requirements. Modern music, which sometimes receives short shrift, is abundantly represented throughout the book and is the subject of special chapters, as are folk and popular music, jazz, and the music of other cultures.

The information presented in the text, combined with the recommended listening, stimulates the formation of broad and discriminating musical tastes. With its emphasis on general principles that can be remembered and listening experiences that can be relished, the *Listeners Guide* launches readers on a program of enduring pleasure and personal enrichment.

An accompanying student manual, *Workbook for Listeners Guide to Musical Understanding*, is designed to supplement and complement the material presented in the textbook from the standpoint of both the student and the teacher.

Explanatory Notes

Listening Guides. Throughout the book listening guides, separated from the body of the text by shaded boxes, provide information regarding each listening example. The composer and the work are identified and dated. Complete identifying information, which is sometimes abbreviated in the guides to conform with the page design, is given in the index of composers, performers, and works. Detailed information concerning the listening guides follows.

PART 1

THE MATERIALS AND ELEMENTS OF MUSIC

- CHARACTERISTICS OF SOUND
- SOURCES OF MUSICAL SOUND
- MEDIUMS OF MUSIC
- ELEMENTS OF MUSIC
- TEXTURE IN MUSIC

2 CHARACTERISTICS OF SOUND

Objects that vibrate when energy is applied to them set the surrounding air in motion. The air transmits the vibrations, and human ears perceive as sound vibrating frequencies between approximately 20 and 20,000 Hz (cycles per second), the limits varying somewhat with individuals and circumstances.

Three conditions are necessary for sound: (1) a *source*, (2) a *medium of transmission*, and (3) a *receiver*. Any object capable of causing the air molecules to vibrate in the appropriate frequency range can serve as a source of sound. The medium of transmission between the sound source and the receiver is normally the air, but water and solids also transmit sound vibrations. The ear serves as the receiver, responding to the vibrations and sending impulses to the brain which are interpreted as sound. Microphones and recording devices are receivers only in the sense that they detect and store vibrations for subsequent reproduction.

The main characteristics of sound are *pitch, loudness, tone color, duration,* and *attack* and *decay.*

Pitch

The first characteristic of sound is *pitch.* Pitch is directly related to the vibrating frequency of the sound source: the faster the rate of vibration, the higher the pitch; the slower the rate of vibration, the lower the pitch.

To experience the perception of pitch differences, listen to several notes played at random on the piano, starting toward the left end of the keyboard and progressing toward the right end. Differences in pitch will be apparent to all who have normal hearing. The keys of the piano produce notes of graduated frequency and pitch from slow and low on the left to fast and high on the right.

When tuned to standard U.S. pitch (A = 440), the lowest note on the piano has a frequency of 27½ vibrations per second. The white key third from the right end of the piano keyboard produces a note with a frequency 128 times greater, 3,520 vibrations per second. The frequency of the highest note on the piano is over 4,000. Even so, the perceived pitches of the piano and all musical instruments fall in the middle and lower portions of the audible range. If the rate of vibration of the lowest note on the piano were halved, it would be below the audible range, but the frequency of the highest note could be doubled twice and still be heard by a young person. The ability to hear high pitches declines with age.

Now listen to the sounds produced alternately by two adjacent keys on the piano, from a white key to a black key or vice versa if they are next to each other. The *interval* (difference in pitch) between the tones of adjacent keys on a piano is a *semitone* (half step), the smallest pitch difference used consistently and systematically in the music of our culture. Nearly everyone can hear the difference and can tell whether the second tone was higher or lower in pitch than the first. Pitch perception this acute is essential for the complete comprehension of music. Actually, most people can distinguish between pitches with much less difference, especially in the middle register. Recognizing small differences in pitch is easiest in the middle register, somewhat more difficult in the high and low registers.

Faulty pitch discrimination can often be improved with a few minutes of drill. It is not that the ability to hear pitches actually improves so much as that one learns what to listen for and how to interpret what one hears. The results of such drill can be measured and general pitch acuity determined by playing pairs of notes, one after the other, in different registers of the piano and with varying distances between them. Students indicate whether the second note is higher or lower than the first. With a few minutes of practice, the percentage of individuals who cannot make a perfect score will be relatively small.

A distinguishing characteristic between tones and noises is the presence or absence of pitch. Musical tones are produced by regular vibrations at a constant rate and have a definite pitch. Noises are produced by erratic vibrations with variable frequencies and have no precise pitch, though they can be classified generally as high or low. Some sounds combine elements of tone and noise, and sounds acoustically classified as noise are utilized in certain musical styles.

Loudness

The second characteristic of sound is *loudness.* The perception of loudness is the subjective reaction to intensity. The intensity or energy of a sound is related to the area and the amount of displacement in the vibrating body producing it. Other factors being equal, a large vibrating surface produces a louder sound than a small one, and wide fluctuations produce louder sounds than narrow ones. The perceived sound, however, is also affected by the medium of transmission and the distance from the source. Since air is the normal medium of transmission, it may be regarded as constant. Loudness is roughly inversely proportional to the square of the distance from the source of the sound.

Musical instruments are designed to take advantage of the physical properties of sound in the matter of loudness. A string of the length and diameter used on a violin vibrating by itself would be barely audible. The body of the instrument increases the area of vibrating surface and amplifies the tone. A soundboard in pianos serves the same purpose. Also, the amount

Relative durations in music are shown by notes of various shapes (see following illustration). The same note symbols show duration by their shape and pitch by their location on the staff. Note values are expressed as whole notes and various fractions. Only relative durations are established by the note symbols, but a supplementary indication showing how many notes of a specified type occur in a minute (see Tempo, page 69) gives an absolute value to notated durations which is lacking otherwise.

| Whole | Half | Quarter | Eighth | Sixteenth | Thirty-second |
| note | note | note | note | note | note |

Though musical notation is logical, developing the ability to read and write it fluently is difficult. Fortunately, this ability or the lack of it has very little to do with the listening process for either musicians or nonmusicians. Often nonmusicians think they are missing something when they hear a concert or a recording because they cannot read music. They may suspect that the ability to read music makes sounds more meaningful. Such is not the case. If musicians get more out of hearing music than others, it is because they have learned to listen better, not because they read music. They do not sit in a concert visualizing the symbols for the music they are hearing, and even if they tried, it would reduce rather than enhance their pleasure. One who reads language but not music has only to compare one's reaction while watching a play or movie to recognize the validity of this observation.

You do not have to read music to appreciate the experience of listening to a work like the *Prelude* to Act III of Wagner's opera *Lohengrin*. Its exhilarating rhythms, energetic melodies, and colorful harmonies capture the attention and sustain the interest of listeners by their sheer energy and elegance. The sound spectrum encompasses nearly the full pitch range of the orchestral instruments from low to high and the dynamic range from soft to loud. The instruments exhibit their characteristic tone colors and a wide variety of durations and articulations. All of this diversity of sound is heard within the brief duration of the piece (shown in minutes:seconds).

WAGNER: *Lohengrin, opera (1850)*
(1813–1883)   *Act III. Prelude*   2:36

2/17*

The *Prelude* preceding the third act of *Lohengrin* establishes the festive mood of the wedding scene on stage when the curtain rises. The music at the beginning of the act is the universally recognized *Wedding March* that accompanies the bridal procession in the opera and the entrance of the bride in wedding ceremonies to this day.

For a more extended introduction to the luxurious sounds and dynamics of the orchestra, with descriptive comments that can be followed as the music is heard, see Ravel's *Daphnis and Chloé* (page 264).

SUPPLEMENTARY MATERIAL

■ *Musical Notes,* sound film, 12:00, produced by United World Films, distributed by Universal Educational and Visual Arts. From *The Light and Sound Series.*

Demonstrates frequency, amplitude, pitch, and quality of tones using string, wind, and percussion instruments. Uses a sonometer to illustrate the laws of strings and a microphone and oscillograph to show the quality of tones. Explains overtones.

■ *The Science of Musical Sounds,* color film, 11:00, produced and distributed by Paramount Communications.

Explores the basic principles of sound production using three types of musical instruments: harp, flute, and xylophone.

■ *The Science of Sound,* two 12-inch LPs, Smithsonian Folkways Science Series 6007, abridged version 6136. Distributed by Rounder Records.

Recordings produced by the Bell Telephone Laboratories describing and demonstrating the phenomena of sound, including how we hear, frequency, pitch, intensity, loudness, fundamentals and overtones, and quality.

*The symbols in the margin denote a musical selection included in the set of custom recordings on compact discs and cassettes available to supplement this book. The numbers indicate the location of the listening examples in the set: CD-cassette/selection.

3 SOURCES OF MUSICAL SOUND

The first source of musical sound was the human body. It possessed an ideal sound source in the vocal cords, and the body could also produce sounds by stamping, clapping, and slapping. In prehistoric times these innate sources were augmented by external devices, and the development of instruments began.

Instruments expand the dimensions of sound. They can produce sounds that are louder and both higher and lower than those possible with the body unassisted. They add to the available tone colors and make possible the playing of combined pitches by a single performer. Some instruments contribute agility and others sustaining power to the sound resources.

The sounds of music are produced by the body and voice; by striking, plucking, blowing, and bowing an assortment of instruments; and by electronic devices. Keyboard instruments couple one of these basic sound-producing processes with a keyboard mechanism. The functions of instruments are to provide a responsive source of sound, a means of amplifying that sound, and ways of controlling its pitch, duration, and loudness. Modern instruments in the hands of adroit performers attain these objectives to a high degree, but for warmth, intimacy, and immediacy of appeal the human voice remains supreme. The sound sources of concert music are described and pictured in the following pages, and the suggested listening provides an introduction to the great music created for each voice and instrument.

Voices

Voices are classified according to sex, range, and to some extent quality. The basic classifications from high to low are: *soprano, alto, tenor,* and *bass.* Soprano and alto designate, respectively, high and low female and unchanged male voices. Tenor and bass designate high and low changed male voices. The range of changed male voices is about an octave lower than that of the corresponding female voices. The span of pitches from the highest note of a soprano to the lowest note of a bass is almost four octaves (compared with a little over seven octaves for a piano), but the compass of any one singer is considerably less.

The terms *soprano, alto, tenor,* and *bass* are applied not only to voices and singers but also to the parts they sing in ensembles and to corresponding parts in instrumental music.

The most natural range for a woman's voice lies between that of soprano and alto. This intermediate voice is called *mezzo-soprano.* The parallel male voice with a range between that of tenor and bass is known as *baritone.* Mezzo-soprano and baritone voices, together with the four previously named, constitute the six voice types. Further distinctions are made, primarily in operatic music, on the basis of style and quality.

Special types of soprano voices are identified by the terms *coloratura, lyric,* and *dramatic.* Coloratura sopranos have unusually high voices and specialize in performing music characterized by florid ornamentation and rapid passages requiring great vocal agility. Lyric sopranos cultivate a light vocal quality and a melodious, flowing style rather than extremes of range or power. Some voices, such as the one heard in the following example, possess both the agility of a coloratura soprano and the quality of a lyric soprano.

WEBERN: *Three Songs, op. 18 (1925)*	3:25*	3/9–11
(1883–1945) 1. *Schatzerl klein (Sweetheart, Dear)*	:59*	
2. *Erlösung (Redemption)*	1:05*	
3. *Ave, Regina (Hail, Queen)*	1:21*	

The soprano voice heard in the recording of these songs is one of those combining coloratura agility with lyric quality. The capabilities of the voice are exploited in a thoroughly contemporary manner. Translation page 201.

*The duration (minutes:seconds) of a complete work and/or its separate parts.

Dramatic soprano is the designation for sopranos with powerful voices and a flair for acting. Operatic roles portraying intense emotions are assigned to dramatic sopranos.

PUCCINI: *Tosca, opera (1900)*		3/4
(1858–1924) Act II. Vissi d'arte	3:08	

Tosca, in this dramatic aria, sings of her life unselfishly devoted to art and love. Translation page 172.

Mezzo-soprano voices lack both the brilliance of the higher soprano voices and the richness of the lower alto voices. Since more women's voices fall in this category than any other, supreme vocal quality and musicianship are essential for mezzo-sopranos who make a career of singing. Many secondary roles in operas are sung by mezzo-sopranos. *Carmen* is one of the few operas in which the leading role is assigned to a mezzo-soprano.

GEORGES BIZET: *Carmen, opera (1875)*		2/19
(1838–1875) Act I. Habanera	5:37	

Carmen, in the mezzo-soprano title role, sings this taunting *Habanera* as she begins her flirtation with Don José, a soldier.

Voice classifications beyond the basic types are determined more by the particular selection being sung than by the voice. The literatures are not mutually exclusive, and the repertoire of most singers includes songs of various types. Singers for obvious reasons choose numbers that show their voices to advantage, but many are equally at home in two or more styles.

The terms *alto* and *contralto* are used interchangeably in referring to voices, though contralto sometimes seems to carry the connotation of an exceptionally deep alto voice. The distinction between the two terms is more one of usage than of meaning. Common practice is to refer to the singers as *contraltos* and to label the music they sing *alto*. The music for alto voices exploits the low tones of the female voice. The quality, typically, is rich, resonant, dark, and "throaty," but mezzo-sopranos often sing alto parts.

HANDEL: *Messiah, oratorio (1741)*   3:35
(1685–1759)   *49. Then shall be brought to pass*
    50. O death, where is thy sting
    51. But thanks be to God

Number 49 is a passage in declamatory style for alto voice with a simple instrumental accompaniment. Number 50, a duet for alto and tenor voices, provides an opportunity to compare the qualities of a low female and high male voice singing alternately and together. All four basic voice types are represented in the choral singing of number 51.

Tenor voices are sometimes characterized, particularly in operatic roles, as *robusto* (robust) or *heroic*. Robusto is the type of tenor voice with tremendous power in the upper register featured in Italian opera. This is the type of voice to which many young tenors aspire. The tenor roles in certain German operas, more specifically *music dramas* (see page 169), are associated with the heroic type. Heroic tenors may begin their careers as high baritones who, through training and practice, add to their natural range the high tones necessary to sing tenor roles. The difference between robusto and heroic tenors is more in the style of the music they sing than in the quality of their voices, so one example will serve to illustrate both.

GIUSEPPE VERDI: *Rigoletto, opera (1851)*
(1813–1901)   *Act IV. La donna è mobile*   2:12

In the rollicking aria *La donna è mobile* (*How fickle women are*), the Duke sings of women's fickleness in a typical tenor robusto style. Translation page 171.

Lyric tenors are the counterpart of lyric sopranos. Their voices possess the same qualities, and they sing the same types of music, ofttimes the same songs. *If with all your hearts* illustrates lyric tenor quality and style.

MENDELSSOHN: *Elijah,* op. 70, oratorio (1846)
(1809–1847)   *4. If with all your hearts*   2:44

This aria in the oratorio is sung by a tenor in the role of Obadiah, an Old Testament prophet.

    Baritones, like mezzo-sopranos, are in competition with the most prevalent voice type of their sex. They cannot hope to impress audiences with extremes of range or feats of brilliance. They compensate with solid production and skillful interpretation. Baritones often excel in singing art songs like Schubert's *Who Is Sylvia.*

SCHUBERT: *Who Is Sylvia* (1826)   2:40
(1797–1828)

The voice heard in this particular recording is that of a baritone, but this song at different pitch levels is sung by other types of voices. Poem page 194; melody and words of the first stanza in German and English page 337.

    Bass is the general term for all low male voices. Subdivisions, as with other voices, are predicated more upon the role or selection being sung than upon the characteristics of the voice. A bass singer especially proud of his low notes may advertise himself as a *basso profundo.* One who claims a range encompassing that of bass and baritone combined, or who lacks extremes of either, may adopt the title of *bass-baritone.* A bass specializing in a lyric style will be known as a *basso cantante,* and one associated with comic roles will be known as a *basso buffo.*

MOZART: *The Magic Flute, opera* (1791)
(1756–1791)   *Act II. Within these hallowed portals*   4:14

The title of this aria in the original German is *In diesen heiligen Hallen.* In it the High Priest Sarastro, a bass, consoles the despairing Pamina and assures her that Prince Tamino will soon be free to marry her. Translation page 169.

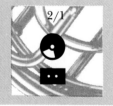

    Specific recordings of the various voice types were cited in the foregoing illustrations to assure their validity. This precaution was necessary, because a common practice is to publish songs with piano accompaniments in high, medium, and low versions. This practice, for better or worse, fosters the interchange of song literature between voice types and even between male and female singers.

    All voice types have the unique ability to combine music and language. Though lacking this ability, traditional instruments have their own special attributes. The characteristics of these instruments, and the new electronic instruments, are described and illustrated in the following pages. The usual classifications of the orchestral instruments are *string, woodwind, brass,* and *percussion,* but more precise classifications are possible on the basis of the way the tones are produced on the instruments.

Instruments Played by Bowing

One method of producing a tone is to draw coarse hair dusted with rosin across a taut string. The hair is fastened at each end to a stick originally curved like an archer's bow but now bent in the opposite direction. The name, however, is retained. The hair is obtained from horses' manes and tails, and most of it comes from Russia. The sticks are made of brazilwood, and the best comes from the state of Pernambuco in Brazil. The venerable bow has gone the way of many modern products, and synthetics are sometimes substituted now for both the hair and the wood. Fittings attached to the stick hold the hair (or synthetic) straight and smooth and make the tension adjustable. The act of drawing the bow over the strings is *bowing,* and instruments played by bowing are *string instruments.*

Modern bowed instruments are the product of a long period of evolution which culminated with the perfection of the violin family around 1600. They all have four strings with one end tied firmly to a tailpiece and the other wrapped around a peg that is turned to adjust the tuning. Near the fixed end the strings pass over a bridge which transmits the vibration of the strings to the body of the instrument. The body serves as a resonating chamber which amplifies the sound of the vibrating strings to useful levels. Its distinctive shape resulted partially from experiments leading to the perfection of its resonating characteristics, but the indentation at the middle of each side was a practical consideration permitting the bow to function on the outside strings. Protruding from the body of the instrument is a narrow neck which allows the left-hand fingers of the player easy access to the strings. Length, tension, and diameter determine the pitch of the open strings. Other pitches are made by depressing the strings with the fingers against a fingerboard on the upper side of the neck. Variations in loudness, tone quality, and style are made by applying the bow to the strings in different ways. Slight variations in tone quality also can be made by a motion of the hand stopping the strings known as *vibrato.* Vibrato affects the pitch slightly but not audibly. It appears as a shaking motion of the hand. Another tone modification is obtained by inhibiting the vibration of the bridge with a small device of wood, metal, plastic, or rubber called a *mute.*

The four bowed string instruments from the smallest and highest pitched to the largest and lowest pitched are: *violin, viola, cello* (also called *violoncello*), and *bass* (also called *string bass, contrabass,* and *double bass*). The strings are the most versatile instruments. Together they have a pitch range almost as wide as that of the piano. Equally at home in rapid pyrotechnics and in slow, sustained melodies, they are capable of great expressiveness and brittle wit. Small wonder that string instruments are both the prima donnas and the workhorses of every instrumental ensemble that includes them.

FIGURE 3.1

Violin and viola

The violin is the most brilliant and agile of the string family. This is partially because its relatively short, thin strings respond instantaneously to the slightest pressure of the bow, and partially because its small size allows a very efficient technique of stopping the strings with the fingers of the left hand. The instrument is held in a horizontal position under the chin, and the bow is drawn at right angles to the string by the right hand and arm. Violins are the sopranos of the string section and more often than not play the melody, but they are just as effective in a variety of supporting roles.

The suggested listening examples give an impression of the violin's versatility as an unaccompanied solo instrument. A substantial body of music featuring the violin was already in existence when Bach composed this partita, a group of pieces in various dance styles.

J. S. BACH: *Partita no. 3 in E for Violin* (1722)
(1685–1750)   *3. Gavotte en Rondeau*   3:05

In this example only the middle and lower registers of the violin are heard. While the writing is thoroughly idiomatic for the instrument, the work was not conceived as a display piece. Theme page 332.

Paganini was renowned as a virtuoso performer (that is, one who excels in technical ability) on the violin. He was one of a long line of virtuoso performers who were also composers. As composers, they tended to write pieces for their own instruments that displayed their technical skills and dazzled audiences with feats of extraordinary difficulty.

PAGANINI: *Caprices, op. 1*
(1782–1840)   *24. Theme and variations*   4:43

Paganini was the greatest violinist of his age. His *24 Caprices* for unaccompanied violin exploit the full range of the violin and every facet of violin technique, including some features he originated. Publication of most of his compositions was withheld during his lifetime to preserve the secrets of his musical and technical innovations. Theme page 338.

The viola is the alto member of the string family. Violas are slightly larger than violins, but not enough to be immediately apparent to the casual observer except by comparison. They are played in the same manner as violins. Their range is lower, more so than the difference in size would indicate. The ideal ratio of string length to pitch is compromised somewhat to keep the instrument within practical dimensions for under-the-chin playing. Heavier strings less tightly strung compensate for the reduced length in producing the desired pitch. These adjustments contribute to the distinctive tone quality of the viola which tends to be more somber than the violin and a bit nasal. Listening is suggested which provides direct comparison with the violin, with which the viola is most easily confused.

MOZART: *Duo no. 2 in B-flat, K. 424 (1783)*
(1756–1791)   *3. Andante con variazioni*   7:45

This duo for violin and viola provides an ideal means for comparing the tone quality of the two instruments, especially when a theme stated by one instrument is imitated immediately by the other.

Martinu's *Three Madrigals* are examples of twentieth-century music for violin and viola.

MARTINU: *Three Madrigals (1947)*
(1890–1959)   *1. Poco allegro*   3:50

This madrigal in a brilliant contemporary style provides additional experience in distinguishing the quality of the viola from that of the violin.

The cello has the same basic shape as the violin and the viola, but it is much larger. It is held between the player's knees and is supported by an end pin resting on the floor. This playing position, which is upside down in comparison with the violin and viola, and the cello's greater size necessitate different fingering and bowing techniques. The highest open string on the cello is tuned just one step higher than the lowest open string on the violin, but a cellist can play many notes in the violin range. Violins and cellos have essentially the same ratio of size to pitch, so a cello in its high register can be mistaken for a violin. The low register is rich, sonorous, and distinctive. The cello is the tenor of the string family, but in ensembles two

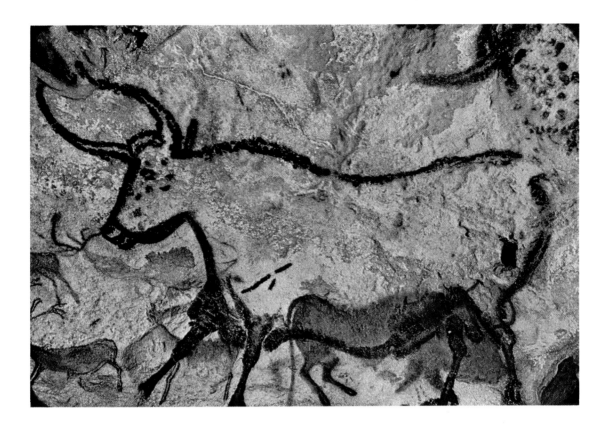

COLORPLATE 1

Lascaux Cave, France:

Rock paintings of reindeer, bulls, horses, and bison (ca. 30,000 B.C.)

These rock paintings were drawn by Cro-Magnons who, at about the same time and place, carved the earliest known musical instrument, a bone flute (see page 217).

Courtesy of the French Government Tourist Office.

COLORPLATE 2
Chartres Cathedral:
Death of the Virgin (ca. 1200)

Stained glass windows, of which this is a magnificent example, were an intrinsic feature of the Gothic cathedrals built in France during the time of the troubadours and trouvères (see pages 224–25). This photographic reproduction illustrates the highly developed state of stained glass art at an early date.

Art Resource, New York.

COLORPLATE 3

Giotto:
Lamentation (1305–1306)

Giotto (1267–1337), acknowledged as the "father of Western painting," is known for his innovative depictions of space, movement, and emotions and for creating three-dimensional illusions. The lifetimes of Giotto and the innovative composer Machaut (see page 225) overlapped thirty-seven years.

Scala/Art Resource, New York.

COLORPLATE 4

Sandro Botticelli:
Birth of Venus (1485)

Botticelli (1440–1510) was a slightly older contemporary of Josquin des Prez (see page 226). Graceful, flowing lines are equally characteristic of Botticelli's paintings and Josquin's music. The *Birth of Venus*, one of Botticelli's best-known works, was painted in Florence for his patron Lorenzo de' Medici.

Scala/Art Resource, New York.

FIGURE 3.2

Cello and bass

parts are often taken by violins, and the cellos are moved down to the bass. The cello is also effective as a solo instrument. In the next example the cello is unaccompanied.

J. S. BACH: *Suite no. 4 in E-flat for Cello,* *(1720)*
(1685–1750)   *2. Allemande*   2:55

The middle and low registers of the unaccompanied cello are featured in this *Allemande,* a dance of German origin included in suites of this period.

The cello is equally effective as a solo instrument with orchestral accompaniment, as in the Haydn concerto.

JOSEPH HAYDN: *Concerto in D for Cello* *(1783)*
(1732–1809)   *2. Adagio*   5:30
                         3. Rondo: Allegro   5:00

These two movements of the concerto, in contrasting tempos and styles, demonstrate the extreme registers of the cello and some of the intricate figurations playable on string instruments. The solo cello is easily distinguished from the instruments of the orchestra.

The double bass, string bass, contrabass, or simply the bass is the largest of the string family. It is so large that the player stands or perches on a high stool beside it, and the full weight of the instrument is borne by an end pin resting on the floor. The lowest bass string is as heavy as a small rope, and its pitch is almost as low as the lowest note on a piano. The other strings are only slightly smaller, and considerable energy must be imparted by the bow to set them in motion. Strong fingers are essential to stop them for the different pitches. Notes higher than the lowest violin pitch are possible but rare on the bass. The normal bass range overlaps the lower cello range and reaches into that of the viola. The tone of a single bass tends to be fuzzy and lacking in focus. This effect is reduced with a group of basses, but even so they seldom are used in a solo capacity or unsupported by other instruments.

SAINT-SAËNS: *Carnival of the Animals* (1886)
(1835–1921)   *5. The Elephant*   1:35

This piece is one of the very few in which the orchestral string basses play the principal melody unassisted.

Instruments Played by Blowing

A number of instruments with quite different shapes, sounds, and mechanisms are played by blowing. Instruments played by blowing are *wind instruments,* and their sound is produced by a vibrating column of air. At one time wind instruments could be divided conveniently on the basis of the material from which they were made—wood and brass. The terms *woodwind* and *brass,* derived from this division, are still used to classify instruments, though metal is now substituted for wood in the manufacture of some "woodwind" instruments.

The sound of all wind instruments stems from a vibrating column of air, but the means of initiating the vibration varies. In playing brass instruments, the lips, activated by the breath, become vibrating membranes, and in contact with mouthpieces of assorted sizes and shapes they energize the air inside the instruments. The lips, breath, and mouth function rather differently in producing sound in woodwind instruments. A stream of air issuing from the lips strikes the edge of a hole in flutes and piccolos and produces the sound in the same way sound is produced by blowing over the top of a small bottle. With clarinets and saxophones a thin, finely shaped piece of cane called a *reed* is the primary source of vibration. The reed is firmly attached to the mouthpiece at one end. The other, parallel with the tip of the mouthpiece, is inserted between the lips. Air passing between the reed and the mouthpiece causes the reed to vibrate. The reeds of oboes, English horns, and bassoons consist of two pieces of cane bound together as double reeds with just enough space between them at the center for the passage of air. The free end of the double reed is inserted between the lips, and both halves vibrate when air is forced between them.

A distinction also can be made between woodwinds and brasses on the basis of their mechanisms. The woodwinds have several holes located along the instrument which are opened and closed by the fingers or by keys and pads activated by the fingers. The pattern of open and closed holes in conjunction with the manner of blowing determines the pitch. There are alternate fingerings for some notes, but most patterns produce only one pitch.

The mechanism of the brass instruments is most clearly illustrated by the trombone. The trombone has a slide that can be extended or shortened to change the length of the tubing through which the air passes. The principle is the same for the other brass instruments, but changes in the tube length are implemented by valves. Each valve is connected to a different length of tubing through which the air passes when the valve is depressed. Otherwise this tubing is bypassed. The air takes the longest route through the horn when the valves are all down and the shortest way when they are all up. Various combinations of three valves suffice for all the pitches on the instrument. The fourth valve with which some brass instruments are equipped serves either to improve the intonation or to change the key of the instrument. Several pitches are obtained with each valve combination by altering the manner of blowing and the formation of the lips. *Embouchure* is the term used to describe the formation of the lips and the placement of the tongue in relation to the mouthpiece of wind instruments.

The tone of brass instruments, like that of strings (but not woodwinds) can be modified by mutes. Brass instrument mutes made of various materials and in assorted shapes and sizes are inserted in the bell, that is, in the flared open end of the instrument. All have the effect of reducing and muffling the tone, the exact quality depending upon the construction and material. French horns are usually muted or *stopped* with the hand rather than with a mechanical device. Unlike the other brass instruments, the shape of French horns is such that the player's right hand can be inserted in the bell. Stopped notes on the horn sound delicate and far away when they are soft, brassy when they are loud and accented.

In table 3.1, the instruments listed in the first column are most common and widely used. Those in the second column are essentially a larger or smaller version of a basic instrument on the same line in the first column. Instruments in the third column are either further modifications of basic instruments or special purpose instruments used mostly in bands and/or popular music.

Instruments on the same line in table 3.1 generally are constructed and their music written in a manner which enables a player to transfer technique from one to another with minimal difficulty. For example, a flute player with a modest amount of practice can play a piccolo or an alto flute. Likewise, a person who plays any one of the clarinets can readily adapt the technique to the others. The same relationship exists among all the saxophones, between oboe and English horn, and so on.

Woodwind Instruments

The flute is the soprano of the woodwind family. It is held horizontally extending to the player's right in a position that permits blowing over an opening near the left end of the instrument. Ancestors of the flute were made of wood, but now flutes are made of silver alloy with an occasional

TABLE 3.1 *W*IND INSTRUMENTS

	Basic orchestra	Large orchestra	Band and/or popular
Woodwind			
Aperture	Flute	Piccolo	Alto flute
Single reed	Clarinet	Bass clarinet	E-flat clarinet
			Alto clarinet
			Contrabass clarinet
			Saxophones
			Alto
			Tenor
			Baritone
Double reed	Oboe	English horn	
	Bassoon	Contrabassoon	
Brass			
Valve	Trumpet		Cornet
			Fluegel horn
	French horn		
	Tuba		Sousaphone
			Baritone
			(Euphonium)
Slide	Trombone	Bass trombone	

specimen of gold or platinum. The flute is very agile and often serves to spin a delicate filigree in the orchestral fabric. The tone is breathy and sensuous in the lower register, clear and bright in the upper register.

DEBUSSY: *Syrinx (1912)*   2:35
(1862–1918)

Syrinx is another name for panpipes, an instrument presumably invented by Pan, Greek god of woods and shepherds. This miniature for flute alone reveals the characteristic beauty of the flute tone.

The flute is capable of producing a wide range of pitches, dynamics, and nuances, many of which are explored in *Density 21.5*.

VARÈSE: *Density 21.5* (1935)   4:13
(1883–1965)

Density 21.5 was written for George Barrère, who owned a custom-made platinum flute. The density of platinum is 21.5. The writing for the flute is not typical, but the extreme registers are well displayed.

FIGURE 3.3

Flute and piccolo

The piccolo is a miniature flute about half the size of its counterpart. Its pitch is the highest of the orchestral instruments, reaching within one

FIGURE 3.4

Clarinet and bass
clarinet

step of the highest note of the piano. Its low register is thin and of limited
usefulness. In its upper register the piccolo has a sparkling tone which becomes shrill and piercing when it is played loudly.

TCHAIKOVSKY: *Nutcracker Suite (1892)*
(1840–1893)   *6. Chinese Dance*   1:00

In this dance the piccolo is employed in the most usual way, playing the same melody
as the flute an octave higher.

The clarinet has a wide practical compass with distinctive colorings in
its low, middle, and high registers. The low register is rich and mellow. The
middle register has a neutral quality which blends well with other instruments and lends itself to accompanying parts and filling in harmonies,
though it is also used for solos. The higher register becomes progressively
more penetrating and, except with expert players, pinched at the top.

C. M. von WEBER: *Concertino for Clarinet (1805)*   8:15
(1786–1826)

Weber exploits the clarinet in all of the traditional ways in this small concerto for
solo clarinet and orchestra.

The clarinet has been a prominent jazz instrument from the beginning, and it remains a standard member of Dixieland bands.

TURK MURPHY BAND: *High Society* (1955)   3:08

In this Dixieland version of an early jazz piece, the clarinet begins playing a harmony part in the background above the trumpet and trombone, but the clarinet has a solo toward the end of the recording.

The bass clarinet, first made in 1793, extends the clarinet sound down into the bass range, where it commonly plays the bass line with other instruments in bands and large orchestras (see the score of Barber's *Symphony no. 1* on page 344). In this capacity its somber tone quality is rarely distinguishable, but it is readily apparent in its occasional solo passages. Wagner used the bass clarinet as a solo instrument in his nineteenth-century music dramas (see page 169) to evoke sinister moods, and Tchaikovsky exploited its velvety low tones in his *Dance of the Sugar Plum Fairy* (see page 40).

The saxophones are too familiar both by sight and sound to require detailed discussion. They are hybrids fusing a single reed (like a clarinet) with a metal body (like the brasses) in a conical shape (like an oboe). The saxophones are the only widely used instruments that can be attributed to one individual. They were developed by Adolphe Sax of Brussels about 1840. The *alto, tenor,* and *baritone* saxophones are the most familiar because of their use in dance bands, but a complete family of saxophones is manufactured. The alto saxophone is heard as a solo instrument in the following work. The literature for solo saxophone is relatively small, but growing.

JACQUES IBERT: *Concertino da Camera* (1935)
(1890–1962)
       2. *Larghetto*   3:50
       3. *Animato molto*   4:00

This little chamber concerto for alto saxophone and orchestra illustrates the legitimate saxophone tone quality and style associated with concert music, as opposed to the more familiar saxophone sound heard in jazz and popular music.

The saxophone section—most often consisting of two altos, a tenor, and a baritone—is responsible for much of the full sound produced by big dance bands and stage bands.

DUKE ELLINGTON: *Old King Dooji* (1938)   2:29
(1899–1974)

In this recording from the big band era, the saxophones are heard playing the melody all together and also playing separate harmony parts.

FIGURE 3.5

Alto saxophone, tenor saxophone, and baritone saxophone

The oboe, with its double reed, has a more reedy sound and plaintive quality than the flute, clarinet, or saxophone, and it is less dexterous. The oboe is associated with simple, pastoral melodies, but it is only slightly less versatile than the other members of the woodwind family. Its lowest note is about the same as that of a flute, but a flute can play higher. In ensembles the oboes customarily play between the flutes and the clarinets, which exceed the oboe range both top and bottom.

MOZART: *Oboe Quartet, K. 370 (1781)*
(1756–1791)   *2. Adagio*   3:45

This quartet for oboe, violin, viola, and cello treats the oboe as a solo instrument accompanied by the three string instruments. The writing for the oboe in this slow movement is fairly typical, unlike the preceding and following fast movements which make extreme technical demands on the oboist.

English horn is a misnomer, since the instrument is neither English nor a horn. The origin of the name is uncertain. There are many theories but few facts. The English horn is an oversized and lower-pitched oboe which emphasizes the reedy and plaintive qualities of that instrument. Except in its lowest register the English horn is difficult to distinguish from an oboe.

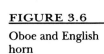

FIGURE 3.6

Oboe and English horn

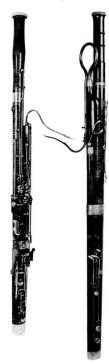

SIBELIUS: *The Swan of Tuonela* (1893)   6:50
(1865–1957)

Tuonela, the land of death in Finnish mythology, is surrounded by a broad, black river upon which floats a swan. The quality of the English horn is admirably suited for this somber tone painting.

The bassoon plays in the same pitch range as the cello, and they frequently are used together in orchestral music. The bassoonist in an orchestra or band is much busier than is generally suspected, because the bassoon part is so often hidden in the background. When the bassoon is used prominently, it is often cast in the role of comedian because of the dry, raucous tone of which it is capable. It is equally at home in lyric melodies and is more flexible than its awkward size and shape would suggest.

MOZART: *Bassoon Concerto,* K. 191 (1774)
(1756–1791)   *2. Andante ma adagio*   4:50

Mozart was a prolific composer of concertos, so it is not surprising to find one for bassoon among them. This movement is essentially lyric, one of the styles in which the bassoon excels.

FIGURE 3.7

Bassoon and
contrabassoon

The contrabassoon, with a range extending almost as low as a piano, supplies the very bottom notes to the woodwind section. Its lugubrious sound is rarely heard alone except for special effects. Its usual function is to play the bass line with the string basses and/or tuba and to double the bassoon part an octave lower. Listeners are seldom conscious of the contrabassoon, but it would be missed if it were not there.

MAURICE RAVEL: *Mother Goose Suite* (1912)
(1875–1937)   *4. Conversations of Beauty and the Beast*   4:15

This movement depicts the *Mother Goose (Ma Mère l'Oye)* fairy tale *Beauty and the Beast* with the beast aptly portrayed by the contrabassoon, first heard about one minute after the beginning.

Brass Instruments
The trumpet is the highest and most brilliant of the brass instruments. Formerly restricted in all but their highest register to fanfarelike figures and inclined to overpower the modest forces of the other sections of the orchestra, the trumpets were reserved (with a few notable exceptions) for rhythmic figures, sustained tones, and climaxes. Mechanical improvements and orchestral resources more in balance with their power now enable trumpets to display the versatility of which they are capable and to utilize their full range of dynamics and pitches.

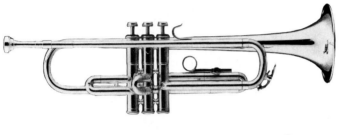

FIGURE 3.8

Trumpet and cornet

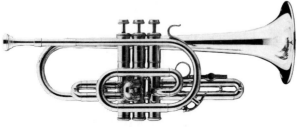

JOSEPH HAYDN: *Concerto for Trumpet (1796)*
(1732–1809)   3. *Spiritoso*   4:45

Haydn's trumpet concerto was written for a then newly invented keyed trumpet rather than for a modern valve trumpet, but the key mechanism allowed Haydn to write for the trumpet in the modern manner. This early trumpet masterpiece nowadays is played on the standard instrument and is learned by every serious trumpet student.

The cornet is similar to the trumpet in size, shape, range, and sound. Its tone is less incisive due primarily to slight differences in the internal shape of its mouthpiece and tubing. Trumpets are the rule in orchestras, dance and stage bands. Cornets are used, usually in conjunction with trumpets, in concert and marching bands and sometimes in jazz groups. Louis Armstrong plays cornet on the Bessie Smith recording of Handy's *St. Louis Blues.*

W. C. HANDY: *St. Louis Blues (1914/1925)**   3:09
(1873–1958)

The cornet sound and blues style, both vocal and instrumental, are aptly illustrated in this example of early jazz in spite of the primitive equipment available at the time of the original recording.

*(Date of composition/date of recording)

The French horn, more often called simply the horn, is a noble instrument with enough power to dominate an orchestra and enough control to blend with a delicate string passage. The horn has by far the widest range

FIGURE 3.9

French horn

of the brass instruments, going almost as high as a trumpet and as low as a trombone. It is an important member of the brass section and an adjunct to the woodwind section, frequently serving as a link between the two. It is a magnificent solo instrument and an admirable accompanying instrument. The horn's versatility in a solo capacity is vividly displayed in Britten's *Serenade for Tenor, Horn, and Strings.*

BRITTEN: *Serenade, op. 31 (1943)*
(1913–1976)   *1. Prologue*   1:20
                2. Hymn   2:00

The *Prologue*, which returns as the *Epilogue*, is played without using the valves on the horn. The pitches thus produced are those of the natural overtone series and do not always correspond with conventional tunings. The extremes of the French horn range, from its highest note to its lowest, are heard in the course of the *Hymn*.

The tuba provides the foundation for the brass section and indeed for the whole orchestra. Its normal function is to reinforce the bass line in loud passages. In the standard orchestra and band literature the tuba practically never has a solo or even an exposed part. This situation is dramatized in Kleinsinger's whimsical *Tubby the Tuba*. The work is intended for children, but adults are not immune to its charm.

KLEINSINGER: *Tubby the Tuba (1942)*   11:45
(1914–1982)

Originally, *Tubby the Tuba* was a Broadway musical for children. It is better known as a concert piece derived from the musical in which Tubby's plight is described by a narrator. Typical sounds of the tuba and several other instruments are illustrated before Tubby finds a melody he can play.

Because the tuba's role in ensemble music is so prosaic and its appearances as a solo instrument so rare, the exotic sounds of *Encounters II* astound most listeners, even musicians.

FIGURE 3.10

Tuba and
sousaphone

WILLIAM KRAFT: *Encounters II (1966)*   6:00
(1923–   )

This avant-garde piece for unaccompanied tuba exploits the extreme range and extraordinary sound effects possible on the instrument in the hands of a virtuoso performer.

Sousaphones are portable, bass, brass instruments named for John Philip Sousa, the March King. Designed for ease of carrying, they take the place of the tubas in marching bands and sometimes in concert bands. The circular shape and forward-facing bell are familiar sights in football halftime shows.

Baritone horns are shaped like small tubas and have valves, but in range, sound, and usage they are closely related to trombones. Euphoniums are similar instruments. Baritones and euphoniums are band instruments exclusively.

Trombones and bass trombones are the only instruments with slides. The two types of trombones can play the same music for the most part, and in their middle registers their tones are indistinguishable. The ordinary trombone plays with greater ease in the high register. The bass trombone

FIGURE 3.11

Trombone and bass
trombone

tone has a little more body, and the instrument is equipped with an attachment activated by a valve that extends the range down four additional
semitones.

HINDEMITH: *Trombone Sonata (1941)*   10:15
(1895–1963)

This sonata is in one movement but four distinct sections, any one of which effectively demonstrates the tone quality and characteristics of the trombone.

**Instruments
Played by
Striking**

Instruments played by striking are *percussion* instruments. The two types of
percussion instruments are those producing definite pitches and those producing indefinite pitches.

   The timpani, also called kettledrums (but not by musicians), are the
most useful and used of the orchestral percussion instruments. They consist of a kettle-shaped, metal body over which a head is stretched. The heads
formerly were made of calfskin, but in recent years plastic heads have been
introduced. At least two timpani are used. The most common sizes are 25
inches and 28 inches in diameter. Large orchestras also have available a
smaller one 23 inches in diameter and a larger one 30 inches in diameter.
Several pitches can be played on each one. The range is determined by the
size and the precise pitch by the tension on the head. The tension is adjusted by hand screws around the rim and by a pedal mechanism. Timpani
are played by two felt-headed sticks, one held in either hand. Notes can be
sustained by a rapid alternate striking by the sticks, called a *roll*. Timpani

are capable of a wide dynamic range by varying the force with which they are struck and of some change of quality by varying the hardness of the stick heads and the location of the striking. A special effect possible only with pedal-equipped timpani is gliding from one pitch to another while the tone is sounding.

A glockenspiel is a percussion instrument with metal bars of graduated sizes arranged in two rows like the black and white keys of a piano. Each bar produces a specific pitch when struck with the hard mallet held in each hand of the player. The pitch is very high, the quality clear and metallic. A bell lyra is a portable version of the glockenspiel with a lyre-shaped frame. This adaptation of the instrument is featured in marching bands.

Xylophones and marimbas are played in the same manner as glockenspiels, but their pitch range is larger and lower and their tone quality is mellower. Their bars are made of hardwood or synthetic material, and resonating tubes of graduated lengths extend down below the bars. Vibraharps and vibraphones resemble xylophones, but they have metal bars and electrically powered rotating discs inside the resonating tubes that produce a vibrato effect.

Tubular bells, also called chimes, are long, metal tubes open on one end and closed on the other. They are made in complete sets, but each tube is individually suspended on a rack. Music written for bells often has but few pitches, and sometimes only the tubes actually required are hung on the rack. When struck with a wooden mallet on the corner of the closed end, the tubular bells produce a sound similar to that of real bells.

Drums in varying depths and diameters have wooden or metal frames covered on both ends by skin or plastic heads. Tension on the heads is adjustable within limits, but no precise pitches result. Drums are struck with assorted sticks and beaters. The snare drum is the smallest. Its name stems from the metal bands or *snares* stretched across the bottom head which create a rattling sound. When the snares are released, a snare drum sounds more like a tom-tom. Side drum is another name for snare drum. The bass drum is the largest drum. The tenor drum is a less frequently used, medium-sized drum. Similar medium-sized drums used in military and marching bands are sometimes given specialized names.

Cymbals are large, plate-shaped instruments of finely wrought brass. They are played in two ways. Holding one in each hand, the player strikes them together in a crash, or one cymbal is suspended and struck with beaters.

A triangle is made from a metal rod bent into a triangular shape. It is struck with a smaller metal rod to produce a light, bell-like sound. A ringing effect is produced by rapid strokes with the beater alternately hitting one side of the triangle and then another near the corner.

Several of the instruments shown in figure 3.12 can be identified from the foregoing descriptions.

The frequently used and some of the less frequently used percussion instruments, divided into definite and indefinite pitch categories, are listed in table 3.2.

FIGURE 3.12

Percussion
instruments

TABLE 3.2 *P*ERCUSSION INSTRUMENTS

Frequently used	*Infrequently used*
Definite Pitch	
Timpani (kettledrums)	Glockenspiel (orchestra bells)
	Xylophone/marimba
	Tubular bells (chimes)
	Vibraphone (vibraharp, vibes)
Indefinite Pitch	
Snare drum (side drum)	Tenor drum
Bass drum	Tambourine
Cymbals	Gong (tam-tam)
Triangle	Castanets
	Wood block
	Temple blocks
	Claves
	Maracas
	Whip (slapstick)
	Ratchet
	Tom-tom
	etc.

The earliest instruments were percussion instruments, and they predominate in the music of many primitive and ethnic cultures, including those of sub-Sahara Africa.

AFRICA/GHANA: *Ceremonial Drums of the Asantehene*   1:02

In this field recording of African tribal music two drums, one large and one small, are heard. Both are made of wood in the shape of a bowl on a cylindrical base. The heads of the drums are skin, traditionally from elephant ears. A metal strip attached to the head of the larger drum sounds when the head is struck.

The percussion instruments on the riser in the center of figure 3.12 are known collectively as a drum set, or *traps*. In jazz and popular music, including rock, all of these instruments and sometimes more are played by the drummer, who is virtually a one-man band. The bass drum and a cymbal device are played with the feet, leaving both hands free for the snare drum and other instruments struck with sticks.

BENNY GOODMAN QUARTET: *Dizzy Spells* (1938)   5:44

The legendary Gene Krupa is the drummer on this recording. Lionel Hampton plays the vibraharp, a definite pitch percussion instrument pictured in the upper left corner of figure 3.12. Benny Goodman on clarinet and Teddy Wilson on piano complete the virtuoso quartet. The recording, made in a concert with a large audience, captures some of the excitement (and extraneous noise) of a live performance.

The imaginative use of percussion instruments produces colorful effects in Bartók's *Sonata for Two Pianos and Percussion*.

BARTÓK: *Sonata for Two Pianos and Percussion* (1937)
(1881–1945)   *3. Allegro non troppo*   6:45

The instruments in order of appearance in this movement are: pianos, xylophone, timpani, cymbal crash (very soft), triangle, side (snare) drum without snares, bass drum, side drum with snares, and suspended cymbal with soft-headed stick.

The infrequently used percussion instruments are employed for special and exotic effects. In addition to those listed in table 3.2, any object that emits a sound when struck can be used as a percussion instrument. Some idea of the possibilities is suggested by the unconventional instruments named in the score of *Ionisation*.

FIGURE 3.13

Harp

*Photo courtesy of Lyon &
Healy Harps.*

> **VARÈSE:** *Ionisation (1931)*   4:50
> (1883–1965)
>
> The score of this work calls for thirteen performers, each playing two or more of
> the following instruments: crash cymbals, suspended cymbal, bass drum (three sizes),
> side drum, snare drum, military drum, string drum (lion roar), gong, tam-tam (three
> sizes), bongos, claves, güiro, maracas, castanets, tambourine, siren (high and low),
> Chinese (temple) blocks, sleigh bells, cowbells, tubular chimes (bells), glockenspiel,
> anvil (high and low), slapstick, triangle, and piano. Both snare and side drums are
> specified, also gong and tam-tams, though the terms are usually synonymous.

Though percussion instruments are used exclusively or predominantly
in the preceding examples, percussion sounds are used sparingly in most
concert music because of their limited and highly specialized nature.

**Instruments
Played by
Plucking**

Several kinds of string instruments can be played by plucking, but the harp
is the only orchestral instrument played exclusively by plucking. The strings
of a harp, strung in an elaborately beautiful frame, produce the same pitches
as the white keys of a piano when the pedals around the base of the instrument are in the middle position. The pitches of the various strings are
raised or lowered a semitone by moving the corresponding pedal up or
down a notch. *Glissando* is a characteristic harp effect in which the player's
fingers are drawn rapidly over the strings sounding all of the pitches between specified limits in rapid succession.

FIGURE 3.14

Acoustic guitar and
electric guitar

TCHAIKOVSKY: *Nutcracker Suite (1892)*
(1840–1893)   *8. Waltz of the Flowers*   6:25

The introduction to this waltz contains one of the most famous harp passages in the
orchestral literature.

Though the usual way of producing the tone on violins, violas, cellos,
and basses is by bowing, tones can also be produced on these instruments
by plucking the strings, called *pizzicato*. The string instruments are played
pizzicato exclusively in the following symphonic movement.

TCHAIKOVSKY: *Symphony no. 4, op. 36 (1878)*
(1840–1893)   *3. Scherzo: Allegro*   4:55

The entire string section of the orchestra is heard playing *pizzicato* in the first part
of this movement and again after the middle part played by the wind instruments.

The most popular plucked string instrument is the guitar. Only the piano
is played by more people. Guitars come in two basic types—acoustic and
electric. The tone of acoustic guitars, used for Spanish, classical, and folk
music, is resonated by the body of the instrument like the orchestral string
instruments. The tone of electric guitars, used in jazz and rock music, is
amplified electronically. Some electric guitars differ drastically from acoustic
guitars in shape and design, but others are merely acoustic guitars with a
pickup unit installed under the strings and connected to an amplifier. In

American folk music the acoustic guitar more often than not is subservient to the voice, but in the flamenco music of Spain the guitar is a featured attraction.

SPAIN/FLAMENCO: *Sevillanas* 2:33

The acoustic guitar and authentic flamenco style are demonstrated in this selection from a collection of flamenco songs and dances recorded by the Lutys de Luz troup.

The sound of electric guitars is too familiar from the saturation exposure in rock concerts, recordings, and videos to require further comment.

Keyboard Instruments

The coupling of a keyboard mechanism with a sound-producing medium is documented in a type of organ found in ancient Greece before 250 B.C. In this and all subsequent keyboard instruments, the purpose of the keyboard is to activate the sound-producing force and to facilitate the striking, blowing, plucking, or electronic response that actually generates the sound. The keys proper neither vibrate nor directly cause vibration.

A long evolutionary period was required to bring the keyboard to its definitive form, and several predecessors of the modern instruments became obsolete in the process. Of the various prototypes, four basic keyboard instruments survive: the piano (more properly the pianoforte), pipe and reed organs, the celesta, and the harpsichord, an instrument which flourished from 1600 to 1800 and is now enjoying a revival. To these must now be added electronic organs and electronic music synthesizers which utilize keyboards as input and control mechanisms.

Striking a piano key activates a felt hammer which in turn strikes a string or strings to produce the sound. The celesta action is essentially the same except that a hard hammer strikes a metal bar. Depressing a pipe organ key opens a valve allowing air to blow through a tone-producing pipe. With a reed organ or harmonium the air blows over a metal tongue which is set in motion to produce the sound. Harpsichord keys are connected with a mechanism which plucks the string in response to a downward motion of the key. Of the instruments with keyboards, only electronic organs and synthesizers produce sounds in a way not found in other instruments.

The piano is used in more combinations and in more different ways than any other instrument. It is a stellar solo instrument; it is used to accompany solo voices and choruses, solo instruments and ensembles; it is combined with other instruments in sonatas and chamber music; it is included in symphony orchestras and dance bands; it serves as a teaching aid in schools; it is found in homes, churches, club rooms, and bars. Because it is so fundamental to the study of music, all serious music students learn to play the piano.

The hammers in the piano mechanism fall back instantly after striking the strings, leaving them free to vibrate until arrested by dampers. Dampers drop on the strings and stop the vibration when the keys are released unless restrained by the action of a pedal. Depressing the right pedal lifts all of the dampers, allowing the strings to vibrate after the keys are released. The left pedal reduces the amount of tone. Grand pianos have an extra pedal in the center which sustains the sound only of keys which are down at the time the pedal is applied.

Ordinary piano sounds are too well known to require illustration, but twentieth-century composers have elicited many new effects from this familiar source. Henry Cowell and John Cage were pioneers in the exploration of new piano resources. In performing Cowell's *Banshee*, the lid of a grand piano is raised, and the sounds are produced directly on the strings by scratching, plucking, striking, and stroking them in various ways.

COWELL: *The Banshee (1925)*   2:40
(1897–1965)

A banshee is a female spirit in Gaelic folklore whose wailing forebodes a death in the family. The eerie sounds of Cowell's *Banshee* are recorded on CRI–109 and Folkways 6160.

A different genre of special piano effects is exploited in Cage's numerous works for *prepared piano,* which he is credited with inventing in 1938. The preparations, specified for each work, consist of applying such things as screws, bolts, nuts, strips of rubber, and weather stripping to the strings in ways that drastically alter the sound even when the notation and manner of playing are conventional, as they are for his *Bacchanale.*

JOHN CAGE: *Bacchanale (1938)*   9:00
(1912–1992)

Cage studied for a time with Cowell and was exposed to new piano sounds early in his career. Between *Bacchanale* and his *Concerto for Prepared Piano and Chamber Orchestra* (1951), Cage produced a substantial body of works for prepared piano.

The pipe organ is the most imposing of instruments. Large models have four keyboards, or *manuals,* each similar in appearance to that of a piano. They have, in addition, a pedalboard with a size and location which permits playing with the toes and heels. All of the keys are connected mechanically, pneumatically, or electrically to thousands of pipes of various shapes and materials ranging in size from smaller than a pencil to larger than a stovepipe. Each type has a distinctive sound. The player selects the desired tone quality and, to an extent, the pitch by means of *stops* located above the keyboards. Air under pressure formerly coming from manually operated bellows but now from electric blowers is supplied to all the pipes. Depressing a key activates a valve allowing air to flow into the pipes selected by the stops and causing the pipe to sound its note. The organ has a tremendous range both in volume and pitch.

Large organs are not mass-produced, and rarely are any two identical. Smaller organs are more inclined toward standardization, having only two manuals and fewer pipes and stops, but they are completely adequate to play most of the organ literature. For those acquainted with the organ only in the restrained atmosphere of a religious service, the resources of the full organ may come as a revelation. The two works suggested for listening, the first church music and the second a concert piece, reveal the broad spectrum of color and dynamics available on the majestic pipe organ.

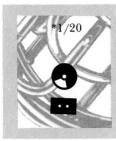

*1/20

J. S. BACH: *Schübler Chorale Preludes (1746)*
(1685–1750)   *1. Wachet auf (Sleepers Awake)**   4:52

Toccata and Fugue in D minor (1717)   9:15

Bach was equally at home playing and writing for the organ and composing sacred and secular music. These works representing the early and late periods of his career are proof of his lifetime devotion to the instrument. Chorale melody page 333.

Electronic organs attempt with varying degrees of success to simulate the sounds of pipe organs. The blowers and pipes of pipe organs are replaced by electrical circuits and speakers in electronic organs. They are no match for the full resources of a large pipe organ, but they have the advantages of economy and compactness, which make them practical for small churches and large cocktail lounges.

The celesta is most easily described as a keyboard glockenspiel. A cabinet supports a small pianolike keyboard and encloses a series of metal bars which sound when struck by hammers connected to the keys. Because of the keyboard, greater dexterity is possible and multiple notes are easier on a celesta than on a glockenspiel. The celesta is a regular member of symphony orchestras where it is grouped with the percussion instruments.

TCHAIKOVSKY: *Nutcracker Suite (1892)*
(1840–1893)   *4. Dance: Sugarplum Fairy*   1:45

This is the first orchestral composition to include the celesta. The tinkling of the celesta solo is placed in sharp relief by the velvety low tones of the bass clarinet.

The harpsichord, supplanted by the piano, all but disappeared from the musical scene though much of the keyboard music written prior to 1800 was intended for it. Musicologists interested in the authentic reproduction of early music sparked a move to take harpsichords out of museums and

FIGURE 3.15
Harpsichord

into recording studios and concert halls. This movement led to a reevaluation not only of the music but also of the instrument itself. Contemporary composers have been stimulated to write for harpsichord, and it has even made a tentative debut in popular music and in radio and television commercials and background music.

In appearance the harpsichord is like a small, angular, grand piano. The keyboard is shorter, and traditionally the black-and-white color of the keys is reversed in relation to the piano. Some harpsichords have two keyboards, one above the other (see figure 3.15). The harpsichord tone is produced by an intricate mechanism which plucks a string when a key is struck. Unlike a piano, hitting a key harder or softer does not influence the tone. This is done by modifying the bite of the plucking device. The old instruments are very fragile, but modern ones are relatively sturdy and durable. In some, nylon is used in place of leather or crow quills for the plectra, and steel frames are used in place of wood.

J. S. BACH: *French Suite no. 4 in E-flat (1722)*
(1685–1750)   *6. Gigue*   2:16

1/17

Bach keyboard works are now standard piano fare, but during his lifetime the piano remained a comparative novelty. The harpsichord, heard on the recording, is the instrument for which works like the *French Suites* were intended. Themes page 332.

Electronic Instruments

Electronic instruments and components capable of generating, modifying, and recording sounds have existed since the beginning of the century, but the ultimate electronic instruments, *music synthesizers,* are of more recent origin. Synthesizers opened up a whole new approach to composition. With a synthesizer, tones of any desired pitch, duration, loudness, and quality could be produced electronically, and eventually the sounds from any source, including conventional instruments, could be duplicated exactly or modified beyond recognition.

Handmade prototypes of electronic music systems were exhibited in 1964, but the term *synthesizer* was not in general use until a few years later. The early instruments were analog (as opposed to digital) synthesizers. Electronic impulses generated by oscillators operating on ordinary electric current were modified by various processing circuits and electronic signals and then converted to sound by loudspeakers. All functions were voltage controlled—that is, determined by varying the amount of voltage. Moog synthesizers were among the first of this type to be mass-produced and widely used. A Moog Modular System 55 synthesizer was the sole sound source for *Switched-On Bach,* no doubt the best known of the electronic music recordings. The synthesizer on which it was realized is now obsolete, but the recording is still available. Its initial sales of more than a million copies propelled electronic sounds into the musical limelight. The listening example (*Wachet auf*) from the album was written for organ in standard music notation, which is reproduced precisely in the synthesized version. Only the tone quality differs from the original as Bach conceived it.

J. S. BACH: *Switched-On Bach (1746/1968)**
(1685/1750)   Chorale Prelude *Wachet auf*   3:37

The complete recording (CBS MK–7194/16–11–0092) contains ten Bach compositions "realized and performed" by Wendy (Walter) Carlos with the assistance of Benjamin Folkman on a Moog electronic music synthesizer. Compare this electronic rendition of Bach's *Schübler Chorale Prelude no. 1, Wachet auf (Sleepers Awake)* with the traditional version for organ cited on pages 40 and 155; LG 1/20. Chorale melody page 333.

*(Date of composition/date of recording)

The next stage in the evolution of analog synthesizers was the substitution of digital (computer) controls for voltage controls. Concurrently with the development of analog synthesizers, programs were devised for computers that enabled them to generate, process, and store sounds digitally. In effect, a computer with suitable peripherals became a synthesizer. Initially the computers were general-purpose computers, and those with sufficient capacity were large, expensive, and rarely available to composers. Additionally, the programs on which they ran were complicated. The situation changed dramatically with the advent of relatively powerful microcomputers. Digital sound generating and control components were

Front panel

Back panel

FIGURE 3.16

MIDI Time Piece II

*Photo courtesy of Mark of
the Unicorn, Inc.,
Cambridge, MA.*

miniaturized and combined in synthesizers small enough to carry with one hand, and prices were reduced to a range comparable to that of conventional instruments.

One of the most significant developments in electronic music has been the adoption of the MIDI (Musical Instrument Digital Interface) as the industry standard device for implementing communication between electronic musical instruments and computers. The MIDI protocol consists of a set of messages representing various aspects of musical performances. A MIDI can accept input from a live performer in real time or step (incremental) time and can pass information between performers, computers, and recorders. MIDIs are being developed, perfected, and exploited at a rate assuring that they will have a significant impact on electronic music for the foreseeable future.

Mark of the Unicorn's MIDI Time Piece II (figure 3.16) is a 1992 model MIDI with many extra functions. Built on a custom MIDI Processor chip, it interfaces with a Macintosh computer or can stand alone. It has eight independent MIDI in/MIDI out terminals, a SMPTE (Society of Motion Picture and Television Engineers) timecode for synchronizing multiple tracks, two flexible footpedal inputs, and a visual display that gives complete information on the configuration and status of the unit. The MIDI Time Piece II is fully programmable from the front panel, and in case of emergency, it even has a "panic" button!

State-of-the-art technology is incorporated in the Synclavier® 9600 synthesizer, promoted as the most powerful integrated digital audio system as yet brought to market. Its features include a customized Macintosh® II graphics workstation, a seventy-six note velocity/pressure sensitive keyboard, a button control panel, SMPTE synchronization, ninety-six polyphonic stereo voices, and memory and on-line sound storage exceeding practical requirements.

FIGURE 3.17

Synclavier® 9600

*Photo courtesy of New
England Digital
Corporation, Lebanon,
NH.*

Synthesizers such as the Synclavier can generate sounds internally, or
they can process sounds originating externally. One treatment of external
sounds is *sampling*, a procedure with many applications. In sampling, a
prerecorded waveform (sample) is analyzed and converted to numerical
representation. This digitized profile of the waveform can then be reproduced with any desired transformations. Sampled flute, French horn, and
percussion waveforms were used by Christian Wolff (1934–   ) in his
Mayday Materials, but only flute-derived sounds are heard in *Part 9.* The
work was realized on a Synclavier in the Bregman Electronic Music Studio
of Dartmouth College.

4/3

CHRISTIAN WOLFF: *Mayday Materials (1989)*
(1934–   )   *Part 9*   4:56

In this selection, one of twenty commissioned by Lucinda Childs for her dance
Mayday, Wolff uses sampled flute tones exclusively in a synthesized and highly stylized version of the Appalachian folk song and square dance tune *Cindy.*

Synthesizers can produce the sounds required for any musical idiom from Bach to rock. The suggested listening examples illustrate just two of the infinite possibilities. Additional information about synthesizers and more examples of electronic music are given in chapter 24. Electronic sounds pervade today's environment. Electronic instruments form the core of rock groups, and digitally generated and processed sounds increasingly dominate the music used in movies and television shows. One has only to turn on a radio or TV set or to attend a local theater to hear music emanating from these newest sources of musical sound.

In Conclusion

The foregoing examples feature a specific voice type or instrument in a complete work or independent part. The suggested listening, therefore, introduces not only the various voices and instruments but also some of the masterpieces of music created for them. For a more concise introduction to the instruments, the following recording is recommended.

BRITTEN: *Young Person's Guide to the Orchestra (1946)*   19:21   3/15
(1913–1976)

In this work, subtitled *Variations and Fugue on a Theme of Purcell* (1659–1695), the theme is played in turn by the full orchestra, the woodwind, brass, string, and percussion sections, and again by the full orchestra before the variations begin. Then each instrument of the orchestra is spotlighted in a variation and again in the fugue (see page 135). A narrator (omitted in some performances) names and describes the instruments before they are heard. Though intended for young people, this composition provides a marvelous introduction to the instruments for initiates of all ages.

Cultivating the ability to recognize specific voices and instruments continues in the following chapter on the mediums of music where the suggested listening examples explore the sounds of voices and instruments in various combinations.

Benjamin Britten

Frequency

27 31 33 37 41 44 49 55 62 65 73 82 87 98 110 123 130 147 165 174 194 220 247 261 294 330 349 392 440 494 523 587 659 698 784 880 987 1046 1174 1318 1397 1568 1760 1975 2093 2348 2636 2794 3138 3520 3950 4186

A B C D E F G A B C D E F G A B C D E F G A B C D E F G A B C D E F G A B C D E F G A B C D E F G A B C D E F G A B C

Instrument/Voice	Low	High
Soprano	C	C
Alto	G	E
Tenor	C	A
Bass	G	E
Violin	G	E
Viola	C	E
Cello	C	A
Bass	E	D
Piccolo	D	B♭
Flute	C	C
Oboe	B♭	G
English horn	E	A
Clarinet	D	B♭
Bass clarinet	D	F
Alto saxophone	D♭	A♭
Tenor saxophone	A♭	E♭
Baritone saxophone	D♭	A♭
Bassoon	B♭	E♭
Contrabassoon	B♭	A♭
Trumpet	E	B♭
Cornet	E	B♭
French horn	B	F
Trombone	E	D
Bass trombone	C	F
Tuba	E	D
Harp	C♭	G♯
Glockenspiel	G	C
Celesta	C	C
Xylophone	C	C
Tubular bells	C	F
Timpani	D	G

Frequencies rounded to whole numbers. Ranges approximate for voices and some instruments, and extremes not always practical.

4 MEDIUMS OF MUSIC

The voices and instruments surveyed in the previous chapter make music in many combinations. There are no restrictions on the types or numbers used together, and at one time or another music probably has been written for almost every conceivable group. Certain combinations by virtue of special qualifications are most prevalent. These are the common mediums of music.

Solo

Solo, literally, means alone. In music it is used both in its literal sense and in the sense of a piece or passage for one predominant instrument or voice with accompaniment. Unaccompanied solos are occasionally written for other instruments, but the one which regularly appears by itself is the piano. The piano is adaptable to old music and new, to brief character pieces and extended major works. Because of the wealth of literature, the abundance of competent performers, and the availability of instruments, the piano undoubtedly is heard more than any other instrument or combination of instruments.

FRÉDÉRIC CHOPIN: *Mazurka no. 24 (1838)*   1:21   2/10
(1810–1849)

Piano solo: piano alone. Themes page 338.

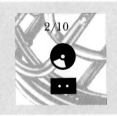

Used in the sense of a piece for one voice or instrument with accompaniment, *solo* is usually modified by the name of the voice or instrument performing the solo part. A safe assumption is that the accompaniment unless otherwise indicated is played by the piano. Thus, a vocal solo or soprano solo is a song for voice and piano; a violin solo is a piece for violin and piano, and so on.

Independent songs for solo voice and piano are called *art songs,* or *lieder* (from the German word for songs). Composers using German texts produced a vast treasury of such songs during the nineteenth century. Franz Schubert is credited with originating the form. His *Erl-King* is a prime example of *lied* (singular of *lieder*).

2/8

SCHUBERT: *The Erl-King (Der Erlkönig),* op. 1 (1815)   4:02
(1797–1828)

Art song or lied: voice and piano. Translation page 195.

Instrumental solos with piano accompaniment are a common medium of musical expression. The solo literature is especially plentiful for instruments such as the violin which are frequently heard in solo recitals. Karol Szymanowski, who was regarded by some critics during the first half of this century as the greatest Polish composer since Chopin, composed extensively for the violin as a solo instrument.

KAROL SZYMANOWSKI: *Romance,* op. 23 (1913)   4:23
(1882–1937)

Violin solo: violin and piano.

Instrumental solos accompanied by orchestra most often fall in the concerto category. In a *piano concerto* the piano is elevated to the solo role, and the accompaniment is provided by the orchestra. The amount of orchestral participation in the presentation and working out of the thematic ideas varies considerably from one concerto to another. The primary function of the orchestra in some is to provide background for the solo. Others are virtually symphonies with one predominant instrument. The following example is between these extremes.

3/14

BÉLA BARTÓK: *Piano Concerto no. 3* (1945)
(1881–1945)   3. *Allegro vivace*   7:19

Piano concerto: solo piano and orchestra.

Chamber Music   Chamber music is the general designation for instrumental ensemble music performed with one player on a part. Since there is only one player for each part in the music, the number of players is never large. A word indicating the number of players or parts (e.g., *duo* or *duet, trio, quartet, quintet, sextet, septet, octet,* or *nonet*) is often included in the title of chamber works. Music for more than nine players usually does not qualify as chamber music, and most chamber music is for groups of two to five players. Musical interest is distributed, more or less equally, among the parts. There is no soloist or leader, and opportunities for displaying individual virtuosity are purely incidental.

Duos or duets for two melody instruments are abundant in the teaching literature, but only a few are programed. The following example is one of the exceptions. The Bartók Duos are progressively arranged teaching pieces using twentieth-century devices. Their musical value makes them an effective source of recital material.

BÉLA BARTÓK: *Duos (44) for Two Violins (1931)*
(1881–1945)   *44. Ardeliana*   1:50
Duo: two violins.

A *sonata* is an extended work in three or four movements (see page 144) for one or two instruments. Sonatas for two instruments, usually a melody instrument and piano, conform to the basic definition given for chamber music, but they are not always included in the classification. This is because the solo-accompaniment relationship between the two instruments in some sonatas is inconsistent with the ideals of chamber music. Sonatas in which the primary function of the piano is to provide an accompaniment for the melody instrument perhaps belong in the solo category, but many are perfectly valid examples of chamber music.

Though sonatas have been composed for piano in combination with virtually every instrument, including another piano, those for violin and piano are most numerous. Both instruments may be named in identifying sonatas, or the piano may be taken for granted in sonatas as it is in solos. The chamber music classification of the following example and similar sonatas is substantiated by the absence of superficial technical display and by the participation of both instruments in the presentation of the musical ideas.

CÉSAR FRANCK: *Violin Sonata in A (1886)*
(1822–1890)   *4. Allegretto poco mosso*   6:06
Violin sonata: violin and piano.

A *trio* may comprise any three instruments, but the only combinations standardized to any degree are the *string trio,* consisting of violin, viola, and cello, and the *piano trio,* consisting of violin, cello, and piano. The piano trio is the only combination of three instruments for which a large and significant body of literature exists.

MENDELSSOHN: *Piano Trio no. 1 (1839)*
(1809–1847)   *1. Molto allegro ed agitato*   7:45
Piano trio: violin, cello, and piano.

The dearth of music for three instruments contrasts with the abundance of music for four. Any combination of four instruments constitutes a *quartet,* but the most usual combination consists of two violins, viola, and cello, the instrumentation of a *string quartet.*

The string quartet is an ideal medium for which Haydn and practically every composer since his time have written. The combination of instruments in a string quartet provides the composer a perfectly balanced, homogeneous medium with a wide range of pitches and dynamic levels. The sounds of a string quartet can be sonorous one moment and ethereal the next. If power and brilliance are limited, clarity and intimacy compensate. String players regard the quartet as the ultimate mode of musical expression, and string quartets are what they play for their own satisfaction. In the next example the melody is played in turn by each of the four instruments.

2/2

JOSEPH HAYDN: *String Quartet,* op. 76 no. 3 (1798)
(1732–1809)   2. *Poco adagio, cantabile*   7:33

String quartet: two violins, viola, and cello. Theme page 335.

The plentiful literature for string quartet is balanced by a bounteous array of stellar performers. Renowned string quartets tour and record regularly and, by playing as a unit through many seasons, achieve perfection as ensembles. University faculty, student, and amateur string quartets, in addition, are numerous and often excellent. The literature and the performing groups are sources of reciprocal stimulation. String quartets are organized to perform the existing literature, and the active performing groups are a constant incentive for composers to write still more for them.

The instrumentation of the string quartet is accepted as the norm, and deviations from this combination are reflected in the designations for works and the groups required to play them. For example, a *piano quartet* consists of a violin, viola, cello, and piano, not four pianos as the name might imply. An *oboe quartet* consists of oboe, violin, viola, and cello. The name in each case is derived from the instrument which replaces one of the violins in the string quartet instrumentation. The piano quartet, particularly, is a standard and frequently heard ensemble. Several quartet combinations of three string instruments and one wind have been used effectively, but no combination of four instruments challenges the supremacy of the string quartet as a medium of musical expression.

Quartets of woodwind and brass instruments are also possible, though less common than those involving string instruments. The usual makeup of a *woodwind quartet* is flute, oboe, clarinet, and bassoon. There are several likely combinations of four brass instruments. A *brass quartet* can consist of two trumpets and two trombones; two trumpets, horn, and trombone; trumpet, horn, trombone, and tuba; or any group of four brass instruments, including those with cornets and baritones. Many brass quartet compositions can be played by more than one combination of instruments. Woodwind and brass quartets are not the perfect chamber music mediums that string quartets are. The tone quality of the various woodwind instruments lacks homogeneity, and the brass instruments by nature are less suited to the performance of intimate music.

A *quintet* often consists of a string quartet augmented by one additional instrument, in which case it is identified by the name of the added instrument. A *viola quintet* is a string quartet with an extra viola. A *cello quintet* is a string quartet with an extra cello, and a *clarinet quintet* is a string quartet plus clarinet. The most popular addition to the basic instrumentation of the string quartet is the piano, resulting in the *piano quintet*.

ROBERT SCHUMANN: *Piano Quintet,* op. 44 (1842)		
(1810–1856)	*1. Allegro brillante*	9:00

Piano quintet: two violins, viola, cello, and piano.

Woodwind quintet is a curious but usual way of referring to a group of four woodwind instruments and one brass. In the interest of accuracy, the name is sometimes shortened to *wind quintet.* Both names apply to a group consisting of flute, oboe, clarinet, bassoon, and horn. This combination lacks the warmth of a string quintet and the power of a piano quintet, but it has greater diversity of tone color than either. Wind quintet music tends to be witty and clever rather than emotional or profound. Contemporary composers have found the medium attractive, and many have composed effectively for it.

JACQUES IBERT: *Trois Pièces Brèves (1930)*		
(1890–1962)	*1. Allegro*	2:25
·	*2. Andante*	1:20
	3. Assez lent—Allegro scherzando	3:00

Woodwind quintet: flute, oboe, clarinet, horn, and bassoon.

Chamber music has been written for groups of six (sextet), seven (septet), eight (octet), and nine (nonet) players. There is no standard instrumentation beyond the quintet, and the literature is not extensive. Isolated chamber works exist for larger ensembles, but the tendency with larger groups is to depart from the chamber music concept and to use more than one player on a part.

Vocal music is ordinarily excluded, by definition and custom, from the chamber music category. However, *madrigals* are a type of vocal ensemble music intended for performance (but not usually performed) with one on a part, which qualifies them for consideration in this context. Madrigals of the most prevalent type are secular works for four to six voices, with five most usual. Four-part madrigals are for soprano, alto, tenor, and bass. Five-part madrigals usually call for an additional soprano; six-part madrigals for these five and another tenor. Madrigal writing flourished in Italy and England during the sixteenth and seventeenth centuries; and the name has been revived by contemporary composers.

1/14   **THOMAS MORLEY:** *My bonny lass she smileth* (1595)   1:45
(1557–1602)

Madrigal: two sopranos, alto, tenor, and bass.

The performances of jazz combos are chamber music of a sort, startling as the idea may seem to purists. The small combos improvise intimate jazz with one player on a part. Emphasis is on group performance, but each member has opportunities to be in the spotlight. Classic chamber music designations—trio, quartet, quintet, and sextet—are common. Instruments to provide melody, harmony, and rhythm must be included in a combo, but otherwise the instrumentation is completely flexible. One possibility is illustrated in the following combo performance of a George Gershwin tune.

4/10   **GEORGE GERSHWIN:** *But Not for Me* (1930/1965)   3:44
(1898–1937)

Modern Jazz Quartet: piano, vibraphone, bass, and drums.

Choirs

A *choir* is a group devoted to the singing of sacred music. A *choir* is also a group of instruments belonging to the same family. It is used here in both senses, though an instrumental choir within an orchestra or a band is usually called a *section*.

Vocal choirs have been an important adjunct to worship since the time people learned to sing together, and the magnificent sound of numerous voices did not go unnoticed by composers of secular music. Composers of both sacred and secular music have written copiously for voices since the beginning of the Renaissance. The enormous quantity of music for voices is in sharp contrast to the relatively meager amount for individual instrumental choirs. Choral music is normally written for soprano, alto, tenor,

COLORPLATE 5

Michelangelo:
Creation of Adam (1508–1512)

The *Creation of Adam*, a detail from the Sistine Chapel ceiling in the Vatican, was painted by Michelangelo (1475–1564) during the High Renaissance period of art in Italy, which preceded the corresponding "golden age of vocal polyphony" in music (see page 228) by about fifty years.

COLORPLATE 6

Mathis Grünewald:
Isenheim Altarpiece (1515)

Incidents in the life of the painter Mathis Gothart Nithart, known as Grünewald
(1480–1528), are dramatized in Paul Hindemith's opera *Mathis der Maler*
(Matthias the Painter). The three movements of the symphony (see page 275)
derived from the opera were inspired by the panels of the Isenheim Altarpiece
shown in the illustration.

COLORPLATE 7

El Greco:
Madonna and
Child with Saint
Martina and
Saint Agnes
(1597–1599)
Oil on canvas,
1.935 × 1.030
(76⅛" × 40½")

El Greco (the Greek)
is the name by which
Domenikos
Theotokopoulos
(1541–1614) of
Crete was known in
Spain where he
created his
masterpieces. In
some of his
paintings, including
this one, the figures
are elongated for
purposes of
emotional
expression. The
expressive qualities
of the paintings by
El Greco match
those of the
compositions by his
contemporaries,
Palestrina and
Lassus (see pages
227–28).

COLORPLATE 8

Peter Paul Rubens:
Rape of the Daughters of Leucippus (1618)

Rubens (1577–1640) was, with the help of many assistants, the most prolific artist of his time. Thoroughly baroque in style and spirit, his canvases exhibit unprecedented energy and movement, characteristics that are reflected in the driving rhythms of many baroque compositions.

Scala/Art Resource, New York.

and bass voices. Each of these can be divided when the music requires more than four parts. Technically, a choir sings sacred music and a chorus secular music, but the distinction is not always observed. Church music was formerly for unaccompanied voices, and *a cappella* (meaning "for the chapel") is now a general designation for unaccompanied vocal music and the groups that perform it.

PALESTRINA: *Pope Marcellus Mass (1555)*
(1525–1594)   *Kyrie*   5:00

A cappella choir: sopranos, altos, tenors (two parts), and basses (two parts).

1/13

Of the instrumental choirs, the string choir is the most versatile. It becomes the string section in an orchestra and a string orchestra when it performs independently. It includes all of the bowed instruments—several of each. Music for strings is normally written in five parts, two for violins and one each for violas, cellos, and basses. The cellos and basses at times play the same part, reducing the number to four. Oftentimes one or more of the five is divided to accommodate additional melodic lines or to provide fuller harmonies. Though the instrumentation of a string orchestra adds only basses to that of a string quartet, the larger number of players and the possibility of dividing the parts affects the style of writing and noticeably alters the tone quality. Tchaikovsky's *Serenade* would not be mistaken for a string quartet, nor would the composer have written precisely the same way for the smaller ensemble.

TCHAIKOVSKY: *Serenade in C,* op. 48 (1880)
(1840–1893)   *2. Waltz*   3:40

String orchestra: first violins, second violins, violas, cellos, and basses.

Many passages in the symphonic literature are assigned exclusively to the woodwind section or to the brass section, but the instruments in these sections rarely function as independent choirs. The instruments of the percussion section, however, have gained recognition as an independent performance medium. A group playing percussion instruments is called a *percussion ensemble.* Any and all percussion instruments may be included. Though relative newcomers on the concert scene, percussion ensembles now exist all over the country, and the amount of music for them is expanding rapidly. The percussion instruments seem to have a special appeal for contemporary composers.

CARLOS CHÁVEZ: *Toccata for Percussion (1942)*　　　11:25
(1899–1978)　　　　*1. Allegro, sempre giusto*　　　4:35
　　　　　　　　　　2. Largo　　　3:40
　　　　　　　　　　3. Allegro un poco marciale　　　3:10

Percussion ensemble: large and small Indian drums, side (snare) drums, tenor drums, bass drum, timpani, large and small gongs, glockenspiel, xylophone, suspended cymbals, chimes, claves, and maracas—six players.

Band

Band is a general term for a variety of instrumental ensembles with woodwind, brass, and percussion sections, but no string section. Bands vary in size from the normal complement of a United States military band, formerly twenty-eight but now forty-three, to well over a hundred in some marching bands. The instrumentation is not uniform. Concert bands normally include all of the wind and percussion instruments described in chapter 3 plus a string bass. In marching bands, instruments that are ineffective outdoors or difficult to carry while marching are eliminated, and the other brass, saxophone, and drum forces are expanded. Large bands—concert and marching—tend to have a fixed instrumentation that is utilized in all works performed.

Symphonic bands and *wind ensembles* are elite bands that have the same three sections and the same instruments as concert bands, but in symphonic bands and wind ensembles the number, distribution, and uses of the instruments are significantly different. There are fewer players and much less doubling (more than one player on the same part), and the instrumentation is adjusted to the precise requirements of each work performed. Table 4.1 shows the basic instrumentation of the Eastman Wind Ensemble, widely known for its recordings. This basic instrumentation is augmented or reduced by the conductor to comply with the specifications of the particular score and to reflect the intent of the composer. Consequently, the exact instrumentation may vary from work to work even on the same program.

A wealth of concert music exists for wind ensembles, but marches are the natural province of bands.

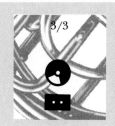

JOHN PHILIP SOUSA: *Hands Across the Sea (1899)*　　　2:42
(1854–1932)

In this Sousa march recording, the Eastman Wind Ensemble is conducted by its founder, Frederick Fennell. The information regarding its instrumentation and performance practices was provided by its present conductor, Donald Hunsberger, who is shown conducting the group in figure 4.1.

TABLE 4.1   *E*ASTMAN WIND ENSEMBLE INSTRUMENTATION

Players	Instruments
4	Flutes, piccolo, alto flute
4	Oboes, English horn
8	Clarinets including E-flat, B-flat, alto, bass, and contrabass
4	Bassoons, contrabassoon
4	Saxophones
6	Trumpets
5	Horns
4	Trombones
2	Euphoniums
2	Tubas
2	Piano, celesta, keyboard
1	Harp
1	String bass
1	Timpani
5	Percussion

FIGURE 4.1

Eastman Wind Ensemble, Donald Hunsberger, Conductor

The participation of marching bands in parades and football halftime shows has won them an exalted position in the realm of entertainment. Concert bands and symphonic wind ensembles in recent years have been recognized by composers and audiences as significant mediums deserving serious attention.

Dance Band

Big dance bands, also known as stage bands and studio bands, have three distinct sections.

1. *Brass:* trumpets and trombones
2. *Reed:* saxophones, sometimes clarinets
3. *Rhythm:* piano and/or electronic keyboard instrument, string bass, usually guitar, and drums

Striving for an individual style, a name band plays special arrangements exclusively, making a unique instrumentation both feasible and desirable. This concept is the exact opposite of that prevailing in symphonic literature. Symphonic composers do their own orchestration, and every orchestra plays the same version.

Brass sections vary from three trumpets and two or three trombones to as many as five of each, with the numbers approximately equal. The lowest trombone part is usually written for bass trombone.

Reed sections have a minimum of four saxophones—two altos, tenor, and baritone—often more. Most saxophone players also play clarinet, so arrangers have at their disposal four or more players to divide between saxophones and clarinets as they wish. The distribution is not necessarily the same for all selections.

The rhythm section provides the steady, underlying beat that renders the intricate rhythms of the other sections meaningful and makes the music danceable. Rhythm players, if they use music, read from parts containing chord symbols rather than complete notation, and they improvise on the harmonic framework indicated by the symbols. A banjo was sometimes used instead of a guitar in the early big bands. The use of electronic keyboard instruments is a recent development. Surrounding the drummer is an impressive array of percussion instruments which are played dexterously using both hands and both feet.

A dance band constituted along these lines is capable of both subtlety and power. To achieve maximum sonority, arrangers write an independent part for each player and distribute the notes so that each chord can be complete in all three sections of the band. This style of writing and this type of band were in vogue during the *swing* era of the thirties and forties. Legendary figures of that generation—Glenn Miller, Benny Goodman, the Dorsey brothers, Count Basie, and Duke Ellington, to name a few—can still be heard on reissues of their recordings, like the following.

DUKE ELLINGTON: *Old King Dooji (1938)*   2:29
(1899–1974)

Duke Ellington's orchestra, as he called it, in this period consisted of two trumpets, one cornet (in place of a third trumpet), three trombones, two alto saxophones (one doubling on clarinet), baritone saxophone, bass, guitar, and drums.

The big band sound no longer dominates the jazz scene as it once did, but neither does it exist only in reissues from its heyday. Harry Connick, Jr., is one of the new generation of composer/performers who continues the big band tradition, complete with vocals.

HARRY CONNICK, JR.: *Blue Light, Red Light (1991)*
(1967–   )   *1. Someone's There*   3:28

The instruments listed for this recording are: piano, bass, drums, guitar, two alto saxophones, two tenor saxophones, baritone saxophone, clarinet, three trombones, bass trombone, and four trumpets. The piano player (Connick) sings the vocal, the baritone saxophone player doubles on bass clarinet and flute, and one of the trombone players doubles on sousaphone.

The big band instrumentation was sometimes augmented to include strings and other symphonic instruments. Paul Whiteman, Duke Ellington, and Stan Kenton in turn evoked favorable, even enthusiastic responses with innovations which combined symphonic and jazz elements, but their pioneering efforts did not lead to enduring traditions.

Orchestra

An *orchestra* consists of four sections: woodwind, brass, percussion, and string. The string section, which distinguishes orchestras from bands, is always the largest. The instrumentation of symphony orchestras, having evolved gradually over an extended period, tends to be relatively stable. Therefore, the approximate distribution of instruments for orchestras of various sizes can be tabulated, as they are in table 4.2.

Orchestral works composed during the second half of the eighteenth century typically are scored for a classic orchestra—pairs of flutes, oboes, sometimes clarinets, bassoons, horns, trumpets, timpani, and a modest body of strings. The full orchestra which became standard during the next century routinely included clarinets; the number of horns was increased to four; trombones and later tuba were added along with an extra percussion player or two and strings to balance. Since the late nineteenth century, composers have had available and have created works utilizing the full resources of the large orchestra shown in table 4.2, where the instrumentation of the various orchestras is given for comparison. Isolated works have been written

Esa-Pekka Salonen, Music Director, Los Angeles Philharmonic

TABLE 4.2   DISTRIBUTION OF INSTRUMENTS IN THE ORCHESTRA

	Classic orchestra	Full orchestra	Large orchestra
Woodwind			
Piccolo			1
Flute	2	2	2–3
Oboe	2	2	2–3
English horn			1
Clarinet	(2)	2	2–4
Bass clarinet			1
Bassoon	2	2	2–3
Contrabassoon			1
Total	6(8)	8	12–17
Brass			
French horn	2	4	4–8
Trumpet	2	2–3	3–5
Trombone		3	3–4
Tuba		(1)	1
Total	4	9–11	11–18
Percussion	1	3	4
Harp and piano		1	2–3
String			
1st Violin	4–8	8–12	14–18
2nd Violin	4–6	6–10	10–16
Viola	2–4	4–8	8–12
Cello	2–4	4–8	8–12
Bass	2–4	4–6	8–10
Total	14–26	26–44	48–68
Grand total	25–39	47–67	77–110

for still larger, gigantic orchestras, but practical considerations inhibit the use of extras beyond the standard large orchestra. The expansion which occurred during the last century and the first part of this one seems to have run its course.

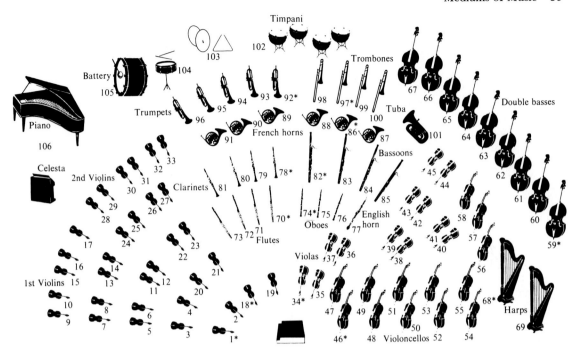

FIGURE 4.2

Seating plan, Philadelphia Orchestra. Asterisks indicate principal or first chair of each section.

The seating plan of orchestras varies, but in general the players are spread in a fan shape around the conductor's podium, which is front and center on the stage. The first violins are always on the left. The leader of the first violin section, the *concertmaster*, sits at the head of the section on the outside and functions somewhat as an assistant conductor. The second violins are usually seated next to the first violins, but they have been placed at the front on the opposite side of the stage. Prevailing practice is to keep all of the violins together and to place the violas and the cellos on the conductor's right. The cellos most often are on the outside and the violas on the inside. The string basses are at the side of the stage behind the cellos. The woodwinds are in front of the conductor. The French horns are usually between the woodwinds and the rest of the brass instruments. The trumpets, trombones, and tuba form a semicircle with the percussion section at the back of the stage. Figure 4.2 shows the seating plan of the Philadelphia Orchestra.

The score of the first orchestral example calls for wind instruments in pairs plus timpani and strings—a typical orchestra of the period when it was composed.

W. A. MOZART: *Symphony no. 35 in D* (1782)
(1756–1791)   *1. Allegro con spirito*   7:59

Classic orchestra: two flutes, two oboes, two clarinets, two bassoons, two horns, two trumpets, timpani, and strings. Also LG 2/6 (Beethoven).

As the orchestra evolved, trombones and later tuba were added to the instrumentation, and the string and percussion sections were expanded. This instrumentation was prevalent during much of the nineteenth century and continued into the twentieth century.

PAUL HINDEMITH: *Mathis der Maler (1934)*
(1895–1963)   2. *Grablegung (Entombment)*   4:08

Full orchestra: two flutes (second switching briefly to piccolo), two oboes, two clarinets, two bassoons, four horns, two trumpets, three trombones, tuba, timpani, percussion, and strings.

Augmenting the woodwind section from two to three of each type brings the instrumentation to that of a large orchestra. Opera scores, like that for the following work, were among the first to introduce the large orchestra instrumentation.

RICHARD WAGNER: *Lohengrin, opera (1850)*
(1813–1883)   *Act III. Prelude*   2:36

Large orchestra: three flutes, three oboes, three clarinets, three bassoons, four horns, three trumpets, three trombones, tuba, timpani, percussion, and strings. Also LG 3/2 (Tchaikovsky).

In large orchestras the third part for each woodwind type may require one of the specialized instruments—piccolo, English horn, bass clarinet, or contrabassoon—as in Barber's *Symphony no. 1 in One Movement.* Harp and piano are also frequently included in the instrumentation.

SAMUEL BARBER: *Symphony no. 1 (1936)*   18:30
(1910–1981)

Large orchestra: two flutes, piccolo, two oboes, English horn, two clarinets, bass clarinet, two bassoons, contrabassoon, four horns, three trumpets, three trombones, tuba, timpani, percussion, harp, and strings. First page of the orchestral score showing all of the instruments except harp, page 344.

Kurt Masur, Music Director, New York Philharmonic

While the instrumentation of the Barber symphony is the largest that can be regarded as standard, much larger orchestras are called for on occasion. Schoenberg originally scored his *Five Pieces for Orchestra, op. 16* for four of each woodwind and six horns, but his subsequent revision, significantly, is for a standard, large orchestra. The added cost of rehearsing and performing works for extraordinarily large orchestras restricts performances, a fact that composers must ponder before embarking on such projects. One work that has survived despite being written for an unusually large orchestra is Stravinsky's ballet *The Rite of Spring* (*Le Sacre du Printemps*).

IGOR STRAVINSKY: *The Rite of Spring (1913)*
(1882–1971)   *Sacrificial Dance*   4:25

Very large orchestra: three flutes, piccolo, alto flute, four oboes, English horn, four clarinets, bass clarinet, four bassoons, contrabassoon, eight horns, five trumpets, three trombones, two tubas, timpani (two players), percussion, and strings.

Instruments are combined with voices in operas, oratorios, cantatas, and musicals. Some masses are for chorus and orchestra, and a few symphonies include voices. Dance band and pop and rock groups have always featured singers. Combining voices with instruments adds to an ensemble the tone colors of voices and the extra dimension of language.

    Carl Orff's *Carmina Burana* effectively combines instruments and voices in a theatrical cantata. It draws its text and dramatic framework from a collection of secular poems written by medieval monks and wandering scholars and discovered centuries later in the library of an ancient abbey in Upper Bavaria. The combined expressive power of the orchestra and chorus are exhibited in *O Fortuna,* a setting of Latin words describing the vagaries of luck.

**Instruments
and Voices**

CARL ORFF: *Carmina Burana (1936)*
(1895–1982)   *1. O Fortuna*   2:19

Orchestra and chorus.

SUPPLEMENTARY MATERIAL

■ *The Symphony Orchestra,* second edition, sound film, 14:00, produced and distributed by Encyclopedia Britannica Educational Corporation.
    Traces the development of the orchestra from an ensemble of five string players to a large symphonic organization. Uses examples from the musical masterworks of three centuries to demonstrate the contribution of each major development in the orchestra.

■ *The Symphony Sound with Henry Lewis and the Royal Philharmonic,* color film, 28:00, produced by IQ Films, distributed by Learning Corporation of America. From the *Introduction to the Performing Arts Series.*
    Henry Lewis discusses the unique characteristics of the symphony orchestra and describes the instruments and their particular roles within the symphony.

5 ELEMENTS OF MUSIC

Individual sounds of varying duration, pitch, loudness, and color are combined simultaneously and in series to form the elements of music. The elements are not isolated in ordinary listening, but considering them separately facilitates study.

Rhythm and Meter

The most primitive element of music is *rhythm*. In a broad sense, the term encompasses all aspects of durations organized in time. The term has more restricted meanings in certain contexts. For example, various dances such as waltzes and tangos are associated with certain rhythms; rhythm in conjunction with pitches is the basis of melody; and the adjective form of the term, rhythmic, is applied to brief patterns of durations.

Meter is the aspect of rhythm relating to the pulses of equal duration ordinarily perceived in music and to their organization in groups defined by accents. The underlying metric patterns of accented and unaccented pulses provide the stimulus to which one responds physically in marching, dancing, and toe tapping. Except when referring specifically to meters or metric patterns, common practice is to use the more general term, *rhythm*.

Rhythm, unlike the other elements of music, can exist independently. Any sound, including noise, can establish rhythm. It is present in speech. Motion can be rhythmic, but rhythm usually implies organized sound. The sound of heels clicking on the pavement as a person walks creates a rhythmic pattern. The steps measure identical units of time, and these units are grouped in pairs by the alternation of left and right. The measured motion of walking has a direct counterpart in the rhythm of a march.

3/3

JOHN PHILIP SOUSA: *Hands Across the Sea* (1899)   2:42
(1854–1932)

This is one of Sousa's many stirring marches. Observe how easy it is to feel the pulse of this piece, as it is in all true marches. Tap your toe or wave your hand in time with the music as this march is played. Themes page 343.

The pulse of music is called the *beat*. With certain types of music, marches among them, responding physically to the beat is almost a reflex action. When the beat is less obvious, tapping or clapping with it focuses attention on the rhythm and aids in sensing the beat.

Music is made up of notes with durations that are longer, shorter, and with the same duration as the beats. The presence of longer and shorter durations does not obscure the perception of the beat or the regular pattern of the underlying rhythm. Quicker notes are heard in groups comprising beats, and slower notes are heard as combinations of beats. The drums and certain lower-pitched instruments usually mark the beat in marches.

Musicians sometimes count with the beats as a teaching device. The counting for a march goes *ONE-two, ONE-two.* The beats in a march are alternately accented and unaccented. *ONE* coincides with the accented beats and *two* with the unaccented beats. The complete pattern, an accented beat plus an unaccented beat, constitutes a *measure* or a *bar* of music. Though marches are also are also written with a four-beat pattern, *ONE-two-Three-four,* it simplifies the discussion to consider all march rhythms as two-beat patterns for the moment.

In addition to the marches originally intended to accompany marching, there are marches conceived as concert pieces. A common practice is to adapt march and dance rhythms for use in concert music. The beat in concert marches is not always as clear and regular as it is in street and military marches. This is true of the following concert march, which is from a suite which in turn is from an opera.

SERGE PROKOFIEV: *Love for Three Oranges (1925)*
(1891–1953)   *3. March*   1:40

The march rhythms in this piece are basically clear and regular, but there are momentary shifts that would be unlikely in a military march.

The preceding march for orchestra and the following march for piano illustrate opposite poles of the march concept. The former is fast and gay; the latter slow and somber. One must probe beneath the surface to detect the common rhythmic source indicated by the titles.

FRÉDÉRIC CHOPIN: *Piano Sonata no. 2 (1839)*
(1810–1849)   *3. Funeral March: Lento*   7:30

This dirgelike funeral march is one of the most familiar concert marches in the literature.

The *ONE-two* beat pattern found in marches also provides the rhythmic basis for dance music of many kinds. The *Russian Dance (Trepak)* from Tchaikovsky's *Nutcracker Suite,* taken from the ballet of the same name, has an obvious duple pattern of beats.

TCHAIKOVSKY: *Nutcracker Suite (1892)*
(1840–1893)   *4. Russian Dance (Trepak)*   1:01

A trepak is a Cossack dance in fast duple meter. The Cossacks were an elite corps of horsemen in czarist Russia.

The duple *ONE-two* beat pattern is only one of numerous possibilities. Waltzes, for example, have a triple *ONE-two-three* rhythmic background. The lilting, supple rhythm of waltzes contrasts sharply with the angular, straightforward rhythm of marches. The traditional *oomp-pah-pah* waltz accompaniment highlights the waltz rhythm with the accented first beat in the low register and the unaccented second and third beats in a higher register. This figure establishes the rhythmic pattern and continues as an accompaniment for the melody in the following example, as it does in most waltzes.

Johann Strauss

JOHANN STRAUSS: *The Blue Danube Waltz* (1867)   9:50
(1825–1899)

The nearly five hundred works of Strauss include several operettas, but he is best known as a composer of waltzes. They were conceived as dance music but endure as concert music. This waltz, one of his most famous, is not a simple dance tune, but a series of sophisticated melodies elaborately scored for full orchestra. An introduction in another rhythm precedes the waltz proper, and in concert performances the strict tempo of the dance is not preserved.

Just as many march rhythms are found in music not intended for marching, waltz rhythms are found in music not intended for dancing. In the following example the name, rhythm, and accompaniment pattern of the waltz have been retained, but other connections with the dance have been severed.

FRÉDÉRIC CHOPIN: *"Minute" Waltz* (1846)   1:25
(1810–1849)

The familiar name of this delightful miniature *Waltz, op. 64 no. 1,* suggests that it should be played in sixty seconds. Double that time is more realistic for most piano students, and the piece would still be too fast for dancing. Listeners hearing it played in the usual way tend to hear the beats in groups and the measure rather than the beat as the rhythmic unit. Concentrating on the typical waltz pattern of the accompaniment instead of the melody makes the waltz rhythm easier to detect.

The rhythmic element is prominent and uncomplicated in marches and dances, so they make a logical point of departure for the study of rhythm and meter. The basic duple and triple beat patterns underlying the rhythm of marches and waltzes, respectively, are also found in music far removed from parades and ballrooms. Music of widely divergent types may share a common rhythmic background. The rhythmic element in concert music is usually less obvious than in march and dance music, but in most instances the beats and groupings are readily perceptible. Try tapping and counting with the beats as you listen to the examples illustrating various rhythms and meters.

NICCOLÒ PAGANINI: *Caprices, op. 1*
(1782–1840)   *24. Theme and variations*   4:43

2/7

This piece has the same underlying *ONE-two* rhythm as a march, and the pace of the beats is nearly the same as in Sousa's *Hands Across the Sea* (LG 3/3). The beats and duple groupings can be perceived even though the solo violin has no accompaniment. During the brief silences between variations the regular beat is not maintained. Theme page 338.

Rhythms with march or dance characteristics are found in vocal as well as in instrumental music. The following aria and a waltz have much in common rhythmically.

GIUSEPPE VERDI: *Rigoletto, opera (1851)*
(1813–1901)   *La donna è mobile*   2:12

2/18

This opera aria has not only the same rhythmic background as a waltz but also a waltzlike accompaniment figure, making its triple meter unmistakable. Translation page 171.

Regular, recurrent patterns of two beats or three beats underlie the rhythm of most music. In a two-beat pattern the first beat is accented and the second unaccented. In a three-beat pattern the first beat is accented and the second and third are unaccented. These are the basic beat patterns.

Each basic pattern may constitute a *measure* of music. Two or more basic patterns are combined in larger measures. A measure of four beats, for example, consists of two groups of two beats. The first of the four beats receives a primary accent. The third receives a lesser, secondary accent, and the second and fourth beats are unaccented. This, at least, is the theory learned by young musicians. From the standpoint of the listener, the distinction is not always clear. The amount of accent is purely relative, and it is not always possible or even desirable in performance to exaggerate the difference between the stresses to the point where the primary and secondary accents are readily distinguishable. As a result, many marches are written in four-beat measures rather than in two-beat measures. When a march has a four-beat pattern, the left foot comes alternately with the first and third beats of the measure and the right foot with the second and fourth beats without noticeable effect. The same is true of dance music, which is written both ways.

The possibility of confusion between duple and quadruple meters exists only for listeners. Musical notation is explicit, and conductors are meticulous about making appropriate gestures, the ones that players expect for a given notation, though such subtleties are lost in radio and recorded performances. The following example is written in measures of four beats, or quadruple meter, but the most obvious aspect of the underlying rhythm is the alternation of strong and weak beats.

TCHAIKOVSKY: *Symphony no. 6, op. 74 (1893)*
(1840–1893) *3. Allegro molto vivace* 9:35

The rhythmic element is pronounced in this symphonic movement, and no difficulty will be experienced in locating the marchlike beats. If you can, distinguish not only between accented and unaccented beats but also between primary and secondary accents. Once you have located the primary accent, count with the rhythm *ONE-two-Three-four*. A certain sensitivity is required to differentiate between qualities of accent, but a reasonable degree of accuracy can be achieved by careful listening when performers are punctilious in their rendition. The distinction between two-beat measures and four-beat measures is not so much a fact to be observed as a suggestion to be sensed.

Just as rhythmic groups of two beats are combined in four-beat measures, rhythmic groups of three beats are combined in six-beat measures. In measures with six beats, the first receives the primary accent as always. The fourth receives the secondary accent, and beats two, three, five, and six are unaccented. The possibility of confusion between the primary and secondary accents and consequently between three-beat measures and six-beat measures is apparent. It is reassuring that appreciation is not impaired by such minor discrepancies in perception and that musicians are not infallible in this regard.

The situation is complicated by the fact that in faster tempos the notated beats tend to be heard as groups of three and the measures perceived as having two beats with divisions in thirds. The opening rhythms of the following example, with a borderline tempo between slow and fast, illustrate both possible interpretations. The durations in the first two measures are shown graphically.

1/17

J. S. BACH: *French Suite no. 4 in E-flat (1722)*
(1685–1750) *6. Gigue* 2:16

Measures of six relatively fast beats:

Durations	——	—	——	—	/	—	—	—	—	—	—	/
Beats	1	2	3	4	5	6	/	1	2	3	4	5	6	/

Measures of two beats, each equal to three in the preceding diagram:

Durations	——	—	——	—	/	—	—	—	—	—	—	/
Beats	1	.	.	2	.	.	/	1	.	.	2	.	.	/

While the music is playing, count the beats one way and then the other. Which seems most natural? Themes page 332.

In written music measures of nine beats and twelve beats also occur, but rarely.

The underlying rhythmic pulses of Western music basically are grouped and divided into duple and triple patterns. These basic duple and triple patterns and combinations of them in measures of four, six, nine, and twelve beats constitute the conventional metric units of familiar music.

The rhythmic possibilities inherent in combinations of duple and triple groupings such as $2 + 3$ and $2 + 2 + 3$ were not exploited in concert music until recent times, but such metric patterns are indigenous to the Balkan region. Rhythms having beats of unequal duration or measures that divide unequally are asymmetric (not symmetric). The following example of traditional Bulgarian dance music is based on a $2 + 2 + 3$ asymmetric rhythm pattern.

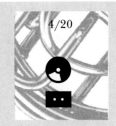

BULGARIA: *Tsone Mile Chedo/Eleno Mome*   2:02   4/20

If the individual rhythmic units in this example are perceived as beats, they are very short, and the measures have seven beats counted *ONE-two-Three-four-Five-six-seven.* If, instead, the groups are heard as the beats, the measures have three beats—two short and one long—counted *ONE-two-threeee.* Either way, the effect of the irregularity is clear and distinctive.

The acceptance of asymmetric meters opened new rhythmic vistas for composers and listeners alike. Tchaikovsky was one of the first composers to use five-beat measures in a symphonic composition.

TCHAIKOVSKY: *Symphony no. 6,* *op. 74 (1893)*
(1840–1893)   *2. Allegro con grazia*   7:15

The five-beat rhythmic pattern of this music may not feel quite as comfortable as the more usual patterns, but one soon becomes accustomed to its regular, though asymmetric, groupings. Five-beat measures divide $2 + 3$ or $3 + 2$. The unequal division of the measures and the irregular spacing of the accents produce an effect quite unlike that of symmetric rhythms.

It is only a short step from the use of asymmetric meters to the abandonment of fixed rhythmic patterns. The constant patterns and regular accents which regulated the rhythmic flow in music of the past are no longer universal. Many works of this century have irregular accents defining unpredictable groupings of beats and notes. The old sense of rhythmic stability and security is replaced by a sense of freedom and excitement. Symmetric rhythms, while still used, can no longer be taken for granted. Contemporary composers have added a new dimension to rhythm and have used it with skill and imagination. As a result, rhythm has been elevated from a role of subservience, a mere handmaiden of melody and harmony, to that of an equal in the hierarchy of musical elements. One of the first to grasp the potential of rhythm for attracting attention and sustaining interest and to feature it in extended passages was Igor Stravinsky.

3/6

IGOR STRAVINSKY: *The Rite of Spring* *(1913)*
(1882–1971) *Sacrificial Dance* 4:25

Every measure of this music from the ballet depicting the spring rituals of pagan Russia contained innovations when it was written, and it breached all of the conventional boundaries with its harmonic complexity and rhythmic intricacy. Irregular measures and shifting accents figure conspicuously in the rhythmic plan of the work. In some passages almost every measure has a different duration than its neighbors. In others the measures are fairly constant, but accents occur in unexpected places. Sometimes there is silence where an accent is anticipated. All of this adds up to rhythm that is as high-tensioned as the twentieth century. Its intricacies are a challenge to both performers and listeners. Many are attracted to this music immediately. Others have to learn to like it, but very few are bored by it.

Accents and obvious rhythmic groupings are not mandatory in music. Notes can be played and sung without perceptible accents or divisions, though this possibility is largely ignored. The tendency to organize sounds in groups seems to be innate. It emerges spontaneously in the writing of composers and in the playing and singing of performers. Listeners are inclined to attach significance to the slightest hint of stress or division and to organize sounds into patterns even when none are intended. Furthermore, avoiding suggestions of division is impossible in traditional notation. Bar lines, originally introduced as an aid to reading, are drawn between measures, and they have an acquired rhythmic significance which musicians are trained to observe. It is difficult for them to overcome this conditioning in the few passages where it is not appropriate. The net result is that few passages and fewer performances are lacking in stresses and groupings, but stresses should not be regarded as perpetual necessities. No music exists without flow and motion, but the obvious type of accent and grouping heard in marches and dances diminishes to the vanishing point at the opposite end of the rhythmic spectrum. The notation of many avant-garde compositions lacks bar lines and conventional metric groupings. Rhythmic relationships are sometimes specified using new notational devices, and sometimes they are left to the discretion of the performer or to chance. Principles of rhythm must be redefined and listening habits reoriented to accommodate the revolutionary rhythmic concepts in the new music of recent years.

At the beginning of each piece of conventional music and wherever changes in the rhythmic framework occur, there is a *time signature,* also called a *meter signature.* The time signature most often consists of two Arabic numerals written on the staff, one above the other, at the beginning of the piece. The lower number shows which note symbol is used to represent the beat. The upper number indicates the number of beats in each measure of the music. The measures are marked in musical notation by vertical lines called *bar lines.* Vestiges of an older system of rhythmic notation persist in two time signatures which have a symbol in place of the two numbers. A large "C" is the equivalent of a 4/4 time signature, and the same symbol with a vertical line through it is the equivalent of a 2/2 time signature.

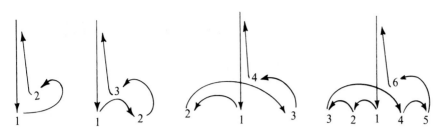

FIGURE 5.1

Conductor's beat
patterns

Conductors, with their right hand or a baton, describe stylized patterns in the air appropriate to the various time signatures. Each conductor makes personalized modifications in the designs, but sufficient uniformity is preserved to make the beats intelligible to players. A stroke straight down directly in front of the conductor is used for the first beat of each measure. For this reason, the first beat of a measure is referred to as the *downbeat*. If there are two beats in the measure, the second is indicated by an upward motion roughly parallel with that of the downbeat. A three-beat pattern approximates the shape of a triangle—down, right, and up to the point of origin. The conductor's beat for four-beat measures is down, left, right, and up. The motion for six-beat measures is down, left, left, right, right, and up. (See figure 5.1.) Unaccented beats at the end of measures come on the up stroke of the conductor's beat and are referred to as *upbeats*. Measures with more than six beats usually are conducted with motions following one of the contours mentioned, with subdivisions as necessary. When the beats are too fast to be conducted individually, one gesture is used for a group of beats. Conversely, when the notated beat is very slow, it may be divided and conducted with two or three motions.

What aspects of rhythm should listeners be able to discern? Distinguishing between two-beat and three-beat patterns presents no formidable problem. Recognizing combinations of basic groups is more difficult, and infallibility cannot be expected. However, attentive listeners will be aware of extended measures in the more obvious examples. Sensitivity to shifting accents, to changes of meter, and to the absence of rhythmic stresses should be cultivated. Rhythm is the foundation of the musical edifice. The realm of listening experience is extended by an awareness of rhythm's patterns and functions.

Tempo

Tempo refers to the rate of speed in music. The ability to establish exact tempos was enhanced in 1816 when Johann Maelzel added a scale of tempos to a previously invented pendulum device and patented it as a *metronome*. The pendulum could be set to swing and tick at selected rates with which the beats of music were coordinated. In modern metronomes the functions of the pendulum are usually performed by electronic timing mechanisms.

Metronome markings are expressed in terms of the number of beats per minute. The Maelzel metronome (M.M.) marking M.M. = 60 indicates a tempo of 60 beats per minute or one per second. Often a note symbol is used in place of the abbreviation M.M. The marking ♩ = 72 indicates a tempo of 72 beats represented by quarter notes (the symbol shown) per minute. At that rate each beat has a duration of 1/72 of a minute, or 5/6 of a second.

Beethoven was intrigued by the possibilities of the metronome, and he provided his symphonies with metronome markings. Contemporary composers are more inclined to use metronome markings than were composers of the period immediately following their introduction. Perhaps because of tradition or the mechanical nature of the metronome, composers continued to use Italian terms introduced early in the seventeenth century as tempo indications. These terms lack the precision of metronome markings, but they convey implications of style as well as of pace. Combining Italian terms with metronome markings is a common practice which secures the advantages of both.

Tempo indications would be of no particular concern to the listener except that they are used to designate the various movements of multi-movement works and sometimes figure in the titles of compositions. This makes familiarity with at least the more common ones desirable. Arranged from the slowest to the fastest with approximate English equivalents, they are:

Largo: Broad, large	*Moderato:* Moderate
Lento: Slow	*Allegro:* Cheerful
Adagio: Comfortable, easy	*Vivace:* Lively, quick
Andante: Going along, walking	*Presto:* Very fast, rapid

Derivative forms of these terms provide shades of meaning. *Larghetto,* a diminutive form of *largo,* indicates a tempo slightly less slow. *Allegretto,* a diminutive form of *allegro,* indicates a tempo slightly less fast. There is disagreement on the interpretation of *andantino,* the diminutive form of *andante.* Some regard *andante* as a slow tempo and *andantino* as somewhat faster. Others class *andante* as a fast tempo and consequently consider *andantino* to be a little slower. No less a personage than Beethoven was puzzled by this question. Though the precise meaning of *andantino* is in doubt, the confusion about its significance establishes the fact that *andante* falls at the center of the scale of tempos and on the dividing line between those classified as fast and those classified as slow. *Prestissimo* is a superlative form of *presto,* meaning extremely fast. Diminutive and superlative forms of other terms also are used.

To provide more explicit and descriptive directions, tempo indications are modified by additional Italian words and phrases such as:

Agitato: Agitated	*Grazioso:* With grace
Animato: Animated	*Ma:* But
Appassionata: Passionately	*Maestoso:* Majestically
Assai: Very	*Marcato:* Marked
Cantabile: Singing	*Molto:* Very, much
Con brio: With vigor and spirit	*Non:* Not
Con fuoco: With fire	*Non troppo:* Not too much

Con moto: With motion	*Più:* More
E or *ed:* And	*Poco:* Little
Espressivo: Expressively	*Sostenuto:* Sustained

Many combinations of these and other terms are used in identifying the examples. See the glossary for additional definitions.

In addition to the words and phrases for rates of speed, there are indications for gradual and sudden changes, both faster and slower. Listeners should be alert to changes of pace, a significant means of musical expression.

Composers from time to time abandon Italian terminology in favor of the vernacular, but this practice has not become general. It is more prevalent now than formerly, but it has two disadvantages. Italian words and phrases through long usage have developed connotations difficult or awkward to express in other languages, and musical terms in Italian are more universally understood than any other.

There are no absolute limits on musical pace, but practical considerations regulate extremes. Sustaining accuracy in extremely slow tempos is difficult. Equally difficult is conducting, counting, and playing extremely fast tempos. Tempos related to the physiological rhythm of the heartbeat seem most natural. These encompass rates between approximately sixty and eighty per minute. Tempos outside these limits are perceived as slow or fast. The tendency is to divide or combine units to bring them within this range, though the points at which this occurs vary with individuals, both performers and listeners.

Tempo is a major factor in setting the mood of music, and it is a prime source of variety. Contrast of tempo is sought between sections of larger works, between movements of multimovement works, and between selections on programs. The usual order of tempos in a four movement symphony is: fast—slow—moderate or moderately fast—fast, the last usually faster than the first. There are, of course, modifications of and exceptions to this plan. A typical sequence of tempos is illustrated in Mozart's *Haffner Symphony.*

W. A. MOZART: *Symphony no. 35* (1782)		19:06	1/22–25
(1756–1791)	*1. Allegro con spirito*	7:59	
	2. Andante	4:26	
	3. Menuetto	3:06	
	4. Presto	3:35	

This music was written in honor of Siegmund Haffner, the son of Salzburg's mayor, at the time he was elevated to the nobility. No tempo indication is given for the *menuetto* (minuet), a practice of the period that leads to diverse interpretations. Originally a rustic dance, the minuet made its way into the French court and from there into concert music. The dance was characterized by grace and dignity, but the minuets in symphonies are often played in a sprightly style. The most usual tempo marking, when one is given, is *allegretto.* Menuetto themes page 334.

Schumann's *Scenes from Childhood* (*Kinderscenen*), a collection of thirteen brief pieces, provide an interesting study in tempo. Each editor (and performer) has different ideas regarding their interpretation. The tempo markings in two editions are given for comparison. The Italian tempo indications are from the G. Schirmer edition. They must have been added by the editor, Harold Bauer, because they do not appear in other editions. The metronome marks immediately following the Italian terms are also from the Schirmer edition. The metronome marks in parentheses are from the Kalmus edition "edited according to manuscripts and from her personal recollections by Clara Schumann," a famous pianist and wife of the composer. The metronome markings for numbers 9 and 12 in the two editions are for different note values, as shown. Comparable metronome marks would be 56 for number 9 in the Schirmer edition and 40 for number 12 in the Kalmus edition. English translations of the original German titles are from the Schirmer edition.

ROBERT SCHUMANN: *Scenes from Childhood* (*1838*)   14:40
(1810–1856)

1. About Strange Lands and People   2/4   1:30
    Andante   ♩ = 72   (♩ = 108)
2. Curious Story   3/4   1:00
    Allegro giojoso   ♩ = 132   (♩ = 132)
3. Blindman's Buff   2/4   :35
    Allegro scherzando   ♩ = 116   (♩ = 120)
4. Pleading Child   2/4   :50
    Moderato   ♩ = 60   (♩ = 88)
5. Perfectly Contented   2/4   :35
    Allegro moderato   ♩ = 84   (♩ = 72)
6. Important Event   3/4   1:00
    Allegro marziale   ♩ = 120   (♩ = 120)
7. Reverie (Träumerei)   C   2:10
    Adagio espressivo   ♩ = 56   (♩ = 80)
8. At the Fireside   2/4   :45
    Allegretto grazioso   ♩ = 104   (♩ = 108)
9. The Knight of the Rocking Horse   3/4   :40
    Allegro con brio   ♩ = 176   (♩. = 76)
10. Almost too Serious   2/8   1:10
    Moderato, poco rubato   ♪ = 100   (♪ = 104)
11. Frightening   2/4   1:30
    Poco allegro   ♩ = 96   (♩ = 108)
12. Child Falling Asleep   2/4   1:25
    Lento non troppo   ♩ = 44   (♪ = 80)
13. The Poet Speaks   C   1:30
    Adagio espressivo   ♩ = 88   (♩ = 92)

For an illuminating comparison of the tempos specified for the *Scenes from Childhood* with those of a recorded performance, count the beats for 15 seconds while the music is playing and multiply by four to give the number of beats per minute. The procedure is complicated somewhat by occasional deviations from the regular tempo indicated by the composer and by liberties taken by artists in their interpretation of the music, without which performances would seem mechanical and uninteresting. Total performance time provides another basis for tempo comparisons, since slower tempos result in longer performance times and faster tempos in shorter performance times.

Unless a composer gives a metronome marking, an approximate tempo is merely suggested, and no two conductors or players will give identical interpretations. Some performers choose to ignore even precise directions. Fast, brilliant tempos are favored by some while others are partial to slower, more deliberate paces. Both schools of thought have many partisans, and tempo is a frequent subject of debate among musicians.

Melody is that inscrutable, magical element of music that captures the imagination and lingers in the memory to be recalled, hummed, and whistled long after words and accompaniments have been forgotten. Melody and music are almost synonymous, yet strangely, countless textbooks are devoted to harmony, counterpoint, and form but few to melody. One reason may be that dissecting and analyzing melodies is not very illuminating. Melody, perhaps more than the other elements of music, is dictated by inspiration and appreciated by instinct. Some questions about melody, however, can be posed and answered objectively.

Melody

What is a melody? How are melodies conceived? What are the characteristics of a good one? How are melodies recognized and remembered? These are questions inquisitive listeners might ask. The first is the easiest to answer.

A melody is a succession of musical tones conveying an impression of continuity—a series of pitches of varying durations arranged in a logical sequence. Random sounds are not perceived as melodies, nor are tones unduly separated in time, register, or color. As usually construed, melodies have definite points of beginning and ending; the latter attended by a sense of completion. The proportions of individual melodies are modest, and most compositions have more than one. Extended works have many, though probably only a few of them are remembered vividly. An essential art of composition is to delineate separate melodies without disturbing the flow and continuity of the whole.

Most melodies are played or sung in their entirety by the same instrument, voice, or group. This is not mandatory, but it is suggested by the requirement of continuity. It also serves the purpose of making the melody easier to follow. Exceptions to this occur in repetitions after a melody is familiar. Then various instruments may share a single statement for variety. In orchestral compositions, contrasting melodies usually are assigned to different instruments.

The principal melody more often than not is higher in pitch than the accompaniment and secondary melodies. This, however, is something which changes with the period, the style, and the form. Occasionally the main

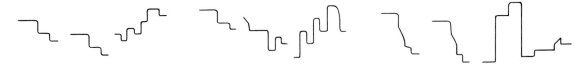

FIGURE 5.2

Melodic contour graph of *Who Is Sylvia*

melody is assigned to the bottom or middle of the musical texture. At other times melodic interest is divided between all the parts. Composers and performers subtly direct the listener's attention to the most important melodic line when it departs from its accustomed position. This is done by making it louder, faster, slower, or different in color from the background.

The exact mechanism by which a person is able to remember and recognize hundreds of different melodies is a mystery, but musical memory is not much different from any other. It is aided by repetition and association. It improves with use and retains best that which it finds most pleasant. Musical memory and musical enjoyment are closely linked. There is satisfaction in hearing familiar melodies and in anticipating well-known strains. Extending the scope of one's listening experience to include both more and better music develops the musical memory and in the process broadens the foundations of musical enjoyment. The full potentials of memory and appreciation are realized when music one initially finds intriguing is heard repeatedly under agreeable circumstances.

Remembering melodies, like remembering words, names, addresses, and telephone numbers, requires the ability to recognize familiar arrangements of a limited number of components—twelve tones in the case of music. Melodies are nothing more than distinctive arrangements of notes selected from the twelve available. Few melodies make use of all of them. More important than the selection and order of tones in melodic recognition is *contour*. Melodic contour results from the interplay of pitches and durations.

A graph of the melodic contour of *Who Is Sylvia* (figure 5.2) is given as an aid in visualizing that aspect of the melody. Follow the graph while a recording of the song is played. The melody in the voice is heard three times with different words.

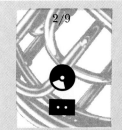

2/9

FRANZ SCHUBERT: *Who Is Sylvia* (1826)   2:40
(1797–1828)

Observe the balance between ascending and descending motion and between conjunct and disjunct movement. Notice also the distribution of high and low points in the line. Small rhythm and pitch patterns, which are repeated literally and varied, provide unifying elements. Schubert demonstrates infallible intuition in achieving these desirable melodic characteristics. Words page 194; notation page 337.

Knowing that a composer draws material from a fundamental stockpile of twelve notes and that melodies can be represented by graphs may make composing sound like fitting pieces of a jigsaw puzzle into suitable patterns of up and down, long and short. This obviously is not the case. What about inspiration? Its role is not as decisive as popular legends would lead one to think. Composers do not experience a powerful emotion and dash wild-eyed to the piano to create, spontaneously, an immortal masterpiece. In reality the creative process is much less romantic and more arduous, but not a mechanical or perfunctory task.

Composition begins with an idea—call it inspiration if you will. Ideas may come out of the blue, but far more often inspiration strikes the composer who is in pursuit of it, pencil in hand. Each composer develops a personal approach to composition, but with most the initial germ is born in the mind without recourse to any instrument. The idea is abstract, conceived mentally, but immediately it is translated into symbols and perhaps into sounds as well. Most often the initial idea for a composition is a motive or a melody, occasionally a rhythm, a chord, or a harmonic progression. A unique fragment envisaged in a flash may contain the seed of an entire symphony, but infinite skill, patience, and imagination are required to bring it to fruition. This is the craft of the composer.

If inspiration dictates any aspect of music, it is melody, but even the most inspired melody rarely springs from the composer's mind full-blown and perfect. Most often initial melodic conceptions require reworking and polishing. Applying technique to inspiration, the composer strives for those melodic characteristics illustrated in the Schubert example: balance between unity and variety and between high and low points. The composer's artistic instinct serves as the sole arbitrator of what constitutes *balance,* and success or failure as a composer depends in large measure upon the ability to make such decisions in a manner acceptable to discerning audiences. Immortal masterpieces and rejected manuscripts are made from the same raw material.

The dividing line between good and bad melodies, like that between good and bad music generally, is blurred by subjective judgments. Beauty and ugliness, order and chaos, and the like are not states of being but reflections of personal opinion. Such opinions are supported more by emotional convictions than by logic, and logic at best is not easily brought to bear upon aesthetic matters. The result is that disparity exists in melodic and musical preferences, in likes and dislikes. This is not only inevitable, but essential. Except for differences in taste, there would be only one kind of music, and what could be more dreary? The vitality of the art is in a large measure a product of its diversity, but the diverse melodic styles illustrated will not prove equally attractive to everyone. Personal inclinations as well as differences in conditioning dictate otherwise. The appeal of some melodies is immediate and almost universal, but the taste for others, like the taste for green olives, must be acquired.

A melody, as most listeners would define the term, is a lyrical and song-like series of musical tones. Consequently, a preponderance of the best-known melodies are for voice, including (naturally) popular songs like the following one.

HARRY CONNICK, JR.: *Blue Light, Red Light* (1991)
(1967–   )   *1. Someone's There*   3:28

The melodic style of this popular song is traditional, though it is of recent vintage. The interlude in the middle of the recording illustrates an embellished performance of a vocal melody by instruments.

The longevity of basic melodic concepts is confirmed by the fact that the general description of melody is valid for both the preceding popular song and the following seventeenth-century opera aria, except that the mood of the latter is less lyric and more somber.

HENRY PURCELL: *Dido and Aeneas, opera* (1689)
(1659–1695)   *Thy hand, Belinda/When I am laid in earth*   4:12

The aria begins after a brief introductory passage. This particular example, serving here as a model melody, takes on added significance when it is heard again later on as an example of continuous variation form with attention focused on the bass line (see page 330). Also LG 2/1 (Mozart).

The lyric, flowing, and songlike characteristics of melodies conceived by composers like Haydn and Mozart in the late eighteenth century were shaped by classic ideals of simplicity and clarity. Romantic composers of the next era replaced these qualities with their own special kind of sensuous emotion to write soaring melodies of breathtaking beauty and grace.

GIACOMO PUCCINI: *Tosca, opera* (1900)
(1858–1924)   *Vissi d'arte*   3:08

Melodies like this one are a significant factor in the continuing popularity of Puccini as an opera composer.

The gift for melodic invention is evident in the instrumental as well as the vocal works of romantic composers.

CÉSAR FRANCK: *Violin Sonata in A* (1886)
(1822–1890)   *4. Allegretto poco mosso*   6:06

Overlapping statements of the same melody by the violin and the piano contribute to the effectiveness of the melodic unfolding without distracting from the sense of continuity.

Twentieth-century composers have been energetic in expanding melodic concepts beyond the types illustrated thus far. Singable melodies are no longer considered essential. Melodies with wide ranges, angular leaps, and disjunct contours are in vogue. Contemporary rhythmic and harmonic resources have exerted strong pressures on melodic designs. The combined effect of these influences has altered recent melodic invention to the point where modern music is accused of being tuneless by some schooled exclusively in the old traditions. A blanket indictment is not justified, though isolated pieces of evidence can be cited to support it. Modern melodies depart radically from traditional means, but their objectives remain the same. The intent of contemporary composers is to achieve greater interest and expressiveness by abolishing arbitrary restrictions and exploiting new freedoms. They may at times sacrifice ordered regularity, tonal stability, the clarity, the simplicity, and the sensuousness of the previous melodic styles in their quest for melodic materials more suitable for their requirements, but they are still striving for successions of musical sounds conveying impressions of continuity and logic. The old ways of achieving these ends have not been entirely discarded, but many new ones have been added. The melodies of Paul Hindemith's *Kleine Kammermusik* (*Little Chamber Music*) are certainly recognizable as melodies, yet they have a thoroughly contemporary flavor. They are capricious, brittle, and fresh.

HINDEMITH: *Kleine Kammermusik (1922)*   13:00
(1895–1963)   *1. Lustig (Merry)*   2:30
                     2. Walzer (Waltz)   2:00
                     3. Ruhig und einfach (Quiet and simple)   4:45
                     4. Schnelle (Quick)   :45
                     5. Sehr lebhaft (Very lively)   3:00

This gay and witty piece is not to be taken too seriously. The clever melodies sparkle, with no pretensions of profundity. Not until the third movement is there a hint of traditional melodic lyricism.

In some avant-garde styles and works the melodic element is missing, in which case interest is concentrated in one or more of the other elements.

Harmony

Different pitches sounding together produce *harmony*. The smallest elements of harmony are *intervals*, which consist of two tones. The harmonic effect of an interval depends upon the relationship between the vibrating frequencies of its two component tones. In general, simple ratios are more harmonious; complex ratios more discordant. The Table of Intervals (table 5.1) shows the intervals above C in relation to the piano keyboard and lists them in order of complexity. The ratios are only approximate because of minor discrepancies between the natural ratios and modern tuning. The descriptive terms given for the quality of the intervals are purely subjective.

To hear the effect of all the intervals, find the note C near the center of the piano keyboard (see table 5.1), and play each interval up from C, progressing from the smallest to the largest. Then play the intervals in order

TABLE 5.1 *T*ABLE OF INTERVALS

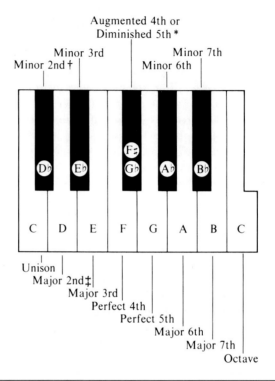

Notes	Interval	Ratio	Description
C-C	Unison	1:1	amplifies sound only
C-C	Octave	1:2	white, transparent
C-G	Fifth, perfect	2:3	barren, open, hollow
C-F	Fourth, perfect	3:4	barren, open, hollow
C-E	Third, major	4:5	clear, bright
C-E♭	Third, minor	5:6	somber, dark
C-A	Sixth, major	3:5	clear, bright
C-A♭	Sixth, minor	5:8	somber, dark
C-D	Second, major	8:9	mildly discordant, rough
C-B♭	Seventh, minor	9:16	mildly discordant, rough
C-B	Seventh, major	8:15	sharply discordant, harsh
C-D♭	Second, minor	15:16	sharply discordant, harsh
C-F♯*	Fourth, augmented	17:24	strident, unstable
C-G♭*	Fifth, diminished	17:24	strident, unstable

Different ways of notating the same relationship.
†Or *half step* or *semitone.*
‡Or *whole step* or *whole tone.*

of complexity, as they are listed at the bottom of the Table of Intervals. After this, you may wish to substitute your own descriptive terms for those given.

Intervals are classified as consonant or dissonant. Those with the simple vibrating ratios, up to and including the minor sixth (5:8), are consonant. The remaining intervals are dissonant, some more so than others. There is an unfortunate tendency to regard consonant intervals as pleasant and dissonant intervals as unpleasant. No musical sound or combination of sounds is intrinsically unpleasant. A more valid association can be made between dissonance and tension and between consonance and repose. Dissonance generates tension which is relieved by consonance. This is analogous to the conflict in a novel produced by problems which are resolved at the end. Consonances and happy endings are meaningful artistically only in terms of the dissonances and conflicts that precede them. Dissonant intervals and chords should not be regarded as distasteful but as the harmonic elements which render consonant intervals and chords imperative. The interaction of consonance and dissonance in the musical matrix gives substance and direction to the composer's ideas.

The various intervals provide several shades of consonance and dissonance. The range of consonance and dissonance is expanded to infinity when the number of tones sounding together and the relationships between them are unrestricted. The music of different styles and periods operates on entirely different harmonic planes. Just as drama runs the gamut of human emotions from the comparative tranquillity of Arcadian idylls to the intensity of Greek tragedies and the horror of explicit violence, music explores the extremes from purest consonance and complete repose to ear-shattering dissonance and electrifying tension. Any harmonic sound can be meaningful and appropriate in the proper frame of reference.

Most harmonies contain three or more tones. Three or more tones sounding together make a *chord*. The foundation structures of harmony are three-note chords built from alternate notes of a scale, C–E–G for example, called *triads*. The three notes of a triad may be arranged in any order and doubled in various octaves without causing the triad to lose its identity, but every detail of order, spacing, doubling, and scoring modifies the sound somewhat. A triad may be constructed on any note, and each one has a distinctive quality and function in relation to the others.

Clear examples of unadulterated triad harmony are not plentiful. During the period when triad harmonies were used exclusively, all of the parts in the prevailing style were conceived melodically, not harmonically. The melodies combined to form triads at strategic points, but between these points notes not belonging to the triad were used. Also, one part sometimes arrived at its triad note slightly after or before the other parts. In listening to such music the ear is attracted to the melodic lines by their independent rhythms, and the harmonic foundation governing the melodic movement goes unnoticed. The following example is typical. Only triad harmonies are used, but this fact is obscured by the motion of the lines except at the end of phrases and sections.

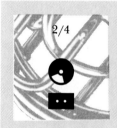

PALESTRINA: *Pope Marcellus Mass (1555)*
(1525–1594)   *Kyrie*   5:00

Triads were the only chord structures acknowledged by Palestrina and his contemporaries, but as the voices move from one triad tone to another, other notes occur melodically. The triad harmonies are most apparent in the final section of this example.

The harmonic resources of music are never static, and it was inevitable that additions to triad structures would be made almost as soon as composers started to think of music in terms of chords and chord progressions rather than in terms of combined melodies. Four-note chords constructed in the same way as triads, from alternate scale tones, began to make tentative appearances early in the seventeenth century. If the numbers 1–3–5 are used to represent triad formations, the numbers 1–3–5–7 represent the components of these four-note chords, called *seventh chords,* a seventh being the interval between 1 and 7. Seventh chords were assimilated gradually into the harmonic vocabulary during the seventeenth and eighteenth centuries but did not challenge the predominance of triads until the last half of the nineteenth century, and then only occasionally. The bulk of the concert music now performed and most universally appreciated was composed using a harmonic language consisting of various triad and seventh-chord structures. Beethoven's *Piano Sonata no. 8,* known as the *Pathétique,* is a prime example of this harmonic language.

BEETHOVEN: *Piano Sonata no. 8 (1799)*
(1770–1827)   *1. Grave—Allegro di molto e con brio*   5:59

Written near the middle of the period just described, this sonata movement illustrates all of the chord structures and progressions in common use at the time. Seventh chords are especially prominent in the slow introductory section and in subsequent appearances of the introductory material. Themes page 335.

In some works composed during the second half of the nineteenth century, seventh chords displaced triads as the most prevalent chord structures. Concurrently, a predilection for chromaticism (that is, the use of the five tones not included in the scale or key of the piece) emerged. Extensive use of seventh chords and chromatic (color) notes led to highly colorful and expressive harmony. Richard Wagner pioneered this trend. Criticized as an undisciplined radical by some of his contemporaries, he is now acclaimed as one of the great innovators in the history of music.

RICHARD WAGNER: *Tristan and Isolde* *(1865)*
(1813–1883)   *Prelude*   10:45

Nowhere are Wagner's revolutionary harmonic ideas employed more effectively than in this *Prelude*. After more than a century, this music is unsurpassed for sheer sensuousness, and the harmonies still have an aura of strangeness. The first performance must have been astounding. Also LG 2/17.

Adding another note, the second note above the seventh, to a seventh chord produces a *ninth chord*. Ninth chords are both too rich and too cumbersome for a steady diet, but they contribute added spice to the musical fare. Claude Debussy exploited ninth chord sonorities around the turn of the century. Later, jazz composers and arrangers discovered these sounds and adopted them as their own.

CLAUDE DEBUSSY: *Nocturnes* *(1899)*
(1862–1918)   *2. Fêtes (Festivals)*   5:45

Ninth chords are used freely, but by no means incessantly, in this atmospheric work. Debussy's tone painting is devoted more to conveying impressions than details, but his depiction of a procession, first approaching and then departing, is unmistakable.

Continuing the process of building chords from alternate scale tones beyond the ninth produces *eleventh chords* and *thirteenth chords*. Eleventh chords are fairly common, especially in popular songs of the Broadway musical variety. Thirteenth chords, which contain all of the notes of a seven-tone scale, are somewhat less useful and less used. One hesitates to suggest a specific selection from the popular field, because most of them are short-lived. Almost any sophisticated arrangement of a popular song will provide examples of this type of harmony. Gershwin's *Rhapsody in Blue* is a more enduring work in a similar vein.

GEORGE GERSHWIN: *Rhapsody in Blue* *(1924)*   16:10
(1898–1937)

Jazz elements of the period when it was written dominate the rhythms, melodies, and harmonies of this work. Seventh chords are the most prevalent harmonic ingredient, but ninth chords, eleventh chords, and occasionally more complicated harmonic structures occur.

The music played by the new big bands combines complex, dissonant harmonies with colorful instrumentation. The following example also uses electronically generated and modified sounds and pitches not heard in conventional music.

4/11

DON ELLIS BAND: *House in the Country (1969)*   2:46

This piece demonstrates convincingly that very strident harmonies can be incorporated in a style that is immediately accessible.

During the twentieth century, harmonic resources have been expanded to include chord structures built in seconds, fourths, and fifths (see the Table of Intervals, page 78) and also combinations of tones and simple chords, such as triads, from different keys. Chords in these categories are heard in the preceding example and in Stravinsky's *Rite of Spring* (LG 3/6—cited as an example of rhythm on page 68). *Sonorities,* a more inclusive term than chords, significantly more complex than those in these examples require revolutionary approaches to combining tones.

One work featuring an innovative concept of sonority is Penderecki's *Threnody for the Victims of Hiroshima.*

KRZYSZTOF PENDERECKI: *Threnody (1960)*   9:00
(1933–   )

This elegy is for fifty-two string instruments, each one with an individual part. It uses *quarter tones,* that is, pitch differences only half as large as the smallest in conventional music. Sometimes every quarter-tone pitch within a specified range sounds simultaneously, producing a solid mass of pitches. Sounds are produced on the instruments in a variety of uncharacteristic ways, vastly expanding the string orchestra's spectrum of tonal colors. In music like this, sonority and tone color are the most salient features. Melody and rhythm are displaced as the elements of primary interest and the focus of the listener's attention.

Though harmonic tension and dissonance at times seem to have reached the saturation point, the quest of composers for new sonorities never ceases, and each generation of listeners is exposed to new sound experiences.

Tonality and Mode

Tonality is that phenomenon which causes music based on a major or minor scale to gravitate to a single focal point. This tendency exists in both melodies and harmonic progressions. The note that emerges as the center of the tonal system is designated the *tonic* or *keynote.* The letter name of the keynote is the *key* of the piece or passage. There is no obvious reason for the supremacy of one tone and the subservience of others, but this orientation around a central pitch occurs spontaneously in tonal music. The function of all other tones and chords is ordained by their relation to the tonic.

Tonality is an elusive quality, difficult to define but easy to demonstrate. Start singing the first stanza of *America (My Country 'tis of Thee)* and stop on the word "I." Notice the sensation of being "up in the air." The impression is stronger if the harmony is added. The phrase demands completion which is accomplished by adding the tonic note and chord with the word "sing." At the end of the stanza, the tonic on "ring" is approached differently, but stopping short of it produces the same effect. A variant of this experiment is to interrupt a recording of a tonal piece before the final chord. In each case a conclusive feeling is demanded which only the tonic can supply. The interaction of tonal relationships which creates this situation is *tonality*.

Any pitch may serve as the tonic. The relation of other tones to it determines the *mode*. Between octaves of the tonic, there are eleven different pitches. Together with the tonic they constitute a *chromatic scale* of twelve tones. Commonly, music is based on scales of seven tones selected from these to form certain patterns of whole steps (major seconds) and half steps (minor seconds). Numbering the scale degrees up from the keynote, the most prevalent pattern has half steps between 3–4 and 7–8, whole steps elsewhere. This is the pattern associated with the syllables *do, re, mi, fa, sol, la, ti, do*. It forms a *major scale*, and music derived from it is in a *major mode* or *key*. *America, The Star Spangled Banner, Home on the Range,* and most familiar songs are in major keys.

After major, the next most common scale pattern is that of *minor*. Natural minor is a seven-tone scale with half steps between 2–3 and 5–6. *When Johnny Comes Marching Home* is a well-known song in minor. The major mode has been so predominant, elements of it customarily are incorporated in pieces which are fundamentally minor. This has led to scale resources referred to as forms of minor but which actually are hybrids combining elements of the two modes. The essential difference between major and all forms of minor lies in the third degree of the scale. It is a major third above the keynote in major and a minor third above the keynote in minor.

Contrast the sound of the two following examples—one major and the other minor.

FRÉDÉRIC CHOPIN: *Preludes for Piano (1839)*
(1810–1849)   *No. 7 in A major*   :42
                          No. 4 in E minor   1:52

2/11–12

Prelude no. 7 is in a major key, and *Prelude no. 4* is in a minor key, as indicated. Both preludes end with a strong return to the keynote in the melody and the bass. See if you can sing the keynote just as the sound of the last chord fades away.

A high percentage of the music written since 1600 is either major or minor. The ability to distinguish between major and minor and to discern the keynote at the end of compositions and at critical points during the course of a work is evidence of perceptive listening.

Prior to the seventeenth century when the major-minor system gained ascendancy, liturgical music was classified according to a system of *church modes* (also known as *ecclesiastical modes*). These modes are seven-tone scales like major and minor but with variable patterns of whole steps and half steps. The modal classifications were applied to the Gregorian chant repertory, of which the following *Kyrie* is a sample.

GREGORIAN CHANT: *Mass IV (Cunctipotens)*
(Codified 590–604)　　　　　　　　*Kyrie*　　　　　　　　2:06

Modal music has a central tone called the *final* that functions like a keynote in defining the mode, but the sense of a tonal center is less decisive in modal music than in major and minor keys. Notation page 329.

The modal scale patterns were also used in the secular music of the period. They are still heard in folk songs, and many of the currently popular rock melodies and harmonies have a definite modal flavor. After centuries of relative obscurity, the church modes were rediscovered and adapted to modern usage by composers both popular and serious. One of the first pieces of chamber music to utilize modal melodies in a deliberate fashion was Ravel's *String Quartet*.

MAURICE RAVEL: *String Quartet in F* (1903)
(1875–1937)　　　　　*1. Allegro moderato—Très doux*　　　　　7:30

The composed modal melodies of this quartet are unlike the chants or folk songs with which they share scale materials. The modal influence does not extend to the harmonies, which are typical of Ravel and turn-of-the-century French music.

Toward the end of the last century, composers seem to have come to the conclusion that the possibilities of musical invention within the major-minor system were approaching exhaustion. In any event the exploration of other scale resources dates from about this time. Besides reviving the church modes, composers devised and exploited new scales. One of the most distinctive of the new scales was the *whole tone scale*. In contrast to major and minor scales and the church modes, whole tone scales have no half steps and only six tones. The following composition draws its material, except for a brief passage in the middle, entirely from a whole tone scale.

CLAUDE DEBUSSY: *Preludes for Piano, Book I* (1910)
(1862–1918)　　　　　*2. Voiles (Sails or Veils)*　　　　　3:54

The whole tone scale is ideal for creating the nebulous atmosphere of this piece.

Fascinating as the whole tone scale is, its usefulness has definite limits. Melodies and harmonies derived from it have a certain sameness of sound, and the very striking quality which initially attracts both composers and listeners soon leads them to tire of it.

Another scale formation that has been explored by twentieth-century composers is an eight-tone or *octatonic* scale constructed of alternating half steps and whole steps. Octatonic scale derivations are not readily recognized by ear, and music theorists have only recently begun scrutinizing scores for evidence of octatonic origins. Some passages in *The Rite of Spring* by Stravinsky (LG 3/6) are based melodically and harmonically on the interval patterns of octatonic scales.

In the first half of this century, composers utilized octatonic and other scales of fewer than twelve tones, but the prevailing trend has been to reject the somewhat arbitrary concept of selective scales and to regard all twelve tones of the chromatic scale as equal in status and accessibility. The net result has been to abolish the previous hierarchy of tones and to expand and free from restraint the available pitch resources.

According equal status to the components of an all-inclusive pitch collection of twelve tones does not automatically eliminate the possibility of tonality. Tonal centers can be established which include in their orbit all eleven remaining tones, rather than the customary six that gravitate to a conventional tonic. Distinctions between major and minor disappear, and the tonality in such music is vague. However, alert listeners can detect the tonal centers in music, like the following example, which embodies the principles of this expanded tonal concept.

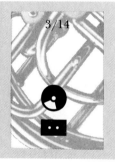

BÉLA BARTÓK: *Piano Concerto no. 3 (1945)*   3/14
(1881–1945)   *3. Allegro vivace*   7:19

The tonal centers in passages of this twentieth-century concerto are almost as obvious as they are in nineteenth-century works, yet all twelve notes are used with equal freedom. A contemporary flavor is attained without undue complexity. Judicious balance between the old and the new have made this concerto a favorite with listeners who are a little tired of the standard repertory but not quite ready to embrace more radical new music.

Many twentieth-century composers have made the final break with tradition, as far as tonality is concerned, and write music which has no key center. Music without a tonal center is said to be *atonal.* Proponents of this type of music eschew the term, but it is descriptive. Arnold Schoenberg evolved a system of "composition with twelve tones related only to one another" which assures the equal use of all twelve tones and eliminates the possibility of any tone inadvertently asserting itself as a tonic, or tonal center. A tone row comprising all twelve notes in a fixed order, with none repeated, serves as the basis for a complete work. The row, subjected to specified manipulations and modifications, is repeated throughout the composition. No note is used except as it occurs in its prescribed order in the series. The technique and philosophy of the system are far more complex than this, but a detailed explanation is beyond the scope of a music appreciation book.

Twelve-tone music, as music written according to Schoenberg's system is commonly called, is not designed for easy listening, but it must be considered by anyone seriously interested in the music of our time. Some of the greatest creative minds of twentieth-century music have regarded serial organization as the most viable compositional procedure. Every living composer is familiar with the system and, it seems safe to generalize, is influenced by it to some degree. No composer active at the present time could or would choose to be insulated from such a significant development, though many do not subscribe to the method. Composers on the whole have been more intrigued by serialism and atonality than have performers and listeners. Performers find it difficult and frequently ungrateful to play. Listeners are rarely able to detect the high degree of organization implicit in the system and are perplexed by the absence of familiar tonal functions. The preceding examples illustrate various kinds of tonality. The following example contrasts with these and demonstrates the difference between music which has a tonal center, however vague, and that which has none.

ARNOLD SCHOENBERG: *String Quartet no. 4* *(1936)*
(1874–1951)   *1. Allegro molto, energico*   8:10

This music is atonal. Unless you have previously heard music by Schoenberg or one of his disciples, you probably have never heard any like it before. It is not performed often, for it is extremely difficult to play. Until recently, there were few performances or recordings of music like this. You will not find singable melodies, toe-tapping rhythms, or sonorous harmonies in it. The melodic motion is disjunct, the rhythm irregular, and each part obstinately independent. Kaleidoscopic convolutions reflect the turmoil of the age which gave this music birth. In listening to it, try to put aside preconceived notions about what music should be, and accept this music on its own terms. It will not recall fond memories, and you will not go away whistling its tunes. It does provide a provocative and stimulating listening experience. Also LG 3/9–11.

Modulation

The same melodic and harmonic devices which cause one note to emerge as a tonal center are used to shift the center from one pitch to another. This process is called *modulation.* Any change of key is a modulation.

Modulation is a constant source of variety in tonal music and a feature of musical form. Excursions to other keys are invariably followed by a return to the original tonic in traditional compositions. One must be aware of changes in tonality, especially the departure from and return to the original key, to comprehend musical structures and procedures completely. The perception of tonality and modulation may be on the subconscious level, but static tonality produces conscious monotony.

Modulations may be made between any two keys, but most often they occur between *related keys.* Related keys are those keys which have five or more of their seven notes in common. Keys with fewer than five notes in common are *foreign* or *remote keys,* and modulations to them are *foreign* or *remote modulations.* Pairs of keys, one major and one minor, which have all seven notes in common but a different keynote are *relative keys.* The major key and the minor key with the same keynote are *parallel keys.*

Modulations are reckoned according to the relationship of the new tonic to the old. In describing key relationships the Roman numerals and the names associated with each scale degree are useful. In scale order, they are:

I—Tonic
VII—Subtonic (Leading tone)
VI—Submediant
V—Dominant
IV—Subdominant
III—Mediant
II—Supertonic
I—Tonic

Either the name or the numeral indicating the scale degree can be used in referring to modulations. For example, a modulation to the dominant key or to V would indicate that the fifth scale degree of the old key would become the new tonic. Modulations throughout a composition are related to the original tonic key established at the outset. Modulations to the dominant key are most common, followed by modulations to the subdominant (IV), supertonic (II), relative major (III), and relative minor (VI). These are closely related keys having six or all seven of their tones in common.

Modulations are illustrated in the examples of Part Two in connection with the study of musical form.

Dynamics and Color

Dynamics and tone color, or timbre, cannot be ignored in a discussion of musical elements. They are not elements in the same sense as rhythm, melody, and harmony, but they are nonetheless essential components of the composer's expressive material.

Dynamics, a composite term for degrees of loudness and softness, are prime factors in determining the emotional intensity of music. Dynamic levels are determined by the number and kind of instruments and/or voices sounding and by the manner of playing or singing. The total dynamic range in music is vast.

Composers' intentions regarding dynamics are conveyed to performers by means of Italian words, more specifically their abbreviations, which are an integral part of music notation. The basic terms, abbreviations, and meanings are:

Word	Abbreviation	Meaning
pianissimo	*pp*	very soft
piano	*p*	soft
mezzo piano	*mp*	moderately soft
mezzo forte	*mf*	moderately loud
forte	*f*	loud
fortissimo	*ff*	very loud
crescendo	*cresc.*	gradually louder
decrescendo	*decresc.*	gradually softer
diminuendo	*dim., dimin.*	gradually softer

Dynamic indications are relative, and very loud for a violin is quite different from very loud for a trombone or a full orchestra. However, composers learn what to expect from each instrument and combination and score accordingly. The imbalance of tone produced by certain categories of instruments is compensated for somewhat by the numbers used. For instance, string instruments produce much less sound than brass instruments, but there are many more of them in an orchestra. In this regard observe that doubling the number of players does not double the tone volume. Two violins playing with equal intensity are only 1.3 times louder than one. Ten are required to double the sound of one. Securing proper dynamic levels and balancing the sound of opposing sections in larger ensembles is a strategic function of conductors.

Color in music results from the fusion of pitches and timbres. Each note on every instrument has a unique sound, even ignoring pitch differences. With various pitches and timbres mingled, the color possibilities of a modern orchestra are infinite. The art of *orchestration* (scoring music for orchestra) and the quest for orchestral color have been carried to new heights during the last 150 years. This trend has been encouraged by mechanical improvements in instruments and by the astounding technical proficiency of large numbers of performers. Performances of scores which would have been deemed impossible to play before the turn of the century are commonplace today. The perfection of instruments and the artistry of players have stimulated composers to write ever more demanding scores and to tap hidden instrumental resources for new colors. Fresh orchestral colors have been produced by instruments playing in extreme registers—very high and very low. Mechanical devices have been used in and on instruments to modify their tone coloring. Unusual ways of producing tones, like strings played with the wood rather than the hair of the bow, have been used for special effects. These variegated tints added to the normal rich coloring of the orchestra provide the composer with a tempting palette.

Recent composers have taken full advantage of bounteous and relatively stable instrumental resources. They have made penetrating studies of instrumental possibilities, limitations, and peculiarities and have cultivated an idiomatic way of writing for each instrument which utilizes its capabilities to the fullest and minimizes its shortcomings. This facet of composing was largely ignored by earlier composers who were inclined to be indifferent toward instrumentation. Many of their scores do not specify the instruments to be used, an unthinkable omission in recent times. Lack of standardization in both instruments and instrumental combinations fostered the practice of writing, on occasion, parts which could be played by any of several instruments. These circumstances, coupled with the preoccupation of composers for an extended period with problems of melody, harmony, and form, delayed the full flowering of orchestral color. Skillful and colorful orchestration and ferreting out latent instrumental possibilities are hallmarks of the nineteenth and twentieth centuries. Certain younger composers going contrary to this trend are reverting to the older practice and producing works with variable or unspecified instrumentation.

Harmony also is a source of musical color. Some combinations of notes are rich, others stark. Some are bright, others dark. Some harmonic progressions are iridescent and some are achromatic. Words are inadequate to describe them, but the hues of harmony are apparent to all who listen.

The full range of dynamic levels from whispering to thundering and the full spectrum of orchestral color from infrared to ultraviolet are exploited in the following example.

RIMSKY-KORSAKOV: *Capriccio Espagnol* (1887)		14:45
(1844–1908)	1. Alborada	1:15
	2. Variations	4:30
	3. Alborada	1:15
	4. Scene and Gypsy Song	4:45
	5. Fandango of the Asturias	3:00

The composer's intention was to create a piece which would "glitter with dazzling orchestral color." He was satisfied with his accomplishment, as well he might have been! He took issue with critics who praised the *Capriccio* as a magnificently orchestrated piece and preferred to think of it as a brilliant composition for the orchestra, a subtle but in his mind an important distinction. The first, third, and fifth movements share thematic material. The fourth and fifth are played without interruption.

Nikolai Rimsky-Korsakov

6 TEXTURE IN MUSIC

There are four types of musical texture—*monophonic, heterophonic, polyphonic,* and *homophonic.* Phonic by itself is defined: *of, pertaining to, or producing sound.* Mono- is a combining form meaning *one, single, alone.* Hetero- is a combining form indicating *other, different.* Poly- is a combining form signifying *many, much, several.* Homo- is a combining form denoting *common, joint, like.* These terms have special connotations in music.

Monophonic Texture

Monophonic texture, or *monophony* to use the noun form, is music consisting of a single, unaccompanied melodic line. It was the first to develop of the four types of texture. Monophonic music occupies such an insignificant position in our culture that it is difficult to realize the large span of music history devoted to its development and how large it still looms on the universal musical scene. Primitive music and that of ancient civilizations, early church and court music, and Oriental music to the present day are essentially monophonic. Most of this music was little known beyond its own time and sphere of influence until musicologists and ethnologists combined their skills with the marvels of recording to discover, collect, re-create, and disseminate music from the distant past and from the far corners of the world.

Acquaintance with old and exotic music has increased recognition of its value. Freedom and interesting detail of line in monophony compensate for its sparseness of texture. It is refreshing to discover the beauty of single lines—rediscover would be more exact. The systematic sounding together of different pitches, dating back only a little over a millennium, is a comparatively recent development.

All of the forty or so extant examples of ancient Greek music are monophonic. With few exceptions they are fragments associated with words for singing, though it is known from other sources that instruments were used in conjunction with voices and independently. When a voice (or voices) and an instrument were combined in performances, they shared a single melodic line. An epitaph inscribed in stone as a tribute to the wife of one Seikilos is a complete monophonic song. Pitches are given for and the rhythm is derived from the words. The performance practices of ancient Greece are revived in the recorded version.

SEIKILOS: *Epitaph* (200 B.C.)   1:51

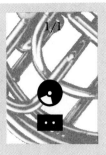

The recording begins with the pitches of the song sounded in descending order, as they are in the notation of Greek scales. Following a brief spoken announcement, the complete melody is played on a *kithara*, a plucked string instrument of the lyre family. The melody is heard again with a solo voice and the kithara together. The recording concludes with a slightly embellished version of the melody played on the kithara and a terminal spoken phrase. Notation page 329; translation page 221.

The largest organized body of monophonic music is the liturgical chant of the Catholic Church. The liturgy crystallized during the pontificate of Gregory the Great (590–604), from whom the chant takes its name. The origins of some of the chants can be traced back to antiquity, whereas others postdate Gregory. There are nearly three thousand chant melodies in the repertory, a treasury no proper study of music can ignore. Music of the remote past should not be equated with music in familiar styles. The very old, like the very new, must be accepted on its own terms. Though the unmeasured rhythm and unaccompanied lines of the chants may sound quaint to modern ears, they were and are monuments in the history of music.

GREGORIAN CHANT: *Mass IV (Cunctipotens)*
(Codified 590–604)   *Kyrie*   2:06

This example of monophonic music is a chant setting of a text from the Catholic Mass, but the words—*Kyrie eleison, Christe eleison, Kyrie eleison*—are Greek, unlike the remainder of the Mass. Notation page 329; translation page 223.

Instrumental melodies are rarely unencumbered in Western music, but in one instance when a composer lavished his talents on a single instrumental line, the result was the following exquisite melody for solo flute.

CLAUDE DEBUSSY: *Syrinx (1912)*   2:35
(1862–1918)

This work for flute alone is one of the very few for an unaccompanied wind instrument. Syrinx is the Greek name for panpipes, a primitive wind instrument associated with the god Pan.

When by accident or design divergent versions of the same melody sound simultaneously, heterophonic texture results.

Heterophonic Texture

Heterophonic texture, or *heterophony,* is the sounding at the same time of differing versions of one melody, especially in improvised or spontaneous performances. Heterophony occurs when a plain and an embellished version of a melody are deliberately combined. It also occurs intermittently in group performances of melodies transmitted aurally with personal and regional variants. Heterophonic traditions exist mainly in primitive and non-Western music such as that of Asia, the Near and Middle East, China, and particularly Japan. The African example cited is only marginally representative.

4/15   AFRICA/SENEGAL: *Greetings from Podor*   1:30

This 1969 recording of tribal music from West Africa is not an example of pure heterophonic texture because of the drum and handclapping rhythms and the solo voices, but heterophony can be heard in the group singing.

Monophonic and heterophonic texture are relatively rare and insignificant in Western art music where their primary function is to provide passages of contrasting texture in works that are predominantly polyphonic or homophonic.

Polyphonic Texture

Chants and melodies were accompanied by stamping, clapping, and percussion instruments from the earliest times, but real polyphonic texture did not result because the rhythm sounds did not have definite pitches. Polyphony requires the sounding together of different pitches belonging to melodic lines.

A kind of prepolyphony occurred early in the development of music as a result of combining male and female or boys' voices. The natural pitch of adult male voices is about an octave lower than that of preadolescent and female voices. When they sing the same melody together, they normally sing in octaves. That is, they sing identical melodic contours and notes with the same letter names, but different pitches. Two pitches in this relationship blend so perfectly that they are barely distinguishable, and the sound is more like an amplification of one pitch than a combination of two. This is the pitch relationship heard in the singing of folk and familiar melodies by mixed groups and also, on occasion, between the male and female leads in dramatic musical works.

Singing melodies in octaves or accompanied by percussion instruments did not lead to polyphony. That development was delayed until different pitches other than octaves were combined systematically and preserved in notation. The earliest specimens with these qualifications date from the ninth century.

Various kinds of polyphony from the ninth to thirteenth centuries are known by the general term *organum.* Organum consists of a chant melody with one to three added parts. In strict *parallel organum* the added parts duplicate the chant melody at constant, consonant intervals (octaves, fifths, and/or fourths) throughout. Less strict but still classified as parallel is organum in which the phrases of the chant and an added part begin and end on the same pitch with intervening motion essentially in parallel fourths. The recording of the *Sit gloria Domini* fits the first description; the recording of the *Rex coeli* the second.

PARALLEL ORGANUM: *Sit gloria Domini/Rex coeli (850)*   :48

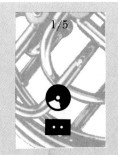

Sit gloria Domini (Glory be to God) is a four-part example of organum. The chant is the second highest part. The basic added part is a fifth lower. The bottom part duplicates the chant an octave lower, and the top part duplicates the other part an octave higher. The intervals between parts 1–2 and 3–4 are fourths. In *Rex coeli* (King of heaven) the chant is the upper of the two parts. Notation and translation in Davison-Apel *Historical Anthology of Music, vol. I.*

Free organum, a somewhat later development, differs from parallel organum in that the contour of the added part is independent. The same intervals sound between the chant and added part as in parallel organum, but they may be approached and left by contrary as well as parallel motion. Rhythmically, the added part coincides with the chant.

FREE ORGANUM: *Cunctipotens Genitor (1050)*   :53

The chant melody of *Cunctipotens Genitor* (All-powerful Father) is from the Kyrie cited as an example of monophonic texture on page 91. The added part is above the chant. Notation and translation in Davison-Apel *Historical Anthology of Music, vol. 1.*

In *melismatic organum* several notes of a rhythmically independent added part sound above a single, sustained note of the chant melody. At the beginning and end of phrases, the intervals between the two parts are the consonances associated with organum. Within phrases the added part is rhythmically and melodically free.

MELISMATIC ORGANUM: *Cunctipotens Genitor (1125)*   2:00

This example of melismatic organum has the same text and is based on the same chant melody as the preceding example of free organum. Notation and translation in Davison-Apel *Historical Anthology of Music, vol. I.*

Though all early music in more than one part is classified as polyphony, the term has a special connotation implying music conceived as a combination of melodic lines rather than as a succession of chords. The texture of music consisting of two or more lines is *polyphonic* or *contrapuntal,* the terms being used interchangeably. The art of combining melodies and the study of contrapuntal music is *counterpoint.*

The simplest kind of counterpoint is created by combining a melody with itself starting at different times so that statements of the melody overlap. This is the kind of counterpoint produced when a group sings rounds like *Are You Sleeping,* also known as *Brother John* and *Frère Jacques.* Nearly everyone knows the tune. It is a four-part round, which means that the melody is sung starting at four different times. The words are aligned to show how the four parts fit together. To experience this type of contrapuntal texture firsthand, sing *Are You Sleeping* with a fourth of the class on each part. It can be repeated any number of times, since the end of the melody leads around (hence the name of the form) and back to the beginning.

ANONYMOUS: *Are You Sleeping*

1. Are you sleeping, are you sleeping, Brother John,   Brother
                                   2. Are you sleeping,   are you

1. John?	Morning	bells are	ringing,	morning bells		are	ringing,
2. sleeping,	Broth-	er	John,	Broth-		er	John?
3. Are		you	sleeping,	are		you	sleeping,

1. Ding,	ding,	dong,	ding,	ding,		dong.	
2. Morning	bells are	ringing,	morning	bells are		ringing,	Ding,
3. Broth-	er	John,	Broth-	er		John?	Morning
4. Are	you	sleeping,	are	you		sleeping,	Broth-

2. ding,	dong,	ding,	ding,	dong.		
3. bells are	ringing,	morning	bells are	ringing,	Ding,	ding
4. er	John,	Broth-	er	John?	Morning	bells are

| 3. dong, | ding, | ding, | dong. | |
| 4. ringing, | morning | bells are | ringing, | Ding, ding, dong, ding, ding, dong. |

When a musical idea stated in one part is immediately repeated in another, the second and any subsequent part is said to be in *imitation.* The imitation is continuous in *Are You Sleeping.* The number of beats or measures between the entrances of the parts is the *distance of imitation.* The distance of imitation between successive entrances in *Are You Sleeping* is eight beats or two measures. The difference in pitch, if any, between the starting notes is the *interval of imitation.* In rounds the imitation is at the same pitch when the parts are sung by voices of the same sex, at the interval of an octave when the entrances alternate between male and female voices.

The old English round *Sumer Is Icumen In* (*Summer Is Coming In*) is not too unlike *Are You Sleeping* in construction. It has four parts in continuous imitation at the distance of four beats plus two accompanying parts in which two elements of a short melodic fragment alternate.

ANONYMOUS: *Sumer Is Icumen In* (1240)   1:39   1/8

A diagram of the form of *Sumer Is Icumen In* is given on page 133.

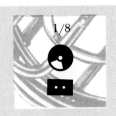

The limitations of continuous imitation like that found in rounds are too severe for extended compositions. In most types of imitative polyphony, the parts enter with the same theme or motive and then become free, or imitative passages alternate with passages in nonimitative *free counterpoint*. Sometimes the imitation consists of no more than an exchange of motives between the parts. Bach explores the full range of possibilities from fragmentary to almost continuous imitation in his *Two-Part Inventions,* of which the following are representative.

J. S. BACH: *Two-Part Inventions* (1720)
(1685–1750)   *No. 2 in C minor*   1:25
               No. 3 in D major   1:10
               No. 7 in E minor   1:25

The two parts of *Invention 2* are in strict imitation at the interval of an octave and at the distance of two measures (eight beats) during most of the invention. The imitation is interrupted briefly in the middle and just before the end. The lower voice imitates the upper for the first half of the piece, and the upper voice imitates the lower in the last half.

In *Invention 3* the second voice enters in imitation two measures (six beats) after and an octave lower than the first voice. The imitation is dropped after two measures and not resumed, though the two parts exchange motives on several occasions. Notation page 331.

Invention 7 is organized around motives which pass from one part to the other carrying the burden of interest.

Attentive listening and repeated hearings are usually necessary before the individual lines of imitative counterpoint can be followed and fully appreciated. The interchange of motives between parts is less difficult to perceive. Perhaps the most common type of contrapuntal texture is that involving exchanges of material between the parts and imitation of limited duration. *Fugues* are prime examples of this type of counterpoint.

The structure of fugues is considered in greater detail in chapter 9, but basically a fugue is a musical form in which each part enters imitatively with the same theme or *subject* and in which subsequently the subject is combined with itself and with other melodies. Melodic interest is distributed between all of the parts, and recognizing the themes wherever and whenever they appear is essential for comprehension of the musical design. The subject is announced alone at the beginning of a fugue. Hearing the subject by itself a few times facilitates recognition of later entrances when it is altered and associated with other melodic lines.

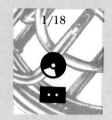

1/18

J. S. BACH: *Well-Tempered Clavier, vol. I* (1722)
(1685–1750)   *16. Fugue in G minor*   2:16

Bach brought the fugue to its highest perfection, and this is a classic example of the form. Counting the statements of the subject as they appear is one way to determine whether or not all of them are being detected. A structural diagram of this fugue is given on page 136. Themes page 332.

Though fugue form was perfected in Bach's time, it has been adapted to changing styles through the years and is still in use. The following example in comparison with the previous one demonstrates that the fugue idea has diverse applications.

JAROMIR WEINBERGER: *Schwanda, opera* (1927)
(1896–1967)   *Polka and Fugue*   7:30

The opera *Schwanda* tells the tale of a jolly bagpipe player who defeats the devil himself with magical music. The complete opera is seldom given in this country, but this excerpt is a favorite. The *Polka* is fundamentally homophonic, though countermelodies are introduced at times. It comes to a close in just over two minutes, and the violins by themselves announce the fugue subject. From this point on, the fugue subject or fragments of it are passed from one section of the orchestra to another in typical fugue fashion, and the texture becomes polyphonic. Toward the end of the fugue, elements of the fugue subject and the polka theme are combined. Also LG 3/15 starting about three minutes from the end.

Some polyphonic texture is entirely nonimitative; that is, it results from combining essentially independent melodies. The prelude to *Die Meistersinger* (*The Mastersingers*) contains a stellar example of this type of polyphony. The three main themes are introduced one after another, then toward the end of the piece all three themes are ingeniously combined. Listeners must learn to recognize and remember the themes as they are heard separately to appreciate fully the marvelous effect when they are heard together.

RICHARD WAGNER: *Die Meistersinger, opera* (1868)
(1813–1883)   *Act I. Prelude*   9:00

The piece and the first theme begin together with an incisive rhythmic motive followed by an ascending scale line. A new rhythmic motive and full chords in the brass and woodwind sections signal the beginning of the second theme (1:35). The first theme returns (2:20) transformed into a lyric melody. The mood changes, and the third theme, the famous "Prize Song" of the opera, enters quietly (3:35). After extensive development, all three themes are combined in the final section (6:25). The "Prize Song" theme is the principal melody. Both versions of the first theme are used in the bass, and the second theme provides the harmonic background. Themes page 341. Also LG 1/20.

Homophony is musical texture in which melodic interest is concentrated in a single part, usually the highest, with the remaining parts in subservient, accompanying roles. Supporting parts in homophonic music are designed to provide a suitable harmonic background for the primary melody.

Homophonic Texture

The homophonic and polyphonic approaches to music differ in emphasis, but they are not mutually exclusive. In the accompanying parts of homophonic music, harmonic (chordal) considerations are paramount, but chord tones sounding in succession constitute lines. In polyphonic music melodic considerations are paramount, but melodic tones sounding at the same time form chord structures. The emphasis in homophony, excluding the primary melody, is on the smooth, unobtrusive, even repetitious connection of chord tones, in contrast with polyphony where the emphasis is on engaging contours in all parts.

Ideally, the vertical and horizonal aspects of musical texture—the chordal and melodic orientation—should be in balance. Any conflicting requirements are reconciled by proficient composers with no apparent compromises.

Few compositions are purely homophonic or polyphonic. One type of texture may predominate, but rarely to the exclusion of the other. The dividing line between them is not always sharp, and intermingling is common. For instance, when the rhythms of combined melodies coincide for a time, as they do on occasion in vocal polyphony of the sixteenth century, the effect is like that of homophony.

The concept of multipart music as a single melody with a harmonic accompaniment originated about 1600 when a group of Italian poets and musicians attempting to re-create Greek drama laid the foundations for both homophony and opera, neither of which was implicit in their model. One aim of the group was to provide dramatic texts with musical settings that would permit clear understanding of the words, a requirement not satisfied by existing styles. Their solution was to project a solo melodic line against a background of slower-moving harmonies, a revolutionary innovation at the time.

A passage in the new style with a declamatory melody accompanied by relatively static harmonies is a *recitative* (as in recitation). Monteverdi was the most distinguished composer of early operas, basic elements of which were recitatives.

CLAUDIO MONTEVERDI: *Orfeo, opera (1607)*
(1567–1643)   *Tu sé morta*   2:35

Tu sé morta is in the recitative style that dominated the first operas and persisted between more lyric sections of operas, oratorios, and cantatas into the nineteenth century.

Within the seventeenth century the practice of setting dramatic texts in a declamatory style with a simple harmonic accompaniment had migrated to England. An introductory passage (recitative) in this style precedes a more extended and lyric lament in the following excerpt from Purcell's early English opera *Dido and Aeneas*.

HENRY PURCELL: *Dido and Aeneas, opera* *(1689)*
(1659–1695)   *Thy hand, Belinda/When I am laid in earth*   4:12

This selection, also known as the *Lament* and *Dido's Farewell,* comes near the end of act III of the opera. Words page 168; ground bass page 330. Also LG 1/21 number 49.

Homophonic texture of the type found in recitatives is rare in compositions other than operas and choral works with soloists. In other categories the prevailing type is characterized by flowing vocal or instrumental melodies and rhythmically animated accompaniments. A third kind of homophony occurs in multipart singing of hymns, chorales, carols, and patriotic songs when all of the parts move together with the melody in block chords. Each of these types is illustrated in the selections from Mendelssohn's *Elijah.*

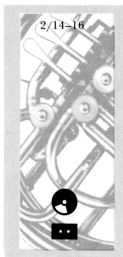

MENDELSSOHN: *Elijah, oratorio* *(1846)*
(1809–1847)   3. *Ye people, rend your hearts*   :55
                     4. *If with all your hearts*   2:44
                     15. *Cast thy burden upon the Lord*   1:24

Number 3 is a recitative with sustained chords in the orchestra accompanying a declamatory vocal line. The style is reminiscent of the chronologically earlier recitatives of Monteverdi and Purcell (see pages 97 and 230). The homophonic texture of number 4 consists of a melody for solo tenor plus an orchestral accompaniment of chord figures, rhythm patterns, and repeated chords. Number 15 is like a chorale in which the words of the text occur synchronously in the four-part chords formed by the voices. The orchestra provides bridges between phrases and brings the number to a close. The themes of number 4 are given on page 338 and the vocal parts of number 15 are given on page 339. The big choral numbers in *Elijah* are too contrapuntal to be appropriate examples in this context, but including one of them in the listening provides a more balanced view of the work.

From the beginning, the texture of jazz and popular music has been homophonic. Both instrumental and vocal versions of Gershwin's song are given congenial settings in this current recording.

GEORGE GERSHWIN: *'S Wonderful* *(1927/1988)*   3:46
(1898–1937)

The full gamut of homophonic texture is displayed in jazz and popular music. The styles are too familiar to require more than an isolated example.

In all musical styles the most obvious way of motivating harmony which otherwise would be static is to repeat the chords in rhythmic patterns. The rhythmic repetition of the chords not only adds interest and animation but also provides, in music for piano, a means of sustaining the sound at equal intensity. The repeated notes in *The Erl-King* accompaniment serve multiple purposes.

FRANZ SCHUBERT: *The Erl-King (Der Erlkönig) (1815)*   4:02
(1797–1828)

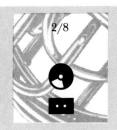

2/8

Goethe's words and Schubert's music together make this art song one of the finest and best known in the entire literature. A translation of the poem is given on page 195. The rapid repeated notes in the piano accompaniment graphically portray the frantic night ride of the father holding his dying son in his arms.

Another way to motivate harmony is to have the notes of the chords sound one at a time in succession, typically in consistent rhythm and pitch patterns. The keyboard music of the last half of the eighteenth century is replete with accompaniment figures fitting this stereotype. Mozart was one of the composers who used this method of motivating harmonies in a basically homophonic texture.

W. A. MOZART: *Piano Sonata no. 15 in C (1788)*
(1756–1791)   *1. Allegro*   3:00
                  2. Andante   4:00
                  3. Allegretto grazioso   1:25

Each movement of this sonata contains accompaniment figures current in Mozart's time. The patterns are varied and interrupted to avoid monotony, but the real interest is in the melody above the accompaniment.

Another attribute of accompaniment figures, aside from those already mentioned, is their capacity to create the illusion of full chords with few notes. This combines the advantages of satisfying harmony with simplicity and clarity. There is no confusion or obscurity in the Mozart sonata, for much of the time only two notes are sounding, one melody tone and one tone of the accompaniment pattern. This fact is camouflaged by the figuration and the use of the sustaining pedal of the piano.

Harmonic progression and motivation were both highly stylized in the 1750–1825 period, leaving composers free to concentrate on melodic invention and organization, a circumstance which contributed to the tremendous fecundity of men like Mozart and Haydn without noticeably impairing the quality of their music. Men of lesser talent relying excessively upon these devices produced a quantity of undistinguished music which is no longer performed.

Composers of the next century were less inclined to settle for stereotyped patterns and harmonies. Their accompaniments generally are more elaborate and imaginative, sometimes approaching the status of secondary melodies, but still serving the same purposes as those of their predecessors. Their harmonies are more colorful, partially as a result of the fancier accompaniment patterns and partially as a product of natural evolution. Chopin was a luminary in this generation of composers.

FRÉDÉRIC CHOPIN: *Preludes for Piano (1839)*
(1810–1849)   *No. 3 in G*   :55

Chopin was a master in conceiving brilliant piano figurations. His music ushered in a style of piano writing which remains at the apex of piano literature. It is a rare piano program on which he is not represented, at least by an encore. This *Prelude* is a small sample of the piano style upon which his reputation is based.

Composers of the present century shun everything that smacks of pattern or stereotype (except the minimalists who capitalize on repetitiousness) and consequently are not attracted to the homophonic accompaniment patterns. Finding substitutes for them magnifies the problems of composition and reduces output, but most composers now seem to feel that the added effort is not only justified, but necessary. Composers continue to write homophonic music, but their rejection of ready-made devices requires them to devote their creative energies as much to the settings as to the melodies and themes.

The evolution of musical texture from monophony and heterophony through polyphony to homophony has been a cumulative process. The emergence of a new type of texture did not cause the preceding ones to disappear. Melodies at first were monophonic, though they sometimes had rhythmic backgrounds. From the beginning some degree of heterophony was inevitable in impromptu group performances, and heterophony is still cultivated in Asia and Africa. Systematically combining different pitches in polyphonic textures originated in the ninth century and is still evolving. The concept of homophony emerged about 1600, and homophonic texture has been predominant in secular and popular music since shortly thereafter. In the music now performed in recitals, concerts, and opera houses, the texture is mostly homophonic or polyphonic. Monophonic texture is used incidentally for variety, but heterophonic texture is rarely detected. The finale of Mozart's *String Quartet no. 14* illustrates the use of polyphonic and homophonic textures in almost equal proportions, with glimpses of monophonic texture.

W. A. MOZART: *String Quartet no. 14 in G (1782)*
(1756–1791)   *4. Molto allegro*   4:00

This movement begins with a four-note melody played by the second violin alone, so the texture is briefly monophonic. The first violin enters with the same melody while the second violin continues with a countermelody, so the texture becomes polyphonic. Both violins continue as the cello and viola enter in turn, also with the same melody, producing four-part imitative counterpoint. After all four instruments have played the opening melody, the first violin plays a new melodic line accompanied by chords, and the texture becomes homophonic. The texture thereafter alternates between being essentially polyphonic or homophonic, with a few unaccompanied notes on occasion. As this music is played, listen carefully to distinguish the three types of texture. Also LG 1/25.

COLORPLATE 9

Rembrandt van Rijn:
The Night Watch (1642)
Oil on canvas, 12'2" × 14'7"

Rembrandt (1606–1669) painted his *Night Watch* the same year that Monteverdi composed his last opera, *The Coronation of Poppea* (see page 232). Dramatic changes in style and technique were occurring in both art and music during this period.

Scala/Art Resource, New York.

COLORPLATE 10

Antoine Watteau:
Mezzetin (1718)

Mezzetin, an amorous and sentimental character in a play, is depicted by the preeminent French artist Watteau (1684–1721) with the elegance, grace, refinement, and restraint typical of the rococo style. The transitional rococo style in music, which came between the baroque and Viennese classic periods, is illustrated by the compositions of Watteau's contemporary, François Couperin (see pages 161 and 239).

The Metropolitan Museum of Art, Munsey Fund, 1934.

COLORPLATE 11

Jacques Louis David:
The Death of Socrates (1787)
Oil on canvas, 78″ × 59″

David (1748–1825), a dedicated French revolutionary and neoclassicist, studied
antiquities in Rome. These studies are reflected in the neoclassic subject and style
of *The Death of Socrates,* which was painted during the corresponding Viennese
classic period in music and the lifetimes of Haydn and Mozart.

COLORPLATE 12

Jean Auguste Dominique Ingres:
La Grande Odalisque (1814)
Oil, 35¼'' × 63¾''

Ingres (1780–1867) is classified as a neoclassicist, though _La Grande Odalisque_ (harem concubine) has the nude female form and voluptuous curves associated with the preceding rococo style and a hint of exotic romanticism, which was then about to emerge in both art and music. The lives of Ingres and Beethoven, the last of the Viennese classic composers, overlapped some forty-seven years.

Scala/Art Resource, New York.

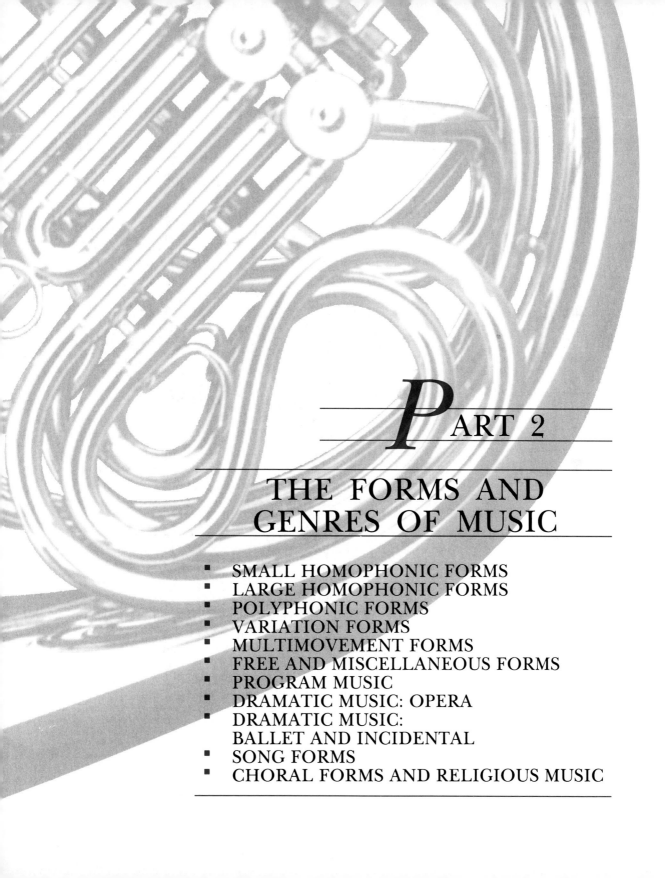

PART 2

THE FORMS AND GENRES OF MUSIC

- SMALL HOMOPHONIC FORMS
- LARGE HOMOPHONIC FORMS
- POLYPHONIC FORMS
- VARIATION FORMS
- MULTIMOVEMENT FORMS
- FREE AND MISCELLANEOUS FORMS
- PROGRAM MUSIC
- DRAMATIC MUSIC: OPERA
- DRAMATIC MUSIC:
  BALLET AND INCIDENTAL
- SONG FORMS
- CHORAL FORMS AND RELIGIOUS MUSIC

7 SMALL HOMOPHONIC FORMS

Form in music can be equated with design or structure. It results from patterns of repetition and contrast. Form refers to the logical organization of musical elements in a sequence of time.

Musical form has points in common with architecture, language, and literature. The structure of music can be likened to the structure of an edifice. The sounds of music create patterns in time as the shapes of material create patterns in space. Phrases and sentences in language have counterparts denoted by the same terms in music. Musical ideas enter, unfold, develop, and reach climaxes in the manner of novels and plays.

In spite of certain similarities to speech and the other arts, musical organization is essentially unique. It does not convey concrete meanings, so it is free from syntactical rules. Its formations are not restricted by the pull of gravity or the necessity of bearing weight. It exists only in time. Its perception is dependent upon remembering and relating a sequence of musical events. Elusive though it may be, form is a primary concern of the composer, the performer, and the listener. Music is not fully comprehended unless its plan of organization is perceived to some degree.

The forms of music cannot be regarded as molds into which the composer pours pitches and rhythms until they are full. In a very real sense each musical idea dictates its own form, and no two are identical. However, in the evolution of music certain recurrent patterns have crystallized. Without being the same they are sufficiently uniform to yield to systematic study. Not every work is cast in a traditional form, but traditional considerations serve as a point of departure for the study of the ways musical ideas are organized.

Motive

Musical organization begins with a note, but a single note cannot be related to a specific work. The smallest identifiable musical unit is a *motive*. A motive may be a rhythm, a pitch pattern, a combination of these, or less often a harmonic progression. Motives are the cells which coalesce into an organic whole. The most useful motives are those easily recognized in manifold modifications and readily adapted to multiple functions. Often they serve like mortar in binding together the other elements. Motives serve to link contrasting ideas, and they may figure in accompaniments as well as in melodies. Motives are particularly useful in *sequences*, that is, repetitions at other pitch levels of rhythmic, melodic, or harmonic patterns. Some themes are constructed by expanding and extending motives sequentially. The opening motive of Beethoven's *Fifth Symphony* fulfills all of these functions and in its many guises permeates the entire first movement.

BEETHOVEN: *Symphony no. 5 (1808)*
(1770–1827)   *1. Allegro con brio*   8:34

The first four notes introduce the motive which consists initially of three short notes on the same pitch followed by a longer note a third lower. The rhythm approximates the letter *V* in Morse code used during World War II as a victory motto. The statement of the motive is followed immediately by a repetition of its rhythm and contour at a slightly lower pitch. Different versions of the motive then are strung together in sequence to form a theme. The motive is still in evidence during a transitional passage, and when a lyric melody enters, it moves to the accompaniment. The rhythm of the motive is always recognizable no matter how its shape is bent or where it appears in the texture. The motive is a primary unifying element of the *Symphony* and the germ from which this movement springs. Motive page 337.

Phrase

The structural unit of music just larger than a motive is a *phrase*, borrowing a term from language. More than one phrase is generally required to complete a musical idea, so the musical idea in a single phrase is usually incomplete. The standard phrase length is four measures, but longer and shorter phrases are uncommon only in dance-inspired music. The setting of each of the following familiar lines is one phrase long. The phrases vary in length from three to six measures, as shown by the number in parentheses at the end of each line. Observe that two or three phrases of text may be set to a single phrase of music and that sometimes there are perceptible subdivisions within a musical phrase.

O say! Can you see, by the dawn's early light, (4)
O beautiful for spacious skies, for amber waves of grain, (4)
Come, Thou almighty King! (3)
My country, 'tis of thee, sweet land of liberty, of thee I sing. (6)

Cadence

Each phrase ends with a *cadence,* the musical equivalent of the vocal inflections in spoken language associated with the end of phrases and sentences. The cadence effect is achieved by appropriate melodic, harmonic, and rhythmic formulas. The strength of cadences varies from a momentary pause within a musical idea to absolute finality at the end of a composition. The cadences within a musical idea are *incomplete cadences.* The cadences at the end of complete ideas and works are *complete cadences.* Cadences are marked in the following form diagrams, and many types are illustrated.

Sentence

Homophonic music, like language, grows by a cumulative process. In language the two parts of a compound sentence are joined to express a complete thought. Similarly, in music the incomplete ideas of two or more phrases are combined to express a complete musical thought. The resulting unit of musical form is a *sentence*, also called a *period*. Among musicians *period* is the more prevalent term, but *sentence* seems preferable for nonmusicians. Sentences in music most often consist of two phrases. The first phrase in two-phrase sentences ends with an incomplete cadence, and the concluding phrase ends with a complete cadence. Interrelationships between the phrases constituting a sentence are the norm.

The most concrete way to examine typical sentence structures is to sing some familiar melodies illustrating them. Several are suggested. The phrase structure of each sentence is described and diagramed. A line under the words extends to the end of a phrase. The diagonal stroke at the end of a phrase line signifies a cadence, incomplete if the abbreviation i.c. appears below the line and complete if the abbreviation c.c. appears below the line. Phrases are identified by lowercase letters. A letter in parentheses following an identifying letter indicates a closely related phrase.

The phrases in two-phrase sentences typically have a question-answer relationship. The two phrases may begin alike and be very similar right up to the cadence points, but the cadences are different. The first phrase closes with the rising inflection of a question and an incomplete cadence. The second phrase closes with the falling inflection of an answer and a complete cadence. The melody of Stephen Foster's *Old Folks at Home* begins with this type of sentence.

Sentence: Two phrases beginning alike

'Way down upon the Swannee River, far, far away,

a   i.c.

There's where my heart is turning ever, there's where the old folks stay.

b (a)   c.c.

In the other type of two-phrase sentences the two phrases begin differently, as in the following example. The question-answer effect results from the contrasting contours of the two phrases. The ascending motion of the "a" phrase is answered by the descending motion of the "b" phrase. Unity is achieved by the repetition of a rhythmic pattern that occurs three times in each phrase. Observe that the meaning of the words and the punctuation have no bearing on the question-answer relationship of the two phrases.

Sentence: Two phrases beginning differently

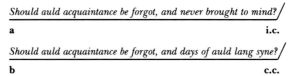

Should auld acquaintance be forgot, and never brought to mind?

a   i.c.

Should auld acquaintance be forgot, and days of auld lang syne?

b   c.c.

Sentences are predominantly of the two-phrase variety with the phrases either beginning alike, like *Old Folks at Home*, or differently, like *Auld Lang Syne*. Less common are sentences of three, four, or more phrases.

In a three-phrase sentence the first two phrases end with incomplete cadences and the third with a complete cadence. The entire melody of *Silent Night* is a three-phrase sentence.

Sentence: Three phrases, all different

> *Silent night, holy night, all is calm, all is bright.* /
>
> **a**   **i.c.**
>
> *Round yon virgin mother and Child, holy Infant so tender and mild.* /
>
> **b**   **i.c.**
>
> *Sleep in heavenly peace, sleep in heavenly peace.* /
>
> **c**   **c.c.**

In sentences of three or more phrases, two of the phrases may be the same. Of the four phrases in the first sentence of *Flow Gently, Sweet Afton,* the first and third are the same except for one note. Modifications, such as this, which do not obscure the identity of a part or alter its function are indicated by adding a prime sign (') to the identifying letter or number. The second and fourth phrases begin alike but end differently. Only the last phrase of a sentence has a complete cadence.

Sentence: Four phrases, first and third alike

> *Flow gently, sweet Afton, among thy green braes;* /
>
> **a**   **i.c.**
>
> *Flow gently, I'll sing thee a song in thy praise;* /
>
> **b**   **i.c.**
>
> *My Mary's asleep by thy murmuring stream,* /
>
> **a'**   **i.c.**
>
> *Flow gently, sweet Afton, disturb not her dream.* /
>
> **c (b)**   **c.c.**

The sentence structures of most music can be related to one of these four patterns illustrated from familiar songs. There are exceptions, of course, and in extended works and especially in developmental and transitional passages the divisions are apt to be vague and the phrases irregular.

Motives, phrases, and sentences—these are the building blocks of the homophonic forms.

One-Part Form

A *one-part form* differs from a sentence only in that a one-part form is complete in itself, whereas a sentence is usually part of a larger whole. All one-part forms, naturally, are sentences, and any sentence which stands by itself as a complete entity is also a one-part form. *Silent Night,* cited as an example of a three-phrase sentence, is also a one-part form. The melody of *When Johnny Comes Marching Home* is a four-phrase sentence and, likewise, a one-part form.

One-part form

> *When Johnny comes marching home again, hurrah, hurrah!* /
>
> **a**   **i.c.**
>
> *We'll give him a hearty welcome then, hurrah, hurrah!* /
>
> **b (a)**   **i.c.**

The men will cheer, the boys will shout, the ladies they will all turn out, /

c   i.c.

And we'll all feel gay when Johnny comes marching home! /

d   c.c.

Other familiar examples of one-part form are: *America the Beautiful, Stars of the Summer Night, Abide with Me,* and *Anchors Aweigh.* Repetitions of the melody with different words do not change the musical form.

Traditional twelve-bar blues are one-part forms with three phrases. The following words from Bessie Smith's *Lost Your Head Blues* taken from the recording in the *Smithsonian Collection of Classic Jazz* are typical.

One-part form (blues)

I was with you baby, when you didn't have a dime. /

a   i.c.

I was with you baby, when you didn't have a dime. /

b(a)   i.c.

Now since you got plenty money you have throw'd your good gal down. /

c   c.c.

One-part forms are common in folk, patriotic, and children's songs and in spirituals and hymns. They are relatively rare in instrumental music, but not unknown. Several of Chopin's *Preludes,* for example, are one-part forms.

FRÉDÉRIC CHOPIN: *Preludes for Piano* (1839)
(1810–1849)   *No. 4 in E minor*   1:52

One-part form

a   i.c. /   b(a)   c.c. /

The tempo is slow, and the phrases are long in this one-part form. The two phrases, which are nearly equal in length, begin alike but end differently. The division between them is marked by the incomplete cadence and by a momentary interruption in the persistent rhythm of the accompaniment.

FRÉDÉRIC CHOPIN: *Preludes for Piano* (1839)
(1810–1849)   *No. 7 in A*   :42

One-part form

a   i.c. /   b   i.c. /   a'   i.c. /   c   c.c. /

In this highly unified one-part form the rhythm is the same in all of its four phrases. The first and third phrases are melodically and harmonically similar but not identical. The melodic contours and harmonics of phrases two and four complement those of phrases one and three.

Binary is the customary designation for musical forms consisting of two distinct parts. Each part consists of a sentence or equivalent and ends with a complete cadence. The first complete cadence comes toward the middle of the form and ends the first part. The second complete cadence closes the second part and ends the work. Binary form is found in the same categories of familiar music as one-part form. The melodies of *Auld Lang Syne, Sweet and Low,* and *Aura Lee* (popularized as *Love Me Tender*) are binary. The first sentence of *Aura Lee* is the setting for the verses, and the second sentence is the setting for the refrain. In all ensuing form diagrams, musical sentences and parts with sentence function are identified by capital letters.

Two-Part Form: Binary

Binary form

As the blackbird in the spring, 'neath the willow tree, /

A-a   **i.c.**

Sat and piped, I heard him sing, singing Aura Lee. /

A-b (a)   **c.c.**

Aura Lee, Aura Lee, maid of golden hair, /

B-a   **i.c.**

Sunshine came along with thee, and swallows in the air. /

B-b   **c.c.**

In concert music, binary form is almost peculiar to the baroque period (1600–1750). It is the traditional form of the dance movements in the suites of that era. As used in the suites the form is known more specifically as *baroque binary.*

Baroque binary form is highly stylized. The tonic key is firmly established at the beginning of the first part, and then a modulation is made to a related key, ordinarily the dominant or relative major. A cadence in the new key concludes the first part. It is repeated immediately. The material of the second part is derived from and closely related to that of the first. There is no contrast of style, mood, or tempo. Frequently the only difference between the beginnings of the two parts is the change of key. The second part begins in the new key to which the first part modulated. Sometimes the second part starts as an inversion, that is, an upside-down version of the first part. After beginning in the related key, the second part modulates back to the original key, sometimes passing through one or more other tonalities en route making it somewhat longer than the first part. A complete cadence in the tonic key concludes the second part. It, too, is repeated immediately. Though repeats are invariably indicated, they are not always observed by performers. Examples of baroque binary form are legion in the suites of Bach and his contemporaries. The ones in the *French Suites* are exceptionally concise and clear. The timings (minutes:seconds) in the form outlines indicate the approximate elapsed time to the beginning of the sentence. Phrases are not shown.

1/17   **J. S. BACH:** *French Suite no. 4 in E-flat (1722)*
(1685–1750)   *6. Gigue*   2:16

Binary form

A   Starts with a lilting figure in one voice, the other   :00*
        two enter imitatively, ends with complete cadence
        in dominant key.

A   Repeated.   :27*

B   Starts with single voice like A but theme inverted   :54*
        and in dominant key, ends with complete cadence
        in tonic key.

B   Repeated.   1:35*

Themes page 332.

*Progressive timings in a series starting with :00 indicate the approximate elapsed time to
the beginning of the part or section.

Immediate repetitions of parts or sections do not affect the basic designations for the forms. The AB pattern of *Aura Lee* and the AA BB pattern of a typical baroque binary dance movement are both binary.

Three-Part Form: Ternary

A three-part design comprising statement-departure-return, represented by the letters ABA, is the most prevalent pattern of musical organization. It occurs in works of all sizes, small and large. When each of the three parts consists of a single idea, the form is simple *ternary*. Many familiar and popular songs are in ternary form. Ternary design is most obvious when there are no repetitions and the three parts are of equal duration, as they are in the following example.

2/10   **FRÉDÉRIC CHOPIN:** *Mazurka no. 24 in C (1838)*   1:21
(1810–1849)

Ternary form

A   Sentence of four phrases, the first and third alike,   :00
        ending with a complete cadence in the tonic key
        (C).

B   Change of key and style. Four phrases of which   :26
        the third and fourth are essentially variants of the
        first and second respectively. Ends with a
        harmonically strong but rhythmically weak cadence
        in the new key (A-flat).

A   Returns abruptly. First note omitted but otherwise   :50
        exactly as before.

Themes page 338.

Mendelssohn's *If with all your hearts* is an example of ternary form with several features, including voice and text, that differ from those of the Chopin piano piece. The phrase structure is less regular. The degree of contrast between the A and B parts is less pronounced, and the end of B is linked to the return of A without a cadence. When a closing cadence is lacking, the end of the contrasting middle part is defined by the clear return of the first part, as in this case. The return of the A material, after the initial clear reference, is altered and abridged (indicated by the prime sign added to the letter), a common occurrence in ternary forms.

MENDELSSOHN: *Elijah, oratorio (1846)*   2/15
(1809–1847)   *4. If with all your hearts*   2:44

Ternary form
A   Four phrases of which the first and third are alike,   :00
        the fourth extended with a repetition in the text.

B   New elements in voice and orchestra with vague   :56
        references to A melodic contour. Three related
        phrases of varying length lead without a cadence
        to . . .

A′   Return of A varied and abridged.   1:46

Themes page 338.

The two preceding examples give some impression of the infinite variety of detail possible within the ternary concept. In general, the function of the B section is to provide contrast with the A section which precedes it and to create a need for the return of A to round out and complete the design. The degree of contrast between the A and B sections varies substantially. In simple, concise examples of ternary form the thematic material of B may be derived from and very similar to that of A and the degree of contrast slight—just sufficient to establish a feeling of departure and return. In other examples of the form, especially more expansive ones, the material of B may be completely new, and the style may contrast sharply with that of A. The options are multiplied when repetition is included among the variables.

All of the homophonic forms are routinely expanded by repetition. According to an established principle the immediate repetition of a part or group of parts does not alter the analysis of the underlying form. As previously stated, an AB pattern and an AA BB pattern are both regarded as binary. One explanation is that a literal repetition is usually indicated by a sign, and the music is only written out once. Baroque binary forms with an AA BB pattern are written with repeat signs as shown.

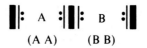

(A A)   (B B)

Literal repetitions and repeat signs are comparatively rare in recent concert music, and the repeat signs prevalent in older music are not always observed in contemporary performances, perhaps reflecting our accelerated pace of living. When repeat signs are observed, the underlying structure of the piece is more readily apparent to one reading the score than to one relying on aural perception unassisted. Though immediate repetitions do not change the name or the basic organizational plan of a form, they do alter the actual sequence of musical events. Becoming familiar with the conventional patterns of repetition simplifies the problem of identifying the forms containing them.

The standard form for popular songs is ternary with the first A repeated immediately, resulting in an AA B A pattern. The words are usually different with each appearance of the A melody, so the repetitions are written out over the words. Duke Ellington's *Solitude* is a clear example of this popular song form.

DUKE ELLINGTON: *Solitude (1934)*   1:00
(1899–1974)

Ternary form

A	Eight-measure sentence ending with a cadence in the tonic key.	:00
A	Melody repeated with different words.	:15
B	Two four-measure phrases; contrasting material and tonality.	:30
A	As before, but with different words. A repeat sign at the end indicates a repetition of the entire song as a unit.	:45

The timings do not reflect any repetitions of the complete song that are heard in performances. *Solitude* is included in the *Duke Ellington Songbook.*

The form of Ellington's *Solitude* and Schumann's *Träumerei* are similar but different in critical respects. In *Träumerei* the first A modulates to the dominant key, as in binary form, and the repetition is indicated by a repeat sign. Because of the modulation, the return of A after B is modified to remain in the tonic key. The modification is indicated in the form diagram by a prime sign added to the letter (A′).

ROBERT SCHUMANN: *Scenes from Childhood* (1838)
(1810–1856)   7. *Träumerei (Reverie)*   2:10

Ternary form

A	Two phrases beginning alike, the second phrase ending with a complete cadence in the dominant key but the rhythmic motion continues in the bass.	:00
A	Literal repetition indicated by a repeat sign.	:30
B	Closely related to A, two phrases with similar contours, the second higher; both cadences incomplete but the end of B confirmed by the return of A.	1:00
A′	First phrase the same as before, second phrase modified to cadence conclusively in the tonic key.	1:30

All of the phrases in this piece begin with the same melodic contour. Emphasis is upon unity rather than variety, which is usual in small forms. Theme page 338.

When the first sentence in a ternary form modulates and cadences in a new key, as it does in *Träumerei,* the return of A is altered to end the piece in the same key as it began. It is traditional to begin and end tonal compositions in the same key and, except in the simplest forms, to explore other tonalities in between. Thus the principle of departure and return applies to tonality as well as to thematic material.

A preliminary *introduction* may precede the basic structure of a musical form. The popular song *Someone's There* begins with an instrumental introduction. The complete song in a typical ternary form (AA B A) is then performed as a vocal. Similarities between this song and Ellington's *Solitude* are apparent. The sheet music for *Solitude* indicates a repetition of the entire song. *Someone's There* is heard twice in the recorded performance, with the first part of the repetition an instrumental version. Because of their brevity, pop and rock songs are usually extended by repetition in performances.

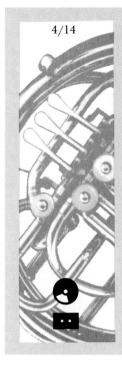

4/14

HARRY CONNICK, JR.: *Blue Light, Red Light* (1991)

(1967–   )   *1. Someone's There*   3:28

Ternary form

Introduction—Instrumental   :00

A   Vocal begins, three phrases.   :23

A   Repetition with slightly more conclusive cadence.   :47

B   Two contrasting phrases.   1:09

A′   Return of A extended to four phrases and ending   1:23
         with a complete cadence.

A   Instrumental version of A begins repetition of   1:53
         complete ternary form.

A   Instrumental version of A varied and embellished.   2:16

B   Vocal with same words as before.   2:38

A′   Vocal with same words as before, instrumental tag   2:52
         ending.

The words are different with each A in the AA B A′ pattern except for the refrain
" 'Cause I know someone's (you're) there."

Between the end of one part of a musical form and the beginning of
the next there may be a *transition*. A transition is a passage that functions
as a bridge between two structural units of a form. For this reason transitions are also called *bridges*. A modulation (change of key) normally occurs
within a transition, and transitions also serve to prepare the way for changes
of tempo, mood, and style. Transitional passages are usual between the parts
of the larger musical forms; less usual but not uncommon between the parts
of ternary forms. The transition in the following ternary form leads from
the end of the B section in a contrasting key back to the tonic key and the
return of the A theme.

3/2

TCHAIKOVSKY: *Nutcracker Suite* (1892)

(1840–1893)   *4. Russian Dance (Trepak)*   1:01

Ternary form

A   Four phrases with an a-b-a-c(b) design.   :00

A   Repeated with somewhat fuller scoring.

B   Melody moves to the bass, four phrases with the   :22
         same design as A.

Transition based on motive common to the two parts.

A′   First three phrases essentially as before, last phrase   :38
         extended several measures without a cadence
         until the end.

Themes page 342.

A *coda* is a section sometimes added to the basic design of a form to bring a composition to a more conclusive or satisfactory close. *Codetta* is a diminutive form of the term meaning "small coda" but frequently used to designate a closing section appended to a principal part within a work. Codas are not usually found in one-part or binary forms but are common in ternary and all of the larger forms. The following twentieth-century work is a relatively sophisticated example of ternary form with a coda. In it the return of A is represented by a substantially modified version of its first phrase, and the two transitions plus the coda account for almost half of its duration.

PAUL HINDEMITH: *Mathis der Maler* (1934)   3/12
(1895–1963)   *2. Grablegung (Entombment)*   4:08

    Ternary form

A   Three phrases of which the first and third are   :00
          related.

Transition   :45
B   Oboe and then flute and oboe play two related   1:20
          phrases accompanied by pizzicato strings.

Transition using elements of both A and B.

A′   First phrase of A modified and extended.   2:15

Coda   2:50

See colorplate 6. Themes page 343.

Additional uses of introductions, transitions, and codas are illustrated in the listening guides that follow for the larger forms.

The three parts of ternary forms theoretically can be repeated individually, but the usual practice when there is more than one repeat is to repeat the first part by itself and to repeat the second and third parts together as a unit. The pattern then becomes AA BA BA. The ternary design is apparent when the repetitions are indicated by repeat signs.

$$\|: \ A \ :\|\|: \ BA \ :\|$$
$$\text{(A A)} \qquad \text{(BA BA)}$$

The pattern of repetitions shown for ternary form with the repeat signs was undoubtedly derived from the pattern of repetitions associated with baroque binary form (see page 107), and those who regard the pattern of repetitions as decisive in determining the form call this form *rounded binary.* The rounded binary designation is particularly appropriate when the initial A modulates to the dominant or relative major key, as in baroque binary, and the modified return of A is abbreviated. The distinctions between binary and ternary forms are not always clear, and experts sometimes disagree on terminology. For listeners, the critical factor in recognizing ternary form is the perception of the return, after a departure, to the material of the beginning.

The following example of ternary form with the repeat pattern just described was selected for its clarity. It also illustrates additional features found in ternary forms. The initial statement of A does not modulate. B is a single contrasting phrase with three subdivisions, not a sentence or two phrases as in the preceding examples. The third subdivision leads without a cadence directly to the return of A, a procedure not unusual in ternary forms. The return of A is complete and unchanged except for the first melody note and the last measure accompaniment figure, changes that are barely perceptible.

ROBERT SCHUMANN: *Scenes from Childhood* (1838)
(1810–1856)   *1. About Strange Lands and People*   1:30

Ternary form

A	Opening melodic motive appears three times in succession followed by a cadence in the same key.	:00
A	Repetition indicated by a repeat sign.	:15
B	Almost as long as A but just a phrase.	:30
A	Return virtually unchanged.	:45
BA	Repeat signs indicate repetition as a unit.	1:00

Themes page 338.

For additional examples of binary and ternary forms with and without repeats, see the marches, minuets, scherzos, and trios in the listening guides for the compound forms pages 115–19.

Free Part Forms

Small part forms that deviate from the patterns of repetitions and returns shown for binary and ternary forms or that have an extra thematic element can be classified as *free part forms*. In this category are patterns such as A B C A, the form of Chopin's *Mazurka no. 41 in C-sharp minor, op. 63 no. 3*, and AA BB CC A coda, the form of Schubert's *Moment Musical in F minor, op. 94 no. 3*. Also in this category is the *Prelude to Act III of Lohengrin*.

RICHARD WAGNER: *Lohengrin, opera (1850)*
(1813–1883)   *Act III. Prelude*   2:36

Free part form

A   Vigorous fanfarelike motive begins a sentence of   :00
      two similar phrases.

B   Melody in bass derived from A motive.   :20

A′   Reduced to a phrase.   1:02

C   Quiet, lyric melody initially in oboe. Cadences of   1:12
      A, B, and C related.

Transition with reminiscences of C over repeated chords in brass.

A″   Sudden return of first phrase.   2:00

B′   Abbreviated return.   2:10

Coda

Themes page 340.

Just as phrases are joined in sentences and sentences are combined in binary and ternary forms, binary and ternary forms are united at the next level of musical organization. The resulting forms have specialized applications, and there is no universally accepted terminology for them. *Compound binary* is a descriptive designation for the musical form consisting of two parts, each of which is simple binary or ternary. This form is typical of marches and rarely encountered elsewhere, so *march form* is another name for it.

The first part of a compound binary form in march style is sometimes referred to as the *march* (as it is in the following diagram) to distinguish it from the second part, which is customarily labeled and called the *trio*. There is no logical reason for calling the second part a trio, but the usual explanation is that the corresponding part in a minuet is called a trio. March trios are traditionally in the subdominant key, and the trio concludes the form. Marches, therefore, are the one consistent exception to the rule that a piece ends in the same key as it begins. The trios in marches are usually lyric in style. Their lyricism is sometimes interrupted by a contrasting middle section, after which the lyric style returns.

In the listening guides for compound forms, the trios are treated as separate parts, and the sentences are identified by the letters A and B as in simple binary and ternary forms, not C and D, though the themes are different.

March forms, among others, often begin with brief introductions that are useful in capturing the attention of listeners, in establishing the tempo, mood, and key of the piece, and in preparing for the entrance of the first thematic idea.

March Form: Compound Binary

Sousa's *Hands Across the Sea* is a march in compound binary form. It adheres to the conventional march plan throughout.

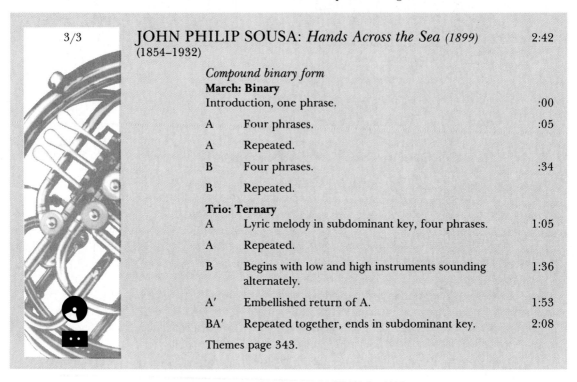

3/3   JOHN PHILIP SOUSA: *Hands Across the Sea (1899)*   2:42
(1854–1932)

Compound binary form
March: Binary
Introduction, one phrase.   :00

A   Four phrases.   :05

A   Repeated.

B   Four phrases.   :34

B   Repeated.

Trio: Ternary
A   Lyric melody in subdominant key, four phrases.   1:05

A   Repeated.

B   Begins with low and high instruments sounding alternately.   1:36

A′   Embellished return of A.   1:53

BA′   Repeated together, ends in subdominant key.   2:08

Themes page 343.

Composers of marches generally follow the basic plan of organization utilized by Sousa. The march proper is nearly always binary, and the trio is usually binary or ternary but is occasionally one part. Each sentence traditionally is repeated.

A plan of organization very similar to that found in marches is more or less standard for rags, which is not surprising. Marches and rags have much in common. Joplin even indicates *Tempo di marcia* (march tempo) for his *Maple Leaf Rag* and labels the second part "trio." Sousa and his famous band played a band version of this rag throughout Europe the year after it was published (coincidentally the same year as Sousa's *Hands Across the Sea*). Each *strain* (sentence) is sixteen bars long, the same as most march strains. Since all strains of a rag are similar in style, they are sometimes represented by consecutive letters and not grouped in parts. The usual pattern of themes and repetitions is then AA BB A CC DD. The similarity of this pattern to the compound binary form of marches is apparent in the following diagram of a typical rag.

SCOTT JOPLIN: *Maple Leaf Rag (1899)*   3:01   4/4
(1868–1917)

Compound binary form
Tempo di marcia: Ternary

A	Syncopated rag rhythm, tonic key.	:00
A	Repeated.	
B	Rhythmically similar to A and in same key.	:41
B	Varied.	
A	As before.	1:21

Trio: Binary

A	Different rhythm patterns, key changes to subdominant.	1:41
A	Repeated.	
B	Syncopated rag rhythm like the beginning, modulates back to tonic key.	2:21
B	Varied.	

A form with an overall A B A design in which each part is a simple binary or ternary form is a compound ternary form. Compound ternary is the usual form for minuets (French, *menuet;* German, *Menuett;* Italian, *minuetto;* in German scores, *Menuetto*). Each part of a minuet is most often ternary. The middle part, like the second part of a march, is a trio. The trio designation apparently originated when it was the practice to write the middle part of minuets for three instruments. The name persisted long after the reason for it had disappeared. The word *minuet* is used in two ways—to identify a complete piece or movement and more specifically to refer to the parts of a minuet that precede and follow the trio. Minuet-trio-minuet is the sequence of parts in a complete minuet. The first appearance of the minuet and the trio ordinarily have a full complement of repeats, and the return of the minuet has none, producing the following pattern.

Minuet and Trio Form: Compound Ternary

Minuet		Trio		Minuet
‖: A :‖	‖: BA :‖	‖: A :‖	‖: BA :‖	A B A
(AA)	(BA BA)	(AA)	(BA BA)	

The third movement in classic four-movement symphonies, sonatas, and quartets typically is a minuet, as in Mozart's *Symphony no. 35.*

1/24

W. A. MOZART: *Symphony no. 35 in D (1782)*
(1756–1791)   *3. Menuetto*   3:06

Compound ternary form
Minuet: Ternary, D major

A	Two phrases—the first loud, vigorous, ascending; the second quiet, lyric, descending.	:00
A	Repeated.	
B	Two phrases which parallel the stylistic relationships of A.	:21
A	As before.	
BA	Repeated together.	:44

Trio: Ternary, A major

A	Two phrases that begin alike.	1:06
A	Repeated.	
B	Two phrases, the second extended.	1:29
A	As before.	
BA	Repeated together.	1:59

Minuet: Ternary without repeats, D major

A	As before.	2:29
B	As before.	
A	As before.	

Themes page 334.

Starting with Beethoven, the minuet in multimovement works sometimes was replaced by a *scherzo.* Scherzos have the same form and meter as minuets but differ in tempo, which is faster, and style, which is less graceful. Scherzo is an Italian word meaning "joke" or "play." In keeping with the name, scherzo movements may contain elements of whimsy, humor, and surprise in their bustling rhythms. The following is an extremely concise but perfectly valid example of scherzo form and style.

BEETHOVEN: *Violin Sonata no. 5 in F (1801)*
(1770–1827)   *3. Scherzo: Allegro molto*   1:15

Compound ternary form
Scherzo: Ternary

A	Piano alone.	:00
A′	Material repeated with violin added.	
B	Just a phrase, full chords in piano.	
A′	First phrase only.	
BA′	Preceding two phrases repeated together, slightly extended.	

Trio: Binary

A	Running figure in both violin and piano.	:28
A	Repeated.	
B	First phrase with running figure in piano, second phrase with running figure in violin.	
B	Repeated.	

Scherzo: Ternary

A	As before.	:50
A′	As before.	
B	As before.	
A′	First phrase only, slightly extended.	

Themes page 336.

When the return of the minuet or scherzo after the trio is literal and complete except for the repeats, it is not necessary for it to be written again. This repetition is indicated by the sign *D.C.*, abbreviation for the Italian words *da capo* meaning "from the beginning." On seeing this sign, performers go back to the beginning and play to the end of the minuet or scherzo proper (up to the trio), where the word *fine*, meaning "end," appears. Repeat signs are ignored when playing a da capo.

In vocal music compound ternary structures are found in the *da capo arias* of cantatas, oratorios, and operas. Da capo arias are songs for solo voice with instrumental accompaniment in which the first part returns, sometimes with improvised vocal embellishment, after a contrasting section. The return of the first part corresponds to the return of the minuet or scherzo after the trio. The repetition of part I is indicated by the abbreviation for da capo, giving the form its name. Da capo arias were common in the music of earlier periods, although their musical design resulted in text repetitions at the expense of dramatic continuity. In the score of Handel's *Messiah, He was despised* is written as a da capo aria with the contrasting middle part and return of the first part shown on the diagram, but the aria is not always performed in its entirety.

Da Capo Aria Form

G. F. HANDEL: *Messiah, oratorio (1741)*
(1685–1759)   23. *He was despised*   10:53

Da capo aria form
Part I: Binary, major
A   Motives of part I introduced in orchestra, voice   :00
        repeats first phrase and continues with an
        extended phrase that modulates and cadences in
        the dominant key.

B   Same text and motives as A, orchestra starts in new   1:52
        key, voice enters after one phrase and modulates
        back to tonic key, repeated cadences before
        concluding orchestral phrase.

Part II: Binary, minor
A   Contrasting style and mode, agitated rhythmic   4:35
        figure in accompaniment.

B   Accompaniment figure continues uninterrupted as   5:18
        background to vocal declamation, part ends with
        two chords in orchestra.

Part I: Da capo, from the beginning as before.   6:00

Themes page 333.

On some recordings of this aria part II and the da capo are omitted. It is complete as diagramed on Telarc 2–CD–80093–2.

ADDITIONAL EXAMPLES

One-Part Form
   Chopin: *Preludes, op. 28* numbers 1,
   2, 9, and 20
   Verdi: *Rigoletto,* opera
        La donna è mobile
        (introduction, three phrases,
        extension; repeated)
        LG 2/18

Binary Form
   Bach: *French Suite no. 5 in G, BWV.
   816,* all movements
   Handel: *Concerto Grosso, op. 6 no. 1
   in G,* last movement
   Mozart: *The Magic Flute,* opera
        Within these hallowed
        portals (A B, repeated)
        LG 2/1

Ternary Form
   Brahms: *Waltzes, op. 38 no. 2 in E*
   Rachmaninoff: *Prelude in C-sharp
   minor, op. 3 no. 2*

Schumann: *Scenes from Childhood,
op. 15 no. 2*

Compound Binary Form
   Sousa: *Manhattan Beach,* march
        Fairest of the Fair, march

Compound Ternary Form
   Beethoven: *Piano Sonata no. 11 in B-
   flat, op. 22*
        3. Menuetto
   *Symphony no. 3 in E-flat,
   op. 55, "Eroica"*
        3. Scherzo
   Haydn: *Symphony no. 104 in D*
        3. Menuetto

Da Capo Aria Form
   Handel: *Rinaldo,* opera
        Cara sposa
        Semele, oratorio
        Where e'er you walk

8 LARGE HOMOPHONIC FORMS

The terms *large* and *small* are relative as applied to musical forms. A large form in a fast tempo may be of shorter duration than a small form in a slow tempo. A greater number of parts and a higher degree of organization distinguish the large forms from the small forms. The various *rondo forms* and *sonata form* are the large homophonic forms.

Rondo is the general designation for musical forms in which the theme stated at the beginning returns after each departure. In their use of a fixed element that alternates with variable elements, the rondo forms are similar in design to the poetic form of songs that begin and end with an unchanging refrain or chorus which, in between, alternates with multiple verses. The words of Woody Guthrie's *This Land Is Your Land* as usually performed have an A B A C A D A pattern, though the refrain and all three verses are set to the same one-part melody.

In the fourth song of Schumann's *Frauenliebe und Leben (Woman's Love and Life)*, both the first lines of the stanzas and the musical setting reflect the rondo principle. The first lines are given in the original German and a free English translation.

The Rondo Principle

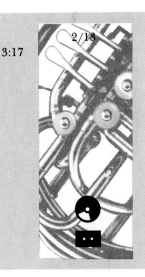

ROBERT SCHUMANN: *Frauenliebe und Leben (1840)*
(1810–1856)   *4. O ring upon my finger*   3:17   2/13

Rondo design

A   Du Ring an meinem Finger,
    O ring upon my finger,

B   Ich hatt' ihn ausgetraumet,
    I had awaked from dreaming,

A   Du Ring an meinem Finger,
    O ring upon my finger,

C   Ich will ihm dienen, ihm leben,
    I'll live for him, I will serve him,

A' Du Ring an meinem Finger,
    O ring upon my finger,

The rondo principle is clearly illustrated in the instrumental pieces of the baroque period (1685–1750) that have *rondeau* in the title. In these old rondos each part is a single sentence ending with a complete cadence, after which the next part follows immediately. As in all rondos the recurring A theme in the tonic key is heard first and after each digression. The number of digressions or contrasting parts in different keys is not fixed. Bach's *Gavotte en Rondeau (Gavotte in Rondo Form)* has four. These four plus the five appearances of A, called the *rondo theme,* make a total of nine parts—AA B A C A D A E A. The immediate repetition of the rondo theme after its initial statement does not constitute an additional part.

1/19

J. S. BACH: *Partita no. 3 in E for Violin* (1722)
(1685–1750) *3. Gavotte en Rondeau* 3:05

Rondo design

A	Rondo theme in tonic key, E major.	:00
A	Repeated.	
B	Contrasting sentence in relative minor key.	:27
A	As before.	
C	Contrasting sentence in dominant key.	:55
A	As before.	
D	Contrasting sentence in supertonic key.	1:34
A	As before.	
E	Contrasting sentence in mediant key.	2:15
A	As before.	

This *partita,* a group of movements with dance characteristics, is number 6 when Bach's sonatas and partitas for solo violin are numbered together. The gavotte is a dance in duple meter with a moderate tempo which first became popular in France during the seventeenth century. Rondo theme page 332.

The archaic rondeau form was superseded by the classic rondo forms. The parts in classic rondos, as compared with those in the Bach rondeau, are fewer in number and tend to be larger in size. Classic rondos have five or seven parts, and the individual parts more often than not have a binary or ternary design, sometimes with repeats. Transitions between parts are common, and they may be extensive. Classic rondos customarily end with a coda.

The classic rondo form with five parts, called a *five-part rondo* or a *simple rondo,* has a basic A B A C A design. Since the themes in a rondo are generally larger than a single sentence, they are represented in the form diagrams by Roman numerals and are sometimes known by descriptive names, as follows:

Five-Part Rondo Form

A = Theme I = Rondo theme
B = Theme II = Subordinate theme I
A = Theme I = Rondo theme
C = Theme III = Subordinate theme II
A = Theme I = Rondo theme

Within the themes, sentences and parts with sentence function are represented in the form diagrams/listening guides by letters, starting with A for each theme. All statements of the rondo theme traditionally are in the tonic key, and themes II and III are in different related keys.

The third movement of Brahms's *Second Symphony* is an example of five-part rondo form. On a surface level the structure is unusually clear. The five parts are delineated by changes in tempo and meter: moderate 3/4—fast 2/4—moderate 3/4—fast 3/8—moderate 3/4. Analysis on a deeper level reveals a degree of integration that defies description. It is not an exaggeration to state that every thematic element is generated by a single motive heard in the first two measures. The initial statement of the motive in this movement (it has appeared previously in the first movement) consists of an initial pitch which is repeated, motion up a step and back to the original pitch, followed by a leap up to a higher pitch. The contour of the motive also appears in inverted (mirror) form with the step up becoming a step down and the leap up becoming a leap down. Both contours are subjected to multiple modifications in rhythm and articulation (see graphs). With the aid of the following form outline and the graphs of the motive, attentive listeners should be able to perceive the main structural divisions in the rondo form and at least some of the subtle interrelationships, though additional hearings may be necessary.

2/20

JOHANNES BRAHMS: *Symphony no. 2 in D* (1877)
(1833–1897)   3. *Allegretto grazioso*   5:38

Five-part rondo form

Theme I (rondo theme), ternary, moderate 3/4   :00

A   Melody in oboe begins with motive.

B   Motive inverted, rhythmically altered, and leap
         filled in.

A′   Return altered and abbreviated.

Theme II, ternary, fast 2/4   1:09

A   Motive in violins, soft and staccato.

B   Motive inverted, new rhythm, loud and
         vigorous.

A′   Motive, first in strings and then in woodwinds,
         serves as return of A.

Transition with strings and woodwinds sounding antiphonally.

Theme I (rondo theme), one part, moderate 3/4   2:00

A″   Reduced to two similar phrases.

Transition based on new form of motive leads to faster tempo.

Theme III, three parts, fast 3/8   2:49

A   Motive in woodwinds, soft and staccato.

B   Like II-B except for 3/8 meter, loud and
         vigorous.

C   Like II-A′ (not III-A) except for 3/8 meter.

Transition similar to that following theme II.

Theme I (rondo theme), ternary, moderate 3/4   3:36

A   Melody in violins begins deceptively in foreign
         key but returns to tonic for B.

B   Essentially as before except for scoring.

A′   As before.

Coda with one final reference to the motive.   4:50

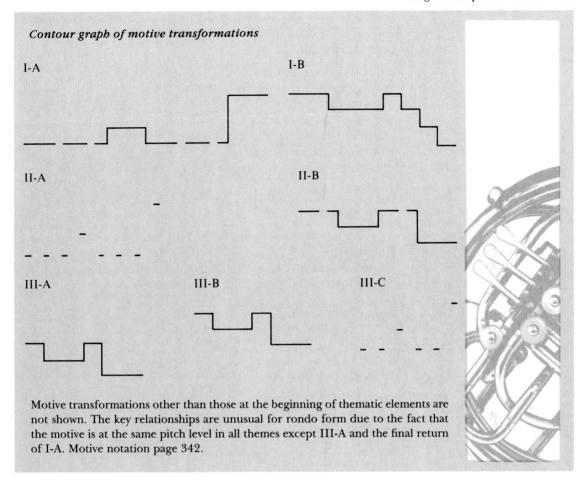

Contour graph of motive transformations

I-A

I-B

II-A

II-B

III-A

III-B

III-C

Motive transformations other than those at the beginning of thematic elements are not shown. The key relationships are unusual for rondo form due to the fact that the motive is at the same pitch level in all themes except III-A and the final return of I-A. Motive notation page 342.

Compositions and movements that are labeled "rondo" by the composer usually have seven parts. *Seven-part rondo* form is also known as *rondo-sonata* form and *sonata-rondo* form, because it has features in common with sonata form, discussed next. Seven-part rondos theoretically have two more parts than five-part rondos but have the same number of themes. The two additional parts come from a return of theme II (subordinate theme I) transposed to the key of the rondo theme (the feature derived from sonata form),

Seven-Part Rondo Form

and an extra statement of the rondo theme. In practice the final statement of the rondo theme is often merged with the coda. The basic plan of a seven-part rondo form is:

A   Theme I (rondo theme), tonic key.

B   Theme II (subordinate theme I), related key.

A   Theme I (rondo theme), tonic key.

C   Theme III (subordinate theme II), new key or keys, sometimes replaced by a development section.

A   Theme I (rondo theme), tonic key.

B′   Theme II (subordinate theme I), transposed to the key of theme I, tonic.

A   Theme I (rondo theme), this return customarily merged with the coda, tonic key.

Seven-part rondo form is frequently used for the final movements of sonatas and concertos, less frequently for the final movements of symphonies and chamber works such as string quartets. Beethoven ends his *Piano Sonata no. 2* characteristically with a clear example of the form.

2/3

BEETHOVEN: *Piano Sonata no. 2 in A (1795)*
(1770–1827)   *4. Rondo: Grazioso*   6:34

Seven-part rondo form

Theme I (rondo theme), ternary   :00
    A   Soaring figure begins both phrases of this sentence.

    B   Contrasting phrase.

    A′   Reduced to a phrase.

Transition, running figures modulate to dominant key.

Theme II, one part   :47
    A   Extended sentence in the dominant key.

Transition, undulating figure in low register.

Theme I (rondo theme), ternary   1:16
    A   Slightly embellished.

    B   As before.

    A′   As before.

Theme III, ternary   1:48
    A   Loud and vigorous, starts in parallel minor key and modulates to its relative major.

    A   Repeated.

    B   Continues style of preceding sentence.

A′	Modified and shortened version of A.	
B	Same material as before, but now the style is soft and smooth.	
A′	Partial return which dissolves into . . .	

Transition, single descending line leads to return of . . .

Theme I (rondo theme), ternary   3:29

A	With additional embellishment.
B	Embellished.
A′	Soaring figure filled in but otherwise as before.

Transition, same material as that following first statement of rondo theme, but this time it does not modulate.

Theme II, one part   4:17

A′	Transposed to the tonic key but otherwise essentially as before.

Theme I (rondo theme) and coda merged   4:40

This section, which is developmental in character, functions as the final statement of the rondo theme and as the coda. Ornate versions of the rondo theme at the beginning and end of this section are separated by contrasting material derived from theme III.

Themes page 334.

Sonata Form

A certain amount of confusion about the term *sonata* is inevitable, since it has different meanings in different contexts. Originally, sonata simply meant a "sound piece" which was played, as opposed to a *cantata* which was sung. This usage is no longer current, but sonata is still used to designate (a) a multimovement work for one or two instruments, and (b) a specific plan of musical organization within one continuous unit. The second definition applies to *sonata form* proper.

Sonata form emerged as a distinct plan of musical organization around the middle of the eighteenth century and was in general use by 1780. The form was ideally suited to the requirements of the classic era (1750–1825) and readily adaptable to the changing styles of subsequent periods. Sonata form seems to have evolved from baroque binary form, but its overall design is essentially ternary. The three large sections of a sonata form are devoted in turn to the presentation, the working out, and the return or summing up of its thematic material. The three sections are the *exposition,* the *development,* and the *recapitulation,* respectively.

In the exposition at least two and generally three thematic ideas are stated. The first theme is the principal theme; the second theme is the subordinate theme; and the third theme is the closing theme. The principal theme and the subordinate theme differ in character and tonality to provide the essential element of contrast. The principal theme is commonly but not invariably dramatic and vigorous in nature, and the subordinate theme lyric and graceful. The closing theme may be little more than a series of cadential formulas bringing the exposition to a close, or it may be a group of thematic ideas equal in scope and importance to the first two themes. When the closing theme has distinct parts, it may be called a *closing group*. Some composers, notably Beethoven, are fond of recalling motives of the principal theme in the closing group at the end of the exposition. At this point in typical early examples of sonata form, until about 1830, a repeat sign in the score indicates a repetition of the entire exposition. These repeat signs are frequently ignored in modern performances, and the practice of writing a repeat sign at the end of the exposition was gradually abandoned.

The development section, as the name implies, is concerned with combining the themes, placing them in new keys and settings, manipulating them, and working them up to a climax.

In the recapitulation readily recognizable versions of the three themes return in their original order. The significant difference between the recapitulation and the exposition is in the keys of the second and the third themes. A transition following the first theme in the exposition modulates to the new key of the second theme, and from that point on the tonic key is avoided until the recapitulation. The beginning of the recapitulation is signaled by the obvious return of the first theme in the tonic key. The tonality is essentially tonic throughout the recapitulation, with the second and third themes transposed and the transitions adjusted as necessary.

A coda, which may amount to a second development section, customarily follows the recapitulation. First movements in sonata form frequently have an introduction. If the introduction is more than a few measures long, it normally is in a slow tempo, contrasting with the fast tempo of the body of the movement.

Beethoven's *Piano Sonata no. 8,* the *"Pathétique,"* is one of his best-known works and an unmistakable masterpiece. The first movement provides a perfect introduction to sonata form.

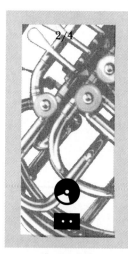

2/4

BEETHOVEN: *Piano Sonata no. 8* (1799)
(1770–1827)   *1. Grave—Allegro di molto e con brio*   5:59

Sonata form
Introduction   :00
  Slow tempo, somber mood.

Exposition
  Principal theme (I)   1:34
    Fast tempo, ascending phrase answered by
    descending phrase in first sentence, second
    sentence begins like first but dissolves without
    a cadence.
  Transition
    Partially based on first phrase of principal theme.

Subordinate theme (II)   2:00
  Three related sentences, the third extended to lead
  directly into closing theme.
Closing theme (III)   2:25
  A   Repeated notes in the bass and soprano with
       a busy figure between.
  B   Running figure in high register.
  C   Reminiscent of principal theme.
(The repeat sign in the score at this point is rarely
observed in modern performances.)

Development   2:56
  Section 1
    Brief return to tempo and material of introduction.
  Section 2
    Fast tempo, principal theme developed to a climax.
  Transition
    Rapid single line.

Recapitulation
  Principal theme (I)   4:04
    One sentence exactly as in exposition, partial
    repetition dissolves into . . .
  Transition
    Based on second phrase of principal theme, only the
    last two measures are like the exposition.
  Subordinate theme (II)   4:20
    Transposed to the tonic key but otherwise as in the
    exposition.
  Closing theme (III)   4:43
    Transposed to the tonic key but otherwise all three
    parts return essentially as in the exposition.

Coda   5:15
  Section 1
    Tempo and material of introduction.
  Section 2
    Final reference to the principal theme.

Themes page 335.

The design of sonata form is such that many details can be varied without destroying the identity or the logic of the plan. A theme may consist of a single idea or a group of related ideas, or may be cast in the mold of a small form. The transitions may be perfunctory or as attractive and imaginative as the themes. New material may be introduced in the development section, or the development section can be omitted, in which case the form is abridged and the exposition is followed immediately by the recapitulation. In the recapitulation the order and tonality of the themes may be changed. All of these variations are possible within the broad concept of sonata form. Most of them are illustrated in the Additional Examples listed at the end of the chapter.

A standardized modification of sonata form attributed to Mozart occurs regularly in the first movements of classic concertos. The special adaptation of sonata form used in concertos has a *double exposition* instead of a repeated exposition. In the first exposition the orchestra presents the thematic material all in the tonic key. After remaining silent during the first exposition, the solo instrument makes an ear-catching entrance to begin the second exposition, and thereafter dominates the musical scene. In the second exposition, which takes the place of the usual repetition, the key relationships and the order of the themes are normal for sonata form. The development and recapitulation are perfectly regular, but at the end of the recapitulation, where a cadence is anticipated, the progress of the movement is interrupted to provide an opportunity for the soloist to exhibit virtuosity. This passage for the solo instrument unaccompanied is a *cadenza.* Originally improvised spontaneously on themes of the movement, cadenzas are now composed, but the free, improvisatory style is preserved. After a brilliant cadenza a mundane coda would be anticlimatic, so the movement usually ends summarily. Mozart's *Piano Concerto no. 27* begins, like his other concertos, with a movement in modified sonata form which has a double exposition and a cadenza.

W. A. MOZART: *Piano Concerto no. 27* (1791)		
(1756–1791)	*1. Allegro*	12:25
Sonata form, double exposition		
Exposition I		:00
Orchestra, tonic key.		
Exposition II		2:15
Piano and orchestra, usual sonata form key relationships.		
Development		5:15
Piano and orchestra, typical developmental procedures.		
Recapitulation		7:10
Piano and orchestra, tonic key as usual in the form.		
Cadenza		10:40
Piano, brilliant passage work using thematic elements.		
Coda		12:05
Orchestra.		

In twentieth-century examples of sonata form, the order of the themes in the recapitulation sometimes differs from that of the exposition. For example, the order of the themes may be reversed, producing an A-B-C—development—C-B-A design. This form is regarded by some as a modification of sonata form, by others as a distinct *arch form* or *bow form.* Arch forms also exist with a middle theme in place of the development section and with just five parts, A-B-C-B-A. In its various guises sonata form has survived through an extended period of music history.

ADDITIONAL EXAMPLES

Rondeau Form
 F. Couperin: *Pièces de Clavecin, Fifth Ordre*
      La Bandoline (AA B A C A D A)

Five-Part Rondo Form
 Bartók: *Piano Concerto no. 3*
     3. Allegro vivace (see page 137)
       LG 3/14
 Beethoven: *Bagatelle in A minor, "Für Elise"*
 Beethoven: *Piano Sonata no. 10 in G, op. 14 no. 2*
     3. Allegro assai (long coda)

Seven-Part Rondo Form
 Beethoven: *Violin Concerto in D, op. 61*
     3. Rondo: Allegro
 Saint-Saëns: *Introduction and Rondo Capriccioso, op. 28*
 Brahms: *Symphony no. 4 in E minor, op. 98*
     3. Allegro giocoso (with development)

Sonata Form
 Beethoven: *Symphony no. 5 in C minor, op. 67*
     1. Allegro con brio
      LG 2/6
 Mozart: *String Quartet in G, K. 387*
     1. Allegro vivace
 Haydn: *Symphony no. 94 in G, "Surprise"*
     1. Adagio cantabile—Vivace assai (with introduction)
 Mozart: *The Marriage of Figaro, K. 492,* opera
     Overture (without development)
 Tchaikovsky: *Nutcracker Suite, op. 71a*
     Overture Miniature (without development)
 Beethoven: *Violin Concerto in D, op. 61*
     1. Allegro ma non troppo (double exposition)
 Hindemith: *Mathis der Maler*
     1. Engelkonzert (order of themes changed in recapitulation)
 Bartók: *String Quartet no. 5*
     1. Allegro
   (arch form with the themes inverted—ascending motion becoming descending motion and vice versa—and their order reversed in the recapitulation)

9

POLYPHONIC FORMS

Both homophonic and polyphonic forms are based on the principle of repetition, but the applications of the principle are different. In the homophonic forms, repetitions of previously stated thematic elements alternate with contrasting material to establish patterns. In the polyphonic forms, immediate repetition in another part (imitation) produces patterns of alternating thematic entrances.

Polyphonic forms are conceived for a fixed number of parts, all of which participate in the unfolding of the thematic material. The number of parts dictates certain critical aspects of the organization, so the integrity of the various voices is maintained. Conflicting requirements of clarity, fullness, and freedom of movement restrict the number of parts in truly polyphonic music to a narrow range. Two-part texture tends to be sparse and harmonically incomplete. Four-part texture is more cumbersome, and following four individual melodic lines taxes the listener's ear. Three seems to be the ideal number of parts for polyphonic music, though single lines and passages in more than four parts have their place in the polyphonic forms. Rests are distributed through the parts in most polyphonic music, reducing the number of parts actually sounding together at a given instant below the total number participating. Polyphonic forms written for more than five parts are rare, but this does not preclude their being scored for orchestra and the larger ensembles. Any number of instruments can play a given part.

Canon

Continuous imitation between two or more parts produces a *canon*. Strict canonic imitation is the most rigid formal procedure in music, and even the momentary lapses allowed within the definitions of the form do not appreciably loosen the bounds. The severe limitations of canonic form make it unsuitable for extended works, but it is effective in short compositions and in brief passages of larger forms.

The part that begins a canon is called the *leader*, and those that imitate are called *followers*. The followers imitate the leader continuously at a fixed distance and interval up to a cadence point, where a momentary lapse may occur and where the leader and followers may change positions.

The following example shows the use of a canon as one part of a compound ternary form. The minuet proper (excluding the trio) is a strict and obvious two-part canon.

JOSEPH HAYDN: *String Quartet,* op. 76 no. 2 (1798)
(1732–1809)   3. *Menuetto: Allegro ma non troppo*   3:05

Overall, this minuet is in a regular compound ternary form. Individually, the minuet proper and the trio are simple ternary forms. In addition, the minuet is a canon in two parts with exact imitation throughout. The violins play the leader in octaves, and the viola and the cello play the follower in octaves, starting a measure (three beats) later and an octave lower. The trio is purely homophonic, but the canon is resumed on the return of the minuet. Haydn's fusion of polyphonic and homophonic forms is a stroke of genius.

Canons in which the end leads back to the beginning are *round canons,* *perpetual canons,* or *rotas.* All three names are used. Round canon, or just *round,* is most familiar because of its association with children's songs like *Are You Sleeping, Lovely Evening, Three Blind Mice,* and *Row, Row, Row Your Boat.* While problems of notation delayed the development of other types of polyphonic music for a time, notation presented no serious barrier to early composers of rounds. Rounds could be, and were, written as single line melodies with just an indication of the point at which the second and subsequent voices were to enter. As a result the form was highly developed at an early date. The old English round *Sumer Is Icumen In* (*Summer is Coming In*) is remarkable for its sophisticated handling of complex polyphonic texture.

ANONYMOUS: *Sumer Is Icumen In* (1240)   1:39   1/8

Structural diagram

    Part 1
    _____

        Part 2
        _____

            Part 3
            _____

                Part 4
                _____

    Part 1
    ●●● — — ● — — — — — ● — — — — — ● — — — ● — — — ● — — —

    Part 2
    ●●● — — — ● — — — ● — — — ● — — — ● — — — ● — — ● — ●●●

This is the oldest piece of secular music available in modern editions and still performed. It is an isolated example of this period and style, but its perfection attests to a considerable prior development. It consists of a four-part canon accompanied by two additional voices which continuously exchange short melodic fragments as shown in the diagram. All six parts can be repeated infinitely, and no real ending is provided.

In the absence of a composed ending, rounds and canons conclude after an indefinite number of repetitions as each voice comes to the end of the melody and drops out until none is left. Canons may be accompanied by free melodic lines or by chords. Participation in the canonic imitation is not required in all of the parts.

Certain manipulations of melodic lines traditional in contrapuntal music can be illustrated succinctly in canons. Interest in these manipulations is renewed because of their extensive application in twentieth-century music. The theory is that melodic lines preserve their identity when played backward, upside down, in longer or shorter rhythmic values (but the same proportions), and in any combination of these. Musicians have precise names for the original form of a melody and the various transformations. They are:

original—the initial unmodified form of a melody.
retrograde—the reverse of the original from the end to the beginning.
inversion—contrary motion or as seen in a mirror. Ascending lines
    become descending lines and vice versa. Skips become equivalent
    skips in the opposite direction.
retrograde inversion—the combination of retrograde and inversion.
augmentation—increased rhythmic values, usually doubled.
diminution—decreased rhythmic values, usually halved.

Most of these devices figure in the canons of Bach's *Musical Offering*.

J. S. BACH: *Musical Offering* *(1747)*   19:30
(1685–1750)

	Perpetual canon on the royal theme	1:25
	Diverse canons on the royal theme	
	1. Two parts	:45
	2. For two violins at the unison	:45
	3. Two parts in contrary motion	:50
	4. Two parts in augmentation and contrary motion	2:15
	5. Two parts	2:35
	Canonic fugue	2:00
	Two-part canon in inversion (two versions)	2:35
	Four-part canon	4:50
	Perpetual canon for flute, violin, and continuo	1:30

(The canons are listed in the order of the *Collected Edition.* The sequence is altered in some recordings.)

While one of J. S. Bach's sons, Philipp Emanuel, was employed as a musician in the court of Frederick the Great, the elder Bach was invited to the Potsdam palace to display his fabled powers of improvisation. Frederick provided a theme upon which Bach extemporized. After returning to Leipzig, he worked out and wrote down these canons and three other works which together constitute his "musical offering" to the king. The "royal theme" is present in all of the canons, sometimes as part of the canon and sometimes as a free voice. The canons have two voices in imitation and one free voice except the two-part canons, which have no free voice, and the four-part canon which has all four parts in imitation. Bach took the liberty of altering and embellishing the king's theme, so it is not always apparent. Canons involving inversion and retrograde forms of the theme are virtually impossible to detect without access to the score. Imitation of this sort serves to unify and organize musical sounds even though it functions largely on a subconscious level. Do not be disturbed if you are not consciously aware of it. Royal theme page 333.

Canons are most effective when used for passages within a larger framework. Canonic imitation figures prominently in many development sections. Occasionally it is used in thematic statements. One such instance is in the Franck *Sonata for Violin and Piano.*

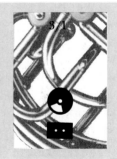

CÉSAR FRANCK: *Violin Sonata in A (1886)*
(1822–1890)   *4. Allegretto poco mosso*   6:06

The theme with which this movement opens is stated as an accompanied canon. In its first appearance the piano plays the leader and the accompaniment while the violin plays the follower. Each entrance of this theme is imitated canonically, with the violin and piano sometimes exchanging roles as leader and follower. The other themes of the movement are either homophonic or in free, nonimitative counterpoint.

Fugue

Fugue form occupies the same position of eminence in the baroque period (1600–1750) as sonata form does in the classic period (1750–1825). It is the form in which composers of the time cast many of their most exalted musical ideas. Fugue form embodies the principle of imitation, but in a much more imaginative and flexible manner than does canon.

The germ cell of a fugue is a pithy thematic idea called a *subject.* Fugue subjects typically contain one or more motives which are readily recognized and capable of sustained development. The subject is announced alone in one voice. It is answered immediately in another. The answer is not an exact repetition of the subject. It is on different pitches, and sometimes the shape is altered slightly, but for listening purposes the subject and answer may be considered the same and are so regarded in this discussion. Each voice of the fugue enters in turn with the subject. If it is a three-voice fugue, there will be three such entrances. If it is a four-voice fugue, there will be four. Regardless of the number, each enters in its assigned register. When all of the voices have stated the subject, the first section or main exposition is concluded.

The next section consists of a series of expositions in different keys separated by passages without the complete subject called *episodes*. Episodes normally contain fragments of the subject or of counterpoints associated with the subject.

In the final section there is a return to the tonic key and traditionally a passage with overlapping statements of the subject called a *stretto*.

A fugue is, strictly speaking, a monothematic form, but frequently a counterpoint consistently associated with the subject achieves the status of a secondary thematic idea and is designated a *countersubject*. Following the diagram of a typical fugue while it is being played does more to explain the form than multiplying words. A structural diagram of a very regular Bach fugue is provided for this purpose.

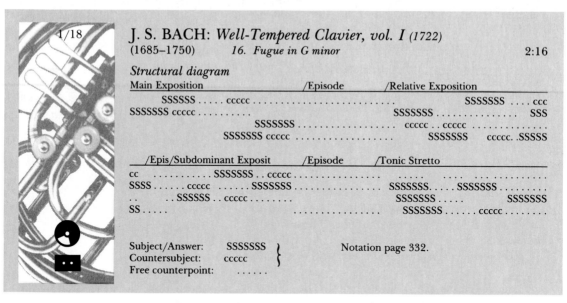

J. S. BACH: *Well-Tempered Clavier, vol. I* (1722)
(1685–1750) *16. Fugue in G minor* 2:16

Structural diagram

Main Exposition /Episode /Relative Exposition

```
    SSSSSS . . . . . ccccc . . . . . . . . . . . . . . . . . . . . . . . . .         SSSSSSS . . . . ccc
SSSSSSS ccccc . . . . . . . . . .                   SSSSSSS . . . . . . . . . . . . . .   SSS
                        SSSSSSS . . . . . . . . . . . . . . . . . . ccccc . . ccccc . . . . . . . . . . . . .
                SSSSSSS ccccc . . . . . . . . . . . . . . . .     SSSSSSS   ccccc. .SSSSS
```

/Epis/Subdominant Exposit /Episode /Tonic Stretto

```
cc  . . . . . . . . . . . SSSSSSS . . ccccc . . . . . . . . . . . . . . .   . . . . .    . . . . . . . . . . . . . . . . . . .
SSSS . . . . . . ccccc  . . . . . . SSSSSSS . . . . . . . . . . . . . . . SSSSSSS. . . . . SSSSSSS . . . . . . . . . . . . . . .
. .   . . SSSSSS . . ccccc . . . . . . . .           SSSSSSS . . . . .          SSSSSSS
SS . . . . .                  . . . . . . . . . . . . . . . SSSSSSS . . . . . . ccccc . . . . . . . .
```

Subject/Answer: SSSSSSS }
Countersubject: ccccc   } Notation page 332.
Free counterpoint: . . . . . . }

Fugal passages occur in forms other than fugues, particularly in the development sections of sonata forms. Less frequently, themes in other forms have a fugal design. A fuguelike passage within a form other than a fugue is called a *fugato*. Fugatos most often follow a plan similar to the first section (main exposition) of a fugue, though some contain all of the elements of a complete fugue. The last movement of Bartók's *Piano Concerto no. 3* is in five-part rondo form, but one theme and part of another are elaborate fugatos.

BÉLA BARTÓK: *Piano Concerto no. 3 (1945)*

(1881–1945)   *3. Allegro vivace*   7:19

3/14

Five-part rondo form

Theme I (rondo theme)   :00
Rapid ascending figure in piano leads to theme featuring short-long rhythms.

Transition: Timpani alone.   :52

Theme II—Fugato   1:02
Exposition starts in piano, is completed in strings.
Subject subsequently appears in inversion and stretto.

Theme I (rondo theme)   2:20
Theme in piano varied and much abridged.

Transition: Timpani alone, as before.   2:45

Theme III, ternary

A   Full chords in piano, figure in strings related to theme II.   2:55

B   Fugato. Subject enters in strings, then inverted form appears in woodwinds before original and inverted forms are played simultaneously by the piano.   3:20

A′   Modified return of A with string figure now played by the piano.   4:00

Theme I (rondo theme)   4:42
Thematic material in the orchestra with embellishing figures in the piano.

Coda: Abrupt break and brief silence separate theme from beginning of coda.   5:58

ADDITIONAL EXAMPLES

Canon
Bach: *Goldberg Variations, BWV. 988* (every third variation is a two-part canon, most with one free voice)
Bartók: *Duos (44) for Two Violins*
        22. Dance of the Fly
Bartók: *Mikrokosmos, vol. I*
        28. Canon at the Octave
        30. Canon at the Fifth
        31. Little Dance in Canon Form

Fugue
Bach: *The Art of Fugue, BWV. 1080*
Bach: *The Well-Tempered Clavier, vols. I & II, BWV. 846–893*
Hindemith: *Ludus Tonalis*

10 VARIATION FORMS

Variation is ever present in the music of virtually all periods and styles, but the number of forms actually governed by variation principles is small. Unity in variation forms is provided by one or more constant elements such as melody, bass line, harmony, or structure. Interest is sustained by modifying the remaining elements. The type of variation is determined by the choice of fixed elements, the kinds of alteration made in the variable elements, and the manner of connecting or separating the variations.

A theme stated at the beginning of a variation form introduces the constant elements. The theme may be original with the composer or it may be borrowed from a preexistent source. *Theme and variations* is a more complete title appropriate for many sets of variations. The theme is announced in a simple, direct fashion calculated to impress its characteristics on the mind of the listener. The variations follow, ranging in number from one to more than thirty, each with a direct though sometimes obscure relationship to the theme. A set of variations may conclude with a restatement of the theme or with a final section departing from the variation scheme, such as a fugue or coda.

Sectional Variations

Sectional variations begin with a theme which usually is a simple tune in one-part, binary, or ternary form sixteen to thirty-two measures in length. The parts of the theme may be repeated, and the repetitions, if any, normally are preserved in the variations. The theme comes to a full close, and there is a momentary interruption between it and the first variation and between all subsequent variations. Each variation duplicates the structure of the theme, and pauses between them divide the work into segments of equal length, though duration may vary with changes in tempo and the omission or addition of repeats.

Variations in which the melody is preserved more or less intact are the easiest to hear. Changes are restricted to the setting of the theme and to the registers and instruments in which it appears. The possibilities for variation are limited, so the number of variations is small. The Haydn example, with four, is typical.

JOSEPH HAYDN: *String Quartet,* op. *76 no. 3 (1798)*
(1732–1809) 2. *Poco adagio, cantabile* 7:33

Theme and variations
Theme—In first violin. :00
Variation I—Theme in second violin. 1:24
Variation II—Theme in cello. 2:48
Variation III—Theme in viola. 4:12
Variation IV—Theme in first violin. 5:36

This quartet receives its familiar name, *Emperor,* from the theme of these variations, which was the Austrian national anthem. The theme was not borrowed, however, for Haydn composed the anthem. The theme is a five-phrase sentence with an a-a-b-c-c design. The plan of the variations is simple. Each member of the quartet plays the theme in turn, and in the fourth variation the theme returns to the first violin where it started. Theme page 335.

A more flexible type of variation results when the melody of the theme is grouped with the variable elements. The same general plan of the previous example is followed, but the melody is embellished, altered, broken into fragments, and at times all but disappears. The structure and harmonic scheme remain as fixed elements, and the influence of the melody often is sensed even when it cannot be heard and isolated. The key center usually is constant, though changes back and forth between major and minor are common. Paganini's *Caprice no. 24* (see page 141) falls in this category, as does the variation movement of Beethoven's *Piano Sonata no. 12.*

BEETHOVEN: *Piano Sonata no. 12* (1801)
(1770–1827) 1. *Andante con variazioni* 7:10

Theme and variations
Theme—*Andante* :00
Variation I—*Un poco più mosso* 1:15
Variation II—*Più animato, ma non troppo* 2:30
Variation III—*Più sostenuto* (minor) 3:30
Variation IV—*Con moto* 4:30
Variation V 5:35
Coda 6:40

The theme is ternary. The melody is suggested in each of the variations, but it is never restated in its original form. The structure and cadence pattern of the theme are retained in all of the variations. Within phrases the harmonies are sometimes varied, and tempo is another variable element. In the absence of a tempo indication for a variation, the preceding tempo continues. Theme page 336.

In some sectional variations only the structure and broad harmonic outline are constant. Details of harmony are changed, and allusions to the theme melody may be so vague that they go undetected by all but the initiated. The theme serves as a point of departure for almost free composition, but enough of its spirit is preserved to assure the necessary unity. Brahms excelled in writing variations of this type. For him the theme functioned as a fount of inspiration, never as a millstone on his creative imagination.

BRAHMS: *Variations on a Theme by Haydn* *(1873)*   17:00
(1833–1897)

Theme and variations

Theme—*Andante*	:00
Variation I—*Andante con moto*	2:00
Variation II—*Vivace* (minor)	3:15
Variation III—*Con moto*	4:10
Variation IV—*Andante* (minor)	5:50
Variation V—*Poco presto*	7:45
Variation VI—*Vivace*	8:35
Variation VII—*Grazioso*	9:45
Variation VIII—*Poco presto* (minor)	12:30
Finale—*Andante*	13:30

This work exists in two structurally identical versions, op. 56a for orchestra and op. 56b for two pianos. The St. Anthony Chorale melody upon which the variations are based is an old hymn of unknown origin. Brahms copied it from the second movement of a *Divertimento in B-flat* for wind instruments by Haydn.

The theme is a ternary form with repeats, giving it an AA BA′ BA′ design. The structure of the theme, including the repeats and the characteristic extension at the end, is retained in all of the variations. The bass line and the melody of the theme figure in the variations, but not in ways that inhibit their striking originality.

The finale is a set of continuous variations (discussed in the second part of this chapter) over a constantly reiterated five-measure motive freely derived from the theme melody. The motive is stated several times in the bass before migrating to the soprano. A final statement in the bass gives way to a triumphant return of the chorale melody and a brief coda, which conclude the work. It is a tribute to Brahms's ingenuity that the repeated motive never becomes obtrusive. On the contrary, it may not even be detected by melody-oriented listeners who do not know about it in advance. Theme page 341.

The ultimate freedom in sectional variation form is displayed when the variations depart from the structure of the theme. In variations of this type, the theme serves as a source from which the composer draws thematic material. The variations have at least a subsurface unity by virtue of their common ancestry, but they may be only "kissing cousins" with highly individual personalities. Such is the case in Rachmaninoff's *Rhapsody on a Theme of Paganini*. Though Rachmaninoff calls his work a rhapsody, it is actually a set of very free sectional variations. Since the theme used by

Rachmaninoff was taken from a set of variations for solo violin by Paganini, listening to Paganini's variations provides an effective introduction to the longer and more complex Rachmaninoff composition.

NICCOLÒ PAGANINI: *Caprices, op. 1*
(1782–1840)   24. *Theme and variations*   4:43

The theme is a one-part form of sixteen measures with an a-a-b (4+4+8) design. The form, key, harmonic scheme, meter, and tempo of the theme are retained in all eleven variations; the rhythm and melody are uniquely varied in each. The last variation leads directly into a brief finale which concludes the piece. Theme page 338.

Free variations like those in Rachmaninoff's *Rhapsody on a Theme of Paganini* differ from the strict variations of the preceding examples in several respects. The variations do not necessarily adhere to the form of the theme in either length or design. Contrasting tempos and tonal centers are usual between variations. A derived motive may be the only element linking a variation to the theme, and secondary themes may be introduced. No two sets of free variations are alike, but all of these characteristics are illustrated in Sergei Rachmaninoff's *Rhapsody*.

RACHMANINOFF: *Rhapsody, op. 43 (1934)*
(1873–1943)   *Introduction, theme, 24 variations, and coda*   21:45

The rhapsody begins with a short introduction based on a motive from the theme. A skeletal outline of the theme, which perhaps should be regarded as the first variation, follows immediately. The theme proper comes next. Rachmaninoff repeats the last eight measures of Paganini's sixteen-measure theme, extending it to twenty-four measures with an a-a-b-b (4+4+8+8) design. Most of the variations are longer than the theme, but a few are shorter. Well-defined cadences separate some variations, some are fused together, while others are linked by cadenza-like passages. The tonic key and minor mode predominate, but other keys, including some major and very remote ones, are explored in variations 12 through 18. Rachmaninoff adds a melody from the Requiem Mass, *Dies Irae* (Day of Wrath), to the original theme in variations 7 and 10 and again in the coda. Theme page 338.

Procedures used by Rachmaninoff in his *Rhapsody*, such as using more than one theme, fusing variations, and delaying the statement of the theme, have been used in other recent variations. Liberties such as these have released variation form from confining limitations and preserved it as a viable means of musical expression for contemporary composers and listeners.

In contrast to sectional variations, *continuous variations* flow from one into another without interruption. The requirement of continuity influences the choice of fixed elements, or perhaps the other way around, the selection

Continuous Variations

of certain fixed elements is conducive to continuity. In any event, the persistent feature of continuous variations is either a bass line or a scheme of harmonic progressions rather than the melody or structure typical of sectional variations.

A *ground, ground bass,* or *basso ostinato* (literally, obstinate bass) are designations for short melodic phrases repeated over and over in the bass as a foundation for continuous variations. The possibility of transferring the phrase to a part other than the bass is not precluded, but it is exceptional. The finale of Brahms's *Variations on a Theme of Haydn* (see page 140) illustrates the procedures of continuous variation over a ground. Similar procedures are employed in the closing scenes of many early operas, among them the final aria in *Dido and Aeneas,* known variously as *When I am laid in earth, Lament,* and *Dido's Farewell.*

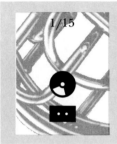

HENRY PURCELL: *Dido and Aeneas, opera* (1689)
(1659–1695)   *Thy hand Belinda/When I am laid in earth*   4:12

After an introductory recitative, a descending chromatic bass line five measures long typical of seventeenth- and early eighteenth-century grounds is heard a total of eleven times, first alone and then supporting full harmonies. The ground bass and chords accompany an independent melody with an AA BB design in the voice. Ground page 330.

Passacaglia and *chaconne* are names for specific types of continuous variation forms. Their development since their emergence in Spain around 1600 has recently been studied in depth, but attempts to distinguish between the two terms in actual usage has produced contradictory evidence. The themes of both are traditionally in the minor mode, eight measures long, and in triple meter. The theme may be a melody introduced in the bass or a series of harmonies. Bach wrote one of each type. He called the one with a continuously repeated line initially heard in the bass a passacaglia and the one which starts with an eight-measure pattern of chords a chaconne, but this distinction is not always observed by other composers. It is of no great importance, for bass and harmony are closely related. In the period when these two forms developed, a prescribed bass line would exert a strong influence on the chord structures erected above it, and a prescribed harmonic progression would almost determine the choice of bass tones.

As with sectional variations, continuous variations may end with a section which departs from the variation process. Bach's *Passacaglia and Fugue in C minor* for organ ends, as the title suggests, with a fugue.

J. S. BACH: *Passacaglia and Fugue* (1705)   13:45
(1685–1750)

The passacaglia begins with the theme by itself. Becoming thoroughly familiar with it is a great help in following the variations. The end of the theme leads directly back to its beginning, and there is no break in the continuity between its twenty varied appearances. The passacaglia reaches a climax, which subsides suddenly for the start of the fugue about two-thirds of the way through the work. The subject of the fugue is the bass theme of the passacaglia with the ending changed. Since the subject is already known, the countersubject enters with the first statement of the subject, unlike most fugues in which the subject is stated initially alone. Theme page 330.

Though not usually associated with variation forms, jazz improvisation based on the melody, harmonic progressions, and/or form of a popular song conforms to the general principles of variation form and perhaps should be included as an addendum.

ADDITIONAL EXAMPLES

Sectional Variations
  Brahms: *Variations on a Theme by Paganini, op. 35*
    Brahms wrote two books of *Studies for Piano*, better known by their subtitle given above, based on the same theme as Paganini's *Caprice no. 24* and Rachmaninoff's *Rhapsody on a Theme of Paganini.* Each book consists of fourteen variations preceded by the theme and followed by a coda. Brahms, like Rachmaninoff, added a repetition of the last eight measures to the original version of the theme. Theme page 338.
  Mozart: *Variations on Ah, vous dirai-je, maman, K. 265*
    The theme of these variations for piano is the French nursery tune named in the title. The same tune is sung by children in this country with the words of *Twinkle, Twinkle Little Star*, the *Alphabet Song*, and *Baa, Baa, Black Sheep.*
  Dohnanyi: *Variations on a Nursery Song, op. 25*
    The theme of these variations for piano and orchestra is the same nursery song used by Mozart, *Ah, vous dirai-je, maman.*
  Gershwin: *I Got Rhythm Variations*
    These variations for piano and orchestra are based on the hit tune from Gershwin's 1930 Broadway musical *Girl Crazy.*
Continuous Variations
  Bach: *Partita no. 2 in D minor for Violin, BWV. 1004*
        5. Chaconne
  Vitali: *Chaconne for Violin*
  Bach: *Mass in B minor, BWV. 232*
        16. Crucifixus (ground bass)

11 MULTIMOVEMENT FORMS

In the preceding chapters each form is considered as a separate entity, but some of the examples are components of more expansive works. The individual components of such works are *movements*, and movements are combined in *multimovement forms*. Each movement closes with a final cadence, and a moment of silence separates the movements in performance. Applause is customarily withheld until the end of the last movement, but lapses occur on occasion when audience enthusiasm is high.

The degree of standardization in multimovement forms varies from type to type. The sequence of types within the chapter is in descending order of standardization.

Complete Sonata Form

The emergence of sonata form proper in the last half of the eighteenth century together with the plan for the multimovement *complete sonata form* marked an epoch in the history of music. These interrelated schemes have provided a supreme mode of musical expression for generations of composers. Untold numbers of masterpieces have been spawned in the matrix of the complete sonata form. The durability of this plan of musical organization through the radically changing styles of the last two-hundred-plus years attests to its adaptability and vitality.

Complete sonata form embraces far more works than those which bear its name. A trio (referring to the form and not the medium) is a sonata for three instruments. Likewise, a quartet is a sonata for four instruments; a symphony is a sonata for orchestra; and a concerto is a sonata for a solo instrument with orchestra. These works are variously titled according to the performing medium, but structurally they are all essentially the same.

A complete sonata, regardless of medium, consists basically of three movements with a fast-slow-fast tempo scheme. A fourth movement is often inserted between the slow and fast movements. The first movement is, with rare exceptions, a sonata form, and certain forms are associated by tradition with the other movements, as shown.

Movement	Tempo	Form
First	Fast	Sonata
Second	Slow	Compound ternary, sonata, variation, or rondo
Third (optional)	Moderate/fast	Compound ternary
Last	Faster	Rondo or sonata

Haydn favored a four-movement plan with a minuet as the third movement. Mozart ordinarily included a minuet in symphonies and quartets but not in sonatas. Beethoven was partial to scherzos, which he included as the third of four movements, but reverted on occasion to the older minuet. Brahms was committed to the four-movement plan, but his third movements usually are without dance or scherzo connotations. An exception to these basic plans, which occurs when the first movement tends toward the slow side, is to reverse the order of the second and third movements, placing a faster rather than a slower movement after the opening movement.

A sonata, a quartet, a symphony, and a concerto will serve to illustrate various types of complete sonata form as written for the different mediums by composers of widely separated periods. By 1789 when Mozart composed the following piano sonata, the concept of complete sonata form as described was well established, but it had not been for long.

W. A. MOZART: *Piano Sonata no. 17 (1789)*		14:20
(1756–1791)	*1. Allegro—sonata form*	4:45
	2. Adagio—compound ternary form	5:25
	3. Allegretto—rondo form	4:10

In this sonata (no. 17 in D, K.576) the pattern of tempos and forms is typical for three-movement complete sonatas, but the internal structure of the first and third movements is somewhat irregular. The first two themes of the first movement begin with the same motive, and the order of the second and third themes is reversed in the recapitulation. The third movement structure is like a seven-part rondo with the second return of the rondo theme suppressed, a modification of rondo form used by Mozart in other works. The thematic design is A B A C B′ A. The same motive is prominent in each of the three themes, producing a highly integrated movement.

In relation to the preceding piano sonata, the following string quartet example is by a slightly older composer at a slightly later date but within the same period and style.

JOSEPH HAYDN: *Quartet, op. 76 no. 2 (1798)*		16:30
(1732–1809)	*1. Allegro—sonata form*	4:40
	2. Andante o più tosto allegretto—	5:00
	compound ternary form	
	3. Menuetto: Allegro ma non troppo—	3:05
	compound ternary form	
	4. Finale: Vivace assai—sonata form	3:45

This string quartet is known as the "Quinten" because the interval of a fifth is prominent in the themes of the first movement. The quartet as a whole follows closely the traditional plan of complete sonata forms with four movements. In the second movement the return of the first part after the contrasting middle section is elaborately embellished in the manner of a variation rather than a literal return. The menuetto was cited previously as an example of canon (see page 133).

The symphony example is an early twentieth-century work that pays homage to classical (1750–1825) style.

PROKOFIEV: *Classical Symphony* *(1917)*   12:40
(1891–1953)   *1. Allegro con brio—sonata form*   3:30
                     2. Larghetto—five-part rondo form   3:30
                     3. Gavotte: Non troppo allegro—ternary   1:30
                     4. Finale: Molto vivace—sonata form   4:10

Those who think of a symphony as something ponderous and formidable will be surprised by the sprightly character of this one. Though adhering to classic form, as the title indicates, this work is not without its twentieth-century flavor. The gavotte is substituted for the more usual minuet or scherzo, but otherwise the structural concept is very close to that of Mozart and Haydn. Also LG 1/22–25.

The Bartók concerto example is thoroughly modern in style and spirit, but its plan of organization has been in use for more than two hundred years.

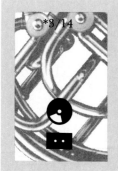

BÉLA BARTÓK: *Piano Concerto no. 3* *(1945)*   21:35
(1881–1945)   *1. Allegretto—sonata form*   6:10
                     2. Adagio religioso—compound ternary form 8:05
                     *3. Allegro vivace—five-part rondo form**   7:19

The three-movement plan is usual in concertos. The first movement sonata form of this one has but a single exposition and no cadenza, and thus adheres more closely to the structural plan of a classic symphony than a classic concerto. The third movement follows the second immediately without any pause, which is not unusual in concertos.

Cyclic Form

The movements of a complete sonata form have a certain underlying unity of style as a natural consequence of having been written by the same composer, but the only organic unifying element consistently present between movements of classic complete sonatas is that of key. The first movement is in the tonic key, the key indicated in the title, as are the third and fourth movements. The second (slow) movement normally is in a different but closely related key. Some composers have felt the need for stronger bonds between movements, for integrating devices beyond a plan of tempos, forms, and keys. This motivation led to the use of common material in the various movements. The shared material may be only a motive which appears in more than one movement, or a common body of themes and motives may permeate all of the movements. The purpose is to achieve a higher degree of unity in multimovement compositions. Works in which the same thematic material is used in more than one movement are *cyclic*. Cyclic form is not a plan of organization but a principle that is used in conjunction with other forms. Dvořák employs the cyclic principle effectively in the complete sonata form of his *New World Symphony*, formerly known as no. 5 but listed as no. 9 in the thematic catalog of his works and current sources.

ANTONIN DVOŘÁK: *Symphony no. 9* (1893)   37:55
(1841–1904)   *1. Adagio, Allegro molto—sonata form*   9:35
                     2. Largo—compound ternary form   10:20
                     3. Scherzo: Molto vivace—   7:20
                     seven-part rondo form
                     4. Allegro con fuoco—sonata form   10:40

The structures of the individual movements are fairly regular. Common material shared by the movements is in addition to the normal complement of distinctive themes. A *motto theme,* which occurs in each of the four movements, is first heard in the opening adagio played by the low strings. Its contour and rhythm are easily recognized and remembered. The melodic line ascends by leaps in notes of unequal duration to a high point, then abruptly descends to or near the starting pitch.

The motto theme, faster and somewhat modified from the version in the introduction, becomes the principal theme of the first movement proper and as such figures prominently in the movement.

In the second movement the motto theme is sounded by the trumpets and trombones in an episode which functions as a transition leading to the return of the opening material of the compound ternary form and a partial restatement of the famous "Going Home" melody by the English horn.

The form of the third movement borrows features from rondo and compound ternary forms. It has an A B A C A B A design like a seven-part rondo, but the A B A at the end is written as a *da capo* like a scherzo-trio-scherzo. The motto theme makes fleeting entrances in two of the transitions and appears again in the coda, principally in the French horns.

Thematic elements from all three preceding movements are recalled in the fourth movement, both in the development section and in the coda. The themes of all four movements are combined in a sort of recapitulation of the entire symphony. In addition to the obvious recurrences of the motto theme and the general summing up at the end, similarities of rhythm and contour can be traced between several of the thematic ideas in the four movements. All of this adds up to a highly integrated multimovement work and a convincing argument for the values of cyclic form. Motto theme page 343.

Antonin Dvořák

Baroque Suite

The *suite* as it crystallized during the baroque period (1600–1750) was an important instrumental form consisting of a series of movements, all in the same key. Most movements bear the name of a dance from which they derive a characteristic rhythm and style. The number and order of the dances vary, but one pattern is more prevalent than any other. It consists of the four following dances in order:

Allemande—A dance of German origin with four-beat measures in a moderate tempo, running figures and short upbeats typical, style serious but not ponderous.

Courante—A quick dance frequently paired with an allemande even before both were incorporated in suites; basic three-beat rhythmic pattern sometimes obscured by shifting accents; differing French and Italian versions produce a variety of styles.

Sarabande—A dignified dance in a slow triple meter in which the second beat may be stressed; spread from Spain across Europe but may have originated in the Orient or the New World.

Gigue—A lively dance which originated in the British Isles; six (or a multiple of three) beats in measures often containing long-short rhythmic patterns.

These four dances are standard in baroque suites. Between the sarabande and the gigue one or more optional dances is usually inserted. A prelude or overture may precede the dances, and a nondance movement is occasionally included in the optional group. The form of all the dances typically is binary. The following suite contains the four standard dances in their normal order and a typical selection of optional dances.

J. S. BACH: *French Suite no. 6 in E* (1723)		17:30
(1685–1750)	1. *Allemande*	3:00
	2. *Courante*	1:45
	3. *Sarabande*	3:45
	4. *Gavotte*	1:25
	5. *Polonaise* } optional group	1:40
	6. *Bourrée*	1:55
	7. *Menuet*	1:30
	8. *Gigue*	2:30

The dances of baroque suites were of international origin. The spelling of the names varied from country to country, and even within a country the spellings were not consistent. Minor discrepancies in spelling and style aside, the same dances were known and accepted throughout the British Isles and the Continent.

Dramatic Suite   When the baroque dances went out of style, suites as conceived by composers of that period were no longer written, but the name continued as a designation for collections of movements not classified as symphonies or complete sonatas. A common type of suite consists of excerpts from a dramatic work such as a ballet, an opera, or the incidental music for a play. Tchaikovsky's *Nutcracker* is a ballet, and the suite derived from the ballet music is a *dramatic suite*.

TCHAIKOVSKY: *Nutcracker Suite* (1892)		22:00
(1840–1893)	1. *Overture Miniature*	3:10
	2. *Characteristic Dances*	
	a. *March*	2:40
	b. *Dance: Sugarplum Fairy*	1:45
	c. *Russian Dance (Trepak)**	1:00
	d. *Arabian Dance*	3:50
	e. *Chinese Dance*	1:01
	f. *Dance of the Toy Flutes*	2:10
	3. *Waltz of the Flowers*	6:25

*Themes page 342.

Kodály's *Hary Janos Suite* is an example of a dramatic suite excerpted from an opera.

ZOLTÁN KODÁLY: *Hary Janos Suite* (1926)	21:35
(1882–1967)	
1. *Prelude: The Fairy Tale Begins*	3:10
2. *Viennese Musical Clock*	2:10
3. *Song*	5:10
4. *The Battle and Defeat of Napoleon*	3:45
5. *Intermezzo (Czardas)*	4:25
6. *Entrance of the Emperor and His Court*	2:55

Dramatic suites do not have any fixed plan. They customarily are arranged by the composer with due consideration for the requirements of balance and variety in style and tempo. More recent suites, unlike those of the baroque era, have changes of tonality between movements. Movements derived from dramatic works are assured a certain underlying unity by their common source. Composers are motivated to excerpt suites from their dramatic works for concert performance and recording, because the problems of presenting the stage versions of operas and ballets limit the number of performances. *Hary Janos* is a case in point. The suite is one of Kodály's most popular works, yet the opera is rarely staged outside of Hungary. Language, casting, and staging, formidable barriers to performances of the opera, are no problem with the suite.

Independent Suite

A work initially conceived as a suite is an *independent suite.* Like complete sonatas, independent suites are multimovement works, but they are inclined to differ from the sonata type in several respects. They are generally less profound, depart from the prescribed forms and movements in both style and number, and sometimes have literary or pictorial connotations. Since the time of Bach, suites have not been sufficiently homogeneous to yield to further generalizing regarding either style or content. Milhaud's *Scaramouche* exhibits many features associated with independent suites.

DARIUS MILHAUD: *Scaramouche Suite* (1937)	8:10
(1892–1974)	
1. *Vif*	2:40
2. *Modéré*	3:20
3. *Brazileira: Tempo of a Samba*	2:10

This suite exists in two versions—one for two pianos and the other an arrangement by the composer for saxophone and orchestra. Scaramouche was a Robin Hood type character in French comedies.

Several other terms have been applied to suitelike compositions. Terms like *divertimento, partita, serenade,* and *cassation* are sometimes almost synonymous with suite, but sometimes have special implications. Divertimentos usually consist of several short movements and are written for instrumental combinations smaller than full orchestra. A partita originally was a set of variations, but in the seventeenth and eighteenth centuries the term came to be used more or less interchangeably with suite. Serenade and cassation are names which suggest performance out-of-doors. Many works besides those with suite or one of the alternate terms in the title fall in this general category. Most multimovement instrumental compositions which are not complete sonatas can be called suites according to current usage.

ADDITIONAL EXAMPLES

Complete Sonata
    Beethoven: *Symphony no. 5 in C minor, op. 67*
    Franck: *Symphony in D minor* (cyclic)
    Franck: *Violin Sonata in A* (cyclic)

Suite
    Haydn: *Cassation in C for Lute, Violin, and Cello*
    Milhaud: *Suite Française* (independent suite for band)
    Mozart: *Divertimento no. 11 in D, K. 251*
    Mozart: *Serenade in G, K. 525, "Eine kleine Nachtmusik"*
    Sessions: *Black Maskers* (suite from incidental music for the play)
    Mendelssohn: *A Midsummer Night's Dream, op. 61* (incidental music for the Shakespeare play)

12

FREE AND MISCELLANEOUS FORMS

The homophonic, polyphonic, variation, and multimovement forms considered thus far encompass the most prevalent plans of organization in instrumental music. There remain, however, a few additional instrumental forms sufficiently common and standard to warrant attention. These, and some categories of instrumental music that are more properly genres than forms, are considered in this chapter.

Overture

The term *overture* originally was applied to the instrumental introductions to operas, oratorios, ballets, plays, and the like. Such overtures are often included on concert programs detached from the complete work. The meaning of the term has been extended to include the first movement of suite-type compositions and independent, one-movement compositions for both orchestra and band.

The earliest overtures consisted of two or three sections in contrasting tempos, usually slow-fast or fast-slow-fast. Though historically important, few overtures of this type remain in the concert repertory. Sectional overtures as a type were superseded by two types of overtures reflecting subsequent developments. For one of the successive types, the principles of sonata form were adapted. For the other type, melodies from the ensuing work were strung together in a medley.

Overtures in sonata form have the advantage of a highly developed plan of organization, especially important in concert performances. The form does not preclude the possibility of using thematic ideas from the body of the work or of foreshadowing the mood and action of the drama. The overture to Mozart's opera *The Magic Flute* incorporates these features in its sonata form and is equally effective as a prelude to the opera and as a concert piece.

W. A. MOZART: *The Magic Flute, opera (1791)*		
(1756–1791)	*Overture*	8:00

Composers of the Mozart-Beethoven period were partial to sonata form in their overtures.

In the nineteenth century the other type of overture, which is simply a potpourri of melodies from a dramatic musical work, emerged. A potpourri overture affords the theater attendee a preview of the tunes which are to follow and gives the concertgoer an abridged version of the work's thematic content. An overture of this type is essentially lacking in unity, because it consists of a series of unrelated melodies isolated from their dramatic context and loosely held together by transitional passages. Its melodies, culled from the best of the complete work, are the source of its strength. Medleys serve as overtures for many French and Italian operas and for most Broadway musicals. The overture to *My Fair Lady* is representative of the type.

FRÉDÉRICK LOEWE: *My Fair Lady (1956)*
(1901–1988)   *Overture*   3:10

Lerner and Loewe's Broadway musical *My Fair Lady* is based on George Bernard Shaw's play *Pygmalion*. The overture for the musical is made up from the melodies of three songs plus a motive from a fourth. A brief introduction captures the listener's attention before the theme of *You Did It* is heard. *On the Street Where You Live* and *I Could Have Danced All Night* follow, with only a perfunctory transition between them. A motive from *Show Me* serves as a coda to the overture and leads directly into the opening song, *Why Can't the English*, sung by professor Henry Higgins.

Concert overtures generally are cast in the mold of sonata form. They provide composers with a substantial vehicle less extensive than a symphony and serve a very practical purpose on concert programs—avoiding interruptions in multimovement works while latecomers are being seated. Overtures are ideal in this capacity. They become, in effect, overtures to the concert. It is customary to provide concert overtures with names, often with pictorial or literary implications as in Mendelssohn's *Fingal's Cave Overture*.

MENDELSSOHN: *Fingal's Cave Overture (1832)*   9:15
(1809–1847)

Mendelssohn conceived the opening of this overture while visiting Fingal's Cave, the largest cave on Staffa, a small, uninhabited island of the Hebrides archipelago off the coast of Scotland. The overture is also known as *Hebrides Overture*. Its sonata form did not inhibit the composer's romantic tone painting from vividly conveying his impression of the surging sea, the barren coastline with its precipitous basaltic cliffs, and the yawning mouth of the mammoth cave.

Prelude

The term *prelude* in some instances is almost synonymous with overture, designating an instrumental introduction to a musical or an opera. For example, the musical *La Cage aux Folles* begins with a prelude that is very similar in design to the potpourri overture of *My Fair Lady*. The lone distinction is that the curtain rises after the overture to *My Fair Lady* and before the prelude to *La Cage*.

JERRY HERMAN: *La Cage aux Folles* *(1983)*
(1933–   )   *Prelude*   3:00

During the prelude, a street scene in St. Tropez is seen on stage. As the sun goes down and the lights come on in the buildings, a nightclub, La Cage aux Folles, is seen in the distance. The prelude begins with an introduction consisting of motives from three songs—*La Cage aux Folles, Song on the Sand (La da da da),* and *The Best of Times.* Then succinct versions of the songs *La Cage aux Folles, With Anne on My Arm, Song on the Sand,* and *We Are What We Are* are heard in succession, followed by a brief coda.

Wagner also used the term *prelude,* or at least its German equivalent, *Vorspiel,* for instrumental introductions that lead directly into the first and sometimes subsequent acts of his operas and music dramas. Endings are provided for concert performances.

RICHARD WAGNER: *Lohengrin, opera* *(1850)*   2/17
(1813–1883)   *Act III. Prelude*   2:36

In nondramatic works the term *prelude* is applied to the first movement of suites and to the first piece of a pair as in prelude and fugue. The most famous examples in the latter category are the forty-eight preludes and fugues of Bach's *Well-Tempered Clavier.* Introductory preludes are apt to be based on a single motive and often make extensive use of scale and arpeggio figures (successions of chord tones). Bach's *C Major Prelude,* the first of the forty-eight and probably the best known, utilizes one arpeggio pattern and a constant rhythm throughout.

J. S. BACH: *Well-Tempered Clavier, vol. I* *(1722)*
(1685–1750)   *1. Prelude in C*   2:10

Some composers, ignoring the literal meaning of the term, have written collections of piano pieces all of which are called preludes. Not much can be said about independent preludes except that they are brief character pieces. In Chopin's collection there are twenty-four preludes, one in each key with the major and minor modes alternating.

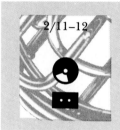

2/11–12

FRÉDÉRIC CHOPIN: *Preludes for Piano (1839)*
(1810–1849)

	No. 4 in E minor	1:52
	No. 7 in A major	:42

Debussy wrote two books of preludes. Each book contains twelve preludes, matching Chopin's total. All of these preludes have descriptive titles. The second prelude in the first book is *Voiles,* which can mean either sails or veils, but the music is more suggestive of the latter.

3/5

CLAUDE DEBUSSY: *Preludes for Piano, book I (1910)*
(1862–1918)   2. *Voiles*   3:54

A *chorale prelude* is a special type of composition for organ which developed as an introduction to the singing of a chorale (hymn) by the congregation in Protestant church services. The form, originally intended for a specific function, has since been used detached from religious services and varied. A chorale prelude is basically an elaboration of the chorale melody, a kind of variation before the theme. In concert performances organists sometimes play the chorale before the prelude, reversing the normal order and placing the prelude in a curious position. This ordering has the advantage of stating the theme, which otherwise might be unfamiliar, before the variation.

Several methods of elaboration are employed in chorale preludes. Some are merely enriched settings of the chorale melody, which may be in any voice, and which usually moves slowly against a more animated background. In others the melody itself is embellished. A third procedure is to derive fugue subjects from the chorale, usually one from each phrase, and to use them in a succession of fugatos. Overlapping of methods is not unusual.

J. S. BACH: *Schübler Chorale Preludes (1746)*
(1685–1750)   *1. Wachet auf (Sleepers Awake)*   4:52

The chorale *Wachet auf* by Philipp Nicolai (1556–1608) was published in 1599. More than a hundred years later, Bach used the chorale as the basis for his *Cantata no. 140* of the same name. Bach transcribed one part of the cantata for organ, and this version is included as the first of six chorale preludes in a collection published by Schübler in 1746. In the cantata and the organ prelude an independent flowing melody, announced at the beginning, continues uninterrupted while the chorale melody is projected against it a phrase at a time. Chorale melody page 333.

Though it is unique rather than one of a type, no discussion of preludes is complete without mentioning Debussy's incomparable *Prelude to the Afternoon of a Faun*. Being an independent descriptive work for orchestra, it neither fits the literal meaning of the word nor bears any resemblance to traditional prelude types, but it illustrates the latitude with which the term has been used by composers.

DEBUSSY: *Prelude to the Afternoon of a Faun (1894)*   9:00
(1862–1918)

Prélude à l'après midi d'un faune, to use the original French title of this work, was inspired by the poem of the impressionist poet, Stéphane Mallarmé. Its content may be summarized: "A faun is lying on the borderland of waking and sleeping in a grove. The atmosphere is palpitating with the golden midday heat. He has seen some slender-limbed, light-footed nymphs flit by; he would perpetuate the lovely vision. But he asks himself, am I in love with a dream? Fully awake, he begins to reflect and analyze, to dissect his sensations and emotions. His thoughts become exaggerated, distorted; his senses predominate. Delicate imagery takes shape in his mind. Had he seen a flight of swans? The current of his ideas becomes more realistic, and he imagines himself under the shadow of Etna with Venus in his arms. While anticipating punishment for such desecration, sleep visits his eyelids once more; he bids adieu to facts and reality and in the shades of oblivion goes in quest of the shadowy, vanished dream."

Rhapsody and Fantasia

Rhapsody and *fantasia* are terms generally applied to freely and often loosely constructed works which follow no prescribed plan of organization. Often they are improvisatory in style, and composers writing them indulge in flights of fancy without the usual regard for conventions of form and style. Liszt's *Hungarian Rhapsodies* served to popularize the form.

FRANZ LISZT: *Hungarian Rhapsody no. 2* *(1851)*   9:20
(1811–1886)

In Liszt's *Hungarian Rhapsodies* Hungarian and Gypsy elements are incorporated in several vividly contrasted, tenuously connected sections. Of the nineteen rhapsodies Liszt composed for piano, the second is most famous. It is included as the fourth of the six he arranged for orchestra.

The English composer Ralph Vaughan Williams wrote two of the better-known fantasias.

VAUGHAN WILLIAMS: *Fantasia on a Theme by Tallis*   15:45
(1872–1958)   *(1910)*

This fantasia is based on a theme by a countryman of Vaughan Williams, Thomas Tallis (1505–1585), but the theme serves only as a point of departure. The theme is freely molded and expanded without regard for preconceived notions of structure, unlike the composer's familiar *Fantasia on Greensleeves* which, despite the title, has a broad ternary design.

Ritornello Form

Ritornello is a form peculiar to the baroque era when texture and tonality were paramount considerations in musical organization. A ritornello form ordinarily has a solo voice, instrument, or small group of instruments that is assigned certain responsibilities in the musical design, the other responsibilities being assigned to the accompanying ensemble. A ritornello form starts with an incisive *ritornello theme* played by the ensemble. The solo voice or instrument enters at the close of the ritornello theme and predominates in a passage that ultimately modulates to a new key. The ritornello theme, or a fragment of it, is then stated in the new key. Modulatory passages, called *episodes,* alternate with partial or complete statements of the ritornello theme in various keys until the last episode modulates back to the tonic key, and the final (usually complete) statement of the ritornello theme in the tonic key completes the form. The number of keys is flexible, and the basic plan is subjected to many modifications. The last movement of Vivaldi's *Violin Concerto in A minor, op. 3 no. 6* is one of the clearer examples of ritornello form.

ANTONIO VIVALDI: *Violin Concerto,* *op. 3 no. 6 (1712)*   1/16
(1678–1741)   *3. Presto*   2:18

Ritornello form
Ritornello theme   :00
  Tonic key (A minor), orchestra.

Episode   :27
  Solo prominent, starts with embellishment of ritornello
  theme, modulates to dominant key.

Ritornello theme   :45
  Starts in dominant key (E minor), orchestra with solo
  interspersed.

Episode   1:04
  Solo prominent, modulates to relative major key.

Ritornello theme   1:22
  Fragment in relative major key (C) followed by same
  fragment in dominant key (E minor), orchestra.

Episode   1:39
  Solo prominent, modulates back to tonic key.

Ritornello theme   1:45
  Tonic key (A minor), solo and orchestra.

Coda   2:06
  Solo and orchestra.

This concerto, one of twelve known collectively as *L'Estro Armonico* (*The Harmonic Whim*), is scored for one solo violin, string orchestra, and harpsichord. When the solo violin is not playing an independent part, it joins in with the violins of the orchestra. Ritornello theme page 330.

The *concerto grosso* is a genre in which the distinguishing characteristics are the medium and the way it is used. The medium consists of a small group of solo instruments—most often two violins, cello, and a keyboard instrument—and string orchestra. The solo group may be constituted differently, and wind instruments are occasionally included in both the solo group and the orchestra. The essential feature of the genre is the contrast alternately between the rich sonority of the full ensemble and the sparser sound of the solo group when the other instruments are silent.

Concerto Grosso

A concerto grosso normally has at least three movements, usually more. The individual movements may be simple part forms, ritornello form, or fugal. The concerto grosso flourished from the end of the seventeenth century to the middle of the eighteenth century, and it has been revived in the twentieth century. Corelli was one of its leading exponents, perhaps its originator. The following "Christmas" concerto grosso is one of his best known.

CORELLI: *Concerto Grosso,* op. 6 no. 8		15:00
(1653–1713)	1. Vivace—Grave	1:30
	2. Allegro	2:00
	3. Adagio—Allegro—Adagio	3:50
	4. Vivace	1:10
	5. Allegro	2:45
	6. Pastorale: Largo	3:45

This concerto grosso bearing the inscription, "Composed for the night of the Nativity," was published posthumously in 1714. The date of composition is unknown. The scoring is for the standard solo group—two violins, cello, and a keyboard instrument—and string orchestra. The contrast between the solo group and the larger body of strings is exploited with special effect in the first and last *allegro* sections and in the *vivace* following the *adagio*.

In Conclusion

Many other terms such as *toccata, impromptu, pastorale, song without words, ballade, nocturne,* dance-inspired names, and a host of others too numerous to mention, are used as designations for musical works. Toccatas are usually brilliant, idiomatic works for keyboard instruments and, by extension, for other mediums as well. The other appellations are used for brief character pieces reflecting the mood or style indicated by the title but otherwise without special distinctions.

In addition there are compositions, especially from the romantic and contemporary periods, which do not follow any prescribed plan of organization. This is true in a sense of rhapsodies and fantasias, but works in these categories have enough in common to create a type if not a pattern. Unique design is relatively rare in conventional music, but not unknown or undesirable. Setting a text or depicting a story may provide the impulse for an unusual sequence of musical ideas. Composers in this century have revolted against the conventions of form as well as those of harmony, tonality, and line. Their new musical language has demanded a new syntax. Musical structures are now more than ever before a product of their content, and free forms—those with no standard organizational plan—are the rule rather than the exception. Even in jazz styles musicians are exploring the possibilities of free form improvisation.

Free or unique form is not to be confused with lack of form. On the contrary, the most skillfully integrated musical expression may defy classification. Works in which ties with traditional patterns are absent or stretched beyond recognition are grouped together as free forms. Their eccentric nature renders impossible generalization and illustration.

A special kind of free form results when the sequence of events and the precise nature of the events in a musical work are not predetermined by the composer. In such cases the compositional decisions not made by the composer are made by the performers or left to chance and presumably differ in each performance. Leaving some elements of a composition indeterminate in notation and variable in performance has emerged as a major trend in avant-garde music. Works of this genre in which responsibility for the ordering of musical events is delegated to the performers and/or dictated by chance tend to be unique in concept and to have in common only their indeterminacy. Representative indeterminate compositions and procedures are described in chapter 24.

ADDITIONAL EXAMPLES

Overture
  Rossini: *William Tell Overture* (opera)
  Rodgers: *The King and I Overture* (musical)
  Beethoven: *Egmont Overture, op. 84* (drama)
  Barber: *Overture to the School for Scandal* (drama)
  Brahms: *Academic Festival Overture, op. 80* (concert)
  Berlioz: *The Corsair, Overture for Orchestra, op. 21*
            (concert overture inspired by Byron's narrative poem)

Prelude
  Wagner: *Prelude to Tristan and Isolde* (opera)
  Bach: *Orgelbüchlein Chorale Prelude no. 10, BWV. 608*
            In Dulci Jubilo (In Sweet Jubilation)

Rhapsody and Fantasia
  Enesco: *Roumanian Rhapsody no. 1, op. 11*
  Bruch: *Scottish Fantasy for Violin and Orchestra, op. 46*

Ritornello Form
  Handel: *Messiah*
            45. I know that my Redeemer liveth

Concerto Grosso
  Vivaldi: *L'Estro Armonico, op. 3 no. 11 in D minor* (violin concerto)

13
PROGRAM MUSIC

Program music is the genre of music inspired by, depicting, or suggesting extramusical ideas. Music without any such associations is *absolute music*. The category in which a composition belongs is sometimes reflected in the way it is identified. A work called a symphony, a string quartet, or a sonata, for example, would ordinarily be in the absolute category. A work known by a title is more apt to be programmatic to some degree, though the designation is commonly used only for instrumental compositions with literary or pictorial connotations or which imitate the sounds of nature.

In program music the influence of the extramusical elements ranges from the merest suggestion of a mood to the graphic representation of specific incidents and scenic details. The most obvious examples of program music portray natural sounds, events, and things realistically. At the opposite end of the spectrum are works with descriptive titles but no other evidence of programmatic influence. Program music of all types can be cast in any of the usual forms or in a free form determined by the program.

Since the sounds of music are not well suited to conveying concrete visual or dramatic impressions, the perception of the program underlying a piece of music is dependent in large measure, if not entirely, upon providing the listener with sufficient clues in advance. When descriptive titles are inadequate for the purpose, composers resort to verbal descriptions of what the music is about. Pertinent sections or résumés of literary works are sometimes quoted in scores and reprinted in program notes and record booklets as an aid to comprehending program music. The need for program notes supports the view that music is incapable of expressing ideas, or at least that it is a poor substitute for words. An unrivaled attribute of absolute music is that its total abstraction makes it unique among the arts. On the other hand, many acknowledged musical masterpieces have a program, and the program music category includes some of the most popular works in the literature.

For many listeners a program serves as a bridge to the realm of music. Its mysteries seem somehow less formidable when the emotions and imagination are provided a more tangible point of departure than abstract sound. There can be no objection to the composer's sharing the source of inspiration with the listener. However, the practice of inventing stories to go with music when none is intended is undesirable, even as sugarcoating for music presented to the very young. False values thus established eventually if not immediately defeat the avowed purpose of making abstract music more palatable.

An undeniable advantage of program music is that fanciful titles derived from the programs are more easily remembered, even by musicians, than the keys and opus numbers formerly used to identify examples of absolute music. One wonders if it is coincidental that of Beethoven's thirty-two piano sonatas, all of the most famous are included in the half-dozen or so associated with names. In an age when keys and opus numbers are virtually things of the past, contemporary composers are finding distinctive titles the best way to identify their works, and most titles have programmatic implications.

Tone Painting

The beginnings of *tone painting* can be traced back to fourteenth-century vocal music, but in these early examples the music merely illustrates words or ideas occurring more or less simultaneously in the text. One of the first examples of instrumental program music is a fantasia by John Munday (d. 1630) in the *Fitzwilliam Virginal Book*. It depicts thunder, lightning, and fair weather. Kuhnau's six *Biblical Sonatas* (1700) are somewhat later and more sophisticated examples of program music for a keyboard instrument. The meaning of each movement is described explicitly in the score. Kuhnau must have anticipated opposition to his ideas, for he explained and defended his approach in a preface to the sonatas. Couperin carried the programmatic concept a step further and correlated his musical ideas with both human attributes and colors in *Les Folies Françoises* (*Follies of the French*).

COUPERIN: *Les Folies Françoises* (1722)		10:20
(1668–1733)	1. *Virginity—invisible*	:00
	2. *Modesty—red*	:40
	3. *Ardor—scarlet*	1:20
	4. *Hope—green*	2:10
	5. *Loyalty—blue*	2:55
	6. *Perseverance—flaxen gray*	4:10
	7. *Languor—violet*	4:50
	8. *Coquetry—various colors*	6:05
	9. *Aged gallants—purple*	6:35
	10. *Benevolent cuckoos—yellow*	7:30
	11. *Jealousy—dark gray*	8:20
	12. *Frenzy or despair—black*	9:35

Couperin composed four volumes of pieces for harpsichord (*pièces de clavecin*) grouped in twenty-seven suites (*ordres*). *Les Folies Françoises* is number four in volume three, fourteenth ordre. Title and color designations notwithstanding, this piece is a series of variations on a harmonic-bass theme. Virginity is the theme, and each following attribute is a variation. The similarity of the variations to each other and to the theme is especially apparent in the cadences which separate them. The variation form and the program are not only compatible, but complementary.

Program music occupied an insignificant place in the music of the classic era, but with the rise of romanticism in the nineteenth century it assumed a position of importance. Music of every dimension from diminutive to monumental and for every medium from one instrument to full orchestra would be embraced by a catalog of romantic program music. The suggested listening barely hints at its magnitude and scope.

Modest Mussorgsky's *Pictures at an Exhibition* is a piece of nineteenth-century program music in the tradition of Kuhnau and Couperin, but with some added touches.

MUSSORGSKY: *Pictures at an Exhibition* (1874)   29:30
(1839–1881)

Promenade   :00
  Depicts the viewer (Mussorgsky) as he moves between pictures in
  the art gallery; theme provides a connecting and unifying element
  between sections, and appears in the finale.

The Gnome   1:30
  A misshapen, comical figure supposedly fashioned as a Christmas
  tree ornament.

Promenade   4:00

The Old Castle   4:50
  A troubadour sings his lay before a medieval castle.

Promenade   8:30

Tuileries   9:00
  The famous gardens with children and their nurses.

Bydlo   10:10
  A two-wheeled ox-drawn cart lumbering across the fields.

Promenade   12:50

Ballet of the Unhatched Chicks   13:25
  Dancers costumed as chicks emerging from their shells.

Samuel Goldberg and Schmyle   14:45
  A dialogue between a rich Jew and a poor one.

The Market Place at Limoges   17:00
  Women wrangling furiously.

The Catacombs   18:20
  The artist exploring the catacombs of Paris by lantern light.

Baba-Yaga   21:55
  A grotesque clock representing the house of Baba-Yaga,
  a witch character of Russian folklore.

The Great Gate of Kiev   25:20
  Hartmann's design for a triumphal arch through which
  passes a pageant of Russian history.

A posthumous exhibition of paintings by Mussorgsky's friend, Victor Hartmann, included the ten canvasses which inspired this composition. It was composed for piano but is better known in transcriptions for orchestra. The recurrent promenade theme serves as an overall unifying element. The other parts have independent themes and their own internal structures. Promenade theme page 342.

The sounds of nature are still heard—sometimes subtly, sometimes humorously—in nineteenth-century program music. Animal and bird sounds are imitated by instruments in *The Carnival of the Animals*. These are served up with parodies of borrowed melodies and engaging original tunes to make musical fare which is certain to entertain children and amuse adults. Ironically, Saint-Saëns regarded this, his most popular work, as such a trifle that he did not allow it to be published or publicly performed during his lifetime.

SAINT-SAËNS: *The Carnival of the Animals* (1886)	21:00
(1835–1921) *1. Introduction and Royal March of the Lion*	:00
2. Hens and Cocks	1:35
3. Fleet-Footed Animals	2:40
4. Tortoises	3:20
5. The Elephant	5:00
6. Kangaroos	6:30
7. Aquarium	7:20
8. Personages with Long Ears	9:40
9. Cuckoo in the Woods	10:15
10. Aviary	12:30
11. Pianists	13:45
12. Fossils	14:55
13. The Swan	16:10
14. Finale	19:00

Borrowed melodies are heard in Sections 4, 5, 11, and 12. "Tortoises" begins with the cancan melody from Offenbach's *Orpheus in Hades* and ends with a few measures from Act I of the same opera. "The Elephant" has a parody of the "Dance of the Sylphs" from *The Damnation of Faust* by Berlioz and a hint of the *Midsummer Night's Dream* "Scherzo" by Mendelssohn. Exercises à la Czerny (a piano pedagogue) are practiced in "Pianists." The themes of "Fossils" are from Saint-Saëns' *Danse Macabre* and Rossini's *Barber of Seville*, with added bits from the French folk songs *J'ai du bon tabac, Ah! Vous dirai-je maman*, and *Partant pour la Syrie*. Material from previous sections is recalled in the finale.

Symphonic/ Tone Poem

The *symphonic poem* or *tone poem* is an important type of nineteenth-century program music. A symphonic or tone poem is a large-scale, single-movement, programmatic work for orchestra. The concept is attributed to Franz Liszt (1811–1886), who composed twelve works in the form (see page 251). His innovation was enthusiastically received and widely imitated. The symphonic poem ranks as the most characteristic expression of the romantic impulse in instrumental music.

Goethe's ballad *The Sorcerer's Apprentice* is such a natural subject for a symphonic poem that someone was bound to use it. Dukas did, and it is difficult to decide whether the music or the story contributes most to the success of the piece. The details of the story are graphically portrayed without sacrificing musical values in this inimitable tone painting.

PAUL DUKAS: *The Sorcerer's Apprentice (1897)*   11:30
(1865–1935)

This work tells in tones the story of an apprentice sorcerer who, in his master's absence, repeats a magic formula he has overheard which enables him to bring a broomstick to life. He commands it to carry water from the well, and it obeys perfectly until the task is completed. Then the apprentice discovers that he does not know the formula to stop it. The broomstick carries bucket after bucket of water until the room is overflowing. In desperation the apprentice chops the broomstick in two, and to his dismay both halves carry water faster than ever. At last the sorcerer returns, pronounces the magic words, and restores order.

Program Symphony/ Suite

Multimovement counterparts of the symphonic poem are the *program symphony* and the *program suite*. Because of the less rigid application of structural principles in program music generally, distinctions between program symphonies and suites are not so well defined as between absolute symphonies and suites. Evidence of the closer relationship between program symphonies and suites is manifest by the addition of movements beyond the normal four in some program symphonies. Berlioz's *Symphonie Fantastique,* with five movements, is deservedly one of the most celebrated.

BERLIOZ: *Symphonie Fantastique (1831)*   48:10
(1803–1869)   *1. Dreams and Passions:*   12:50
                 Largo—Allegro agitato e appasionata assai
              2. A Ball (Waltz): Allegro non troppo   5:40
              3. Scenes in the Country: Adagio   15:30
              4. March to the Scaffold: Allegretto non troppo   5:00
              5. A Witches' Sabbath: Larghetto—Allegro   9:10

Berlioz himself outlined the story of the symphony in a preface to the work:

A young, morbid, ardent musician in a state of amorous despair poisons himself with opium. The dose, insufficient to kill him, plunges him into a delirious sleep during which his sensations take the form of musical ideas in his sick brain. His beloved becomes a melody, an *idée fixe* (fixed idea) which he hears everywhere.

Dreams and Passions.   He at first recalls the vague melancholy and joy which alternated without apparent reason before he met his beloved; then the volcanic passion with which she inspired him, his jealous fury, his return to tenderness and religious consolation.

A Ball.   He finds his beloved waltzing in the tumult of a brilliant fete.

Scenes in the Country.   On a summer evening in the country he listens to two shepherds playing a pastoral duet to summon their flocks. The rustic scene, the gentle rustling of the trees in the breeze, hopeful prospects he has recently entertained, all combine to produce an unaccustomed calm but with a bitter tinge. The beloved returns again . . . his heart throbs . . . he is disturbed by forebodings that she might deceive him . . . one of the shepherds resumes his naive melody . . . the other no longer answers . . . the sun sets . . . in the distance thunder rumbles . . . solitude . . . silence . . .

March to the Scaffold.   He dreams he has killed his beloved, that he has been condemned to death and is being led to the scaffold. The procession advances to the sound of a march now sombre, now wild, now brilliant, now solemn. Loud outbursts are followed without pause by the plodding sounds of marching feet. The *idée fixe* appears for a moment like a last thought of love cut short by the fatal blow of the guillotine.

Witches' Sabbath.   He finds himself at a witches' revel in the midst of a horrible group of spectres who have come to attend his funeral. Strange noises are heard—groans, bursts of laughter, distant shrieks to which other shrieks seem to reply. The melody of the beloved appears once more but transformed from its character of nobility and gentleness to a common, grotesque dance tune. Howls of joy accompany her arrival and participation in the diabolic orgy . . . funeral bells . . . parody on the *Dies Irae* . . . witches' dance . . . witches' dance and the *Dies Irae* together.

Berlioz departs from the traditional sequence of movements in this symphony, but his procedures are not unrelated to convention. He substitutes a waltz and a march for a minuet or scherzo, but this is a logical extension of the basic concept. A minuet or corresponding movement usually follows the slow movement, but sometimes precedes it. Berlioz places the one before and the other after. This provides an ideal balance with the slow movement, longest of the five, flanked on each side by a shorter movement in a relatively moderate tempo. The first and last movements correspond both in tempo and duration. In spite of the program, Berlioz abandons typical structural patterns only in the last movement. The first movement is in sonata form. The second, third, and fourth movements have compound ternary designs. The final movement has a free sectional structure of four large parts.

The appearance of the *idée fixe* in each movement provides a cyclic element. It is announced after the slow introduction of the first movement by the violins and flutes in the prevailing fast tempo of the movement. It is the principal theme of the sonata form. In the second movement this theme appears, rhythmically transformed, in the middle section of the waltz played first by flute and oboe and then by flute and clarinet. The *idée fixe* in a different rhythmic transformation serves as an answering phrase in flute and oboe in the middle section of the third movement and enters briefly at the end. The hero's memory of his beloved is recalled by her theme just before the end of the fourth movement. The *idée fixe* completely transformed into a derisive and sarcastic dance tune by grace notes and trills immediately follows the opening *larghetto* section in the final movement. Thus the *idée fixe* provides a cyclic as well as a programmatic element. *Idée fixe* page 337.

Ives's programmatic *Three Places in New England* has been called a "New England Symphony," but it could just as aptly be called a "New England Suite." Unlike most symphonies, the forms of the individual movements are very free, and the pattern of tempos—slow-fast-slow—is the reverse of that found in three-movement complete sonata forms. The tempo markings of the three movements are:

1. *Very slowly*
2. *Allegro: Quick-step time*
3. *Adagio molto (very slowly)*

*3/7

CHARLES IVES: *Three Places in New England (1914)*   18:17
(1874–1954)   *1. The "St. Gaudens" in Boston Common*   8:55
    *2. Putnam's Camp, Redding, Connecticut**   5:37
    3. The Housatonic at Stockbridge   3:45

Each of the movements is vividly descriptive of the place in New England specified in the title. The first movement, subtitled *Col. Shaw and His Colored Regiment*, is prefaced by a poem (probably by Ives) which contains the lines, "Moving—Marching—Faces of Souls! . . . Slowly, restlessly—swaying us on with you Towards other Freedom!" As fragments of Civil War melodies are projected against a hauntingly dissonant background, one can easily visualize a spectral procession marching to the beat of the drum.

The second movement is a musical fantasy depicting a child's Fourth of July outing at the Revolutionary Memorial located at the site of General Israel Putnam's 1778–79 winter quarters. Snatches of familiar tunes are heard as two bands playing different marches in different tempos and keys approach from opposite directions, pass each other, and depart.

The summer after they were married, Ives and his wife took a walk through the meadows along the Housatonic River near Stockbridge. This walk and a poem by Robert Underwood Johnson which begins, "Contented river! in the dreamy realm. . . ." inspired the third movement of this program symphony or suite.

Many of the staple items in the current repertoire and some of the most widely accepted and appreciated compositions of all time were products of program music's heyday during the romantic period of the last century. As suggested by *Three Places in New England,* the tradition of program music continues in the twentieth century up to and including the electronic compositions of the present.

ADDITIONAL EXAMPLES

Tone Painting
    Debussy: *Preludes for Piano, book I*
       2. Voiles (Sails or Veils)
       LG 3/5
    Ellington: *Harlem Air Shaft*
       (in the Smithsonian Collection of Classic Jazz)

Symphonic/Tone Poem
    Smetana: *Ma Vlast (My Fatherland)*
       2. The Moldau
    Strauss, R.: *Till Eulenspiegel's Merry Pranks, op. 28*
       (see page 255)

Program Symphony/Suite
    Beethoven: *Symphony no. 6 in F, op. 68, "Pastoral"*
    Rimsky-Korsakov: *Scheherazade, op. 35, Symphonic Suite after the Thousand and One Nights*

14 DRAMATIC MUSIC: OPERA

Dramatic music is the general classification for music associated with stage presentations and their more recent counterparts, motion pictures and television. Ideally, dramatic music should be experienced as it was originally conceived. In the case of opera this means, with rare exceptions, a live performance on stage, but film and television versions are reasonable facsimiles, as are the videotapes and laser discs now readily available. The essential combination of aural and visual elements is preserved.

Introduction to Opera

Opera is a prime type of dramatic music. Broadly defined, opera is sung drama with orchestral accompaniment and all the adjuncts of staging—action, sets, costumes, and lighting. An opera is a play set to music, and many operas are based on successful plays. If an undue portion of the American public reacts negatively to the composite form, perhaps it is because of misconceptions regarding opera and a certain dichotomy between traditional operatic fare and current taste. A survey of the genre should help to clarify how opera functions as an art form, and how recent developments in both the creation and production of opera have moved it closer to the requirements of mainstream entertainment. Indeed, it has arrived if Andrew Lloyd Webber's stage works are classified as operas. Webber's works, including *Jesus Christ Superstar, Evita, Cats, Starlight Express,* and *Phantom of the Opera,* are as popular and more widely performed than were those of Verdi, the most successful operatic composer of the nineteenth century, at the zenith of his career.

Enjoyment of opera is contingent upon accepting it as a highly artificial art form. It is not natural to burst into song under the impact of emotional stress or to hit a high C with one's dying breath, but these are conventions the operagoer must be prepared to accept. Opera is remote from reality, but realism in any art is only relative. Frames around landscape paintings and rhymes in play dialogue are equally artificial but widely accepted conventions.

The particular conventions of opera have a long history. The association of music with drama dates back to the ancient Greeks. Their musical achievements were not handed down, but in attempting to revive Greek tragedy, a group of Florentine noblemen known as the *Camerata* laid the foundations of modern opera just before 1600. This group, conforming to their concept of Greek drama, evolved a musical style which consisted of vocal declamation with careful attention to the natural rhythm, accent, and inflection of the text. This vocal declamation, a sort of intensified speech, was carried out over a simple, instrumental harmonic background. The concept was revolutionary in its time, and though its influence on the course of music was immense, the limitations of melodies inseparably bound to natural speech were apparent as soon as the novelty wore off. The advantages of this style were that the text could be understood and that the action progressed almost as fast as in spoken drama. Subsequent attempts to enhance the musical value with more appealing melodies and more expressive harmonies invariably sacrificed these virtues.

From the beginning of opera, scenes occasionally closed with metric songs and choruses and with dancing. These features became increasingly prominent as opera developed. Soon there were distinct sections. *Recitatives* (see page 230) in declamatory style were followed by lyric and metric *arias*. Recitatives and arias are well defined in one of the first English operas, Purcell's *Dido and Aeneas*.

Purcell/*Dido and Aeneas*

The story of *Dido and Aeneas* comes from the fourth book of *The Aeneid* by Vergil. The Trojan hero Aeneas, having been sent by the gods from the ravaged Troy to establish a new empire, is blown off course in a storm. He lands in Carthage where he is welcomed by Queen Dido, and they fall in love. Through sorcery Aeneas is reminded that he must leave Carthage to fulfill his destiny. He departs, and the desolate Dido sings the recitative *Thy hand, Belinda* and the aria *When I am laid in earth* before dying heartbroken in the arms of Belinda, her maid.

1/15

HENRY PURCELL: *Dido and Aeneas, opera* (1689)
(1659–1695)   *Thy hand, Belinda/When I am laid in earth*   4:12

> *Recitative*
>> Thy hand, Belinda! darkness shades me,
>> On thy bosom let me rest,
>> More I would, but death invades me.
>> Death is now a welcome guest.
>
> *Aria*
>> When I am laid in earth,
>> May my wrongs create no trouble in thy breast.
>> Remember me, but ah! forget my fate.

Ground page 330.

As the concept of opera progressed, the instrumental resources and functions were expanded beyond providing accompaniments and to include the performance of overtures and interludes.

The relative emphasis on the various components of opera varied widely with the region and the period. Arias, choruses, entr'actes, and ballets contributed musical interest at the expense of the drama. Plot development was suspended during these episodes and advanced mainly in the recitatives. The portions between recitatives tended toward closed, structurally complete forms. This situation facilitated not only extracting discrete segments from an opera but also exchanging them between operas. In the absence of copyright restrictions, unauthorized borrowing of whole sections was a flagrant eighteenth-century practice that reached a ridiculous extreme in *pasticcios* (from the Italian for pie, pastry, or hodgepodge). These entertainments consisted simply of a succession of favorite operatic selections without regard for the source or sequence.

The demand by singers and audiences alike for vocal display vehicles was another factor distracting attention from the dramatic aspect of operas, and abuses persisted in varying degrees during the formative phases of the genre. In spite of certain dramatic limitations, genuine masterpieces were conceived within a framework encompassing a series of numbers—recitatives, arias, ensembles, choruses, ballets, and instrumental interludes. As a composer of operas fusing these features into a coherent whole, Mozart has no peer, and *The Magic Flute* (*Die Zauberflöte*) is a classic example of a *number opera*.

One of the better-known arias in *The Magic Flute* is sung by the High Priest Sarastro in the second act, set in and around the Temple of Isis and Osiris. At this point in the opera the Queen of the Night is plotting to kill Sarastro, and his servant is threatening the Queen's daughter if she will not accept his love. Though fully aware of these machinations, Sarastro responds by advocating friendship and love, not vengeance, in the aria *Within these hallowed portals* (*In diesen heiligen Hallen*).

Mozart/The Magic Flute

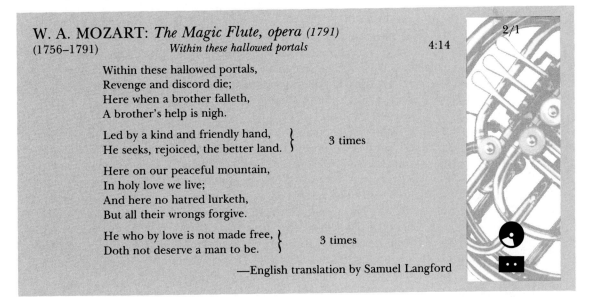

W. A. MOZART: *The Magic Flute, opera (1791)*
(1756–1791)   *Within these hallowed portals*   4:14

2/1

Within these hallowed portals,
Revenge and discord die;
Here when a brother falleth,
A brother's help is nigh.

Led by a kind and friendly hand, }
He seeks, rejoiced, the better land. }   3 times

Here on our peaceful mountain,
In holy love we live;
And here no hatred lurketh,
But all their wrongs forgive.

He who by love is not made free, }
Doth not deserve a man to be. }   3 times

—English translation by Samuel Langford

Richard Wagner (1813–1883) revolted against traditional opera and united music and drama in a new relationship which he called *music drama*. The Wagnerian concept of music drama as a transcendental art form required

Wagner/Music Drama

Richard Wagner

the subjugation of the constituent arts and some negation of their special properties. He composed the music to his own librettos and regarded them as complementary equals in the finished product. There are no divisions or interruptions within scenes of his music dramas. Melodies are continuous and, in a conventional sense, formless. The orchestra participates, almost competes, in the drama, underlining not only the vocal melodies but the emotions and actions as well. Musical motives, called *leitmotivs* in music drama, are associated with particular characters, objects, emotions, or ideas. Leitmotivs, varied and transformed in response to changing dramatic situations on stage, often explain and reinforce the mood and action of the drama in addition to serving as unifying elements. The leitmotiv concept was one of Wagner's outstanding contributions to music, and he was an innovator in the realms of harmony and orchestration as well. Wagner's ideas are most fully realized in the four monumental music dramas forming *The Ring of the Nibelung,* but as an initiation to his dramatic music *Die Meistersinger von Nürnberg* is recommended.

In Wagner's music dramas there are no interruptions between numbers or musically sterile recitatives as there were in earlier operas, but his approach left many of the problems of opera as an art form unsolved for those not completely sold on the idea of music drama as the successor to traditional opera. For many opera buffs the separate numbers in which musical interest is concentrated are the reason for an opera's existence, and music dramas do not have them. The plot of Wagner's music dramas unfolds continuously, but at a snail's pace, and his preoccupation with mythical subjects, which he regarded as the proper province of music drama, is out of vogue. Though Wagner's music dramas are performed regularly in the major opera houses of the world, no other composer has wholeheartedly adopted his philosophy, and no other work conceived along similar lines has achieved notable success. Richard Strauss (1864–1949) perpetuated and developed a style and technique inherited from Wagner but without subscribing to all tenets of Wagner's artistic credo.

Verdi/*Rigoletto*

Giuseppe Verdi

During the time Wagner was formulating the principles of music drama, Giuseppe Verdi (1813–1901) was composing more conventional operas with melodramatic plots and separate numbers but at the same time striving for unity between the music and drama, elimination of extraneous elements, vivid characterization, and effective dramatization. His success in achieving these aims and his apparently inexhaustible supply of captivating melodies have established his operas as international favorites. Of the twenty-four that can be heard on recordings, *Aida, Il Trovatore, La Traviata,* and *Rigoletto* are among the most familiar. One of Verdi's many celebrated arias, *La donna è mobile,* is from the fourth act of *Rigoletto.*

Based on Victor Hugo's drama *Le Roi s'amuse,* the title character of *Rigoletto* is a deformed jester in the court of the Duke. Rigoletto's daughter Gilda has been deceived and seduced by the Duke, but she is still in love with him. In an attempt to reveal the Duke's true nature, Rigoletto induces Gilda to observe the Duke surreptitiously as he makes love to another woman and laughingly sings of woman's fickleness while ignoring his own.

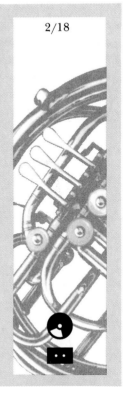

GIUSEPPE VERDI: *Rigoletto, opera (1851)*   2/18
(1813–1901)   *La donna è mobile*   2:12

How fickle women are,
    Fleeting as falling star,
Changing forever;
    Constant, ah! never.

Like feathers flying,
    On the wind hieing,
Even in motion,
    Like waves of ocean.

Yet there's no feeling
    Love's pleasure stealing
Like that of sealing
    Their lips with a kiss,
    Their lips with a kiss,
    Their lips with a kiss!

Though the format of the original is not retained in this very free (but singable) translation, the Italian text of this aria consists of six stanzas in an a + b + a / c + d + a pattern. The musical setting, after an orchestral introduction, is a three-phrase sentence with an a a b structure and an extension. The entire setting is repeated with the three additional stanzas indicated (not included in the translation).

Puccini/*Tosca*

Verdi's successor and the composer in whose operas many find the ideal fusion of music and drama is Giacomo Puccini (1858–1924). His operas, in relation to those of Verdi, are characterized by greater continuity and more emphasis upon the realistic treatment of contemporary subjects. *Madame Butterfly, La Bohème,* and *Tosca* are representative of his stellar achievements as a composer of operas.

The opera *Tosca,* based on a play by the French playwright Victorien Sardou, is set in Rome in June 1800. Tosca, an opera singer, and Cavaradossi, a painter, are lovers. He is sentenced to death by Scarpia, the chief of police, for assisting an escaped prisoner. Scarpia desires Tosca and deceitfully suggests that he will free Cavaradossi in return for her favors. Tosca sings the poignant *Vissi d'arte* in the second act as Scarpia awaits her reply. Outside the gallows are being prepared for the execution.

Giacomo Puccini

GIACOMO PUCCINI: *Tosca, opera (1900)*
(1858–1924)   *Vissi d'arte*   3:08

3/4

> Love and music, these have I lived for,
>> nor ever have harmed a living being . . .
> The poor and distressful, times without number,
>> by stealth, I have succoured . . .
>
> Ever a fervent believer, my humble prayers
>> have been offered up sincerely to the saints;
> In this, my hour of sorrow and bitter tribulation,
>> oh! Heavenly Father, why dost Thou forsake me?
>
> Jewels I gave to bedeck Our Lady's mantle;
> I gave my songs to the starry hosts
>> in tribute to their brightness . . .
> In this, my hour of grief and bitter tribulation,
>> why, Heavenly Father, why hast Thou forsaken me?
>
>   —English translation by W. Beatty-Kingston

The opera ends tragically with Cavaradossi executed, Scarpia stabbed to death by Tosca, and Tosca fleeing from Scarpia's guards and throwing herself over the parapet.

Bizet/*Carmen*   By virtue of one fantastically successful work, *Carmen*, Georges Bizet must be listed with the opera composers of the first rank. The story of the opera is adapted from the novel by Prosper Mérimée. The locale is in and around Seville, and the time is 1820 (figure 14.1). The opera begins with an instrumental prelude which, like a potpourri overture, quotes themes from the body of the work.

GEORGES BIZET: *Carmen, opera (1875)*
(1838–1875)

*2/19

Prelude   3:23
A festive mood is established at the beginning of the prelude with music that accompanies the procession to the bullring in the fourth act of the opera. The first theme is lively and rhythmic. The second theme, from the same scene of the opera, is quieter and more graceful. After a brief return of the opening material, a contrasting theme, derived from the *Toreador Song* of Act II, is heard. A final return of the first theme completes a simple five-part design—AA B A CC′ A. Carmen's fate motive serves as a coda to the prelude and as a transition to the first scene.

    The setting of Act I is a square in Seville with a guardhouse on one side and a cigarette factory on the other. Soldiers and townspeople come and go and pass the time. Micaela enters and shyly inquires about Don José, a corporal who is not there but is soon to come on duty. She departs before he arrives with the relief guard.

    At noontime the girls pour out of the cigarette factory. The last one out is the beautiful Gypsy, Carmen, who sings the seductive *Habanera.*

FIGURE 14.1

Scene from *Carmen*

Georges Bizet

Habanera   5:37

In the *Habanera* Carmen compares love with a bird that cannot be tamed and with a Gypsy child that knows no law and warns anyone who loves her to be on guard.

Don José is seemingly the only one oblivious to Carmen's charms, and that intrigues her. The fate motive sounds in the orchestra; she tosses him a flower and, with a fateful glance, departs. He picks up the flower and is musing on its fragrance when Micaela returns to deliver a letter from Don José's mother. Micaela withdraws, and while Don José reads the letter he promises to abide by his mother's wishes and marry Micaela in spite of his infatuation with Carmen.

The tender mood is interrupted when Carmen wounds a companion in a scuffle. Don José is ordered to arrest Carmen and take her to jail. When he forbids her to talk, she sings the provocative *Seguidilla*.

Seguidilla and Duet   3:50

In this aria Carmen sings of Lillas Pastia's Inn where she goes to dance the seguidilla and drink manzanilla. She offers Don José her love and suggests meeting him at the inn. Drunk with desire, Don José allows Carmen to escape.

Act II is set in Lillas Pastia's Inn, a hangout of Gypsies, smugglers, and soldiers. The act opens with a Gypsy dance that leads directly into the *Gypsy Song* sung by Carmen and two companions. The words of the song describe the Gypsies and their music.

Gypsy Song   3:45

In the recitative following the *Gypsy Song*, Carmen learns from the captain that Don José, who was imprisoned because of her, has been released. Just then, the toreador Escamillo and his entourage enter the inn to wild acclaim, and he responds with the famous *Toreador Song*.

Toreador Song   4:25

Escamillo, in the *Toreador Song,* sings of the thrill of combat shared by toreadors and soldiers, of love awaiting the victorious, and of events in the bullring. At the conclusion of the song Escamillo and the captain both seek Carmen's favor, and both are repulsed.

Two smugglers enter and tell Carmen and her companions that their assistance is needed. The five of them join in the *Quintet.*

Quintet   4:56

In the *Quintet* it is agreed that when it comes to trickery, duplicity, and larceny, it is good to have women with you and without them nothing can be done right.

Carmen's companions agree to go with the smugglers, but Carmen says she cannot go because she is in love and love comes before duty. The others depart. Don José approaches and professes his love to Carmen. Her attempt to entertain him with singing and dancing is interrupted by a bugle sounding retreat in the distance. When Don José says he must return to the barracks, Carmen taunts him. He begs her to listen to him and takes from his jacket the flower that she had tossed to him in Act I.

Flower Song   3:15

In the *Flower Song* Don José reveals that he saved the flower all through his stay in prison and that it retained its fragrance even after it was withered and dry. It came to symbolize Carmen, whom he both loved and hated while in prison, but in the end he confesses that he is completely under her spell.

Carmen insists that he does not love her, because if he did he would follow her to the mountains where they could be free. Don José refuses to desert the army, but before he can leave, the captain returns to see Carmen. The captain orders Don José back to the barracks, and when he defies the order, they draw their swords. Carmen intervenes and calls the smugglers, who rush in. The captain is disarmed and escorted out. Don José reluctantly joins the band of smugglers as the act ends.

Act III is set in a mountain hideout of the smugglers and Gypsies. They sing of the perils and rewards of their trade. When Carmen joins her companions who are reading their fortunes in the cards, she foresees death, first hers and then her lover's.

The smugglers decide the time is right to take their goods through the pass. They exit, with Carmen and her companions leading the way to distract the customs officers. Don José is left to guard the camp. Micaela, seeking Don José, enters the camp fearfully and, when she does not see him immediately, sings a tender air asking God to give her courage.

Micaela's Air   4:25

Micaela sees Don José just as he fires a shot that narrowly misses Escamillo, who loves Carmen and has come for her. Don José says that one who takes a Gypsy girl pays with his life and is about to stab Escamillo when Carmen returns and stops him. As Escamillo is leaving he invites everyone, with special attention to Carmen, to come and see him perform in the arena in Seville.

Micaela, who has been hiding, is discovered. She urges Don José to return with her to see his dying mother and receive her forgiveness. Don José does not want to leave Carmen, but she tells him to go. In the distance Escamillo is heard singing strains of the *Toreador Song.* Carmen attempts to join him, but Don José blocks the way.

Act IV is set outside the arena in Seville where bullfights are held. Street vendors are hawking their goods to the smugglers and Gypsies. A parade of toreadors and their attendants passes by to the cheers of the crowd. Carmen is in her glory beside Escamillo, the favorite toreador and her new love.

Carmen ignores a warning that the jealous Don José is lurking in the crowd. When all the others enter the arena, she remains behind to confront him in the fatal *Duet*.

Duet and Final Chorus 11:04

In the *Duet* Don José pleads with Carmen to return to him and start a new life. She remains completely indifferent and swears that even in the face of death she will not yield. When she hears the crowd cheering Escamillo in the arena, she shows her delight. She starts toward the arena, but Don José stops her. In a final gesture of defiance she tears his ring off her finger and throws it at him. Infuriated, he stabs her and, with her name on his lips, she dies in his arms.

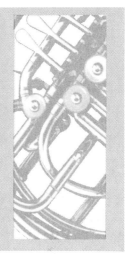

The operas surveyed thus far have been limited to those composed between 1689 and 1900 in Europe—England, Austria, Germany, Italy, and France. Attention is now directed to twentieth-century operatic works in America.

Opera combines the elements of the various forms of stage entertainment—music, drama, and dance—and has many devotees, but it has been slow to attract a wide audience in this country. Parodies and stereotypes have created misconceptions in the minds of some who have never been exposed to the real thing, and admittedly something is lost in each of the arts when they are combined. Music tied to a text and the human voice sacrifices the abstract quality of absolute instrumental music, and an orchestra supporting singers from a pit lacks the power and eloquence of a symphony occupying the full stage. Words that are sung as compared with words that are spoken proceed at a slower pace, impeding the flow of the drama, and are more difficult to understand. Dancing as an element of opera adds color and variety but interrupts the drama except when fully integrated. Anyone expecting to find in an opera all of the attributes in full measure of a concert, a play, and a ballet will be disappointed. To be properly appreciated, opera must be accepted as a distinct medium separate and apart from its components.

In the past, language has been a deterrent to the widespread popularity of opera. The Continental masterpieces were written in languages other than English, and a schoolbook knowledge of a foreign tongue is insufficient for comprehension of an opera libretto as it is sung. The situation is ameliorated by a growing tendency to perform operas in English translations. Excellent translations of several standard works issued in recent years reflect this trend. Another option is to perform operas in the original language with English subtitles as in foreign language films. This practice is routine in televised performances, and it has been introduced in some opera houses. As implemented at the New York City Opera, an English version

Opera in America

of a libretto is stored in a computer, synchronized with the action, and continuously projected above the stage. Electronic technology thereby assists the process of making foreign operas, and sometimes even operas in English, more accessible to initiates.

No language or cultural barrier exists between American audiences and Gershwin's indigenous folk opera *Porgy and Bess*.

Gershwin/ *Porgy and Bess*

George Gershwin is best known by the general populace as a composer of popular songs written for Broadway and Hollywood musicals, but he also composed solo and symphonic concert works during his tragically brief career that began with his first published song, written when he was about seventeen, and ended with his untimely death of a brain tumor at the age of thirty-eight. The idea of composing an opera first occurred to Gershwin when he read DuBose Heyward's 1925 novel *Porgy*, but it did not come to fruition for almost a decade. In the meantime Heyward and his wife, Dorothy, had collaborated on a stage version of the work which ran for 367 performances on Broadway. This stage version, which included many spirituals, became the basis for the opera libretto.

The story of *Porgy and Bess* takes place in the early part of this century in and around Catfish Row, a poor tenement on the Charleston, South Carolina, waterfront (figure 14.2). All of the singing characters are black, and the only spoken dialogue is by four minor white characters. The following synopsis places several numbers from the opera in their dramatic context.

George Gershwin

GEORGE GERSHWIN: *Porgy and Bess, opera* (1935) 3:00:24
(1898–1937)

Synopsis: In the quiet of the early evening on Catfish Row, Clara sings a lullaby, *Summertime* (2:20), to her baby. Her husband Jake leaves a crap game to take the baby and sing it to sleep with the admonition *A Woman Is a Sometime Thing* (1:51). Porgy, a cripple who gets about in a cart pulled by a goat, is teased about being soft on Bess, which he denies. Bess, a lady of easy virtue, enters on the arm of Crown, a burly stevedore who is drunk and belligerent. He joins in the crap game and kills one of the opposing players when he loses. He goes into hiding, telling Bess that he will return when the trouble blows over. When others refuse her, Bess seeks shelter in Porgy's room and in time comes to love him and make him happy. As fishermen repair their nets, a joyous Porgy looks out of his window and sings *I Got Plenty o' Nuttin* (1:29). A drug dealer, Sporting Life, tries to entice Bess to go with him to New York. Porgy overhears her refusal and drives him away. Porgy and Bess join in the love duet, *Bess, You Is My Woman Now* (5:08). Bess is persuaded to attend a picnic at which Sporting Life sings *It Ain't Necessarily So* (3:05). As Bess attempts to return from the picnic, she is accosted by Crown who forces her to stay with him temporarily as she sings *What You Want Wid Bess* (1:56). Bess, now back in Porgy's room, is seriously ill until a neighbor prays successfully for her recovery. Despite fears of Crown's return to claim her, Bess sings *I Loves You, Porgy* (2:06). Crown, forced out of hiding by a violent storm, returns to Catfish Row and is involved in an altercation with Porgy over Bess. Crown mocks everyone else's fear of the storm and sings *A Redheaded Woman* (1:08). Clara rushes out in search of her husband, Jake, whose fishing boat has been sighted upside down in the river. To prove his

FIGURE 14.2

A scene from
Gershwin's *Porgy
and Bess*

manhood, Crown goes after her, but not before exchanging threats with Porgy. The storm ends at dusk, and the chorus mourns those presumed lost in *Clara, Clara* (2:10). Crown stealthily crosses the deserted courtyard, and as he passes beneath Porgy's window, Porgy reaches out, stabs him in the back with a long knife, and then strangles him to death. Porgy, not a suspect but summoned as a witness, is dragged off by two policemen. Left behind, Sporting Life forces dope on a reluctant Bess before describing the high life they can have together in *There's a Boat That's Leavin' Soon for New York* (2:15). After a week in jail, Porgy returns to Catfish Row laden with gifts. When he inquires about Bess, everyone is evasive. He sings *Oh, Where's My Bess* (2:30). Porgy is finally told that Bess is back on dope and that she has gone to New York with Sporting Life. All efforts to dissuade him from trying to find her fail, and Porgy sets out for New York in his cart singing *I'm on My Way* (1:47).

The timings for the individual numbers in the synopsis are the approximate durations of these songs as they occur in excerpts and selections from the opera. The timing for the opera is from a recording of the complete score printed before rehearsals began. The production that opened in New York on 10 October 1935, after a brief trial run in Boston, was much shorter. Gershwin made extensive cuts and approved others during rehearsals and the early weeks of the production, according to an article by Charles Hamm. *Porgy and Bess* closed in New York after 124 performances, a commercial failure by Broadway standards but a phenomenal season for an opera. This production then went on the road with stops in Philadelphia, Pittsburgh, Chicago, and Detroit before finally closing in Washington on 21 March 1936. It is the only production Gershwin lived to see, but the work is now in the repertoires of the leading opera houses of the world.

A significant development in the field of American opera has been the proliferation of opera productions by college music departments and community opera associations. Many areas that could never support a resident professional company are now being offered high-caliber performances, and increasing numbers of talented students and semiprofessionals are gaining valuable training and experience. The number of groups currently performing opera in the United States exceeds one thousand. During a recent season, according to statistics provided by the Central Opera Service, 13,208 opera performances in this country attracted audiences totaling more than 13 million. Grass roots opera played before relatively unsophisticated audiences by young performers has special requirements. In response to this demand, a virtually new concept of opera has emerged.

Operas are being composed to English texts with plots designed to appeal to contemporary audiences. Extraneous elements are eliminated and the dimensions scaled down to practical limits. Composers are writing chamber operas requiring few principals, small choruses or none, small orchestras, and a modest staging budget. Far from suffering from these limitations, operas in this new style are thriving. Making opera a believable and exciting dramatic experience is part of the movement, and in this too it is achieving striking success. With these developments a more general acceptance of opera as a form of entertainment seems assured.

Menotti/*Amahl and the Night Visitors*

A pioneer librettist-composer in this field who has several successful operas to his credit is the Italian-born, American-trained Gian-Carlo Menotti. He has combined his dramatic and melodic gifts with a real flair for the theater to produce a series of flourishing operas. His works have been produced by the Metropolitan Opera Company and innumerable college opera workshops, broadcast on radio and television, and filmed. Perhaps his most spectacular success and the opera probably seen by more people than any other in a comparable span of time is his *Amahl and the Night Visitors.* The NBC telecasts of *Amahl* were annual Christmas events for many years following its first performance in 1951. It certainly is one of the most appealing operas of this new type.

Gian-Carlo Menotti
staging *Amahl and
the Night Visitors*

GIAN-CARLO MENOTTI: *Amahl and the Night Visitors*   45:45
(1911–   )   *(1951)*

The full worth of this small masterpiece is perceived only when it can be seen as
well as heard. Menotti displays rare skill in creating a setting, developing a plot,
delineating character, working up emotional intensity, and bringing off a stunning
climax. The music and text contribute in equal measure to the unfolding of this
simple yet powerful drama.

The opera is extremely concise, but it has all the ingredients of traditional opera
including chorus and dancing. For performance it requires only a modest number
of principals, a small chorus and orchestra, a few dancers, and one stage setting.
The scene is the interior of a humble dwelling on the road to Jerusalem on the night
of the Nativity. Amahl, a crippled shepherd boy, and his widowed mother are visited
by the Three Kings. The memorable events of that night in the lives of Amahl and
his mother provide the material of the story. The English text and the fine diction
of the singers on the recording render further comment unnecessary.

Musicals

Broadway *musicals* represent America's best claim to a national tradition in the theater arts, combining as they do distinctive styles of music and drama. The basic concept originated centuries ago in Italian opera, but the differences are more profound than the superficial substitution of spoken dialogue for recitatives. Though the lineage of musicals can be traced back to venerable sources, their character and content are strictly current-popular and change with the seasons.

Among the luminaries who have contributed to the form are Irving Berlin, George Gershwin, Jerome Kern, Cole Porter, Richard Rodgers, Frederick Loewe, and more recently Stephen Sondheim, whose *Into the Woods* won the 1988 Tony Award for best score and whose *Assassins* followed it to Broadway in 1991. The impressive list of smash hits produced over the years proves that musicals can be tremendously popular and financially rewarding. During the 1987–88 season approximately 75 percent of Broadway's receipts were generated by musicals. That which prospers in this country thrives, so the Broadway musical tradition can look forward to a glorious future. There will be no shortage of composers and lyricists searching for the magic formula to create a hit. To improve the odds, versions of previously successful ventures, such as revivals of earlier musicals and transformations of movie scripts, are currently in favor.

Comparatively few shows that reach Broadway have enough substance, value, and commercial success to survive on the stage beyond their initial season, but many of them are preserved on recordings. The stage life of others is more enduring. *A Chorus Line* by Marvin Hamlisch, which won seven Tony awards, was still setting records on Broadway and on the road after thirteen seasons. An added bonus was the sale of the motion picture rights for $5.5 million.

Bernstein/
West Side Story

The sights and sounds of another survivor, *West Side Story,* still resonate in our collective memory nearly forty years after its conception by the late composer/conductor Leonard Bernstein and lyricist Stephen Sondheim, previously mentioned as a composer. The original company gave almost a thousand performances in New York and toured major cities across the country between 1957 and 1960. Since then, in addition to numerous New York revivals, the musical has been presented by virtually every U.S. stock company and internationally in at least nine foreign languages and in English with subtitles. It was made into a motion picture which won ten Oscar awards, including the one for best film of the year. The original cast and sound track recordings and a more recent studio recording are listed in current catalogs, and the movie version, for which the timing is given, is available on videocassette and laser disc.

COLORPLATE 13

Eugène Delacroix:
Arabs Skirmishing in the Mountains (1863)
Oil on linen, .925 × .746 (36⅜″ × 29⅜″)

The romantic painter Delacroix (1798–1863) was a contemporary and friend of
the composer Chopin (see page 250). The paintings of Delacroix, like the music
of the period, broke with the traditions of classicism to express and evoke intense
emotions in new and distinctive ways.

Chester Dale Fund, © 1992. National Gallery of Art, Washington, D.C.

COLORPLATE 14

Winslow Homer:

Breezing Up (1876)
Oil on canvas, .615 × .970 (24⅛″ × 38⅛″)

Boston-born Winslow Homer (1836–1910) worked as a lithographer and for *Harper's Weekly* as an illustrator and Civil War correspondent before becoming a full-time painter in 1876. He achieved success painting American scenes in his personal American style during a time when American composers were going to Europe to complete their studies.

Gift of the W. L. and May T. Mellon Foundation, © 1992. National Gallery of Art, Washington, D.C.

COLORPLATE 15

Claude Monet:

Banks of the Seine, Vetheuil (1880)
Oil on linen, .734 × 1.005 (28⅞″ × 39⅝″)

A Paris art exhibition in 1874 included a painting by Monet (1840–1926),
Impression: Sunrise, from which the term for the style, impressionism, was derived.
In *Banks of the Seine, Vetheuil,* Monet's choice of subject matter and his treatment
of light and color are typically impressionistic. When these oils were painted, the
predominant style in music was romanticism, but impressionism (see page 262)
was to emerge as a distinct musical style shortly thereafter.

Chester Dale Collection, © 1992. National Gallery of Art, Washington, D.C.

COLORPLATE 16

Edgar Degas:
Four Dancers (1899)
Oil on canvas, 1.511 × 1.802 (59½″ × 71″)

Degas (1834–1917) is classified as an impressionist, but he was less dedicated to the principles of the style than Monet. In the paintings of Degas, influences of Japanese prints and photography can also be detected. He shared with impressionist composers Debussy (see page 263) and Ravel (see page 264) an interest in ballet and its performers.

Chester Dale Collection, © 1992. National Gallery of Art, Washington, D.C.

*Leonard Bernstein
conducting the New
York Philharmonic*

LEONARD BERNSTEIN: *West Side Story (1957)*   2:32:00
(1918–1990)

West Side Story is an American version of the *Romeo and Juliet* tragedy in which the antagonists are members of rival street gangs, the self-styled "American" Jets and the Puerto Rican Sharks. They challenge each other for control of the turf, but before violence erupts, one of the Jets, Tony, falls in love with Maria, sister of the leader of the Sharks. In the ensuing rumble and its aftermath, the leaders of both gangs and Tony are killed. The two gangs at the end are drawn together by their shared grief. The simple plot is enhanced by memorable songs and scintillating dance numbers that coalesce into a masterpiece of American musical theater.

Pop Opera

American musicals have provided models for European pop and rock composers seeking to expand their horizons beyond three-minute singles and loosely organized albums. The resulting genre has been appropriately labeled *pop opera*. In this category are the French composer Claude-Michel Schönberg's Les Misérables, with its trendy derivation from a novel/movie, and his *Miss Saigon*.

Webber/
The Phantom
of the Opera

Preeminent among the British composers of pop opera is Andrew Lloyd Webber, who has written an unprecedented string of spectacularly successful stage works. He first attracted the attention of audiences in England and America with the sensational debut of his rock opera *Jesus Christ Superstar*. Distinctly different but stylistically related works like *Evita*, *Cats*, and *Starlight Express* intervened between *Superstar* and what is perhaps his most significant work to date, *The Phantom of the Opera*, which recently celebrated its record-breaking third anniversary on the stage in Los Angeles.

The music of *The Phantom* is of unusual power and eloquence for a musical, and though it plays in theaters, rather than opera houses, it has many of the attributes of traditional opera. But if opera, it is pop opera! Before its New York opening, advance sales of tickets reached $18 million. Webber has become a billionaire and, according to Queen Elizabeth II's 1992 birthday honors list, a knight of the realm.

Andrew Lloyd Webber

ANDREW LLOYD WEBBER: *The Phantom of the*   1:40:15
(1948–   )   *Opera* *(1987)*

The Phantom of the Opera is based on a 1911 novel by Gaston Leroux which is best known in this country through the 1925 silent film version starring Lon Chaney. The story combines elements of two myths—*Beauty and the Beast* and *Pygmalion*. In the musical version the Beauty is a dancer of modest talents in the Paris Opera company of 1861 who is transformed, in the manner of Pygmalion's statue, into a star singer by the machinations of the Phantom, a disfigured, mad genius who inhabits the underground labyrinths of the opera house. The relationship between the singer and the Phantom is saturated with psychological overtones reinforced by scenery and staging of fantastic complexity.

Webber remains active as a composer, with *Sunset Boulevard* the latest addition to his list of stage works.

Operetta

Operettas and *light operas* are in a style somewhere between that of grand operas (or music dramas) and that of musical shows and comedies. Operettas and light operas usually have spoken dialogue and music in a light but not a popular vein. They are staple fare in amateur and outdoor summer productions.

ADDITIONAL EXAMPLES

Opera
  Britten: *Peter Grimes**
  Wagner: *Lohengrin**
  Ward: *The Crucible*
  Weill: *The Three Penny Opera*

Musicals
  Herman: *La Cage aux Folles*
  Loewe: *My Fair Lady*
  Sondheim: *Assassins*

Operetta
  Lehar: *The Merry Widow*
  Romberg: *The Desert Song*
  Strauss, R.: *Die Fledermaus (The Bat)**

*Available on Home Vision videocassettes at local retailers; also *The Magic Flute, Tosca,* and *Carmen* cited elsewhere in this chapter.

15 DRAMATIC MUSIC: BALLET AND INCIDENTAL

The dramatic music genre includes, in addition to opera, music written to accompany ballets, stage plays, motion pictures, and television shows. A distinction between ballet music and incidental music for plays, movies, and TV is that ballet music is continuous and incidental music is intermittent. Incidental music may come before, during, and after scenes but is often discontinued during dialogue. There is no occasion to interrupt music that accompanies dancing.

A performance by a troupe of dancers in costume to the accompaniment of music is a *ballet*. Ballet exists in four more or less distinct types: *classic ballet*, *modern ballet*, *modern dance*, and *incidental ballet*.

Classic Ballet

Classic ballet is often adapted to existing absolute music. The attire of the dancers is without special significance, but its color and design may contribute indirectly to the general mood of the dance. The stage customarily is bare except for a plain backdrop. The highly stylized steps, gestures, and movements of the ballet are executed with absolute precision. Episodes featuring individual dancers and small groups alternate with those involving the entire company. The motions are graceful and restrained. Evidence of effort is carefully concealed. The ballerinas wear special slippers which permit them to dance on the very tips of their toes, and steps executed in this manner are a characteristic feature of ballet.

Classic ballet is abstract. It tells no story and conveys no message. The aesthetic experience derives from the perception of the elegant bodily movements of the individual dancers, the fluid patterns and designs created by the disposition of the individuals and groups, and the music. The choreographer selects the music and designs the action on the stage. The music independently has no special properties, and thus can only be illustrated in conjunction with the dance.

The preceding description of classic ballet is subject to interpretation and deviation, but it is valid for *Les Sylphides (The Sylphs)* as choreographed by Michel Fokine for Sergei Diaghilev's Ballet Russe. According to George Balanchine, a colleague of Fokine and subsequently founder of the New York City Ballet, in *Les Sylphides* "instead of characters with definite personalities, we have simply dancers in long white dresses and a dancer in white and black velvet whose movements to music invoke the romantic imagination to a story of its own." Sylphs are mythical beings inhabiting the air. The music is a selection of Chopin piano pieces orchestrated by Alexander Glazunov in 1909.

FRÉDÉRIC CHOPIN: *Les Sylphides* (1909)   30:00
(1810–1849)   1. *Nocturne*
                                          (Op. 32 no. 2 in A-flat)
                                       2. *Waltz*
                                          (Op. 70 no. 1 in G-flat)
                                       3. *Mazurka*
                                          (Op. 33 no. 2 in D)
                                       4. *Mazurka*
                                          (Op. 33 no. 3 in C)
                                       5. *Prelude*
                                          (Op. 28 no. 7 in A)
                                       6. *Pas de Deux (Waltz for two dancers)*
                                          (Op. 64 no. 2 in C-sharp minor)
                                       7. *Waltz*
                                          (Op. 18 "Grande valse brilliante" in E-flat)

The selections listed are for an abridged version of the ballet on the Home Vision videocassette *American Ballet Theatre at the Met* (AMEO2).

Modern Ballet

The most obvious difference between classic and *modern ballet* is that modern ballet dramatizes a story in pantomime. Costumes are used to delineate characters, but they are often more fanciful and suggestive than realistic. Ballerinas wear the same shoes as for classic ballet, and all of the classic steps are employed, plus any others required by the story. Because of the limitations of pantomime, plots are relatively uncomplicated. Even so, audiences usually are provided an outline of the story in the program. The stage is kept relatively unobstructed, but scenery, stage properties, and lighting contribute to the total effect. Colorful stories suggestive of varied actions and solo, small group, and full company scenes are most likely to be used.

Music for modern ballets ideally is specifically composed for a given story with the composer and choreographer working in close collaboration. Several of the most celebrated works of the twentieth century were created in this way on commissions from Sergei Diaghilev (1872–1929), impresario of the renowned Russian Ballet. Among them is *The Firebird,* with music by Igor Stravinsky and choreography by Michel Fokine. This is the work which first brought Stravinsky international acclaim. It was followed by a series of ballets which solidly established his reputation as the leading composer of his time.

STRAVINSKY: *The Firebird* (1910)	18:58
(1882–1971) *Introduction*	:00
The Firebird and Her Dance	2:51
The Dance of the Princesses	4:28
Kastchei's Infernal Dance	8:24
Berceuse	12:37
Finale	15:56

In the ballet, based on a Russian legend, young Prince Ivan wanders at night through the enchanted forest and captures the radiant Firebird. In return for her release the Firebird rewards him with one of her feathers. The darkness dissipates and twelve beautiful princesses are seen playing with the golden fruit of a silver tree in front of an imposing castle. The princesses warn Ivan that the castle is the abode of the infernal monster, Kastchei, who casts spells over intruders in his domain. Ivan is saved from destruction by the magic feather. The Firebird lulls the demon to sleep and reveals to the Prince the source of the monster's evil power, an egg hidden in the trunk of the silver tree. Ivan smashes the egg, vanquishing the monster and freeing his captives. The most beautiful of the princesses becomes his bride.

Stravinsky arranged three different concert versions of the *Firebird* ballet music. Of these, the 1919 version with revised orchestration of the six sections listed is the best known. Also LG 3/6.

A contemporary adaptation of the *Firebird* story choreographed by the American Glen Tetly and danced by the Royal Danish Ballet is available on Home Vision videocassette (FIRO2, 55:00).

Music from preexisting scores is sometimes used for modern ballets. This is feasible especially when the music itself suggests a story. Ballets using the music of Debussy's *Prelude to the Afternoon of a Faun* and Rimsky-Korsakov's *Scheherazade* are in this category. There are instances, too, in which music from various sources is arranged and adapted to accompany the intended story and action.

Modern Dance

The distinctions between modern ballet and *modern dance* are by no means clearly defined. In general, modern dance has in common with modern ballet a pantomimed story, specially composed and arranged music, stage effects, and costumes. Differences lie in the types of movements and gestures used by the dancers. Modern dance places more emphasis on realism and less on stylized motions. Ballet dancers are thoroughly schooled in the traditions of classic ballet, whereas modern dancers stress individual expression through bodily movement. The subject matter of modern dance tends to be more earthy and the action more violent, but tender and sentimental moods are not excluded. Ballet slippers are an artifice usually discarded by modern dancers, and bare feet are common. Precision of group movement is less in evidence in modern dance, as rigid order yields to spontaneity. Martha Graham was a leading exponent of modern dance. Her *Appalachian Spring* with music by Aaron Copland is a magnificent example both musically and choreographically. Modern dance is not a separate art, of course, but an aspect of ballet, and no distinction between types can be detected in the music.

Aaron Copland

AARON COPLAND: *Appalachian Spring (1944)*
(1900–1990)   23:05

Appalachian Spring was commissioned by the Elizabeth Sprague Coolidge Foundation for Martha Graham. It received the 1945 Pulitzer Prize for music and the Music Critics Circle Award for the outstanding theatrical work of the 1944–45 season. Originally scored for a chamber ensemble of thirteen instruments, the music was subsequently arranged by the composer for full orchestra. This version, heard in concerts and on recordings, is in eight sections played without pause. The action of the ballet is summarized in the Boosey & Hawkes score of the music as follows:

A pioneer celebration in spring around a newly built farmhouse in the Pennsylvania hills in the early part of the last century. The bride-to-be and the young farmer-husband enact the emotions, joyful and apprehensive, their new domestic partnership invites. An older neighbor suggests now and then the rocky confidence of experience. A revivalist and his followers remind the new householders of the strange and terrible aspects of human fate. At the end the couple is left quiet and strong in their new house.

The tradition of commissioning music to accompany modern dance continues into the electronic age. Lucinda Childs commissioned Christian Wolff to provide music for her dance *Mayday*. Twenty synthesized pieces were produced from which a selection was made to suit the dance's time and structure. Further selection reduced the number to nine parts included as *Mayday Materials* on the CD recording (CDCM Computer Music Series, vol. 6—CRC 2052) of which LG 4/3 is Part 9.

CHRISTIAN WOLFF: *Mayday Materials (1989)*
(1934–   )   *Part 9*   4:56

According to the composer's notes, "the spirit of the dance and music is, among other things, a mix of abstraction, lightheartedness, and perhaps political suggestiveness, having something to do with China and May Day as a worker's holiday."

Another aspect of modern dance music is jazz. Jazz trumpeter/composer Wynton Marsalis collaborated with choreographer Garth Fagin and sculptor Martin Puryear on the stage extravaganza *Griot New York,* an exploration of the African-American experience presented at the Brooklyn Academy of Music during the 1991 Next Wave Festival. A griot is a storyteller.

Incidental ballet is dancing incorporated in a larger theatrical or film production. One of the most remarkable instances of incidental ballet is in Wagner's opera *Tannhäuser*. Interestingly, the original 1845 version of the opera premiered in Germany did not have a ballet. The *Venusberg Music* which accompanies the ballet was added sixteen years later for the Paris premiere, and though the revised version failed to please the Parisian audience, it is the one now available on recordings and staged in the larger opera houses.

Incidental Ballet

RICHARD WAGNER: *Tannhäuser, opera (1845–1861)*
(1813–1883)   *Venusberg Music*   16:45

The *Venusberg Music*, also known as the *Bacchanale*, begins immediately after the overture. The curtain rises revealing the mountain abode in legendary medieval times of Venus, goddess of love and beauty. Voluptuous mythological characters recline provocatively about the stage in pairs and small groups. Tannhäuser, an errant knight and minstrel who has left the world in pursuit of the sensual pleasures Venus has to offer, lies with his head on her lap. In this setting bacchantes—followers of Bacchus, god of wine and revelry—dance erotically to the passionate music of the ballet.

Incidental ballet figures prominently in *The Red Shoes*, a British motion picture with a ballet milieu and a cast of renowned dancers in which complete scenes from several ballets are shown. The film is no longer in theatrical release, but it is available on a Paramount Pictures home videocassette.

In the popular realm, music and dancing are combined in a wide range of styles that one would not think of as ballet. *Theatrical dance* is a more comprehensive term used to encompass all incidental dancing, including that in Broadway and Hollywood musicals. Several recent motion pictures have contemporary dance themes, and videos combine rock music with the dance steps and interpretive movements associated with it. These popular forms of theatrical dance are beyond the purview of this chapter.

Music which is subservient to drama is *incidental music*. In the past, music composed for plays included music to be performed before, between, and during acts, but incidental music is rare in the legitimate theater these days. Incidental music now usually implies music heard in conjunction with motion picture and television productions.

Incidental Music

The use of incidental music can be traced throughout the history of drama. It figured prominently in Greek drama, in the mystery and miracle plays of the Middle Ages, and in the Elizabethan theater. If practical limitations restrict its use currently on the legitimate stage, its expanded role in motion pictures and television more than compensates. Sound motion pictures and sound recording techniques have revolutionized concepts of incidental music and have added a fascinating new tangent to the art of music. Dramatic television shows are filmed or videotaped, so there is no distinction between the uses of music in the two mediums.

A paramount function of incidental music is to intensify the emotional impact of important scenes. Whether the emotion conveyed is one of joy or sorrow, elation or dejection, appropriate music has an uncanny power to evoke greater audience response. Used in this manner, incidental music supplements and augments the effect of words and actions. It underlines turning points and heightens climaxes in the story line.

Closely related to music intended to provoke emotional responses is music with psychological significance. Music in this category is used to suggest subconscious thoughts and emotions and the presence of the unseen. Also included is music employed to create moods, to develop suspense, and to foreshadow impending action.

Music has utilitarian functions, too. It serves to indicate the passage of time. It fills voids when dialogue and sound effects are suspended. It smooths transitions between contrasting scenes. It aids in establishing the locale by exploiting indigenous musical devices—for example, native drums for Africa, Spanish rhythms for the Iberian peninsula, and oriental scales for the Far East. In these capacities incidental music helps to maintain the pace and continuity of the drama and to place it in the proper time and setting.

Actions sometimes are portrayed musically in an exaggerated and ludicrous manner for humorous effect. In this case the music has no psychological implications but simply mimics in an obvious fashion the visual elements. This procedure, called "Mickey Mousing" the action, is the stock approach to scoring cartoons and certain types of comic situations.

Incidental music can be performed with the musicians visible. Anonymous performers may provide music required for a scene, or leading characters may sing or play instruments on camera in their roles. Music in the latter category may be an essential part of the plot, a diversion from the main argument, or a contrived device to display special talents of a star. Incidental music of this type is of necessity confined to situations where it is not inconsistent with the requirements of the story.

Finally, *title music* occupies the two spots where film music is most likely to command the listeners' attention, during the credits at the beginning of a picture and during the notice of completion at the end. *Opening title* music provides background for the studio trademark, the title of the picture, the list of characters and actors, credit lines, and notices. It is interesting to observe the location of the musical climax in this section, whether it coincides with the name of the star, the producer, the director, or perhaps with that of the composer! Besides providing background for the preliminaries, the opening title music establishes the tenor of the drama or the mood of the opening scene. *End title* music rarely is more than a cadence swelling up under the fadeout of the last scene and reinforcing the sense of finality at the end.

Recording the sound track of a motion picture is an intricate and demanding process, requiring care and effort rarely evident to the casual viewer. The composer's work really begins after the final editing of the film is completed. A product costing millions awaits his or her crowning touch before it can be marketed, putting considerable pressure on the composer to work fast. The first step is to decide where music is to be used. This is done by production executives in collaboration with the music staff. The amount of music averages about half the total running time of the picture, but it may be much more or less. The location and extent of the music is largely a matter of personal taste, but in general it appears wherever it can provide one of the functions outlined above.

The film composer is furnished a *cue sheet* giving a synopsis of the action and the dialogue with timing to a fraction of a second for scenes involving music. From this the composer knows whether the music is to be under voices, with sound effects, or *in the clear.* The composer has unlimited access to the film and views the scenes to be underscored as the work progresses. Though some preliminary sketching of thematic ideas may have been done before, only now is the composer ready to start composing music for specific scenes.

Music cues vary in duration from a few seconds to a few minutes. Composing within rigid time limits poses a problem, but those with experience working in the medium do not find this restriction burdensome. The episodes are brief, and the predetermined mood and function of the music stimulate the composer's imagination. Music's mission in relation to drama is achieved more readily than innate artistic merit, and incidental music is not subjected to the same scrutiny as concert music. On the whole, dramatic music is written faster and less laboriously than nondramatic music.

Nonelectronic film music is turned out on a sort of assembly line by a small group of specialists. The composer's draft is handed to an orchestrator who arranges it for orchestra or for whatever instrumentation is to be used. A copyist then prepares parts for the individual players. Before the ink is dry on the last page, a recording time is set.

The required performers are assembled on a sound stage equipped with state-of-the-art recording facilities. The conductor, usually the composer or the music director of the studio, faces a screen on which the picture is projected during the recording. The picture is started a bit before the music entrance, and preparatory signals—streamers and punch marks—are flashed on the screen. On motion picture film the signals are on the film with the images. With videotape the signals are superimposed by computer and a special editing program. The conductor starts on cue and synchronizes the music with the action, assisted by a battery of timing devices including, when necessary, a *clicktrack* that produces clicks at a preset rate in an earphone in the conductor's ear. A runthrough just before recording is the only rehearsal, so superb players are essential. Each scene is recorded as many times as necessary to achieve a "perfect take."

The procedures for composing electronic and nonelectronic film music are essentially the same except that the composer of electronic music works directly with a synthesizer, and the need for conventional notation, orchestrators, copyists, performers, and conductors is eliminated, advantages that are not lost on producers. Electronic music is increasingly evident in motion picture and television sound tracks.

Digital sound processing computers and sequencers (MIDI recorders and programs that store sounds as individually editable events) have been developed that enable composers to synthesize separate sound tracks in real time or step time (virtually note by note) and to record the information on a hard disc by means of an analog-to-digital converter (ADC). The sounds can then be manipulated like words in a word processor. When the editing tasks are completed, the tracks are combined and the information converted back to sound by means of a digital-to-analog converter (DAC). The music cues are then combined with the dialogue and sound effects, and all facets of the sound are synchronized on film or videotape with the visual elements, generally using a SMPTE (Society of Motion Picture and Television Engineers) time code, to complete the production.

The procedures are different when singing, playing, or dancing is shown on the screen. Music for these scenes is prerecorded. The recording is then played back while the action is being filmed, and the action is synchronized with the music. Performances of professional musicians are *dubbed in* when the musical ability of the actors is inadequate. The dubbing technique is used most frequently when a movie star is shown singing a song. Though the *lip sync* (synchronization of the lips with the music) may be flawless, odds are that the voice heard on the film is that of a professional singer.

Except in musicals, incidental music is a subsidiary of the drama. How conscious should the audience be of its presence? Ideally, the viewer should not be aware of the music as such but as an enhancement of the drama. Incidental music which intrudes or competes with the dramatic events is undesirable. The endeavors of film composers are rather menial but well rewarded, in comparison with composers of concert music, and their contribution to the success of dramatic works is substantial. Drama as used here is intended in the broadest sense, including comedies and all mediums of presentation.

Cinema composers, following the lead of ballet and opera composers, have arranged excerpts from film scores for concert performance and have released recordings taken from original sound tracks. On sound track recordings the musical excerpts are usually identified by the scenes they accompany in the film or by the names of the characters with which they are associated, as in the music from *Star Wars/Return of the Jedi*.

JOHN WILLIAMS: *Star Wars/Return of the Jedi* (1983)   44:59
(1932–   )

1. *Main Title (The Story Continues)*	5:09
2. *Into the Trap*	2:36
3. *Luke and Leia*	4:44
4. *Parade of the Ewoks*	3:25
5. *Han Solo Returns*	4:10
(At the Court of Jabba the Hutt)	
6. *Lapti Nek (Jabba's Palace Band)*	2:49
7. *The Forest Battle*	4:01
8. *Rebel Briefing*	2:22
9. *The Emperor*	2:41
10. *The Return of the Jedi*	5:02
11. *Ewok Celebration and Finale*	8:00

The *Star Wars* pictures are produced by Lucasfilm, Ltd., a pioneer in the use of computers to produce special visual effects and to generate, process, and record sound digitally. Composer-conductor John Williams, with more than fifty film scores and a host of awards to his credit, is one of the most active and acclaimed film composers. He is also renowned for his television appearances and recordings as conductor of the Boston Pops Orchestra.

Sound track music can be effective in concert and recorded versions without the visual elements, but as incidental music it is best appreciated in context as part of the total dramatic experience. The next time you go to a movie or watch a dramatic show on TV, concentrate on the music. If you are among the many who have always taken it for granted, its scope and importance will probably come as a revelation.

ADDITIONAL EXAMPLES

Ballet
    Bernstein: *Fancy Free*
    Falla: *El Amor Brujo (Love, the Sorcerer)*
        Ritual Fire Dance
           LG 3/8
    Khachaturian: *Gayane*
    Stravinsky: *The Rite of Spring*
           Sacrificial Dance
             LG 3/6

Tchaikovsky: *The Nutcracker*
Russian Dance
LG 3/2
Several ballets and ballet scenes are available on videocassettes from Classical Video and Home Vision.

Incidental Music

Mandel/Jamal: *M*A*S*H* (television sound track)
Mendelssohn: *A Midsummer Night's Dream* (incidental music for the Shakespeare play)
Prokofiev: *Lieutenant Kijé Suite, op. 60* (from the film score)
Walton: *Henry V Suite* (from the film score)

Music for the Movies

A 54-minute sound film with Aaron Copland narrating and conducting excerpts from *The Red Pony, Something Wild, The City,* and *Our Town* as a framework in which to show the purpose and meaning of background scores for motion pictures. Produced by CBS TV, distributed by McGraw-Hill Films. From *The Young People's Concert Series.*

The Score

A 59-minute color film (also an abridged 30-minute version) in which composers discuss and illustrate various aspects of film scoring. Segments of a television series and three motion pictures are shown. Available from Broadcast Music, Inc., 40 West 57th Street, New York, New York 10019.

16 SONG FORMS

The forms used for instrumental music are also used in music for voices, and the small forms, even in instrumental music, are sometimes called song forms. The song form classification as used in this book, however, encompasses only the three plans of musical organization peculiar to music with words and found in song literature.

When each stanza, or strophe, of a poem is set to the same music, the form of the resulting song is *strophic*. Strophic form is common in folk and familiar songs, children's songs, patriotic songs, hymns, and chorales, as well as in art songs. In art music this type of setting is appropriate only for simple, lyric poems with a limited number of uniform stanzas. From a musical point of view, strophic form has several limitations, consisting as it does of an uninterrupted series of literal repetitions. There is no provision in the form for departure, return, variation, or development. The emotional range of the music, and consequently of the text, cannot be great. Musical interest must be concentrated in a single, cogent statement which fits all of the stanzas of the poem. Within the relatively narrow confines of strophic form, many gems of the song literature, both traditional and art, have been conceived. One such gem, *Who Is Sylvia,* is a perfect example of the form, with identical music for each of its three verses.

Strophic Form

FRANZ SCHUBERT: *Who Is Sylvia* (1826)   2:40
(1797–1828)

Strophic form

A   Who is Silvia, what is she,
        That all our swains commend her?
    Holy, fair, and wise is she;
        The heavens such grace did lend her,
    That she might admired be.

A   Is she kind as she is fair?
        For beauty lives with kindness.
    Love doth to her eyes repair
        To help him of his blindness,
    And, being helped, inhabits there.

A   Then to Silvia let us sing,
        That Silvia is excelling;
    She excels each mortal thing
        Upon the dull earth dwelling;
    To her let us garlands bring.

                    —William Shakespeare: *Two Gentlemen of Verona*

Schubert's setting is of a German translation of Shakespeare's poem, and the spellings of the name do not agree. In the song the last line of each stanza is repeated. Melody page 337.

Through-Composed Form

The procedures in a *through-composed form* are just the reverse of those in a strophic form. For each part of the text a distinctive musical setting is created which is uniquely suited to the rhythm and sentiment of the words. Unifying elements may appear more than once, but there is no systematic repetition of sections. The sequence of musical ideas is dictated by the logic of the words rather than by the requirements of abstract musical design. This type of setting is appropriate for dramatic and narrative poems and those expressing a wide range of emotions. It is the only feasible way of setting blank verse and poems in which the rhythms are inconsistent or the stanzas irregular.

The fact that a through-composed song is organized around the text does not mean that the music lacks unifying elements. Tonality, style, and tempo give a sense of direction and purpose to musical events, even in the absence of a preconceived structural design. Melodic, motivic, rhythmic, and harmonic elements may be repeated, modified, and adapted in the process of illuminating the text. Literal repetitions inspired by textural rather than musical considerations do not violate the concepts of through-composition.

Goethe's *The Erl-King* (*Der Erlkönig*) is a poem that demands a through-composed setting, and Schubert masterfully delineates every feature of the dramatic text in his music. The musical style changes with each shift from narration to dialogue and for each character—the father, the son, and the Erl-King, a symbol of death. The first stanza is preceded by an introduction in which the piano establishes the mood and states the leading motive four times. This motive is heard throughout the song, but always in the piano for which it was conceived, never in the voice part. The complete fusion of poetic and musical ideas produces a spectacular example of through-composed form.

FRANZ SCHUBERT: *The Erl-King (1815)* 4:02 2/8
(1797–1828)

Through-composed form
Introduction

A   Who rides there so late through night so wild?
     A loving father with his young child;
     He clasped his boy close with his fond arm,
     And closer, closer to keep him warm.

B   "Dear son, what makes thy sweet face grow so white?"
     "See, father, 'tis the Erl-King in sight!
     The Erl-King stands there with crown and shroud!"
     "Dear son, it is some misty cloud."

C   "Thou dearest boy, wilt come with me?
     And many games I'll play with thee;
     Where varied blossoms grow on the wold,
     And my mother hath many a robe of gold."

D   "Dear father, my father, say did'st thou not hear,
     The Erl-King whisper so low in mine ear?"
     "Be tranquil, then be tranquil, my child,
     Among withered leaves the wind bloweth wild."

E   "Wilt come, proud boy, wilt thou come with me?
     Where my beauteous daughter doth wait for thee;
     With my daughter thou wilt join in the dance every night,
     She'll lull thee with sweet songs to give thee delight,
     And lull thee with sweet songs to give thee delight."

D′   "Dear father, my father, and can'st thou not trace
     The Erl-King's daughter in yon dark place?"
     "Dear son, dear son, the form you there see
     Is only the hollow gray willow tree."

F(D) "I love thee well, with me thou shalt ride on my course,
     And if thou art unwilling, I'll seize thee by force!"
     "Oh father, my father, thy child closer clasp,
     Erl-King hath seized me with icy grasp!"

G   The father shuddered, his pace grew more wild,
     He held to his bosom his poor swooning child,
     He reached that house with toil and dread,
     But in his arms, lo, his child lay dead!

—J. W. von Goethe
(Translation by Theodore Baker)

Song Cycle

A *song cycle* is a group of songs related by text, thought, medium, or style which collectively constitutes a musical entity. Songs joined together in a unified group expand the scope and dimensions of the art song concept. The texts for a song cycle are usually the work of one poet, but they may be selected by the composer from random sources. The number of songs in a cycle varies considerably. There are three in Hugo Wolf's *Michelangelo Songs* and twenty-four in Franz Schubert's *Winterreise* (*Winter Journey*). In other respects song cycles are similarly lacking in uniformity, so to attempt to generalize about them is futile.

The number of existing song cycles is not large as compared with, for instance, the number of symphonies. Each one tends to be a law unto itself and unlike any other. If any cycle can be regarded as typical, it is Schumann's *Frauenliebe und Leben* (*Woman's Love and Life*). Its eight songs collectively constitute a model song cycle and individually illustrate three distinct approaches to setting a text. Two songs are essentially strophic; one is through-composed; and the other five are in forms associated with instrumental music.

---

*2/13

SCHUMANN: *Frauenliebe und Leben* (*1840*)   24:48
(1810–1856)

1. Ever since I saw him	2:22
2. He of all mankind	3:05
3. I can't believe it	1:45
*4. O ring upon my finger**	3:17
5. Help me dear sisters	1:56
6. Dearest man	5:02
7. Here at my breast	1:19
8. Now hast thou hurt me first	4:01

Song cycle

1. Strophic, tonic key (B-flat)

A   Ever since I saw him,
I seem blind to be,
For whate'er I look at,
Only him I see;
Stays his face before me
As in waking dream,
In the deepest darkness
Brighter, brighter doth it gleam.

A   All the world without him's
Colorless and bare,
For my sister's pastimes
No more can I care,
To my little chamber
I would weeping flee;
Ever since I saw him,
I seem blind to be.

2. Rondo design, subdominant key (E-flat)

A   He, of all mankind the noblest,
     And so gentle, and so kind!
     Lips of frankness, eyes of crystal,
     Steadfast courage, flashing mind.

A   As, in those blue heights above us,
     Bright and noble is yon star,
     So is he, in my own heaven,
     Bright and noble, high and far.

B   Forward, forward on thy highway;
     Let me but thy glory see,
     In all humbleness but see it,
     Blessed in my sadness be.

A   Do not hear my silent prayer,
     Thy high fortunes follow free;
     Heed not me, a lowly maiden,
     Lofty star of majesty!

C   None but worthiest of women
     May deserve thy happy choice;
     I will bless high heaven always,
     Thousand times rejoice!

C′   I will joy then in my weeping,
     Blessed, blessed will I sit;
     And if my poor heart be breaking—
     Break, my heart! What matters it?

A′   He, of all mankind the noblest,
     And so gentle, and so kind!
     Lips of frankness, eyes of crystal,
     Steadfast courage, flashing mind.
          And so gentle, and so kind!

3. Free part form, supertonic key (C minor)

A   I can't believe it, conceive it,
     'Tis all a dream and a lie,
     For how could he over others
     Poor me have set happy and high?

B   Methought his voice was speaking:
     "Forever I love thee!"
     Methought—I must have been dreaming,
     It never, never can be!

C   So dreaming, fain would I die now,
     Here cradled upon his breast;
     How welcome were death, by rapture
     Of tears everlasting caressed!

A I can't believe it, conceive it,
  'Tis all a dream and a lie,
  For how could he over others
  Poor me have set happy and high?

Coda I can't believe it, conceive it,
  'Tis all a dream and a lie!

*4. Rondo design, subdominant key (E-flat)

A O ring upon my finger,
  My little ring of gold,
  Dear jewel, devoutly I kiss thee,
   Devoutly I kiss thee,
  To my heart I hold.

B I had awaked from dreaming
  My childhood's dream of peace and grace;
  I found me lost and forsaken
  In boundless untenanted space.

A O ring upon my finger,
  'Twas taught to me first by thee,
  From thee the revelation
  How precious a jewel our life can be.

C I'll live for him, I will serve him,
  Belonging to him whole,
  Will give him myself, and discover transfigured
  Discover transfigured in him, my soul.

A' O ring upon my finger,
  My little ring of gold,
  Dear jewel, devoutly I kiss thee,
   Devoutly I kiss thee,
  To my heart I hold.

5. Rondo design, all parts begin alike, tonic key (B-flat)

A Help me, dear sisters,
  Help to adorn me,
  Me, the fortunate, tend me now;
  Busy your fingers,
  Daintily wreathing
  Myrtle flowers about my brow.

B(A) When, with a tranquil
  Heart and a happy,
  Safe in the arms of my love I lay,
  Often he whispered
  All his impatience,
  All his longing to hasten the day.

A   Help me, dear sisters,
         Help me to banish
         Foolish fears that my heart oppress,
         That with unclouded
         Eyes I may greet him,
         Him, the fountain of happiness.

C(A)   When, my beloved,
         Thou art before me,
         When thou, my sun, dost on me shine,
         Let me devoutly,
         Let me all humbly,
         Let me bow down to thee, lover mine.

A′   Strew for him, sisters,
         Strew for him flowers,
         Bring for him beautiful rosebuds too.
         And to you, sisters,
         Love and leave-taking;
         Sadly, gladly I part from you.

6. Ternary, major submediant key (G)

A   Dearest man, thou eyest
         Me with wonder deep;
         Dost not guess the reason
         Why today I weep?
         See the liquid pearl-drops,
         Gems I seldom wear,
         Tremble bright and happy
         On my eyelid there!

A   Why my bosom flutters,
         Why my heart is proud,
         Would my lips were able
         To confess aloud;
         Come and hide thy face here
         On my trembling breast—
         In thine ear I'll whisper
         How our love is blest.

B   Now thou knowest the reason
         Of the tears that ran,
         Though thou canst not see them,
         My beloved, beloved man!
         Stay upon my heart here,
         Feel it beat and thrill,
         So that close and closer
         I may clasp thee still!
              Close and closer!

A   Look, beside my bed here
Will the cradle bide
Where the pretty picture
Of my dream I'll hide;
Soon will come the morning,
Waked the dream will be;
There will lie thine image
Laughing up at me!

Coda   Thine image!

7. Strophic, modified, parts begin alike, end differently, major mediant key (D)

A   Here at my breast, my beautiful boy,
Thou art my treasure, thou art my joy.
O love it is gladness, and gladness is love;
So have I said, and so it will prove.

A'   I deemed my fortune all too high,
But still more happy now am I;
Only the heart, only the breast
That baby lips have sweetly pressed.

A''   Only a mother knows full well
What love and happiness may spell.
Pity on man I must bestow,
Who mother's joy can never know.

A''' My darling, darling angel, thou,
Thou lookest at me and smilest now!
Here at my breast, my beautiful boy,
Thou art my treasure, thou art my joy!

8. Through-composed, mediant key (D minor)

A   Now hast thou hurt me first since love began,
And wounded deep!
Thou sleepest, O cruel, most unpitiful man,
Death's endless sleep.

B   The world is empty now for me, a wife
Left all alone—alone;
For I have loved and I have lived, but life
I now have none.

C   I shrink away into my heart's recess,
The veil doth fall;
I there find thee and my lost happiness
My world and all!

Coda   The piano part of the first song, complete but without the voice part or the repetition, returns as a coda to the complete cycle; tonic key (B-flat).

—Adelbert von Chamissio
(Translation by Robert Randolph Garran)

It would be inconceivable since the emergence of the feminist movement for a poet to write of a woman's love and life as Chamisso did or for a composer to set such poems in a song cycle. Presumably, Chamisso and Schumann were reflecting the attitudes of the romantic age in which they lived, but the poems are written in the first person from the woman's point of view. Would a woman of that period have expressed the same sentiments in the same way? It is interesting to speculate. Whatever the answer, the cycle remains a prime example of the genre.

Webern's *Three Songs, op. 18,* are not called a cycle, but as multiple songs for the same medium published and ordinarily performed as a group, they satisfy the minimum requirements for a cycle. The texts are from different sources and are in different styles. In the original the first two songs are in German and the third in Latin. The medium is unusual—soprano voice, E-flat clarinet, and guitar.

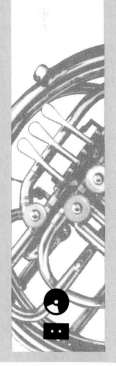

ANTON WEBERN: *Three Songs,* op. 18 (1925)   3:25   3/9–11
(1883–1945)   *1. Schatzerl klein (Sweetheart, Dear)*   :59
                            2. Erlösung (Redemption)   1:05
                            3. Ave, Regina (Hail, Queen)   1:21

1. Sweetheart, dear, mustn't be sad,
    Ere the year is gone you'll be mine.
    Ere the year is gone the rosemary will be green;
    The priest will say: Take each other.
    When the rosemary's green, the myrtle will be green,
    And the wanderer's cane will blossom at home.

2. *Mary:*
    My child, look upon my breasts; let no sinful
        soul be lost.
    Christ:
    Mother, look upon my wounds which I bear at all
        times for your sins.
    Father, accept my wounds as a sacrifice for iniquity.
    Father:
    Son, dear son of mine, all you desire shall come
        to pass.

3. Ave, Mistress of Heaven, ave, Queen of angels,
    Hail Fountainhead, hail Source from which all
        light has come.
    Rejoice, glorious Virgin, most beautiful of all!
    Farewell, o most virtuous one, intercede for us
        with Christ on high.

ADDITIONAL EXAMPLES

Strophic Form
> Schubert: *Die Schöne Müllerin (The Maid of the Mill)*
> > 1. Das Wandern (Wandering)
> Schubert: *Heiden-Röslein (Hedge Rose)*

Through-Composed Form
> Schubert: *Der Tod und das Mädchen (Death and the Maiden)*
> Schubert: *Morgenständchen (Hark, Hark! the Lark)*
> Strauss, R.: *Cäcilie (Cecily), op. 27 no. 2*

Song Cycle
> Beethoven: *An die ferne Geliebte (To the Distant Beloved), op. 98*
> Brahms: *Ernste Gesänge (Serious Songs), op. 121*
> Britten: *Serenade for Tenor, Horn, and Strings, op. 31*
> Debussy: *Chansons de Bilitis (Songs of Bilitis)*
> Schumann: *Dichterliebe (Poet's Love), op. 43*

17 CHORAL FORMS AND RELIGIOUS MUSIC

Choral music is inevitably linked with religion. The arts have occupied a central position in sacred ceremonies from their beginnings down to the present. Music, painting, architecture, poetry, prose, drama, and the dance all have drawn nurture and sustenance from the font of religion. In turn the arts have given expression to the faith and aspirations of humankind through the ages. Art and religion are almost synonymous in primitive societies. The striving for beauty independent from service to divinity and the cultivation of art for art's sake are characteristics of advanced civilizations. Varying concepts of deity in different places and times have led to the development of appropriate modes of worship with attendant arts. Those displayed only within the confines of a holy edifice are of interest primarily to communicants of a particular faith. Between the sacred and the profane lies a body of art, religiously inspired but universal in appeal, which reaches beyond the place of worship and into the museums and concert halls of the world. What is true of the arts and music in general is especially apropos in regard to choral music. The choral repertory is preponderantly of religious derivation.

Mass

The *Mass* is a solemn rite of the Roman Catholic church commemorating the sacrifice of Christ. The complete ritual has a complex structure of many sections only part of which are sung. Some portions of the text change with the day and the season, while others are constant. The items of the Mass that remain the same throughout the liturgical year constitute the *Ordinary,* as distinct from the variable items of the *Proper.* Composed Masses provide settings for five unchanging texts, the *Kyrie, Gloria, Credo, Sanctus/Benedictus,* and *Agnus Dei.* The Mass (Latin *missa*) derives its name from an ancient phrase *Ite, missa est* (Go, the Mass is ended). This phrase, sung or intoned by the priest or deacon at the conclusion of the service, dismisses the congregation.

The texts of the composed portions of the Mass are drawn from several sources. The Kyrie, a supplication for mercy, is part of an old Greek litany. Originally the Kyrie was in Greek and the remainder of the Mass in Latin, but the vernacular was authorized by Vatican Council II (1962–65). The Gloria, a series of acclamations, is from Luke 2:14 and Eastern liturgies. The Credo is the profession of faith formulated by the First Council of Nicaea in 325. The Sanctus/Benedictus text is derived from Isaiah 6:3 and Mark 11:9–10. In the Agnus Dei, petitions are addressed to Jesus as He is characterized in John 1:29. These texts, which have inspired some of the most eloquent pages in the annals of music, are given in the traditional languages and in English. The Kyrie, Gloria, Credo, and Sanctus/Benedictus translations are based on the English version by the International Consultation on English Texts, but with adjustments as necessary to parallel the original Latin. The translation of the Agnus Dei is a more literal alternate version prepared by the International Commission on English in the Liturgy.

Text of the Mass

Kyrie

Kyrie eleison. — Lord, have mercy.
Christe eleison. — Christ, have mercy.
Kyrie eleison. — Lord, have mercy.

Gloria

Gloria in Excelsis Deo,
*   et in terra pax hominibus*
*   bonae voluntatis.*
Laudamus te, benedicimus te,
*   adoramus te, glorificamus te.*
Gratias agimus tibi propter
*   magnam gloriam tuam.*
Domine Deus, rex coelestis
Deus pater omnipotens.
Domine Fili unigenite Jesu Christe,
Domine Deus, agnus Dei,
Filius Patris,
qui tollis peccata mundi:
*   miserere nobis;*
qui tollis peccata mundi:
*   suscipe deprecationem nostram;*
qui sedes ad dexteram Patris:
*   miserere nobis.*
Quoniam tu solus sanctus,
tu solus Dominus,
tu solus altissimus,
*   Jesu Christe,*
*   cum sancto spiritu,*
*   in gloria Dei Patris. Amen.*

Glory to God in the highest,
    and on earth peace to men of
        good will.
We praise you, we bless you,
    we worship you, we glorify you.
We give you thanks for your
    great glory.
Lord God, heavenly King,
God the Father almighty.
Lord Jesus Christ, the only-begotten Son,
Lord God, Lamb of God,
Son of the Father,
you take away the sin of the world:
    have mercy on us;
you take away the sin of the world:
    receive our prayer;
you are seated at the right hand of
    the Father: have mercy on us.
For you alone are the Holy One,
you alone are the Lord,
you alone are the Most High,
    Jesus Christ,
    with the Holy Spirit,
    in the glory of God the Father. Amen.

Credo

Credo in Unum Deum,
*   Patrem omnipotentem,*
factorem coeli et terrae,
visibilium omnium et invisibilium.
Et in unum Dominum, Jesum Christum,
*   Filium Dei unigenitum,*
*   et ex patre natum ante omnia saecula.*
Deum de Deo, lumen de lumine,
Deum verum de Deo vero.
Genitum, non factum,
consubstantialem Patri,
Per quem omnia facta sunt.
Qui propter nos homines et
*   propter nostram salutem*
*   descendit de coelis:*
et incarnatus est de Spiritu
*   Sancto ex Maria virgine,*
*   et homo factus est.*

We believe in one God,
    the Father, the Almighty,
    maker of heaven and earth,
    of all that is, seen and unseen.
We believe in one Lord, Jesus Christ,
    the only Son of God,
    eternally begotten of the Father,
    God from God, Light from Light,
    true God from true God,
    begotten, not made,
    of one Being with the Father.
    Through him all things were made.
For us men and
    for our salvation
        he came down from heaven:
by the power of the Holy Spirit
    he became incarnate from the
        Virgin Mary, and was made man.

Crucifixum etiam pro nobis,
sub Pontio Pilato passus,
et sepultus est.
Et resurrexit tertia die
secundum scripturas;
et ascendit in coelum sedet
ad dexteram Patris.
Et iterum venturus est cum gloria
judicare vivos et mortuos,
cujus regni non erit finis.
Et in Spiritum Sanctum,
Dominum et vivificantem,
qui ex Patre Filioque procedit.
Qui cum Patre et Filio simul
adoratur et conglorificatur.
Qui locutus est per Prophetas.
Et unam sanctam catholicam et
apostolicam ecclesiam.
Confiteor unum baptisma in
remissionem peccatorum.
Et expecto resurrectionem
mortuorum, et vitam
venturi seculi. Amen.

For our sake he was crucified under
Pontius Pilate; he suffered
death and was buried.
On the third day he rose again in
accordance with the Scriptures;
he ascended into Heaven and is
seated at the right hand of the Father.
He will come again in glory to
judge the living and the dead,
and his kingdom will have no end.
We believe in the Holy Spirit,
the Lord, the giver of life, who proceeds
from the Father and the Son.
With the Father and the Son he is
worshiped and glorified.
He has spoken through the Prophets.
We believe in one holy catholic and
apostolic Church.
We acknowledge one baptism for
the forgiveness of sins.
We look for the resurrection of the
dead, and the life of the world
to come. Amen.

Sanctus/Benedictus

Sanctus, sanctus, sanctus Dominus,
Deus Sabaoth,
pleni sunt coeli et terra
gloria tua.
Hosanna in excelsis.
Benedictus qui venit in
nomine Domini.
Hosanna in excelsis.

Holy, holy, holy Lord,
God of power and might,
heaven and earth are full
of your glory.
Hosanna in the highest.
Blessed is he who comes in the
name of the Lord.
Hosanna in the highest.

Agnus Dei

Agnus Dei, qui tollis peccata
mundi: miserere nobis.
Agnus Dei, qui tollis peccata
mundi: miserere nobis.
Agnus Dei, qui tollis peccata
mundi: dona nobis pacem.

Lamb of God, you take away the sins
of the world: have mercy on us.
Lamb of God, you take away the sins
of the world: have mercy on us.
Lamb of God, you take away the sins
of the world: grant us peace.

Palestrina's *Pope Marcellus Mass* is often cited as a model liturgical Mass. The words are projected with exceptional clarity by unaccompanied voices, and the refined contrapuntal lines and ethereal harmonies perfectly reflect Palestrina's reverence for the sacred text. The five sections of the Mass text are usually subdivided when they are set to music. In the *Pope Marcellus Mass* the Sanctus and Benedictus are treated as separate parts, and the Agnus Dei is divided into Agnus Dei I and Agnus Dei II.

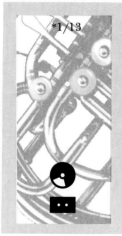

PALESTRINA: *Pope Marcellus Mass* (1555)	34:30
(1525–1594) Kyrie*	5:00
Gloria in excelsis Deo	5:50
Credo in unum Deum	8:08
Sanctus	4:19
Benedictus	3:00
Agnus Dei I	4:13
Agnus Dei II	4:00

Palestrina is regarded as the greatest sixteenth-century composer of church music, and the *Pope Marcellus Mass* is one of his most famous works. It presumably was composed during or immediately following the brief pontificate in 1555 of Marcellus II for whom it is named. The first known performance was in the Sistine Chapel ten years later. It was published in 1567.

Many composers have used the text of the Mass for works not intended for liturgical use. Concert Masses range all the way from the monumental *B minor Mass* of Bach and the *Missa Solemnis* of Beethoven to the *Jazz Mass* of Joe Masters (recorded on Discovery 785). Where liturgical Masses originally were for unaccompanied voices, concert Masses usually are for chorus, soloists, and orchestra. In the more expansive examples the Mass texts, especially the lengthy ones of the Gloria and Credo, are sectioned, with phrases and sentences being treated musically as distinct parts. Masses of this type require resources not ordinarily available for religious services, but they illustrate another facet of music inspired by the rituals of religion.

Requiem

A *Requiem* is a Mass for the dead. It differs from the usual Mass in that the joyous Gloria and the Credo are omitted, and the sections peculiar to the Requiem are inserted. The first item, the Introit *Requiem aeternam* (Rest eternal) from which the service takes its name, precedes the Kyrie. A long Latin hymn, *Dies irae* (Day of wrath), and the Offertory *Domine Jesu Christe* (Lord Jesus Christ) follow the Kyrie. The Requiem concludes with the Communion *Lux aeterna* (Light eternal).

Mozart's last work, left unfinished at his death, was his *Requiem in D minor*. It is scored for a quartet of solo voices (of which the soprano is most prominent), chorus, and orchestra. The five large sections of the text are subdivided and set as twelve distinct parts. The setting of the Kyrie does not conform to liturgical usage. The phrases *Kyrie eleison* and *Christe eleison* are sung simultaneously as the two subjects of a double fugue. This *Requiem* is a superlative example of religious music not intended primarily for liturgical use.

W. A. MOZART *Requiem in D minor (1791)*	53:38
(1756–1791) *Requiem and Kyrie*	:00
Dies irae	8:13
Tuba mirum	10:08
Rex tremendae	13:53
Recordare	16:35
Confutatis	22:30
Lacrimosa	25:20
Domine Jesu Christe	28:25
Hostias	32:32
Sanctus	37:07
Benedictus	38:57
Agnus Dei and Lux aeterna	44:50

An anonymous stranger under conditions of absolute secrecy commissioned Mozart to compose a Requiem just five months before his untimely death. Mozart became obsessed with the idea that the stranger was an emissary of death and that the Requiem was his own. He was obliged to interrupt his labor on this work, and it was incomplete when he died. The night of his death he gave the score to his friend and pupil, Franz Xaver Süssmayr, who finished the composition and delivered it to the mysterious stranger. The stranger proved to be an undercover agent acting for a nobleman, Count Franz von Walsegg, who wished to pass off the Requiem as his own composition. The Count actually was listed as the composer on the program of the first performance.

The *German Requiem* by Brahms is a noteworthy exception to the usual Requiem plan. Brahms selected the text for his Requiem from the German Bible without reference to the traditional content of the Roman Rite. It is in every respect a unique work.

Motet

The meaning of the term *motet* has varied considerably during the seven hundred years that it has been in use, and no single definition covers all of its ramifications. Motets are most often unaccompanied choral compositions with sacred Latin texts and polyphonic texture, but there are exceptions. Motets were an important adjunct of the Catholic service during the Middle Ages and the Renaissance when the genre flourished. Such motets, of which the following by Josquin is representative, have great historical significance.

JOSQUIN DES PREZ: *Ave Maria (1497)*   4:38
(1440–1521)

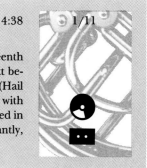

The style of this *Ave Maria* is typical for motets of the late fifteenth and sixteenth centuries. It is for unaccompanied voices in four parts with a sacred Latin text beginning with the couplet *Ave Maria, gratia plena/Dominus tecum, Virgo serena* (Hail Mary, full of grace/The Lord is with you, gentle Virgin). The melody associated with these words is introduced imitatively, and freely modified elements of it are used in the setting of subsequent couplets in the poetic form. The texture is predominantly, but not exclusively, polyphonic.

Madrigal

Madrigals are the secular counterpart of motets. Though the term was used for a fourteenth-century poetic form and its musical settings, it now implies unless otherwise qualified a type of vocal music that flourished in the sixteenth and seventeenth centuries, primarily in Italy and England. The texts for these madrigals are mostly contemplative and idyllic poems, in the vernacular, with amorous or pastoral subjects. The settings are for unaccompanied voices in four to six parts. The texture is less consistently polyphonic than in motets.

The high order of concurrent Italian and English poetry available as texts gave impetus to the madrigal movement. The words inspired the music, and the music reflects directly the moods and thoughts of the text, sometimes portraying a particularly piquant word or phrase realistically.

Madrigals were intended principally as a source of entertainment for those participating in the performance. The ability to sing a madrigal part at sight was a social grace expected of every gentleman and lady. The singing of madrigals was one of the most prevalent forms of entertainment at intimate social gatherings of the period. The vocal skills of a vast public must have been unusually well developed, for the intricate music customarily was performed with the singers seated around a table reading from part books with no conductor and with only one on a part.

The madrigal originated in Italy, and Orlandus Lassus (also known as Roland de Lassus and Orlando di Lasso) is generally grouped with the Italian madrigalists, though he was born in the Netherlands and died in Munich. His formative years were spent in Italy, and his first printed music—a collection of twenty-two madrigals to poems of Petrarch—was published there. *Matona mia cara (Matona, my dear)* was a product of his youth, but the musical style is mature and representative of both the composer and the Italian madrigal.

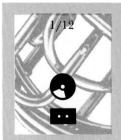

1/12   ORLANDUS LASSUS: *Matona mia cara (1550)*   2:44
(1532–1594)

Lassus was a precocious musician, so the date of composition given for *Matona mia cara* is conceivable though it was not published until 1581. The frivolous text relates in very earthy terms the attempts of an amorous suitor to seduce an Italian maiden. Each of its five stanzas ends with a musical refrain to the nonsense syllables *don don don, diri diri don, don don don.*

Influence of the Italian madrigal was evident in England during the last half of the sixteenth century. Lassus may have visited there briefly in 1554 or 1555. A collection of Italian madrigals provided with English texts, *Musica*

Transalpina, was published in 1588 and widely disseminated. It firmly established the Italian madrigal style in England. The time was ripe for the new form. English poets and composers were of a high order. They adapted the Italian madrigal style to the English language and tastes and produced a large number of indigenous madrigals that are still sung and enjoyed. A feature of the English madrigal school was the use of the nonsense syllables "fa la la" in the texts. Thomas Morley was a first-generation English madrigalist.

THOMAS MORLEY: *My bonny lass she smileth (1595)*   1:45
(1557–1602)

Written just seven years after the publication of *Musica Transalpina,* this example illustrates all of the characteristic features of the English madrigal style, including "fa la las" between phrases of the text.

Cantata

No precise and all-inclusive definition for *cantata* is possible, but in general cantatas are works consisting of several distinct sections for one or more voices with instrumental accompaniment. The sections often contrast in style and medium, with recitatives, arias, duets, choruses, and instrumental episodes common ingredients. The texts of the various sections are related parts of a single narrative which may be sacred or secular in subject matter, lyric or dramatic in style.

Bach's cantatas (almost two hundred extant out of a much larger production) represent the largest body of relatively consistent works in the form. A typical Bach sacred cantata opens with a polyphonic chorus followed by a series of recitatives and arias and closes with a harmonized Protestant chorale. The chorale with which a canata closes often provides a basic source of material, both textual and musical, for the entire cantata. One practice is to use each stanza of the chorale text or a paraphrase of it as the basis for one section of the cantata. The chorale melody, too, may figure in the various sections. Embellished versions of the chorale tune sometimes are used, and at other times phrases of the chorale melody in long notes are given a florid contrapuntal setting. These procedures are illustrated in Bach's Cantata no. 1, *Wie schön leuchtet der Morgenstern (How brightly shines the morning star).*

J. S. BACH: *Wie schön leuchtet der Morgenstern* (1725)   24:50
(1685–1750)   1. *Chorale fantasia*   :00
                    (chorus and orchestra)
                 2. *Recitative*   10:16
                    (tenor with continuo)
                 3. *Aria*   11:17
                    (soprano with oboe da
                    caccia and continuo)
                 4. *Recitative*   15:54
                    (bass with continuo)
                 5. *Aria*   16:48
                    (tenor with two solo violins,
                    strings and continuo)
                 6. *Chorale*   23:25
                    (chorus and orchestra)

This cantata is based on a hymn tune by Philipp Nicolai (1556–1608) and a six-stanza text from which it takes its name. The six sections of the cantata correspond with the six stanzas of the text. The chorale fantasia begins with an instrumental introduction, after which the chorus sopranos sing the words of the first stanza to the hymn tune (doubled by the horns) in an elaborate contrapuntal setting provided by the other voices and instruments. The words of the tenor recitative are a paraphrase of the second stanza of the text. The soprano aria is in effect a duet between the voice and the oboe da caccia, an obsolete instrument resembling an English horn (which is often substituted in modern performances). In the tenor aria two solo violins form a trio with the solo voice. The cantata concludes with a straightforward chorale-style harmonization of the hymn tune. The instruments double the voices in the chorale except for a brilliant countermelody in the horn.

The numbers used to identify Bach cantatas are derived from their order in the collected edition of his works and have no chronological significance. This cantata, though numbered 1, is a product of his maturity. It was written for the Feast of Annunciation, March 25, and reflects the joyous mood appropriate to the occasion. Chorale melody page 332.

At the opposite end of the spectrum from Bach's *Wie schön leuchtet der Morgenstern,* but still classified as a cantata, is Orff's *Carmina Burana (Profane Songs).* This theatrical cantata, a "happening" in contemporary terminology, consists of secular songs for soloists and choruses accompanied by instruments and magic images, dancing girls, and festive drinking scenes. The poems of the text were arranged from a collection written during the Middle Ages by monks and itinerant scholars. Their writings were discovered during the last century in the library of a medieval Bavarian abbey. Translations of the section titles and first lines of the poems serve as clues to the substance of the cantata.

CARL ORFF: *Carmina Burana, scenic cantata (1936)*   60:04   *3/13
(1895–1982)

Fortune, Empress of the World

1.	O Fortune, changeable as the moon*	2:19
2.	I lament Fortune's blows	2:41

I. *Springtime*

3.	The smiling face of spring	4:32
4.	The bright, keen sun	2:37
5.	Behold, welcome	2:30
6.	Dance	1:47
7.	The noble forest blooms	3:16
8.	Hawker, give me the rouge	3:32
9.	Dance/Here, all in a circle/Come, come, my love	4:39
10.	If all the world were mine	:49

II. *In the Tavern*

11.	Boiling inside	2:21
12.	Once I lived in the lakes	3:46
13.	I am the Abbot of Cucany	1:29
14.	When we are in the tavern	2:55

III. *The Court of Love*

15.	Love flies everywhere	3:09
16.	Day, night, and all things	2:29
17.	There stood a girl in a red tunic	1:56
18.	My heart is filled with many sighs	1:55
19.	If a boy is with a girl	1:05
20.	Come, come, come	:58
21.	Opposite courses hang in the balance	1:58
22.	The season is pleasant	2:22
23.	Sweetest boy, I give myself to you	:48

Blanziflor and Helena

24.	Hail, most beautiful one	1:38

Fortune, Empress of the World

25.	O Fortune, changeable as the moon	2:33

This stage cantata divides into three main sections depicting in turn the encounters of humanity with nature, with the gifts of nature, and with love. These three sections are framed by a symbolic parable of life—the wheel of fortune alternately bringing good luck and bad luck in its perpetual rotation.

Oratorios in general are dramatic compositions of large dimensions for soloists, chorus, and orchestra based on religious but nonscriptural texts. They are distinguished from operas by the absence of scenery, costumes, and action as well as by subject matter and from sacred cantatas by their size. The chorus is prominent, more so than is customary in either operas or

Oratorio

cantatas. An overture or opening orchestral introduction is usual. Recitatives by the soloists carry the burden of the narrative. One of the soloists sometimes is a narrator who explains the action, introduces the characters, and provides continuity between the various numbers, all in recitative. Arias generally follow the recitatives. Choral numbers usually are comments on or reactions to the immediately preceding passage, frequently with the chorus representing a crowd in the dramatic situation.

Not all oratorios conform to this plan. Some have secular subjects, and some are done in costume. These must be regarded as departures from the norm, which is represented perfectly in the most famous of all oratorios, Handel's *Messiah* with a text derived from the Bible by Charles Jennings.

*1/21   **G. F. HANDEL:** *Messiah (1741)*   2:19:50
        (1685–1759)

Part I
1. Overture
2. Recitative (Tenor): Comfort ye
3. Air (Tenor): Every valley shall be exalted
4. Chorus: And the glory of the Lord
5. Recitative (Bass): Thus saith the Lord of hosts
6. Air (Bass): But who may abide the day of His coming
7. Chorus: And He shall purify the sons of Levi
8. Recitative (Alto): Behold, a virgin shall conceive
9. Air (Alto and chorus): O thou that tellest good tidings to Zion
10. Recitative (Bass): For, behold, darkness shall cover the earth
11. Air (Bass): The people that walked in darkness
12. Chorus: For unto us a Child is born
13. Pastoral Symphony (Orchestra)
14. Recitative (Soprano): There were shepherds abiding in the field
15. Recitative (Soprano): And the angel said unto them, "Fear not"
16. Recitative (Soprano): And suddenly there was with the angel
17. Chorus: Glory to God in the highest
18. Air (Soprano): Rejoice greatly O daughter of Zion
19. Recitative (Alto): Then shall the eyes of the blind be opened
20. Air (Alto): He shall feed His flock
    Air (Soprano): Come unto Him
21. Chorus: His yoke is easy and His burden light

Part II
22. Chorus: Behold the Lamb of God
23. Air (Alto): He was despised and rejected of men
24. Chorus: Surely He hath borne our griefs
25. Chorus: And with His stripes we are healed
26. Chorus: All we like sheep have gone astray
27. Recitative (Tenor): All they that see Him, laugh Him to scorn
28. Chorus: He trusted in God
29. Recitative (Tenor): Thy rebuke hath broken His heart

30. Air (Tenor): Behold, and see if there be any sorrow
31. Recitative (Tenor): He was cut off out of the land of the living
32. Air (Tenor): But Thou didst not leave His soul in hell
33. Chorus: Lift up your heads
34. Recitative (Tenor): Unto which of the angels said He
35. Chorus: Let all the angels of God worship Him
36. Air (Bass): Thou art gone up on high
37. Chorus: The Lord gave the word
38. Air (Soprano): How beautiful are the feet of them that preach
39. Chorus: Their sound is gone out into all lands
40. Air (Bass): Why do the nations so furiously rage together
41. Chorus: Let us break their bonds asunder
42. Recitative (Tenor): He that dwelleth in heaven
43. Air (Tenor): Thou shalt break them with a rod of iron
44. Chorus: Hallelujah

Part III
45. Air (Soprano): I know that my Redeemer liveth
46. Chorus: Since by man came death
47. Recitative (Bass): Behold, I tell you a mystery
48. Air (Bass): The trumpet shall sound
49. Recitative (Alto): Then shall be brought to pass the saying that is written*
50. Duet (Alto and tenor): O death, where is thy sting*
51. Chorus: But thanks be to God*
52. Air (Soprano): If God be for us
53. Chorus: Worthy is the Lamb

Amen

Messiah ranks as one of the great artistic creations of all time. It was received enthusiastically at its first performance, and its appeal has continued undiminished through the years. In performances and recordings sometimes numbers are omitted and the order rearranged. It is complete with the timing indicated on Telarc 2CD-80093-2.

Several passages of scripture and liturgy have been used repeatedly in choral compositions. Among them are: the Gospels of Matthew, Mark, Luke, and John, which provide the texts for *Passion Music;* the *Te Deum,* a hymn of praise and thanksgiving in the Catholic liturgy which is freely set, often commemorating joyous occasions; the *Magnificat,* canticle of the Virgin in both the Catholic and Anglican rites; and the *Stabat Mater,* a thirteenth-century poem sung at the Feast of the Seven Dolors. The Jewish *Sacred Service* is represented in one superlative example by Ernest Bloch (1880–1959). Specific works in these categories and some more recent and less traditional examples of the types of choral music discussed in the chapter are included in the list of additional examples.

ADDITIONAL EXAMPLES

Mass and Requiem
Bruckner: *Mass no. 3 in F minor, "Great"*
Stravinsky: *Mass*
Bernstein: *Mass, A Theatre Piece for Singers, Players, and Dancers*
Fauré: *Requiem, op. 48*

Motet
Bach: *Motet no. 5, Komm, Jesu, komm, BWV. 229*
Byrd: *Ego sum panis vivus*

Madrigal
Gesualdo: *Tu m'uccidi, o crudele*
Byrd: *I thought that love had been a boy*
Pinkham: *Madrigal*
Musgrave: *Four Madrigals*

Cantata
Bartók: *Cantata Profana*
Prokofiev: *Alexander Nevsky, op. 78* (cantata arranged from the film score)

Oratorio
Mendelssohn: *Elijah, op. 70*
Walton: *Belshazzar's Feast*

Passion
Schütz: *St. John Passion*
Bach: *St. Matthew Passion, BWV. 244*
Penderecki: *Passion According to St. Luke*

Te Deum
Kodály: *Te Deum*

Magnificat
Bach: *Magnificat in D, BWV. 243*
Hovhaness: *Magnificat, op. 157*

Stabat Mater
Pergolesi: *Stabat Mater*

Sacred Service (Jewish)
Bloch: *Sacred Service, "Avodath Hakodesh"*

PART 3

THE PERIODS AND STYLES OF MUSIC

- MUSIC BEFORE 1600
- THE BAROQUE PERIOD (1600–1750)
- THE VIENNESE CLASSIC PERIOD (1750–1825)
- THE ROMANTIC AGE (1815–1900)
- NATIONALISM AND IMPRESSIONISM
- MODERN MUSIC TO 1950
- THE NEW MUSIC
- JAZZ
- FOLK AND POPULAR MUSIC
- THE MUSIC OF OTHER CULTURES

 CHRONOLOGY

B.C.

28,000   Cro-Magnon bone flute

18,000   Archaic percussion instruments

2900   Egyptian notation

2700 Ur string and wind instruments

2400   Sumerian poem in praise of music

1400   Hurrian cult hymn

1200   Chords in Egyptian music

1000   Pre-Mayan bird ocarina

900 Aulos and lyra used in Greece

800   Sumerian hymn

675 Terpander?

620 Sappho 565

300   Hydraulis invented

200   Seikilos epitaph

190 Terence 159

137   First Delphic hymn

A.D.

200   Christian hymn to the Trinity

540   Gregory 604

850   Beginnings of polyphony

1100 Troubadours and trouvères

?   Raimbaut 1207

1170   Walter   1230

1200   Minnesingers

1240   *Sumer Is Icumen In*

1245 Adam 1288

1300   Machaut 1377

1440   Josquin 1521

1501   Music printing

1501   Tallis   1585

1525   Palestrina   1594

1532   Lassus   1594

1546   Caccini   1618

Note: Composers and milestones of music mentioned in the text. Some of the dates are approximate and earliest date given for disputed time spans.

18 MUSIC BEFORE 1600

The origins of music are shrouded in mystery. Scholars can only speculate regarding its beginnings, but recent research has expanded our knowledge of early music and pushed back the date for the earliest evidence of music. Anthropologists and musicologists are studying the music of primitive cultures to shed light on music in its early stages of development, and archaeologists are making exciting discoveries of early instruments and notation in their excavations.

An exhibition of late Ice Age/Upper Paleolithic period artifacts in 1986–87 at the American Museum of Natural History in New York, as reported in *Newsweek* magazine, displayed a bone flute carved by the Cro-Magnon inhabitants of what is now France about thirty thousand years ago. If the dating is correct, this bone flute is the oldest known musical instrument. Since these early people were capable of making a sophisticated wind instrument with holes to control the pitch, it seems safe to assume that they also had percussion instruments, though evidence is lacking.

The Earliest Music

Percussion instruments have been preserved from a somewhat later time and another region. Soviet archaeologists report that they have unearthed musical instruments made from mammoth bones twenty thousand years ago. The instruments found near Chernigov in the Ukraine are described as a drum, kettle drums, and xylophones.

There is ample evidence that music flourished in the earliest civilizations as an adjunct of rituals, ceremonies, festivals, and entertainments. Singing and dancing were accompanied by a variety of percussion, wind, and string instruments. These activities are well documented in archaeological discoveries and pictorial representations that have been known to scholars for decades. Only more recently have attempts been made to decipher the ancient notations and re-create the music.

An article by Maureen M. Barwise in *The Consort,* a British periodical, has transcriptions of twelve examples of Egyptian music dating from the fourth dynasty (2900–2750 B.C.) to the twentieth dynasty (1200–1090 B.C.). According to Barwise, the melodies were "deciphered from ancient notation, which exists in at least two forms—one based on numbers, and one on heirogliphic signs." The music is mostly monophonic, but "Chords, mostly of two notes, occasionally three, are used to mark important words such as 'divine names,' and are more freely used in the later periods."

During the dynastic periods of Egypt the Sumerians to the north and east in the region of modern Iraq excelled in the construction and decoration of musical instruments. Excavations of the death pits of Ur, a Sumerian city-state, yielded the remains of court musicians buried with their

FIGURE 18.1

A Sumerian banquet with music and song from the Royal Standard, Ur, ca. 2700 B.C.

From The Music of the Sumerians, Babylonians and Assyrians *by Francis W. Galpin. Used by permission of Cambridge University Press.*

lyres and harps which were richly ornamented with gold, silver, shell, lapis lazuli, and red stone. Singers and various instruments are included in the depiction of a Sumerian banquet on the Royal Standard from Ur ca. 2700 B.C., now in the British Museum (figure 18.1).

Sumerian uses of music are reflected in a few lines praising music taken from a long poem inscribed ca. 2400 B.C. on a clay cylinder of Gudea, a peaceful priest-king who ruled at Lagash, about fifty miles north of Ur. The poem excerpt is given in the original cuneiform script (figure 18.2) and Francis Galpin's translation rendered in modern English.

Music's Ministry

To fill with joy the temple court,
And chase the city's gloom away,
The heart to still, the passions calm,
Of weeping eyes and tears to stay.

From Francis W. Galpin, *The Music of the Sumerians, Babylonians & Assyrians.* Used by permission of Cambridge University Press.

Musical practices similar to those at Ur and Lagash apparently existed concurrently throughout the region. Five clay tablets with cuneiform inscriptions excavated during the last century in modern Iraq and Syria, to the west, have yielded specific information about scale structures and tuning systems as early as 1800 B.C. and a complete song from about 1400 B.C. The tablets are now scattered in the museums of Philadelphia, London, Berlin, and Damascus, where they have been deciphered in stages by international scholars, including Ann Draffkorn Kilmer of the University of California, Berkeley.

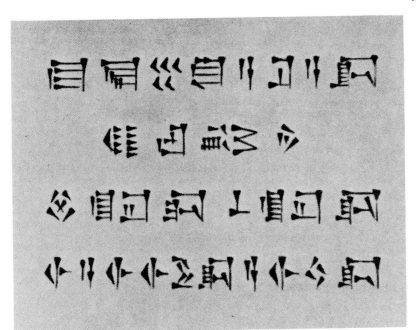

FIGURE 18.2

"*Music's Ministry*" in Sumerian cuneiform script, ca. 2400 *B.C.*

From The Music of the Sumerians, Babylonians and Assyrians *by Francis W. Galpin. Used by permission of Cambridge University Press.*

FIGURE 18.3

Cuneiform notation of Hurrian cult song on clay tablet from Ugarit, ca. 1400 *B.C.*

From Sounds from Silence *by Kilmer, Crocker, and Brown. Used by permission of Bit Enki Publications, Berkeley, California.*

Kilmer, in association with Richard L. Crocker, also of the University of California, used the information inscribed on four of the tablets to reconstruct the ancient tuning system and scales. Interestingly, the scales contain seven tones with varying patterns of whole steps and half steps like modern major, minor, and modal scales.

The fifth cuneiform tablet (figure 18.3) was unearthed in three fragments between 1950 and 1955 at the site of the ancient city of Ugarit on the seacoast of modern Syria. On it are inscribed the words and music symbols of a Hurrian cult hymn from ca. 1400 B.C. The hymn concerns the goddess Nikkal, the wife of the moon god, and probably is addressed to her, according to Kilmer. Present-day knowledge of the Hurrian language is too limited to provide a complete translation of the words, but the musical terms, consisting of a series of intervals and numbers, are in a Hurrian version of the more familiar Akkadian language of Assyria and Babylonia. Kilmer has transcribed the music in modern notation and has matched the Hurrian words with the notes. In order to transcribe the perplexing ancient notation, several assumptions had to be made. Kilmer's most remarkable assumptions are that the notes of the specified intervals are to be sounded together and that the upper notes constitute a vocal melody and the lower notes an instrumental accompaniment. The numbers indicate the number of times each interval is to sound. As transcribed, the song uses notes from the modern C-major scale exclusively, though the effect is more like one of the church modes (Phrygian). The sound is less strange than one might expect in music from a time so remote from our own. The most striking aspect of the transcription, from a historical point of view, is its two melodically independent lines, a feature otherwise undocumented in musical notation until more than two thousand years later.

Scale resources not unlike those inscribed on the Middle Eastern cuneiform tablets apparently were in use during the same millenium halfway around the world. The tones associated with the syllables *do, re, mi, fa,* and *sol* are sounded by a clay ocarina in the form of a bird from a pre-Mayan site about three thousand years old. The site, on the Yucatan peninsula along the east coast of Mexico and Central America, was excavated by a team of National Geographic Society archaeologists. The widespread use of similar scale resources over an extended period of time attests to their universality.

Galpin's *Music of the Sumerians, Babylonians & Assyrians* contains a transcription of the extended (six-page) Sumerian *Hymn on the Creation of Man.* The hymn, from about 800 B.C., was inscribed on a cuneiform tablet found at Asshur, far to the north of Ur. The transcription gives the syllables of the original harp notation and their staff equivalents, a voice part derived from the harp part using notes with the same letter names but usually in a different octave, and the words in Sumerian and English. The notes of the hymn constitute a major scale, like the notes of the Hurrian hymn, but the usage is like that of a church mode (*Lydian*).

The accuracy of transcriptions and the authenticity of performances of ancient music are subjects about which there is much speculation by experts. Questions regarding accuracy and authenticity arise in all recreations of music from the distant past, and definitive answers are rarely possible.

The Sumerians, their immediate neighbors and successors, and the Mayans were not the only early peoples to cultivate music extensively. Music was highly developed and widely practiced in the ancient civilizations of Arabia, India, China, and throughout the Orient. Jewish musical traditions date back to 2000 B.C. Influences of pre-Christian Hebrew chants have survived in the synagogues of isolated Jewish tribes and in Christian chants, though none of the actual music has been preserved. Knowledge of these early musics is of comparatively recent origin and had no direct impact on the development of Western music. Our musical traditions can be traced back only as far as ancient Greece.

In Greek culture, music occupied an exalted position. Music was included in the quadrivium of liberal arts, along with arithmetic, geometry, and astronomy. Greek philosophers wrote in detail about music theory and the place of music in society. The Greeks believed that music was capable of influencing character and behavior and associated certain modes and instruments with specific qualities.

Sharply contrasting musical styles are attributed to the cults of Apollo and Dionysus. The followers of Apollo played the *lyra* and the *kithara*, both plucked string instruments producing soft sounds, in a manner intended to promote the ideal of harmonious moderation. The followers of Dionysus played the *aulos*, a double-pipe reed instrument with a shrill tone, in a manner intended to incite the passions. Both cults used their instruments alone and in conjunction with singing.

During the seventh century B.C. Terpander established the first music school in Greece. He is regarded as the father of Greek lyric poetry and was credited with being the first to set poetry to music, but in light of recent discoveries this honor would now seem to be undeserved. The poems of Sappho, a Greek poetess and musician born in Lesbos ca. 620 B.C., were sung, and music figured prominently in Greek drama, which may have developed from Dionysian rituals. The quantity of Greek music must have been great, but only one brief song and some forty fragments survived the collapse of the Hellenic world.

The most significant surviving examples of music from ancient Greece are two hymns to Apollo inscribed in marble and discovered at Delphi. The first Delphic hymn, though incomplete and requiring some reconstruction, is the longest extant piece of Greek music. Two of the hymn's three sections are given in modern notation in Davison-Apel *Historical Anthology of Music, vol. I.* The second hymn, of which only a fragment has been preserved, is dated 127 B.C., about ten years later than the first hymn.

The brief *Epitaph of Seikilos* is the earliest and perhaps the only piece of Greek music preserved complete and intact. It was engraved on the tombstone of Seikilos's wife some time between the second century B.C. and the first century A.D. at Tralles in Asia Minor.

SEIKILOS: *Epitaph (200 B.C.)*   1:51   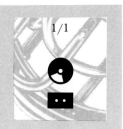 1/1

The poetic words of the *Epitaph of Seikilos,* also known as *Skolion of Seikilos* and *Seikilos Song,* are a timely reflection on the transitory nature of life: "As long as you live, be cheerful; let nothing grieve you, for life is short and time takes its toll." Notation page 329.

The earliest known ancestor of keyboard instruments is the *hydraulis,* a hydraulic organ invented by Ktesibios of Alexandria ca. 300–250 B.C. Water pumped by hand produced the air pressure to activate the organ's nineteen pipes. Its 2″ × 8″ hinged keys, which could be depressed by one finger, were automatically returned to the closed position by a spring mechanism, a remarkable feature for that time. The hydraulis apparently was used primarily for home entertainment by the Greeks, a use continued and expanded by the Romans.

Roman Music

Cicero (Rome, 106–43 B.C.) wrote regarding the use of the hydraulis at banquets and described its sound as "delectable to the ears." The hydraulis, no doubt a louder version, was also played at outdoor Roman spectacles such as the exhibitions of gladiators.

The Romans imported Greek musicians and adopted Greek musical traditions. Brass instruments inherited from the Etruscans, their predecessors in the region, were used lavishly in public entertainments and military maneuvers. The music of the Romans was essentially imitative rather than innovative, but they did cultivate music as an art separate from poetry and drama. Slaves performed music in the homes and theaters of Rome, and the best of them were highly regarded and, for winning competitions, richly rewarded.

Specific information about the music of Imperial Rome is extremely limited, and examples are practically nonexistent, consisting of a single mutilated fragment. That fragment, as reconstructed for the following recording, does not display any uniquely Roman characteristics but is permeated with Greek influence.

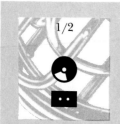

1/2

TERENCE: *Hecyra Verse 861* (160 B.C.)   :24

This example of Roman music is for voice accompanied on the recording by a plucked string instrument. It is very similar in style to the preceding example of Greek music. One can only speculate regarding the distinctly Roman brass and percussion music that initially resounded in the Colosseum and comparable venues, for no trace of it remains.

Early Christian Music

With the rise of Christianity came the need for suitable music. The earliest extant example of Christian chant by several centuries is the *Hymn to the Trinity* from a papyrus discovered at Oxyrhynchus (Egypt). The notation is vocal with solo voice and male chorus alternating, a feature retained in later chants.

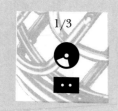

1/3

ANONYMOUS: *Christian Hymn to the Trinity* (A.D. 200)   1:30

The addition of instruments on the recording reflects Greek and Roman practices that were discontinued in Catholic liturgical music.

Between the time of the *Hymn to the Trinity* and about 1300 a supreme body of monophonic vocal music was developed and organized under the patronage of the Catholic Church. This collection of liturgical music is known variously as *plainsong, plainchant, Gregorian chant,* or by its Latin name *cantus planus.* The codification of the chant was accomplished during the pontificate of Gregory (590–604), and it is most often known by his name. The *Kyrie* from *Mass IV* is a representative example of Gregorian chant, though it probably dates from the tenth century.

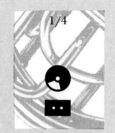

GREGORIAN CHANT: *Mass IV (Cunctipotens)*
(590–604)   *Kyrie*   2:06

This *Kyrie* became a favorite for subsequent polyphonic adaptations. See *Cunctipotens Genitor* (LG 1/6 and LG 1/7). The identification "Cunctipotens" stems from the practice (abolished in 1543) of inserting words between those of the authorized text—in this case inserting the words *Cunctipotens Genitor, Deus* (All-powerful Father, Lord) between *Kyrie* (Lord) and *eleison* (have mercy). Notation page 329.

By the ninth century a second part was sometimes added to a Gregorian melody in a type of polyphonic music called *organum.* In its most archaic form the added part moved parallel with the original at the interval of a fourth or fifth throughout, with both parts often doubled at the octave. *Sit gloria Domini,* which begins the next recorded example, illustrates this type of organum. *Rex coeli,* which follows immediately, illustrates the next step in the evolution of organum. Parallel motion prevails in the middle of phrases, but some deviation occurs at the beginning and end of phrases. As indicated, these are examples of *parallel organum.*

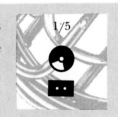

PARALLEL ORGANUM: *Sit gloria Domini/Rex coeli (850)*   :48

Both *Sit gloria Domini* (Glory be to the Lord) and *Rex coeli* (King of heaven) are from a medieval treatise, *Musica enchiriadis,* of disputed authorship.

In the next recorded example, classified as *free organum,* a second part is added above the chant melody of the *Kyrie* from *Mass IV* cited previously. The notes in the two parts sound synchronously. The intervals between them—unisons, fourths, fifths, and octaves—are approached freely by contrary, parallel, or independent motion.

FREE ORGANUM: *Cunctipotens Genitor* (1050) :53

The notation for the chant melody constituting the lower part in this example is given on page 329.

Complete rhythmic and melodic emancipation of the two parts is the distinguishing feature of *melismatic organum.* This type of organum was cultivated in southern France and the Pyrenees Mountain region between France and Spain. The following example is representative. In it the pitches of the *Mass IV Kyrie* in long, sustained notes are heard as the lower part. The motion in the upper part is quicker and more ornate (melismatic). Between the parts the choice of intervals is free.

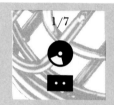

MELISMATIC ORGANUM: *Cunctipotens Genitor* (1125)   2:00

The words and the chant melody are the same in this and the preceding recorded example. Notation page 329.

For additional information regarding early Catholic music, see page 91.

Early Secular Music

During the centuries when the early development of polyphonic music was taking place, both sacred and secular music continued to be preponderantly monophonic. Secular monophonic songs were being disseminated by traveling minstrels and students in minor church orders who roamed Europe. At first the language was Latin as in the music of the church, but by the twelfth century poet-musicians were writing aristocratic poetry in the dialect of southern France and setting it to music. These poet-musicians were the *troubadours.* Raimbaut de Vaqueiras was one of the four hundred known troubadours who left a legacy of some 2,600 poems and 260 melodies. His *Kalenda Maya* was set to a dance tune played on a vielle, an important string instrument of the twelfth and thirteenth centuries.

RAIMBAUT DE VAQUEIRAS: *Kalenda Maya* (1195) :45
(died 1207)

Kalenda Maya is one of the best known and most often cited of the troubadour songs. A recording of it is included in *2,000 Years of Music*, Folkways 3700.

The *trouvères* wrote and sang songs similar to those of the troubadours but using the dialect of northern France. Hundreds of melodies and thousands of poems have been preserved in trouvère manuscripts, some of which are now available in facsimile editions. Richard the Lionhearted (1157–1199) was the most illustrious of the trouvères, but strictly as a poet-musician he was probably surpassed by Adam de la Halle, one of the last in the long succession of medieval minstrels. His most extensive work is a pastoral drama, *The Play of Robin and Marion (Le Jeu de Robin et Marion).* The dialogue and the twelve songs of the play are integrated to maintain continuity in the action. The song *Come with me (Venés après moi)* brings the play to a close.

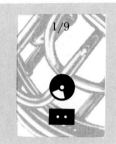

ADAM DE LA HALLE: *The Play of Robin and Marion (1284)*   1/9
(1245–1288)   *12. Come with me*   1:04

The plot of the play is an expansion of a scenario often found in the pastoral songs of the period. The shepherdess Marion is in love with Robin. She is courted and eventually carried off by a knight. Robin's attempt to save her fails, but she persuades the knight to release her. The play ends with Robin and Marion reunited and celebrating with their friends in song and dance.

Starting somewhat later in Germany, the *minnesingers* took up the practices of the troubadours and trouvères, and even some of their melodies. The Germans were less influenced by popular dance music than the French, and the style and subject matter of their songs were sometimes of a religious nature. Walter von der Vogelweide's *Palestine Song (Palästinalied)* commemorates the Crusade of 1228.

WALTER VON DER VOGELWEIDE: *Palestine Song*   :54
(1170–1230)   *(1228)*

The text of this song says, in essence: "Only now, since I have come to the place where God walked as man, do I live a true man's life." A recording and translation of the song are given in *2,000 Years of Music,* Folkways 3700.

The English produced some monophonic songs during this period, but an insignificant number in comparison with the French and Germans. By this time the English were already writing multipart music like the monumental *Sumer Is Icumen In* (see page 133).

Guillaume de Machaut (1300–1377) was a cleric, courtier, poet, and the greatest musician of his age. He composed in a wide range of forms and styles—monophonic, polyphonic, secular, and sacred. He secured a unique place in the history of music by being the first individual to write a complete polyphonic setting of the Ordinary (unchanging sections) of the Mass. The assumption that this Mass was performed in 1364 at the coronation of

Machaut

Charles V of France, whom he served, is not well founded. The entire Mass, sometimes identified as the *Mass of Notre Dame,* is recorded, and excerpts are included in various anthologies. The technical devices characteristic of Machaut's style are evident in the *Agnus Dei.* It is *isorhythmic;* that is, it has rhythm patterns which are repeated with different pitches, a common fourteenth-century practice. The harmonies sound crude to modern ears, because the principles of chord structure and progression we have come to accept were not yet formulated.

MACHAUT: *Mass of Notre Dame (1364)*

1/10

(1300–1377)   *Agnus Dei*   3:18

The first and third sections of the *Agnus Dei* have identical music. The next to the lowest of the four parts, the tenor, is a Gregorian melody for which Machaut has provided a polyphonic setting.

In the century following Machaut the procedures of polyphonic composition were refined and perfected at an accelerated rate facilitated by improvements in the system of rhythmic notation. Music history books list an array of distinguished names and achievements for this period, but the first composer whose music is apt to appeal immediately to twentieth-century listeners is Josquin des Prez (spelled various ways and alphabetized under J, D, and P).

Josquin

Josquin, as he is most often called, was born between 1440 and 1450 in the present Franco-Belgian border region. He studied in Paris and spent thirty years as a musician in the chapels and courts of Italy and France before returning to his homeland where he was provost of a cathedral until his death. He met many of the notables of his day in his extensive travels. His music was sung everywhere, and his influence was enormous. Some of his compositions still display the intricate contrapuntal manipulations typical of his predecessors, but the style for which he is remembered places greater emphasis on harmonic considerations. For the first time chord structures and progressions were consistently governed by principles that later became standard. The horizontal and vertical aspects of his music give the impression of being in perfect balance and under total control.

The *Ave Maria,* previously cited as an example of a motet (see page 207), is typical of the style found in the sacred and serious compositions of Josquin. The texture is predominantly polyphonic and imitative, though there are passages where the voices move synchronously in homophonic texture. The motet is for four voices, but much of the time only two or three of the voices are sounding. Writing for voices in pairs is a feature of Josquin's style illustrated in this ethereal Renaissance vocal music.

JOSQUIN DES PREZ: *Ave Maria (1497)*   4:38   1/11
(1440–1521)

The highly refined techniques of Renaissance motet composition are clearly illustrated in this *Ave Maria.* Overlapping melodic and poetic lines produce a continuous contrapuntal flow between structural divisions delineated by harmonic cadences. Josquin's mastery of chordal writing is particularly evident in the final section of the motet.

Music Printing

The printing of music was first accomplished during Josquin's lifetime. A liturgical book containing monophonic music was printed in 1476, just twenty-one years after Gutenberg's Bible. The first printing of polyphonic music was done by Ottaviano dei Petrucci of Venice in 1501. The publication consisted of ninety-six part-songs of which eight were by Josquin. Subsequent publications by Petrucci contained many works by Josquin. The printing of their music enhanced the reputations of composers and diffused their musical styles throughout Europe.

Prior developments culminated in the sixteenth century with a period known as "the golden age of vocal polyphony" which matched the splendor of Renaissance painting and literature. The art of creating beautiful, euphonious texture by interweaving graceful, fluid, melodic lines was developed to the ultimate degree. Sacred music fostered by the Church and secular music fostered by the courts vied for the first time on nearly equal terms. The two composers who contributed the most to vocal polyphony's golden age were Giovanni Pierluigi da Palestrina and Orlandus Lassus.

Palestrina

Palestrina (1525–1594) has been universally regarded as the greatest composer of Catholic church music for almost four hundred years. He was a choirboy from the age of seven until his voice changed. After a period of study he became an organist and choirmaster. In 1551 he was appointed maestro of the Cappella Giulia, the post he held at his death, but between 1555 and 1571 he held appointments in other churches and was for a time music director of a seminary. He and Annibale Zoilo under a decree issued in 1576 by Pope Gregory XIII prepared a revised version of the Gradual, the variable parts of the Mass sung by the choir. Though Palestrina's creative and professional life was inseparably bound with the Church, he was no ascetic. Emperor Maximilian and the court of Mantua sought his services but would not meet his terms. He was married twice, had two sons, and during the last years of his life ran a successful fur business in addition to holding a church post. He was a prolific composer. His complete works fill thirty-three volumes. His compositions, particularly the *Pope Marcellus Mass*, have been cited repeatedly as models of the purest religious style. In 1903, more than three hundred years after Palestrina's death, Pope Pius X singled out his works for special commendation in the *Motu Proprio* (written reply from the Holy See) on sacred music. The following *Kyrie*, with its free-flowing lines and triadic harmonies, is a magnificent example of Palestrina's music and sixteenth-century vocal polyphony.

G. P. da Palestrina

PALESTRINA: *Pope Marcellus Mass (1555)*
(1525–1594)   *Kyrie*   5:00

This *Kyrie* has served previously as an illustration of the *a cappella* choir medium (page 53), triad harmony (page 80), and the Mass (page 206).

Lassus

Orlandus Lassus

Orlandus Lassus (1532–1594) was an incredibly versatile composer. He wrote in the reserved style of the church and the popular idiom of the day with equal fluency, and he set Italian, French, German, and Latin texts with equal skill. He was born in the Netherlands and, like Palestrina, started in music as a choirboy. By the time he was twelve he was in the service of the Viceroy of Sicily. He held posts briefly in Milan, Laterano, and Naples and perhaps visited England and France before settling in Antwerp in 1555, the year his compositions were first published in Venice. The following year he accepted a court appointment in Munich where he remained, except for occasional journeys, until his death. He wrote in all the styles and forms of his day, and his output totals a phenomenal two thousand compositions. Emperor Maximilian made him a hereditary nobleman, but he may have been even more proud of the title conferred by fellow musicians, "Prince of Music." Two madrigals, *Matona mia cara (Matona, my dear)* written when he was only eighteen years old and *Il grave de l'eta (The burden of age)* composed thirty-seven years later, give some idea of the range of his style in this one type of composition.

ORLANDUS LASSUS: *Matona mia cara (1550)*   2:44
(1532–1594)

This delightful piece is still a favorite of madrigal singers and *a cappella* choirs. The mood of its text, which is humorous and more than a little suggestive, is captured in the musical setting. See also page 208.

A comparison of the preceding and following Lassus madrigals provides a study in contrasts, both in subject matter and musical setting.

ORLANDUS LASSUS: *Il grave de l'eta (1587)*   2:40
(1532–1594)

Lassus dedicated his last volume of madrigals to the physician who attended him during his declining years. The words by Gabriele Fiamma contain the phrases, "In the war of daily living I weaken. In vain do I search for peace or armistice."

When Palestrina and Lassus died, the golden age of vocal polyphony and the Renaissance were drawing to a close. Music was on the threshold of a new era, one that would have to suffer through its growing pains before it could rival the splendor of the past.

Pablo Picasso:
The Tragedy
(1903)
Wood, 1.054 ×
.690 (41½″ ×
27⅛″)

The Tragedy is from the early and brief blue period of Picasso (1881–1973) during which he depicted tragic figures in melancholy hues. The relatively conservative styles of art and music that prevailed in the early years of the century were superseded within a decade by revolutionary new styles—Picasso's cubism, Schoenberg's atonality, and Stravinsky's barbarism (see chapter 23).

Chester Dale Collection,
© 1992. National
Gallery of Art,
Washington, D.C.

COLORPLATE 18

Vasily Kandinsky:
Painting Number
198 (1914)
Oil on canvas,
64″ × 36¼″

Kandinsky (1866–1914) left his native Russia to study, paint, and eventually to teach and write in Germany. He was a leading exponent of abstract expressionism in which vivid colors and free-form shapes were used to evoke emotional responses without reference to representation. Expressionism in art and music (see page 271) evolved in approximately the same time frame.

Collection, The Museum of Modern Art, New York. Mrs. Simon Guggenheim Fund.

COLORPLATE 19

Grant Wood:

American Gothic (1930)
Oil on beaverboard, 76 × 63.3 cm

The American artist Grant Wood (1891–1942) was a student at the Art Institute of Chicago, where his frequently reproduced *American Gothic* is now displayed, before going to Paris and Munich for advanced study. Subsequently, while teaching at Iowa State University and directing government-funded art projects during the depression of the 1930s, he produced paintings of the rural Midwest portraying stylized landscapes and stern people in rigid poses. Wood's realistic American scenes are closely akin in spirit to Aaron Copland's nationalistic compositions (see pages 186 and 262).

COLORPLATE 20

José Orozco:
Zapatistas (1931)
Oil on canvas, 45″ × 55″

Many paintings and murals of Orozco (1883–1949) are nationalistic in the sense that they glorify the common people and causes of an emerging nation, Mexico. His vivid colors, strong lines, and insistent repetition of bold patterns have direct counterparts in the music of Spain and Latin America.

Collection, The Museum of Modern Art, New York. Given anonymously.

CHRONOLOGY

1546 Caccini 1618

 1556 Nicolai 1608

  ? Munday 1630

  1567 Monteverdi 1643

   1582 Allegri 1652

    1588 *Musica Transalpina*

    1590 Florentine Camerata

    1597 Opera

    1600 Figured bass

    1602 *Nuove Musiche*

     1653 Corelli 1713

     1659 Purcell 1695

     1660 Kuhnau 1722

     1668 F. Couperin 1722

      1678 Vivaldi 1741

      1685 J. S. Bach 1750

      1685 Handel 1759

Note: Composers and milestones of music mentioned in the text. Some of the dates are approximate.

19

THE BAROQUE
PERIOD (1600–1750)

The baroque was a period of bustling activity in science, politics, and the arts. Baroque music trailed a similar movement in painting and architecture by half a century. In keeping with the spirit of the times, it is characterized by luxuriant elaboration, grandiose concepts, and spectacular design. Theatricalism, heretofore limited to an occasional picturesque passage, became a significant trend. The period saw decisive changes in the materials, styles, forms, and mediums of music and the birth of the first great universal musical geniuses.

During the baroque era Protestant church music was established on a par with that of the Catholic church. New forms appropriate to the Protestant services evolved. The production of secular music, encouraged by the nobility and upper classes, exceeded that of sacred music. Emphasis on secular music coupled with mechanical and technical improvements in instruments stimulated the writing and performance of instrumental music. For the first time the supremacy of vocal music was challenged by instrumental music. Concurrently an independent instrumental style began to emerge. In this period melodies and harmonies were based almost exclusively on major and minor scales, which supplanted the earlier church modes. Major/minor tonality became a prime factor in musical organization. Loud and soft passages were deliberately juxtaposed, creating patterns of terraced dynamics. Rhythms became more obviously metric, and on occasion incessant streams of equal quick notes produced a sort of perpetual motion. It was, indeed, a time of change and innovation.

That the participants were aware of the revolutionary aspects of their musical activities is apparent from the title of a song collection by Giulio Caccini (1546–1618), *Nuove Musiche* (New Music, 1602), subsequently applied to the whole period and style. A revolt against the mannered polyphony of the previous age generated the impulse which led to the new music. Three basic innovations stemmed directly or indirectly from this revolt: *recitative, figured bass,* and *homophonic texture.*

Recitative was the direct outgrowth of the emphasis placed on the text of vocal music by baroque composers. To quote Claudio Monteverdi (1567–1643), ''The text should be the master of the music, not the servant.'' This was not possible in the sixteenth-century polyphonic style, because the imitative entrances and overlapping phrases made the words and syllables of the text occur at different times in the various parts. With each of four or more voices singing different syllables at the same time, comprehension of the text was impossible. The baroque solution to this problem was recitative, a sort of inflected declamation by a solo voice. This style of singing was used almost exclusively in the first operas and throughout the period in operas, oratorios, and cantatas whenever the text was of primary importance.

The recitative style was ideal for enunciating a text, but it was musically uninteresting. However, the declamatory vocal line had only to be made more lyric and continuous to produce the *solo song* and *aria,* developments which were not long in the making. Musical values were thus enhanced without reducing the text to the status of "servant." The first objective of the new music was accomplished.

This new style was conducive to a kind of musical shorthand. The accompaniment for the voice part involved no carefully prescribed lines, only a simple harmonic background played by instruments. This could be notated by writing just the bass line with numbers below it to indicate the other chord components. This type of notation is called *figured bass* or *thorough bass.* Except for the bass line, it does not indicate the specific notes to be played but does provide a basis for improvisation. The realization, that is the performance, of the figured bass part was done on a keyboard instrument, ordinarily with the bass line reinforced by one or more melody instruments. The complete realization, which customarily proceeded without interruption throughout a composition, was called *basso continuo* (continuous bass) or just *continuo.* It served both as foundation for the musical edifice and as mortar in the musical texture. Its importance can be deduced from the fact that performances were directed by the player at the harpsichord or organ, who often was the composer, who at the same time realized the figured bass part. The practice of writing out the melody and the bass, leaving the inner parts to the discretion of the performer, had the effect of polarizing interest in the outer voices. Because the use of figured bass was general in both vocal and instrumental music, the entire period sometimes is known as the *thorough bass period.*

The vertical concept of chords built over bass tones implicit in the figured bass system is diametrically opposed to the horizontal-linear concept of polyphony. Music conceived as a single, predominant melody supported by vertically ordered harmony is homophonic. *Homophonic texture* is the third basic innovation of the baroque period. The homophonic style did not supersede the polyphonic style. The two flourished side by side. Elements and passages were intermixed. A recitative and aria in the new style might be followed immediately by a fugue in the old. Elaborate polyphonic texture, both instrumental and vocal, often was provided with a figured bass part. After the beginning of the baroque the relative emphasis between homophonic and polyphonic texture varied, but neither disappeared. By 1750 the homophonic style was gaining ascendency, but the baroque era closed with the death of Bach, the greatest contrapuntalist of all time.

Inventiveness in the matter of musical form was also a baroque characteristic. The seventeenth century probably contributed more than any comparable period to the introduction and crystallization of enduring modes of musical expression. Continuous variation, sectional variation, suite, sonata, rondo, concerto, opera, oratorio, overture, chorale, chorale prelude, and fugue all were either conceived or perfected during the baroque period. While it is true that modern examples of these forms are rather different from those of the baroque, the foundations of musical organization were well defined before the period ended. Conventional plans of musical organization not anticipated before 1750 are few in number.

Opera

Opera was the first great achievement of the baroque. Several of the most characteristic features of the period were incorporated in this one composite genre. It was well suited to the exploitation of spectacular theatrical effects. Recitatives and arias were conspicuous elements. Figured bass was used consistently. Rather early the accompanying ensembles of opera were expanded to include large numbers of diverse instruments, paving the way for the future development of orchestras. Instrumental *sinfonias* before and between operatic scenes and dramatic accompaniments utilized distinctive instrumental effects and contributed to the development of an independent instrumental style. The *da capo aria,* in which the opening section is repeated at the end, became a standard pattern. Operatic finales were often continuous variations over a ground bass (constantly repeated melodic pattern in the bass). All in all, baroque opera represented a remarkable artistic achievement which strongly influenced subsequent music, nondramatic and instrumental as well as operatic.

Monteverdi

Claudio Monteverdi

Claudio Monteverdi (1567–1643) was easily the most significant of the early opera composers. Before 1600 he was well established in the court of Mantua as a viol player, singer, and composer in the old style. At middle age he turned from aristocratic chamber music to music for the stage and a wholehearted endorsement of the then revolutionary style of the rising baroque. He composed several operas between his first, *Orfeo* (1607) and his last, *The Coronation of Poppea* (1642). From 1613 until his death he was director of music at St. Mark's Cathedral in Venice, writing much church music. His genius knew no bounds. He was equally adept at writing court, church, and dramatic music, but it is in the field of opera that the striking originality of his genius is most apparent. Though one of the great innovators of music, Monteverdi was astute enough to temper the revolutionary practices of the Florentine Camerata in writing opera (see page 167) with more conventional means. He adopted the new homophonic style for the most part in *Orfeo,* but he breathed the breath of melody into his recitatives and was not disdainful of polyphony when it served his purpose.

Orfeo requires a large and varied orchestra with assorted wind, string, and keyboard instruments. The orchestra contributes to the drama in the accompaniments and supplies many instrumental interludes. The harmonic materials are unusually rich for the period and style. It is a tribute to Monteverdi's creative gifts that so mature an opera could be brought to fruition within a decade after the birth of the form. *Orfeo's* first performance under the auspices of the Duke of Mantua was received enthusiastically. Unlike the first opera which was lost and the other early operas which remained in manuscript, the score of *Orfeo* was published in 1609 and reissued in 1615, spreading the practices of the early baroque.

MONTEVERDI: *Orfeo (1607)*
(1567–1643)   *Act III. Possente Spirto*   9:00

At the point in the opera when *Possente Spirto (Powerful Spirit)* is heard, the mythical Orfeo (Orpheus) is descending into Hades hoping to rescue his dead wife. In this aria he pleads successfully with the boatman to ferry him across the river Lethe. Monteverdi provided two vocal lines for this aria—one simple, the other elaborately ornamented—with instructions to sing one of the two parts. The voice is accompanied by continuo and, except for the last section, specified instruments.

Vivaldi

Antonio Vivaldi (1678–1741) was another Venetian famous during his lifetime as a composer of operas, but now remembered primarily for his concertos, of which about 450 are extant. He began an intensive study of music with his father, who was a leading violinist at St. Mark's Cathedral, and he also prepared for the priesthood. A redhead, he was known throughout his life as *il Prete Rosso* (the Red Priest), though he served actively as a priest for only a year. Thereafter he devoted himself to music exclusively, and until the last year of his life he held a permanent appointment at the Musical Seminary of the Pietà, where orphaned and illegitimate girls were sheltered and trained in music. He played and taught violin, conducted, and served as chief administrator at the school, all the while composing profusely. Many of his works were written for special concerts and festivals at the Pietà and were first performed by the girls under his direction, but he fulfilled other commissions, enjoyed prolonged leaves, and traveled extensively. Attracted by presumably more favorable musical opportunities in the court of Charles VI, Vivaldi moved from Venice to Vienna in 1740. His genius was unrecognized there, and he died in destitute circumstances the next year.

Antonio Vivaldi

Vivaldi wrote concertos for single and multiple solo instruments, that is, for solo concerto and concerto grosso instrumentation (see page 157), with the former outnumbering the latter about two to one. The fast movements are characterized by vibrant rhythms in well-defined meters; the slow movements by singing Italianate lyricism. Drawing on his experience as a violinist and conductor, he wrote equally idiomatic and colorful parts for the solo and accompanying instruments. Typical baroque terracing of dynamic levels is achieved in two ways—by contrasting the full tutti with the solo instrument or group and by marking abrupt dynamic changes in the score. The concertos more often than not are in three movements and have a fast-slow-fast tempo scheme. The formal structures and key patterns are clear and straightforward. Ritornello form (see page 156) predominates in the fast movements, though some are fugal. The slow movements are melodious intermezzos. Vivaldi's opus 3 is a collection of twelve concertos, including both solo concerto and concerto grosso types. *The Concerto no. 6 in A minor* is representative of the solo variety.

*1/16

ANTONIO VIVALDI: *Violin Concerto in A minor* *(1712)*   8:03
(1678–1741)

1. *Allegro*		3:30
2. *Largo*		2:15
3. *Presto**		2:18

The twelve concertos of Vivaldi's opus 3 are known collectively as *L'Estro Armonico* (*The Harmonic Whim*). The first and third movements of this concerto (no. 6) are in ritornello form. The second movement is a small binary form without repeats. The three movements and the fast-slow-fast tempo scheme of this work anticipate the overall plan of classic concertos, but the form and style of the individual movements are pure baroque.

*Ritornello theme page 330.

Vivaldi was paid the supreme compliment when a number of the concertos he had composed for solo string instruments, including six from his opus 3, were transcribed for keyboard instruments by the great J. S. Bach. Bach admired the freshness and vitality of the Italian baroque style, and he was obviously influenced by the intimate knowledge of it he acquired in the process of transcribing the Vivaldi concertos. Baroque stylistic innovations were conceived and nurtured in Italy, but in music they reached their ultimate maturity and fulfillment in the hands of two composers of German birth, Bach and Handel.

Bach

Johann Sebastian Bach

Johann Sebastian Bach (1685–1750) was the most imposing member of a prodigious dynasty of musicians who established the name Bach as a synonym for musician. He was exposed to music at an early age, and his training while unsystematic was typical for the times. His first significant position was as court organist and chamber musician at Weimar (1708–1717) during which time he wrote extensively for organ. In 1717 he was appointed director of chamber music by Prince Leopold of Anhalt at Cöthen, a position he held until 1723. This period was especially rich in the production of chamber and orchestral music. From 1723 on he lived in Leipzig as organist and music director (cantor) of the St. Thomas Church and School and eventually also as director of music in the university. These duties did not require him to relinquish the title of chamber music director in the service of Leopold. He enjoyed further honorary appointments from the Duke of Weissenfels and the King of Poland, Elector of Saxony. His most significant church music was written during his tenure at Leipzig.

A cursory review of Bach's appointments and areas of activity gives little clue to the tremendous magnitude and scope of his genius. Bach's complete works, which due to many losses are by no means complete, fill forty-seven massive volumes. Practically every form, medium, and style of his time with the exception of opera and ballet is represented with incomparable masterpieces. He was a consummate master of contrapuntal technique and achieved an ideal balance between the horizontal and vertical aspects of musical texture. Coming as he did at the end of an epoch when music was on the verge of another metamorphosis, his music was not appreciated by his immediate successors or even by his own sons, distinguished musicians who continued the family tradition. Felix Mendelssohn (1809–1847) is credited with starting the Bach revival which each succeeding year heaps new tribute on his already lustrous reputation. In a poll conducted by Paul R. Farnsworth, Professor of Psychology at Stanford University, the members of the American Musicological Society ranked J. S. Bach as the most eminent composer of all time.

There is no single work which summarizes Bach's creative activity. His range was too broad and his approach too varied to be reduced to generalities and isolated monuments. This volume, as any concerned with the history or literature of music must be, is replete with references to Bach and his music. One final example must suffice for here and now, though volumes and courses devoted to a single phase of Bach's creative life leave much unsaid. The *Brandenburg Concerto no. 3* is one of six for various instrumental combinations commissioned by and dedicated to Christian Ludwig, Margraf of Brandenburg.

J. S. BACH: *Brandenburg Concerto no. 3 in G* (1721)	13:20
(1685–1750) 1. *Allegro moderato*	7:00
2. *Adagio*	:10
3. *Allegro*	6:10

This 1721 concerto, like the others in the group, is of the concerto grosso type but somewhat atypical. It has three parts each for violins, violas, and cellos, plus string bass and continuo. There is no solo group as such, but the scoring contrasts the massive sound of the entire ensemble with the lighter sound of small sections. The first movement is a ritornello form. The Adagio consists of just two chords, which may have been intended as a point of departure for the harpsichord (continuo) player to improvise a slow movement. An elaborate binary form concludes the work, a magnificent example of baroque instrumental polyphony and a prime example of Bach's incomparable contrapuntal technique.

Handel

George Frideric Handel (1685–1759) was born in Halle, Saxony, in close proximity to Bach in both time and place. If the two men had been regarded as competitors, Bach surely would emerge the victor, but their paths never crossed. Bach made a trip to Halle hoping to meet Handel, but Handel had already left for England. Artistically, too, these giants of the late baroque pursued divergent courses. Their temperaments ordained it. Bach was essentially a provincial burgher who never traveled far from his birthplace, a devoted family man who produced twenty children in two happy marriages, a man whose personal tranquillity was ruffled by bickering with local church, town, and school authorities. Handel, by contrast, was a true cosmopolitan who traveled widely and lived and worked in Germany, Italy,

George Frideric Handel

and England. He was a gregarious extrovert who fraternized with artists and persons of rank. His difficulties were with his patrons, the divas who sang his music, and with other composers who vied with him for royal favor. As would be expected, Bach's music is predominantly introspective and contemplative; Handel's is mostly dramatic and theatrical.

Overcoming strenuous parental objections, Handel obtained a broad and thorough musical training including studies in counterpoint, canon and fugue, and lessons on the harpsichord, organ, violin, and oboe. He became in turn a church organist and a violinist in an opera orchestra. While in the latter position he composed his first operas. Before he turned permanently to other forms, he wrote forty-six operas in the Italian language and style in addition to four early ones in German. After 1712 Handel lived permanently in England which placed him in the curious position of being a German composer writing Italian operas for the English. His fortunes fluctuated drastically with the taste and favor of the times. The complete disenchantment of the English with the artificialities of Italian opera brought Handel to bankruptcy. Though a crushing blow at the time, it was a blessing in disguise. With the failure of his operatic ventures, Handel turned to the form which was to assure his immortality—oratorio.

As a young composer in Italy he had essayed the form. In the full maturity of his fifties he returned to it, and though the form was no longer new, his treatment of it was unprecedented. The epic proportions of his scores, the sheer mass of his performing groups, the vigor of his music, and the eloquence of his Biblical heroes combined to overwhelm audiences. The success of his oratorios surpassed by far that of his operas, reestablished his reputation, and recouped his financial position. The greater part of his creative career was devoted to operas, but the vagaries of time and taste consigned them for nearly 250 years to the limbo of forgotten music. After a long period of neglect, some of them are again being staged, and they are receiving enthusiastic receptions by operagoers.

Handel's place in the history of music would be secure if he had written nothing but the English oratorios, but in addition to these and the operas he composed an enormous quantity of chamber music and a large number of concertos which further exalt his position. His productivity surpasses even that of Bach. The collected edition of his works with index runs to 110 large volumes.

Handel's masterpiece unquestionably is his *Messiah* (see page 212). Excluding *Messiah*, one of Handel's most familiar and most performed works, and certainly one of the most ingratiating, is his *Water Music.*

G. F. HANDEL: *Water Music* (1717)   13:50
(1685–1759)   *1. Allegro*   2:25
                      2. Air   4:25
                      3. Bourrée   :45
                      4. Horn pipe   :50
                      5. Andante   2:40
                      6. Allegro deciso   2:45

A fanciful tale persists about the origin of the *Water Music* to the effect that Handel composed it in an attempt to regain the good graces of the King. Handel was granted a limited leave by his employer, the Elector of Hanover, for the purpose of visiting England, so the story goes. Handel overstayed his leave (as a matter of fact stayed in England permanently) and was still in England when his former employer ascended the throne of England in 1714 as George I, placing Handel in an extremely embarrassing position. The truth seems to be that Handel composed some twenty-odd pieces of "water music" over a period of years for various entertainments held on barges floating down the Thames. Several suites have been made from this music, the best known of which consists of the six movements listed, arranged for modern orchestra by the eminent Irish composer and conductor Sir Hamilton Harty.

The similarities and the differences between the styles of Bach and Handel are apparent when the *Brandenburg Concertos* and cantatas of the former are compared with the *Water Music* and oratorios of the latter. These were the styles of instrumental and vocal music at the end of the baroque period.

CHRONOLOGY

1668   Couperin   1733

1714   C. P. E. Bach   1788

1719   L. Mozart   1787

1732   Haydn   1809

1735   J. C. Bach   1782

1756 W. Mozart 1791

1770   Beethoven   1827

1782   Paganini   1840

1786   Weber   1826

1791   Czerny   1857

1792   Rossini   1868

1797 Schubert 1828

20 THE VIENNESE CLASSIC PERIOD (1750–1825)

Three great names dominate the music of the Viennese classic period: Haydn, Mozart, and Beethoven. Their art did not spring full-blown from the ashes of the waning baroque. Portents of the new style were stirring more than a quarter of a century earlier in a transitional preclassic period generally designated as *rococo* or *gallant style* in France (see colorplate 10) and as *expressive* or *sensitive style* (*empfindsamer Stil*) in Germany. In the music of the rococo the majesty and pomposity of the baroque were replaced by aristocratic elegance. The ornate melodic lines typical of the rococo are illustrated in François Couperin's *Les Folies Françoises* (see page 161). The German counterpart of the rococo was more the music of the shopkeepers and merchants than of the nobility and more plain and sentimental than flamboyant. The compositions of J. S. Bach's son, C. P. E. Bach, and particularly his keyboard sonatas are representative of this style. The best elements of these French and German styles were incorporated in the music of Austria coincidentally with the revival of classic ideals.

Classicism is defined as conformity to classic principles of lucidity, simplicity, dignity, symmetry, restraint, refinement, and objectivity. In music these objectives were achieved by: (1) clarification of formal structures with emphasis on sectional homophonic forms, sonata form preeminent, (2) preference for compact, vocally inspired melodies possessing the quality of direct simplicity typical of folk songs, (3) elevation of homophonic texture to a position of dominance with extensive use of patterned harmonic motivation in broken-chord accompaniment figures, (4) employing imitative counterpoint essentially as a developmental device, abandoning contrapuntal forms, (5) giving harmonic clarity and simplicity precedence over complexity and ingenuity, and (6) consistently casting ideas in well-defined, regular phrases of four and eight measures.

Not all contributions of the Viennese classic period were directly inspired by classic ideals. Greater standardization of mediums also was accomplished during this time. The prior practice of scoring for available players in a particular court or church gave way to artistic conviction regarding suitable instrumental combinations. Toward the middle of the eighteenth century fairly uniform orchestras consisting of first and second violins, violas, cellos, basses, flutes, oboes, bassoons, trumpets, horns, and timpani began to take shape. By the end of the century orchestras with these constituents plus clarinets provided composers with a perfected and widely available medium of musical expression. The art of orchestration became an essential adjunct of composition. Basso continuo was discarded, and all of the parts in a composition were written out completely. At the same time the string quartet of two violins, viola, and cello was established as the predominant chamber music medium.

Dynamic shading became an essential feature of musical expression during this time. The terraced dynamics of the baroque typified by the alternating loud and soft passages of the concerto grosso were augmented by gradual changes from soft to loud (*crescendo*) and loud to soft (*decrescendo*), by sudden outbursts, and by moments of silence. These expressive features were introduced by a series of composers in the preclassic era who were the direct forerunners of the Viennese classic masters.

The names (Franz) Joseph Haydn (1732–1809) and Wolfgang Amadeus Mozart (1756–1791) are frequently uttered in the same breath and with the same degree of reverence. The tragic brevity of Mozart's life is illuminated by the fact that Haydn, born twenty-four years earlier, survived him by eighteen years. Influence between them was strong and mutual. Young Mozart learned much from Haydn's music, and the older Haydn learned much from Mozart. Each acknowledged his indebtedness to the other, Mozart by dedicating six string quartets to Haydn. Their personal fortunes were very different. Haydn, starting in more humble circumstances, came along early enough to benefit from the vanishing custom of a court appointment. Mozart, though intermittently attached to a church or court, never enjoyed the security of a suitable permanent appointment. Neither did he profit much from publication or performances of his works, avenues of remuneration newly opened to composers.

Haydn

Franz Joseph Haydn

Haydn's parents were amateur musicians in menial circumstances. There was music in the home, and at an early age his aptitude drew attention. From the age of five he had elementary instruction and soon was furthering his musical training while singing as a boy soprano in a church choir. When a teacher was negligent in his duty to provide instruction in theory and composition, Haydn purchased textbooks and pursued the study on his own initiative. He was dismissed from the choir when his voice changed. For the next ten years he eked out a meager subsistence playing accompaniments and giving music lessons, all the while working assiduously to perfect his own playing and composing. He was already in his late twenties when he obtained his first appointment. A short time later he joined the entourage of the Hungarian Esterhazy princes. His status was essentially that of a servant, but the position provided security and not only the incentive but the necessity for composing. His initial success was not sensational, but he never ceased growing as a composer. Gradually his fame spread throughout Europe. By the time his last patron, Prince Nikolaus, died and his orchestra was dissolved in 1790, Haydn had a pension from the estate and an international reputation. That same year he accepted an urgent invitation from the impresario Johann Salomon to perform in London. He remained there until 1792 and returned to London in 1794–95, scoring spectacular successes both times. The age of the public concert featuring celebrities to attract paying audiences had arrived, but Mozart had not lived to see it. Haydn returned to Vienna where he lived in affluence the rest of his days. Recognized as the grand master of chamber and symphonic music, he turned after hearing the Handel festivals in England to the composition of choral music, producing six great Masses and two oratorios. Though lesser known, the operas he composed while in the employ of the Esterhazys round out a career that embraced every sphere of musical activity and spanned an entire epoch. The *Surprise Symphony* is one of the twelve symphonies Haydn composed for the Salomon concerts in London.

JOSEPH HAYDN: *Symphony no. 94, "Surprise"* (1792)	21:45
(1732–1809) 1. *Adagio cantabile—Vivace assai*	7:30
2. *Andante*	5:40
3. *Menuetto: Allegro molto*	4:50
4. *Allegro di molto*	3:45

As was customary with Haydn, the otherwise brisk first movement in sonata form begins with a slow introduction. The second movement, a set of variations, contains the "surprise"—a sudden loud chord in a soft passage—about which Haydn is reputed to have said, "That will make the ladies jump." Wit and good humor are characteristics of his music. The menuetto is more rustic than courtly. Few conductors play it as fast as Haydn's marking would indicate. Literal interpretation of this tempo marking would result in a pace and mood approaching that of a scherzo. The fourth movement, in rondo form, displays the verve and sparkle expected of a Haydn finale. Also LG 2/2.

Mozart

W. A. Mozart certainly ranks as the most precocious musical prodigy of all time. His father, Leopold (1719–1787), was a violinist, author of a method for violin, and a recognized composer. He started the musical training of his son at the age of four in response to eager and intelligent interest. By the time he was six, young Wolfgang had composed little minuets and had appeared in his first public concert playing the harpsichord. When he was seven he made the first of his many foreign journeys, this one to Paris. His appearances now included giving exhibitions of improvisation in addition to playing concertos on the harpsichord and the violin. His first published compositions, four sonatas for harpsichord with violin ad libitum, were issued in Paris in 1764 when he was eight. That same year the Mozarts were cordially received in England where Wolfgang's first symphonies were written and repeatedly performed. He astounded the King with his ability to read at sight the music of contemporary composers such as Johann Christian Bach (1735–1782), son of J. S. Bach, who was then a leading musician in London. Mozart visited the music capitals of Europe in rapid succession, met most of the prominent musicians of the day, absorbed the latest styles and techniques like a sponge, turned out an uninterrupted torrent of compositions, and dazzled audiences with his performing feats. During a brief respite in Salzburg Mozart devoted himself to serious study and to the composition of his first oratorio. In 1768 he was on the road

Wolfgang Amadeus Mozart

again, visiting Vienna where he wrote his first opera and conducted a performance of his *Solemn Mass* before a large audience. After brief service to the Archbishop of Salzburg, he took leave to visit Italy. The Italian tour was undertaken primarily for the purpose of broadening his musical experience, but it turned out to be an unbroken succession of triumphs. His concerts were jammed, his compositions praised, his genius applauded, and honors were bestowed on him. In Rome Mozart wrote from memory the entire score of the nine-part *Miserere* by Gregorio Allegri (1582–1652) after hearing it only twice. At the age of fifteen his meteoric career was at its zenith.

The next year the Archbishop of Salzburg, his friendly protector, died. The Archbishop's successor was unsympathetic to the young composer and subjected him to totally unwarranted indignities. Mozart obtained a leave of absence to seek another appointment. His efforts were unsuccessful, and he returned to his unhappy position at Salzburg. The situation became unbearable, and in 1781 he resigned and settled permanently in Vienna. The wife whom he married shortly after arriving in Vienna was as improvident as he. The scanty returns from the unending stream of masterpieces that flowed from his pen and a pitifully inadequate stipend tardily granted by the emperor were squandered. Production of some of the greatest music in the entire literature, operas and symphonies which have been played untold thousands of times on programs all over the Western world from that day to this, never succeeded in raising their creator above the level of pecuniary anxiety. At thirty-five he was buried in a pauper's grave without an inkling of the untold fortunes that would be made and spent on his efforts.

Mozart's popularity reached new pinnacles on the two-hundredth anniversary of his death. All 626 of his works were performed during an eighteen-month festival at New York's Lincoln Center. The highly regarded biographical film *Amadeus*, containing extended selections of his music, was shown repeatedly on television. His complete works have been issued on compact discs by both Phillips and Sony, and his recordings sell more than those of any other classical composer.

Mozart's genius knew no limits. He is the one composer whose operas, symphonies, chamber music, and solo works are of equal monumental significance. His concertos for piano and for violin served to crystallize the form. Typical examples of his work could be drawn as easily from one category as another, but the late symphonies epitomize his mature style.

The last seven of Mozart's forty-one symphonies were composed between 1782 and 1788. Of the six (excluding number 37) that have established themselves as enduring favorites in the symphonic repertoire, three were completed in successive summer months of 1788. That three such masterpieces could have been conceived in such a short time seems almost incredible. Even more amazing is the fact that each has a separate and distinct identity, as do the three earlier symphonies of the group. Collectively, they stand as incontrovertible evidence of the depth and strength of Mozart's genius and mark a high point in the Viennese classic period. The concise symphony of 1782 displays the same mastery of technique and invention found in the later symphonies.

W. A. MOZART: *Symphony no. 35 (1782)*	19:06	1/22–25
(1756–1791) *1. Allegro con spirito*	7:59	
2. Andante	4:26	
3. Menuetto	3:06	
4. Presto	3:35	

This work was hastily composed as a serenade to be played on the occasion of Siegmund Haffner's elevation to the nobility. As a serenade it had an introductory march and two minuets. The following year Mozart eliminated the extraneous movements and transformed the work into a standard four-movement symphony. Menuetto themes page 334.

Beethoven

Ludwig van Beethoven

Ludwig van Beethoven (1770–1827), towering giant of music and third in the triumvirate of Viennese classic composers, lived in a period of political turmoil, and the dramatic social changes of the times are reflected in his music. The exalted position he occupies in the minds of both musicians and nonmusicians is due partially to the transcendental power of his musical achievements and the unquestioned authenticity of his genius and partially to the fact that he exemplifies as no other composer before or since the qualities commonly associated with the creative artist.

Beethoven, son and grandson of Flemish musicians of modest abilities who had settled in Bonn on the Rhine, began his musical training at an early age under the strict and stern tutelage of his father, who had pretensions of producing another wonderchild of the Mozartean cast. He displayed remarkable talent but nothing to rival the phenomenal abilities of Mozart. In his early teens he was assistant organist in the church, harpsichordist in the court orchestra, and violist in the theatre orchestra. He attended the public schools in Bonn and continued his studies with the local musicians. He met and elicited praise from Mozart during a short visit to Vienna in 1787. Haydn, on his way back to Vienna in 1792 after his first engagement in England, stopped over in Bonn and warmly praised a cantata by Beethoven. With this encouragement and a letter from the Elector, he left his provincial birthplace and moved to Vienna, capital of the musical world. Beethoven studied with Haydn for a time, but, being dissatisfied with him as a teacher, switched to others. At this stage of development, Beethoven evidently was not a tractable student, and the teachers were not impressed with his scholarship. He was, however, welcomed in the palaces of music-loving aristocrats of Vienna and fraternized as an equal with the social elite of the city. His genius and nobility of character were appreciated and his uncouth appearance and occasional ill manners were tolerated if not forgiven.

Beyond his youth Beethoven never held any of the positions which till then had supported composers and had elicited from them routine quotas of music for immediate consumption. His income was from sales of his works and allowances granted him by the wealthy without exacting tribute. This left him free to compose what, when, and how he pleased and if need be to wait for inspiration, an option he often elected if one were to judge by comparing his output with that of Mozart or Haydn.

But there is more to it than that. His whole manner of working was different. Whereas with Mozart whole symphonies seem to have been conceived in a flash and dashed off at blinding speed, Beethoven started with germ motives in the rough which he inscribed in a series of sketchbooks. Motives and themes often were transformed, polished, perfected and left to season before they found their way into finished works. His monuments were hewn from granite, not molded in clay. Each work is a unique entity which by compelling inner logic forges its own peculiar shape. Beethoven for the most part takes cognizance of conventional forms but strives for a higher degree of integration than his predecessors. Beethoven's form is progressive. There is little literal repetition beyond that accomplished by signs in the traditional places. Otherwise each return of a theme is projected against a different background or exposed to new and more penetrating illumination. Transitions are not perfunctory passages which merely accomplish a change of key or mood. They are occasions for additional development of thematic ideas, opportunities for unexpected modulations and harmonic experimentation. Creative imagination is ever at work in Beethoven's music. Nothing is superfluous. The musical drama unfolds in every measure. He wrote few potboilers. One has the feeling that every time he took his pen in hand it was in a deliberate attempt to create a masterpiece. With a goal so high, his percentage of successes is astounding.

All of his nine numbered symphonies remain in the repertory, as do his two independent overtures and various overtures for his one opera, *Fidelio* (*Leonore*). Opera was admittedly not his forte, but his single attempt in the form is still staged in spite of an absurd libretto. All of his piano music has been recorded and much of it, which includes five concertos and thirty-two sonatas, is programed regularly. All violinists and cellists play his sonatas for these instruments. His one violin concerto is an enduring favorite. His sixteen string quartets are paragons of the form. Considering the quality, it is a respectable list. It is strongly slanted, as was his talent, toward instrumental music. In this realm he has never been equalled. His nine symphonies have been a decisive force in shaping all subsequent development of the form. After Beethoven had composed all of his symphonies except the last, the *Eroica* was still his favorite.

BEETHOVEN: *Symphony no. 3, "Eroica" (1804)*	48:40
(1770–1827) *1. Allegro con brio*	15:15
2. Marcia funebre: Adagio assai	15:45
3. Scherzo: Allegro vivace	5:55
4. Finale: Allegro molto	11:45

In more ways than the inscription on the score, this is a "heroic" symphony. It is heroic in proportions, content, and realization. Paul Henry Lang ranks it as ". . . one of the incomprehensible deeds in arts and letters, the greatest single step made by an individual composer in the history of the symphony and in the history of music in general." One has only to compare it with Mozart's *Symphony no. 35* or Haydn's *Symphony no. 94* previously cited to grasp the magnitude of Beethoven's accomplishment and to perceive the transformation of the form within a span of one generation. This symphony is intensely dramatic, personal, powerful, monumental; terms that would scarcely be applied in the same context to any prior symphony. The music bursts the classic restraints and overflows the traditional forms. Portents of rising romanticism are evident everywhere, even in the somewhat programmatic inspiration for the work. The symphony originally was dedicated to Napoleon Bonaparte, but Beethoven tore up the title page when Napoleon proclaimed himself Emperor, betraying the ideals of equality and liberty that Beethoven held so dear. It was now a tribute "to the memory of a great man," not an individual but an immortal hero. Napoleon was not forgotten, however. When he died seventeen years later, Beethoven is supposed to have said, with reference to the second movement *Funeral March*, "I have already composed the proper music for the occasion." Also LG 2/6.

Beethoven was, in a very real sense, the end of the Viennese classic period and also the beginning of the romantic age.

CHRONOLOGY

1786   Weber   1826

1797 Schubert 1828

1803   Berlioz   1869

1809Mendelssohn1847

1810   Chopin   1849

1810   Schumann   1856

1811   Liszt   1886

1813   Wagner   1883

1813   Verdi   1901

1822   Franck   1890

1824   Bruckner   1896

1825   J. Strauss   1899

1833   Brahms   1897

1835   Saint-Saëns   1924

1838   Bizet   1875

1840   Tchaikovsky   1893

1841   Dvořák   1904

1843   Grieg   1907

1844   Rimsky-Korsakov   1908

1854   Sousa   1932

1858   Puccini   1924

1860   Mahler   1911

1864   R. Strauss   1949

1865   Dukas   1935

1865   Sibelius   1957

1873   Rachmaninoff   1943

21 THE ROMANTIC AGE (1815–1900)

In contrast with the classic era, the *romantic age* was committed to the assertion of imagination and sentiment over logic, emphasis on the personal over the universal, stress of the subjective over the objective, and the preeminence of spontaneous freedom over deliberate formality. The romantic movement in music trailed a similar movement in literature but eventually surpassed it in opulence. Music was an ideal medium for romantic utterances, and it has been referred to as *the* romantic art. In spirit, romanticism is the opposite of classicism, but the traits of one never dominate music to the exclusion of the other. It is more a matter of emphasis.

Romantic composers continued to use the forms and mediums perfected in the classic era, but in a freer and more personal manner. To these they made contributions of their own. The tone or symphonic poem, the character piece, and the art song are innovations of the romantic period molded to conform to its precepts. Music drama is a romantic version of opera.

There are no clear-cut dividing lines between periods in music. The transition from classic to romantic is no exception. Romantic elements are detected readily in works of Beethoven. Carl Maria von Weber (1786–1826), who died a year before him, and Franz Schubert (1797–1828), who died a year after, generally are considered to be the first champions of the new movement. Full realization of the romantic impulse probably was delayed by their untimely deaths. Even so, their contributions to the romantic movement were substantial.

Weber

Weber anticipated many romantic developments. He was among the first to write a large programmatic work (*Konzertstück in F minor, op. 79*), a concert waltz (*Invitation to the Dance, op. 65*), patriotic songs, and occasional pieces for the piano. He broke with the classic Italian opera traditions exemplified by Rossini (1792–1868) and founded German romantic opera, strongly influencing the ensuing music dramas of Wagner (1813–1883). *Oberon*, Weber's last opera, is replete with romantic elements, many of which are evident in the overture.

Carl Maria von Weber

C. M. VON WEBER: *Oberon* (1826)
(1786–1826)   *Overture*   9:30

On the basis of previous triumphs, Weber was commissioned to provide music for an opera to be premiered at Covent Garden in London. *Oberon*, a fairy opera in twenty-one spectacular scenes, was the result. Weber supervised the rehearsals and conducted the first twelve performances before his death. The opera played nineteen more times that season and then slipped into virtual oblivion except for the overture and an aria or two.

Schubert

Franz Schubert

Schubert's symphonies and chamber music are perhaps no more romantic than Beethoven's, but his art songs (see index) and his character pieces for piano are truly romantic expressions. It was a time of extremes—of gigantic works and miniatures. The "Great" *Symphony no. 9 in C* by Schubert is one of the former, and his little *Moments Musicaux* (*Musical Moments*) are examples of the latter.

FRANZ SCHUBERT: *Moments Musicaux* (1827)
(1797–1828)   *No. 3 in F minor*   2:00

Moments Musicaux was one of the designations Schubert used for short piano pieces of a lyrical or improvisatory nature. The third is the most familiar of the six included in the group.

The decade between 1803 and 1813 saw the birth of the first generation of full-fledged romantic composers: Hector Berlioz, Felix Mendelssohn, Robert Schumann, Frédéric Chopin, Franz Liszt, Richard Wagner, and Giuseppi Verdi.

Berlioz

Hector Berlioz

Hector Berlioz (1803–1869) had a stormy career befitting his romantic nature. He defied convention and tradition. He was ever an experimenter and innovator, so much so that most of his works were slow to win favor. His personal life was as hectic as his artistic life. He fell madly in love with an English actress and in the romantic tradition was equally miserable at first when she rejected him and later when she finally accepted him and they were married. Though Berlioz played only the guitar and the flageolet (a whistle flute), neither an orchestral instrument, he was a master of orchestration. His treatise on instrumentation is the earliest orchestration text still in print. His considerable literary talent was put to use in his position as music critic for a Paris newspaper. When he toured Germany and Italy, he reported his activities in two volumes of *Musical Travels*, and he penned the texts for some of his dramatic works. If he was a less complete musician than the masters of the previous periods, his interests ranged further afield. His most illustrious orchestral work, the *Symphonie Fantastique*, was discussed in detail on pages 164–65. More concise and equally engaging is his "ouverture caractéristique" *Le Carnaval Romain* (*The Roman Carnival*).

HECTOR BERLIOZ: *Le Carnaval Romain, overture (1838)*   8:40
(1803–1869)

Berlioz derived the music for this concert overture from his opera *Benvenuto Cellini.*
He made the adaptation for independent performance several years after the 1838
premiere of the opera in Paris.

Felix Mendelssohn (1809–1847) was born into a wealthy and influential
family. The proverbial picture of a struggling artist does not apply in his
case. He was afforded every advantage and grew up in a stimulating intel-
lectual environment. His remarkable talents were evident at an early age.
His compositions never surpassed the quality of his *Midsummer Night's Dream
Overture* which he wrote at the age of seventeen. He was a brilliant pianist,
organist, and conductor. He toured extensively and occupied several important posts. One of Mendelssohn's greatest contributions to music was
fostering the Bach revival, which has been gaining momentum ever since.
It was he who instigated the first performance of Bach's *St. Matthew Passion*
subsequent to the composer's death, and it is a tribute to his perception to
have recognized the value of this neglected masterpiece. His compositions
include oratorios on the order of Handel (see page 212), concertos for violin
and for piano, symphonies, and a quantity of piano and chamber music.
His *Songs Without Words* are not his greatest works, but they are among his
best known. Unlike some of his compositions, which are rather akin to those
of the baroque and classic composers, these character pieces clearly reflect
the romantic spirit of his times.

Mendelssohn

Felix Mendelssohn

MENDELSSOHN: *Songs Without Words, op. 67 (1844)*
(1809–1847)   *4. Spinning Song*   1:55

Mendelssohn created a new genre of piano composition with these slight, lyric piano
pieces. He wrote eight volumes of them between 1830 and 1845, of which opus 67
is the sixth. These sketches are drawn with a sure hand and with infinite charm,
grace, and sensitivity.

Robert Schumann (1810–1856) is another romanticist whose talents were
both literary and musical. His career as a pianist ended abruptly when a
device he was using to develop finger independence permanently injured
his hand. Thenceforth he concentrated on composition and literary activities. He was a founder of the music periodical *Neue Zeitschrift für Musik*
and was its editor from 1835 to 1844. The publication ardently championed liberal and progressive tendencies. Chopin and Brahms, among many
others, benefited from Schumann's perceptive and knowledgeable essays
and criticisms. His writings were potent, beneficial forces in music and
laudable examples of music journalism. The first twenty-three published
compositions of Schumann are for piano. Only later did he turn to songs,
chamber music, and works for orchestra. Though all four of his symphonies

Schumann

Robert Schumann

and several of his large works remain in the repertory, he seems to have been most at home writing in the smaller forms and for piano and voice.

Because of his literary inclination, it was only natural that Schumann should be attracted to the great lyric poets and the art song. An awareness of his personal plight provides added insight to the romantic outpouring of his songs. Schumann and Clara Wieck carried on a tempestuous courtship for several years against the strenuous objections of her father. Their love prevailed against every insidious strategy, but their marriage was delayed. The consummation of their romance opened the floodgates of his inspiration. He turned from the composition of piano music to songs and wrote about 140 within the year to inaugurate his most productive period. The eight songs of the *Frauenliebe und Leben* (*Woman's Love and Life*) cycle are included in that total.

2/13

ROBERT SCHUMANN: *Frauenliebe und Leben* (*1840*)
(1810–1856)   *4. O ring upon my finger*   3:17

The poems of the complete cycle are given in an English translation on pages 196–200.

Chopin

Frédéric Chopin

Frédéric Chopin (1810–1849) was the most highly specialized of the first-rank composers. He wrote almost exclusively in small forms for piano, but in this limited area he is supreme. His relationship to the piano character piece is similar to that of Handel to the oratorio, Mozart to the concerto, Beethoven to the symphony, and Schubert to the art song. Each made a definitive contribution to the particular medium. Chopin's brief character pieces exploit a mode of expression and an instrument which came into vogue with the romantics. Both Mozart and Beethoven played and wrote for the piano, but for the most part in a manner also suited to the harpsichord. A truly distinctive style of writing for the piano utilizing its full capabilities was born with Chopin.

Chopin's fame as a composer rests on a variety of small piano pieces of types designated with fanciful titles: ballades, etudes, mazurkas, polonaises, waltzes, preludes, and nocturnes. The ballades, of which there are four, borrow their name and to an extent their spirit from the poetic form. Chopin published two books of twelve *Etudes* (studies) each, plus a collection of three. They are studies in the sense that they include all the pianistic difficulties and harmonic effects of a revolutionary piano style, but they never degenerate into mere pedantic exercises. On the contrary, they include some of Chopin's most inspired passages. Chopin left his native Poland permanently at the age of twenty, but his Slavic origin and his romantic patriotism inspired a quantity of music. His fifty-six *Mazurkas* and twelve *Polonaises* use Polish dance rhythms. He used waltz rhythm for fourteen famous pieces. Perhaps his most popular creations are included in the cameo-like *24 Preludes*. The very name *nocturne* (night piece) is fraught with romantic suggestions, and Chopin's poetic musical language gave eloquent voice to these suggestions in nineteen pieces with that title. The *Nocturne op. 9 no. 2* is a celebrated gem from this collection.

FRÉDÉRIC CHOPIN: *Nocturnes, op. 9 (1831)*
(1810–1849)   *No. 2 in E-flat*   4:20

For an alternate example, see page 106 and listen to LG 2/11 and 2/12.

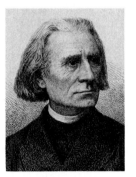

Liszt

Franz Liszt (1811–1886) was without a doubt one of the most influential figures of his time. His career was as long and varied as it was spectacular. It began in his native Hungary when he was only nine with a public performance of a difficult piano concerto and extended to his death sixty-six years later in Bayreuth. His triumphs as a pianist were rivaled by his achievements as a composer, conductor, and teacher. His tours as the greatest piano virtuoso of the nineteenth century took him to the music capitals of Europe where he circulated in the highest circles with the famous, rich, and titled. Aspiring young musicians flocked to him, and deserving ones could count on him for instruction and assistance. During his eleven-year tenure as court conductor at Weimar, it became a center for the new romantic music to which Liszt contributed prolifically as a composer. Only a few of his numerous works are programed regularly, and his popular reputation is secured by the relatively trivial *Liebestraum.* He deserves a better fate, for he has a long list of worthy compositions to his credit. His piano music is brilliant, though sometimes bombastic. His nineteen *Hungarian Rhapsodies* for piano, some of which he transcribed for orchestra, popularized rhapsody as a designation for musical works (see page 155). The twelve symphonic (tone) poems inaugurated a new form (see page 163). In these extended works for orchestra the form and content, liberated from classic restraints, are dictated in large measure by the literary programs which inspired them. The third and best known of the symphonic poems, *Les Préludes,* is Liszt's musical interpretation of philosophical concepts expressed in one of Lamartine's *New Poetic Meditations.*

Franz Liszt

FRANZ LISZT: *Les Préludes (1854)*   16:00
(1811–1886)

The following quotation from Lamartine is printed in the score:

What is our life but a series of preludes to that unknown song, the first solemn note of which is sounded by death? Love forms the enchanted daybreak of every life; but what is the destiny where the first delights of happiness are not interrupted by some storm, whose fatal breath dissipates its fair illusions, whose fell lightning consumes its altar? And what wounded spirit, when one of its tempests is over, does not seek to rest its memories in the sweet calm of country life? Yet man does not resign himself long to enjoy the beneficent tepidity which first charmed him on nature's bosom; when the trumpet's loud clangor has called him to arms, he rushes to the post of danger, whatever may be the war that calls him to the ranks, to find in battle the full consciousness of himself and the complete possession of his strength.

Opera Composers

Richard Wagner (1813–1883) and Giuseppe Verdi (1813–1901) complete the list of first-generation romantic composers. Their contributions to the romantic movement, which were primarily in the field of opera, are discussed in chapter 14. Following Wagner and Verdi, the big names in romantic opera are Georges Bizet (1838–1875) and Giacomo Puccini (1858–1924), also discussed in chapter 14.

Franck

César Franck

César Franck (1822–1890) was temperamentally more of an ascetic and mystic than a romantic, but he adopted and expanded the romantic musical resources of his predecessors and contemporaries. In spite of early promise as a concert artist on the piano and organ, he elected to follow an unspectacular career as a church organist, teacher, and composer. He lived and died in comparative obscurity, yet he exerted a powerful influence on French music. Young composers at the Paris Conservatory who objected to the dominance of opera in French music turned to Franck, who was professor of organ, for their training rather than to the regular composition classes. Many of the big names in French instrumental music received guidance from Franck, and they in turn perpetuated his ideas. Of his compositions only a small number, mostly written when he was in his sixties, are well known. The exquisite *Symphonic Variations* for solo piano and orchestra amply demonstrate his extraordinary mastery of musical organization and the eloquence of his highly personal harmonic idiom. His cyclic *Symphony in D minor* is one of the most played works in the symphonic literature. His lone sonata for violin, also cyclic in form, occupies a similar position in that literature.

*3/1

CÉSAR FRANCK: *Violin Sonata in A* (1886)		27:18
(1822–1890)	1. *Allegretto ben moderato*	6:22
	2. *Allegro*	7:58
	3. *Ben moderato*	6:52
	4. *Allegretto poco mosso**	6:06

The cyclic form (see page 146) of this sonata is readily perceived when all four movements are played in succession, because the thematic quotes from the preceding movements are unambiguous in ensuing movements. The last movement, which is included in the *Listeners Guide* recordings, contains elements of all three preceding movements and summarizes the style and content of the complete sonata.

Brahms

Johannes Brahms (1833–1897) is sometimes referred to as the classic romanticist. His temperament was romantic to the roots, but he opposed in principle and practice the unbridled fervor and the uncritical sentimentality of the ultraromantics. His romanticism was always restrained and disciplined. His musical utterances, no matter how impassioned, are confined to classic patterns. Brahms was the antipode of the extravagant Liszt-Wagner type of romanticism, and as such was championed by and champion of a rabid anti-Wagner clique. Brahms, to his credit, took no part in this and openly admired works of Wagner, particularly the opera *Die Meistersinger*. It was quite against his will that he found himself in the center of the Wagner controversy, and he was neither deterred by his adversaries nor deflected by his advocates. More than most composers, Brahms was free to compose according to his own dictates. He toured as a pianist and accompanist and did some conducting, but most of his life was devoted to composition without sponsorship and consequently without restriction. He eschewed program and dramatic music but wrote magnificently in all the absolute forms for voices, piano, various chamber groups, and orchestra. The quality of his music is of such uniform excellence that it is virtually impossible to choose between works except on the basis of personal preference. He wrote quantities of vocal music, both solo and ensemble, and a *German Requiem* in seven large sections using passages from the German Bible for the text. He is one of the few composers of the romantic period seriously and consistently concerned with chamber music. He wrote numerous sets of variations continuing and elaborating on the traditions of Haydn, Mozart, and Beethoven. His works involving orchestra, generally conceded to be his best, include two overtures, two piano concertos, a violin concerto, a double concerto for violin and cello, and four symphonies. In the realm of the symphony, Brahms inherited the mantle of Beethoven.

Johannes Brahms

JOHANNES BRAHMS: *Symphony no. 2* (1877)		39:45	*2/20
(1833–1897)	*1. Allegro non troppo*	15:36	
	2. Adagio non troppo	9:08	
	*3. Allegretto grazioso**	5:38	
	4. Allegro con spirito	9:17	

Brahms continued the symphonic traditions of Beethoven but in the musical language of the late nineteenth century. It seems inconceivable now that his profoundly emotional music ever could have been considered austere, as it was by early auditors. Adjectives like sombre, contemplative, and elegiac may be apropos for the first symphony, but the second symphony is all sunshine and light and brimming with idyllic melodies. Analysis reveals the penetrating logic of its organization, but its spontaneous beauty is on the surface for all to hear. Allegretto themes page 342.

Tchaikovsky

If any composer of symphonic music requires no introduction to the general listener, it is Peter Ilich Tchaikovsky (1840–1893). It is inconceivable that anyone has not heard some of his music, if not in the original at least in a popular version. Biographers have bared intimate details of his personal life. Tchaikovsky began the study of music very early, but none of his teachers detected signs of genius in their charge. He was trained in law and for a time worked as a clerk in the Ministry of Justice in St. Petersburg, meanwhile continuing his musical studies. He resigned his post to devote himself to music. He taught private lessons to augment his meager financial resources until he was appointed professor of harmony in the Moscow Conservatory. He traveled throughout Europe while still on the staff at the

*Peter Ilich
Tchaikovsky*

conservatory but nevertheless found the position irksome. A curious arrangement with a wealthy widow, Nadejada von Meck, eventually enabled him to resign it. She settled on him a generous annuity, but by mutual consent they never met (except once by accident). Their communication was by correspondence exclusively. The Czar granted Tchaikovsky a pension which, added to his annuity, left him free to travel and compose. He spent much time abroad and in 1891 came to America where he conducted concerts in New York, Philadelphia, and Baltimore.

Tchaikovsky is the most cosmopolitan of the nineteenth-century Russian composers and, with the possible exception of Rimsky-Korsakov, the most polished technically. The emotion of Tchaikovsky's music is more intense than profound. Consequently its appeal is more immediate than enduring. It must be that two new listeners arise to take the place of every one satiated with his music, for its popularity shows no signs of diminishing. Tchaikovsky's music was not sufficiently "Russian" for him to be grouped with the nationalistic composers of his time, but it abounds in Russian characteristics—folk songs and folklike melodies, traditional rhythms, violent and sudden contrasts of mood. He composed for all mediums, but orchestra was his forte. He was a brilliant orchestrator and fecund melodist. These virtues overbalance a rather mechanical application of structural formulas. He wrote operas, ballets, tone poems, concertos, and six symphonies of which the last three are performed profusely. Like most of the late romantic composers, he was inclined toward the classic forms. The overture-fantasy *Romeo and Juliet* is an interesting blend of classic form and romantic content.

TCHAIKOVSKY: *Romeo and Juliet* *(1880)*   19:45
(1840–1893)

This overture-fantasy has a regular sonata form with introduction, exposition, development, recapitulation, and coda. The themes and sections of the sonata form can be related to the characters and situations of the Shakespeare drama from which the work takes its name. The chorale-like introduction is descriptive of Friar Lawrence. The fiery principal theme portrays the feud between the houses of Montague and Capulet, and the subordinate theme is tender love music.

Romeo and Juliet is the earliest work of Tchaikovsky to find a permanent place in the orchestral literature. He revised it twice, and the version invariably heard is the final one.

**Strauss and
Rachmaninoff**

Several composers who were born in the nineteenth century lived well into the twentieth century but continued to write in an essentially romantic style to the end of their creative lives. Two of these were Richard Strauss (1864–1949) and Sergei Rachmaninoff (1873–1943).

Rachmaninoff was perhaps better known during his lifetime as a concert pianist than as a composer, but it is through his compositions that he is now remembered. He composed for orchestra and for voices, but the works that secure his position in the ranks of composers are the ones involving piano (see page 141).

Strauss, born into a musical family, scored spectacular successes with a series of tone poems written while he was still in his twenties. Then he turned his talent for dramatic music to opera, for which it was equally adept. His later years (after 1910) were less productive, and he never again matched his early triumphs. *Till Eulenspiegel* was composed while his creative powers were at their peak.

Richard Strauss

RICHARD STRAUSS: *Till Eulenspiegel* (1895)   13:45
(1864–1949)

The complete title of this tone poem is *Till Eulenspiegel's Merry Pranks,* to which Strauss added the annotation, "After the old-fashioned roguish manner—in rondo form." Till is a puckish character in German folklore. The composer did not provide a detailed account of the adventures portrayed in the music, but others have. Wilhelm Mauke describes it this way:

Once upon a time there was a prankish rogue, ever up to new tricks, named Till Eulenspiegel. Now he jumps on his horse and gallops into the midst of a crowd of market women, overturning their wares with a prodigious clatter. Now he lights out with seven-league boots; now conceals himself in a mousehole. Disguised as a priest, he 'drips with unction and morals,' yet out of his toe peeps the scamp. As a cavalier he makes love, at first in jest, but soon in earnest, and is rebuffed. He is furious, and swears vengeance on all mankind, but, meeting some 'philistines' he forgets his wrath and mocks them. At length his hoaxes fail. He is tried in a Court of Justice and is condemned to hang for his misdeeds; but he still whistles defiantly as he ascends the ladder. Even on the scaffold he jests. Now he swings; now he gasps for air; a last convulsion. Till is dead.

The "once upon a time" music with which the piece begins, serves as a coda and brings it to a close. The rondo form is far from typical.

In the works of Anton Bruckner (1824–1896) and by the time of Gustav Mahler (1860–1911) romanticism was already a little overripe for some tastes. Reverting to classic forms was not enough to stem the tide against it. Widespread nationalism was to revitalize romanticism for a while, but the movement which began so lustily ran its course and expended its energy like the classic period before it in the span of a lifetime. Of the late romantic compositions those by Mahler are currently most in vogue.

Bruckner and Mahler

Gustav Mahler

GUSTAV MAHLER: *Symphony no. 4 in G* (1900)		54:55
(1860–1911)	1. *Deliberately, unhurried*	17:55
	2. *Leisurely, without haste*	10:00
	3. *Peacefully*	18:10
	4. *Very leisurely*	8:50

This is the lightest, brightest, and shortest of Mahler's symphonies, though it is by no means small or trivial. A solo soprano voice introduced in the fourth movement sings a text describing the delights of heaven in childlike terms. English equivalents are given for Mahler's German tempo indications for the movements.

The composers of the period could point to solid achievements. Romantic music accounts for a large part of the current repertory, its popularity unchallenged. Its composers invented new forms, modified old ones, enlarged the orchestra, enriched the harmonic resources, and expanded the emotional range of music. Audiences increased in size. Composers were freed from bondage and obtained if not a more secure at least a more honored position in society. The romantic period was, in its own way, another golden age of music.

CHRONOLOGY

1804   Glinka   1857

1810 Chopin 1849

1811   Liszt   1886

1824   Smetana   1884

1833   Borodin   1887

1835   Cui   1918

1837   Balakirev   1910

1839 Mussorgsky 1881

1840   Tchaikovsky   1893

1841   Chabrier   1894

1841   Dvořák   1904

1843   Grieg   1907

1844   Rimsky-Korsakov   1908

1860   Albéniz   1909

1861   MacDowell   1908

1862   Debussy   1918

1862   Delius   1934

1865   Sibelius   1957

1867   Granados   1916

1874   Ives   1954

1875   Ravel   1937

1876   Falla   1946

1880   Bloch   1959

1881   Bartók   1945

1882   Kodály   1967

1882   Szymanowski   1937

1884   Griffes   1920

1887   Villa-Lobos   1959

1896   Weinberger   1967

1898   Harris   1979

1899   Chavez   1978

1900   Copland   1990

22 NATIONALISM AND IMPRESSIONISM

Nationalism and impressionism are two completely distinct musical styles that overlap chronologically. Both began in the nineteenth century and lasted into the twentieth century, but they should not be confused.

Nationalism is one aspect of romanticism, albeit a rather special aspect warranting separate consideration. Nationalist composers added a variety of dialects to the musical language of romanticism without changing its essentials.

Impressionism is the style that resulted from the reaction of French composers against Germanic romanticism. The impressionists, unlike the nationalists, rejected romantic traditions and introduced new concepts and resources. In retrospect, impressionism seems to have been a brief interlude between romanticism and the more radical styles of twentieth-century music that were to follow.

Nationalism

Rebounding from Napoleon's grandiose schemes of subjugation and domination, a wave of nationalism swept over the ethnic groups of Europe. Small groups struggling for identification and independence and large ones responding to the surge of expansion were equally enveloped. Nationalism is a sort of group romanticism. Composers were quick to seize the banner of the new movement and were active in extolling the virtues of their particular patriotism. A certain amount of geographic and political influence in the arts is almost inevitable, but the conscious cultivation of nationalistic elements was a feature of the romantic and postromantic periods.

Nationalism in music took manifold forms. It was expressed by deliberately incorporating in the musical fabric melodic and rhythmic peculiarities of a particular region. These features usually are established by and derived from the folk songs and dances of the people. The borrowing sometimes was direct, with complete folk melodies appearing intact in composed works. The process had the effect of bringing art music closer to the common folk, another facet of the romantic movement.

National heroes, folk characters, legends, epics, and myths—all were grist in the mill of patriotism. They were glorified in songs and symphonic poems. Operas were based on them. Some composers achieved enviable reputations solely on the basis of works with nationalistic pretensions. Even those not identified with the movement were not immune to its influences.

Nationalism fared better in music than in the other arts. Expressions which in prose or poetry would be blatant propaganda were interestingly exotic in music. Music dedicated to opposing ideologies was not explicit enough to be offensive. The fervent emotions of a piece like Sibelius's *Finlandia,* which might be banned in a subjugated country for inciting the people to revolt, could be appreciated by persons not partisans in the conflict. Strongly nationalistic music, far more than literature and painting, transcends geographic, political, and ethnic borders. The widespread acceptance of pieces written with avowed patriotic intent attests to this. So does the adoption of foreign dialects for specific works, as in the Spanish and Italian caprices of the Russian composers Rimsky-Korsakov and Tchaikovsky respectively.

A significant effect of nationalism in music was to challenge the dominance of music by German musicians and to hasten the demise of Germanic romanticism. In this way nationalism paved the way for impressionism and the modern era, both of which contain residual traces of nationalism.

The list of composers associated with the nationalistic movement contains many familiar names. It will be observed that most of them are from smaller countries and racial groups or from countries previously lacking a thriving indigenous musical tradition, not from Germany, Italy, France, or England.

One of the first countries to turn consciously to nationalism was Russia. Michael Glinka's opera *A Life for the Czar* (1836) was an early example. Around 1875 a group of Russian composers, subsequently known as *The Five,* banded together in a united effort to build a national musical tradition. Alexander Borodin (1833–1887), César Cui (1835–1918), Modest Mussorgsky (1839–1881), Mily Balakirev (1837–1910), and Nikolai Rimsky-Korsakov (1844–1908) were the members of the group. Borodin is best known for his opera *Prince Igor* which contains the famous *Polovtsian Dances* and is the source of the Broadway musical show *Kismet.* Cui and Balakirev are rarely played now. Mussorgsky's masterpiece is the opera *Boris Godounov,* but his *Pictures at an Exhibition* (see page 162), his symphonic poem *Night on Bald Mountain,* and some of his songs are more familiar. Rimsky-Korsakov was the least nationalistic, the most highly trained, and the most successful of the group, with a number of concert favorites to his credit including the colorful *Capriccio Espagnol* (see page 89). Tchaikovsky (1840–1893) was excluded from the group, because his music was not sufficiently "Russian," though it was permeated with Russian qualities.

Adjacent to Russia and much of the time under its domination, Poland had its own distinct style of musical nationalism. Though Frédéric Chopin (1810–1849) left his native Poland and did not return during the last half of his lifetime, a high percentage of his works reflect his intense patriotism in their Polish spirit and rhythms. Karol Szymanowsky (1882–1937), the foremost Polish composer of his time, wrote in various derivative styles before turning to the nationalistic idiom of his maturity and masterworks.

Bedřich Smetana (1824–1884), the great Czech nationalist, is remembered for his comic opera *The Bartered Bride* and for his manifestly nationalistic cycle of six symphonic poems *My Fatherland (Ma Vlast)* of which *The Moldau,* depicting the route of that river through Bohemia, is most famous. Antonin Dvořák (1841–1904) was also a Czech nationalist, but two of his most popular works, the *New World Symphony* (see page 147) and the *American Quartet,* are impregnated with American influences occasioned by his three-year stay in this country.

Hungarian elements lend an authentic ring to the Hungarian Rhapsodies of Franz Liszt (1811–1886) and more recently to the works of Béla Bartók (1881–1945) and Zoltán Kodály (1882–1967).

Spanish dance rhythms are particularly infectious, and they figure prominently in the music of Spanish composers Isaac Albéniz (1860–1909), Enrique Granados (1867–1916), and Manuel de Falla (1876–1946). Iberian rhythms have also attracted non-Spanish composers Emmanuel Chabrier (1841–1894), Rimsky-Korsakov, Debussy, and Ravel. Composers Heitor Villa-Lobos (1887–1959) of Brazil and Carlos Chavez (1899–1978) of Mexico were exponents of Latin American nationalism.

The stirrings of nationalism reached into the Scandinavian countries, and several composers of local importance imparted the flavor of the northland to their music. Edvard Grieg (1843–1907) is the name invariably associated with Scandinavian nationalism. The music of another northerner, Jean Sibelius (1865–1957), is the music of Finland as far as the outside world is concerned. Supposedly he did not use actual folk material, but his music is saturated with the moods and sounds regarded as typical of Finland, though it is he alone who made them so.

Confusion exists as to just what America's indigenous music is and just what constitutes "Americanism" in music. As soon as our musical traditions were sufficiently mature to resent the yoke of European influence, composers' interest in native resources roused. African-American music, Native American music, folk music (especially Western), and jazz were explored. Elements of all four have found their way into worthy compositions, but none has seemed to be ideally suited to a continuing tradition. Obvious folk and traditional elements have been included in serious American music only sporadically. Nationalism has been a peripheral rather than a central aspect of music in the United States, but American composers of late have declared their independence from Europe. It is no longer considered essential, as it was a few generations ago, for American composers to complete their training abroad. It isn't even the fashion. With increasing numbers of American musicians trained on their native soil, an autogenous musical tradition has emerged. Music has been composed which has an American sound. The American sound is too elusive to be defined precisely, but it is heard and recognized in the music of this country. American music has achieved identity without obvious devices, and this perhaps is the best kind of nationalism. Edward MacDowell (1861–1908) used Native American themes but never outgrew his Germanic training. Though Roy Harris (1898–1979) and Aaron Copland (1900–1990) both studied in France, they are regarded as two of the more "American" composers of their generation. The young, domestically trained composers are not as a rule consciously nationalistic in orientation.

The distinctive characteristics of each nation's music are most apparent when selections from various geographic regions are heard in succession. The suggested examples provide a panoramic view of nationalism in music, starting with Russia.

ALEXANDER BORODIN: *Prince Igor, opera (1890)*
(1833–1887)   *Polovtsian Dances*   11:35

Borodin worked on his opera for many years but never completed it. It was finished by Rimsky-Korsakov and Glazunov and given its first performance three years after the composer's death. Borodin said, "*Prince Igor* is essentially a national opera which can be of interest only to us Russians who like to refresh ourselves at the fountain-head of our history, and to see the origins of our nationality revived upon the stage." The setting of the opera is in Central Asia during the twelfth century. The Polovtsi, a Tartar race, have captured Prince Igor in the second act, and the Polovtsian maidens dance in his honor. The music for this most famous scene of the opera compounds savagery, passion, and power in music which belies Borodin's modest estimate of its worth. There are voice parts in the original, but the dances are often played in concerts with instruments taking the vocal lines.

It is unusual for a composer of the first rank to be closely identified with a particular nationalism, but Chopin is an exception. More than a quarter of his compositions are based on Polish dance rhythms, including fifty-three mazurkas of which the following example is one.

FRÉDÉRIC CHOPIN: *Mazurka no. 24 in C (1838)*   1:21
(1810–1849)

2/10

The mazurka is a Polish folk dance in triple time characterized by strong accents on the second or third beats of the measure. Themes page 338.

Bohemia, an area of modern Czechoslovakia, gained a measure of political independence from Austria in 1860. Two years later a national theater dedicated to the performance of Bohemian drama and opera was founded by public subscription. Bedřich Smetana began immediately to compose operas in the Bohemian language and imbued with the nationalistic spirit. After the enthusiastic reception of *The Bartered Bride*, the second of his eight operas, Smetana was appointed first conductor of the theater.

BEDRICH SMETANA: *The Bartered Bride, opera (1866)*
(1824–1884)   *Overture*   6:05

Excerpts from *The Bartered Bride*, and the opera itself in translation, have become international favorites. The mood of the overture and the opera is that of a festive Bohemian village.

When Manuel de Falla returned to Spain at the beginning of World War I after seven years in Paris, his compatriots suspected him of having diluted his Spanish blood with French wine. After a brief period drenching himself in the songs and dances of his native land, he silenced their doubts by composing the thoroughly Spanish ballet *El Amor Brujo* (*Love, the Sorcerer*) for the Andalusian Gypsy dancer Pastora Impero.

MANUEL DE FALLA: *El Amor Brujo (1915)*
(1876–1946)   *Ritual Fire Dance*   *3:33*

The story of *El Amor Brujo* concerns a Gypsy girl who is haunted by her dead lover. His appearance whenever she is about to kiss her new lover is frustrating the romance. The dead man, unable to resist a pretty face in life or death, is distracted during a rendezvous by a girl friend of his ex-sweetheart. The new lovers kiss; the spell is broken; the spectre disappears; and all ends happily. The *Ritual Fire Dance* from this work is one of Falla's most popular creations.

Finland came under Russian control in 1809, but it was not until 1899 when Tsar Nicholas II initiated a Russification program that intensive resistance to Russian domination fanned the flames of nationalism. Jean Sibelius's contribution to the movement was *Finlandia*. The USSR recognized Finland's independence in 1920.

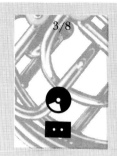

Jean Sibelius

JEAN SIBELIUS: *Finlandia,* op. 26 no. 7 *(1899)*   8:45
(1865–1957)

This work, written while Finland was oppressed by the iron rule of Imperial Russia, so inflamed the Finns that its performance was banned throughout the country. When Finland achieved independence, *Finlandia* became a symbol of triumph and freedom.

Aaron Copland's ballet *Billy the Kid* is as American as apple pie. Not only is the ballet set in the old West with a legendary figure as its central character, but cowboy tunes are dexterously woven into the musical fabric.

AARON COPLAND: *Billy the Kid (1938)*   19:35
(1900–1990)

The Open Prairie	:00
Street in Frontier Town	3:05
Card Game at Night	9:10
Gun Battle	12:50
Celebration after Billy's Capture	14:47
The Open Prairie Again	16:50

This ballet was commissioned by Lincoln Kirstein, director of the Ballet Caravan. The sections listed are included in an orchestral suite extracted from the complete ballet. Among the cowboy tunes heard in the suite are: *Get Along Little Dogies, The Old Chisholm Trail, Old Paint,* and *The Dying Cowboy.* Also LG 3/7.

Having sampled the musical dialects of nationalism, it is time to examine impressionism and its innovative features.

Impressionism

Impressionism began as an art movement. Édouard Manet was using impressionist techniques as early as 1863, but the term was first used in a derisive commentary on a painting by Claude Monet (see colorplate 15). A group of painters which included Renoir and Degas (see colorplate 16) adopted the term officially for their exhibitions starting in 1877. The impressionists, reacting negatively to the prevailing style of painting classical and sentimental subjects, used primary colors in juxtaposition to achieve greater brilliance and luminosity than was possible with the customary blended pigments. Their representation of the effects of natural sunlight blurred outlines. Minor details tended to disappear, and forms were suggested rather than defined. Spontaneous impressions were captured on canvas, not studied renderings.

The symbolist poets Stéphane Mallarmé and Paul Verlaine were kindred spirits with the impressionist painters, and like the impressionist painters they preceded and set the stage for the corresponding style in music.

Debussy

Impressionism in music and the name Claude Debussy (1862–1918) are inseparable. He was the first impressionist composer and almost the only one whose works are regarded as exclusively and purely impressionistic, but perhaps this is because his music sets the standards by which impressionism in music is measured. Debussy drew inspiration from the impressionist painters and the symbolist poets. His music, like their pictures and poems, is subtle and suggestive rather than bold and exuberant. It is sensuous but not passionate, picturesque but not graphic. Color and mood take precedence over line and structure. He was not prolific, but every page of his music is finely wrought. It includes two books of *Preludes* and numerous small works for piano, an opera *Pelléas and Mélisande*, song cycles and cantatas, a small quantity of chamber music, and a few exquisitely colored orchestral works. The quintessence of impressionism is embodied in his *Nuages (Clouds)*.

Claude Debussy

CLAUDE DEBUSSY: *Nocturnes (1899)*
(1862–1918)   *1. Nuages (Clouds)*   7:20

Nuages is the first of three *Nocturnes* for which Debussy provided the following program notes:

The title *Nocturnes* is intended to have here a more general and, above all, a more decorative meaning. We, then, are not concerned with the form of the Nocturne, but with everything that this word includes in the way of diversified impression and special lights.

Clouds: The unchangeable appearance of the sky, with the slow and solemn march of clouds dissolving in a gray agony tinted with white.

Also LG 3/5.

Debussy was not a nationalist in the usual sense, but he did regard impressionism as a French reaction to German romanticism. A clue to his thinking is provided by the way he signed his name: "Claude Debussy, French musician."

Ravel

Maurice Ravel (1875–1937) is invariably linked with Debussy as an impressionist composer. He was influenced by Debussy and impressionism, but he was no slavish imitator. His music is less fragmentary than that of Debussy, more lyric and dynamic. Precision and clarity are characteristics of his art, as it is of the French language and literature. He wrote brilliant music for piano and made equally brilliant transcriptions of some of it for orchestra, in addition to his original orchestral compositions. Among Ravel's best-known works are *La Valse,* and *Bolero* for orchestra, two piano concertos, a string quartet, *Pavane* and *Mother Goose* (see page 28) which exist in both piano and orchestral versions, and the ballet *Daphnis and Chloé* from which he derived two suites. The following example is *Suite no. 2,* the one which is most frequently programed.

MAURICE RAVEL: *Daphnis and Chloé* (1911)		15:00
(1875–1937)	*1. Daybreak*	:00
	2. Pantomime	5:15
	3. General Dance	10:45

The great Russian impresario, Diaghilev, commissioned Ravel to compose music for a ballet. *Daphnis and Chloé,* from which this suite is taken, was the result. The story, based on a Greek myth, concerns the love of the shepherd Daphnis and the shepherdess Chloé who exchange vows of love in the opening scene. Chloé is abducted by pirates and is forced to entertain them by dancing. The god Pan intercedes, and Chloé is liberated. The music of *Suite no. 2* begins just before Daphnis and Chloé are reunited. The score contains clues to the action in the ballet.

Daybreak. No sound except the murmur of dew condensing and trickling from the rocks . . . Daphnis lies sleeping before the grotto of the nymphs . . . little by little day breaks . . . the songs of birds are heard . . . shepherds seeking Daphnis find and awaken him . . . he looks about anxiously for Chloé . . . finally she appears surrounded by shepherdesses . . . the two lovers rush to each other's arms . . . Daphnis sees Chloé's crown as a sign of Pan's intervention in the abduction.

Pantomime. Daphnis and Chloé mime the adventure of Pan and the nymph Syrinx, with whom the god was enamored . . . Chloé impersonates the young nymph wandering in the meadow . . . Daphnis appears as Pan and declares his love . . . she rejects him . . . he persists . . . she disappears in the rushes . . . in desperation he picks some reeds and makes a flute on which he plays a melancholy air . . . Chloé reappears and dances to the accent of the flute . . . the dance becomes more and more animated and, spinning wildly, Chloé falls into the arms of Daphnis.

General dance. (Introduction) Before the altar of the nymphs Daphnis and Chloé pledge their troth . . . a group of girls costumed as bacchantes enters shaking tambourines . . . Daphnis and Chloé embrace tenderly . . . a group of young men enters the scene . . . joyous tumult . . . general dance . . . Daphnis and Chloé.

Impressionism was almost, but not quite, a French monopoly. The Germans were not receptive to the new style, as would be expected since it was a reaction to their romanticism, but impressionist influences can be detected in many English, Italian, Spanish, and American works written during the first third of the century. Though several non-French composers were influenced by impressionism, about the only ones classified as impressionists, and these not consistently, are Frederick Delius (1862–1934) and Charles Tomlinson Griffes (1884–1920). Delius lived in France after the age of twenty-six, so he scarcely qualified as non-French, though he was born in England of German parentage and studied music in the United States and Germany. This leaves Griffes as the one composer without French connections who can be regarded as an impressionist. The first of his *Roman Sketches* is the best known, and the fourth makes an interesting comparison with Debussy's *Nocturne* of the same title.

CHARLES GRIFFES: *Roman Sketches (1917)*
(1884–1920)

1. The White Peacock	5:20
4. Clouds	4:20

The four *Roman Sketches* originally were for piano. Griffes scored the first and last for orchestra before his untimely death. A quotation from the mystic poet William Sharp prefaces each of the sketches. The one preceding *The White Peacock* begins:

Here where the sunlight
Floodeth the garden,
Where the pomegranate
Reareth its glory
Where the oleanders
Dream through the noontides;

and ends:

Pale, pale as the breath of blue
    smoke in far woodlands,
Here, as the breath, as the soul of this beauty,
Moves the White Peacock.

The lines quoted in the score of *Clouds* are:

Mountainous glories,
They move superbly;
Crumbling so slowly,
That none perceives when
The golden domes
Are sunk in the valleys
Of fathomless snows.

Impressionism brought the nineteenth century to a close and remained as the first distinctive twentieth-century style, but other, radically different, musical idioms were in the making.

CHRONOLOGY

1872	Vaughan Williams	1958
1874	Schoenberg	1951
1874	Ives	1954
1876	Falla	1946
1880	Bloch	1959
1881	Bartók	1945
1882	Kodály	1967
1882	Stravinsky	1971
1883	Webern	1945
1883	Varèse	1965
1885	Berg	1935
1887	Villa-Lobos	1959
1890	Ibert	1962
1891	Prokofiev	1953
1892	Milhaud	1974
1895	Hindemith	1963
1895	Orff	1982
1896	Weinberger	1967
1897	Cowell	1965
1898	Gershwin	1937
1898	Harris	1979
1899	Chavez	1978
1900	Copland	1990
1906	Shostakovich	1975
1908	Carter	
1908	Messiaen	1992
1910	Barber	1981
1911	Menotti	
1912	Cage	1992
1913	Britten	1976
1914	Kleinsinger	1982
1918	Bernstein	1990

23 MODERN MUSIC TO 1950

During the first half of this century the more innovative and progressive styles of music initially suffered varying degrees of rejection, a fate shared by contemporary painting. A more normal situation would be for each generation to be most receptive to the arts and crafts of its own time, which is essentially the case in literature, drama, and architecture. It is unlikely that a novel by Dickens will turn up as a book-of-the-month club selection, that Shakespeare will replace Neil Simon on Broadway, or that baroque architecture will be revived. Unfortunately, the parallel does not extend to serious music. Plausible reasons for the persistence of older works on programs and the delayed recognition of newer music are worthy of investigation.

Conductors and performers are inclined to place the blame on audiences who presumably demand familiar music without conceding that the familiarity of the old music is the result of its having been programed in preference to new music. With the masterpieces of the past being played because they are familiar and being familiar because they are played, the chances of contemporary works breaking into the charmed circle are reduced, and practical considerations retard the process.

Modern music on the whole is technically more demanding on the players and, as with audiences, less familiar. Readying a new work for performance requires more practice and rehearsal time than the quick review needed for the standard repertory, and rehearsal time at union scale is expensive. Performance fees for works protected by copyright are not prohibitive, but works in the public domain (in this country those published before 1906) are free. In addition to these obstacles, complex modern idioms make greater demands on the perception of listeners.

The harsh dissonances, unsingable melodies, and irregular rhythms added to the musical vocabulary after the turn of the century require substantial adjustment on the part of listeners. The adjustment is complicated by the rapidity with which musical resources expanded and the inadequacy of time for assimilation. Though the disparity between the old and the new in retrospect was more apparent than real until midcentury, widespread acceptance was not immediate. It was not always so!

Before 1800 most composers were attached to a court or a church which provided a ready outlet for their latest creations. Auspicious occasions of church, court, and state were commemorated with special compositions. As a result of their institutional connections, composers had both the time and the incentive to produce voluminous amounts of music and in the process to become masters of their craft. That some of their works are enduring masterpieces is a purely gratuitous circumstance. A natural corollary of placing a premium on new works was that old ones were short-lived. The repetition of familiar favorites season after season was unknown in that period. Many compositions since rediscovered were discarded in their own time after a few performances. *The Art of Fugue* by J. S. Bach, now universally regarded as a monument of musical art, sold only thirty copies in the eighteenth century, and the plates for it were melted for their metal by Bach's sons, themselves reputable composers.

By the second decade of this century the situation was reversed. Works of the past were venerated at the expense of contemporary compositions. No one suggests consigning the music of previous centuries to oblivion, but bringing into balance the performance of newer music is not only a desirable but a necessary objective if the art is to remain a vital cultural force. The process of integrating mainstream twentieth-century music with the standard concert fare is belatedly under way, stimulated by the currency and freshness of the musical materials and styles that evolved between 1900 and 1950.

Rhythm

The rhythmic limitations observed in music conforming to fixed metric patterns and in which constant pulses are divided in prescribed ways must be regarded as arbitrary. That these limitations were honored for so long is more amazing than that they were abandoned early in this century. With rhythm exploited for its own sake, as it has been increasingly during the past ninety years, it was inevitable that rhythmic possibilities would be expanded to include asymmetric meters, shifted accents, and complex and irregular divisions of rhythmic units. The existence of duple and triple meters and pulses divided in regular fractions ultimately suggests alternating and combining duple and triple meters in various ways and dividing pulses irregularly, standard features of modern music. Accents displaced in relation to the metric organization of the music have been used for centuries but are now more conspicuous. The organization of durations according to serial procedures, found in some post-Webern (1883–1945) compositions, traces its origins back to the isorhythm (see page 226) of the fourteenth century. The principles of augmentation and diminution (increasing and decreasing rhythmic values) practiced for centuries have been expanded, updated, and systematized by Olivier Messiaen (1908–1992). He writes music with no fixed metric scheme in which certain notes in a succession of more or less uniform values are prolonged or reduced by a fraction, often by adding a dot to or withdrawing a dot from the note symbol, which increases or decreases its value by half. In the music of Elliott Carter (1908–   ) there are passages in which the tempo (pace) is systematically changed by precise degrees at small time intervals. This concept adds a new dimension to the old idea of ritardando (gradually decreasing the tempo) and accelerando (gradually increasing the tempo). Though ties between rhythmic practices present and past are readily established, learning to accept the unexpected along with the expected is the only requirement for responding to the rhythms of twentieth-century music.

Learning to appreciate contemporary melody is more of a problem. The **Melody**
concept of melody has evolved over the centuries, but in the minds of music
lovers generally the word implies a succession of tones which is singable
and easily remembered. Such a description is valid for most of the melodies
of the past and for the popular and familiar music of the day, but it is a
narrow view of melody. Melodies that are singable by untrained voices of
necessity have a restricted compass and predominantly conjunct motion.
Melodies are more easily remembered when they are based on familiar scale,
chord, and rhythm patterns, but limitations of this sort artificially inhibit
creativity in an age of freedom and unlimited resources. Composers who
give free rein to their imaginations or apply advanced principles in the creation of wide-ranging, angular, disjunct, instrumental lines free of traditional scale and chord influences are accused of writing music which is
tuneless. Such accusations should not be leveled at music containing lines
of inherent logic and beauty which do not conform to traditional concepts
of melody. The definition of melody rather should be broadened to embrace all tonal successions of inherent logic and beauty. The problem is that
the perception of beauty is largely in the eye of the beholder, and complex
logic may be incomprehensible to all but the most avid scholars. Casual
listeners therefore should approach contemporary music with an open mind
regarding the essential attributes of melody, and when they find none should
look elsewhere in the sound spectrum for the essence of the particular work.

Counterpoint, the art of combining melodies, has been renovated, but the **Counterpoint**
results have been less startling than the melodies themselves. The melodies
used in contrapuntal associations display the same characteristics as other
melodies, but the old ideal of fitting them together in a happy blend is replaced by one in which combined melodies pursue conflicting paths with
obstinate independence. When the ear is conditioned to follow the lines of
contrapuntal music, clashes between them whether momentary or perpetual do not attract much attention.

Harmony evolved slowly and systematically from the time pitches were first **Harmony**
sounded together up to the end of the nineteenth century, by which time
the most complex harmonies in common use were seventh chords consisting of four alternate scale tones. The ratios of their vibrations were relatively simple, and they blended into thoroughly agreeable sounds. Then
the evolutionary process exploded. Within twenty-five years harmonic materials were expanded to include chords of seven and more tones and the
most complex relationships possible between the twelve available notes. The
suddenness of the expansion eliminated the possibility of gradual adjustment. Before the first of these new dissonant chords had been assimilated,
newer and more strident ones were introduced. Traditional concepts of
consonance and dissonance were upended. Though the dissonant harmonies of the twentieth century are the logical culmination of evolutionary
processes set in motion when two tones were first sounded together, most

listeners were unprepared for the burst of speed at the finish. Much antagonism toward new music stems from a reluctance to accept the more complex tonal relationships as legitimate sonorities. If consonance is equated with beauty and dissonance with ugliness, then certainly modern music is not very pretty. However, if consonance is equated with repose and dissonance with tension, which is more valid, the high-powered music of this century makes that of the past seem almost idyllic. There is no reluctance on the part of contemporary composers to use any conceivable combination of tones, but most vertically conceived combinations of tones can be analyzed in terms of their relationship to conventional arrangements. Some are conventional chord structures with notes omitted or with foreign tones added. Some combine two conventional structures, and some build chords from intervals other than those found in traditional harmonies. An infinite number of sonorities are available to contemporary composers compared with a mere handful in use less than a hundred years ago. The composer's art has become more involved and the listener's art more exciting with the harmonic innovations in the first half of this century.

In the matter of harmonic progression, too, recent composers have explored new possibilities. They eschew the stereotyped harmonic formulas which abound in conventional music. Freedom of chord relationship as well as structure is constantly exploited. Dissonant chords are juxtaposed as independent entities, not bound by archaic principles of progression and resolution. Beyond this, simultaneous sounds are unordered—the product of independent linear motion, systematic procedures not primarily concerned with harmonic considerations, or coincidence. To appreciate music in the newer idioms, the composer's premises, which may reject all traditional concepts of harmony, must be accepted.

Tonality

Contemporary concepts of melody and harmony inevitably weaken the bonds of tonality. Whereas traditional music gravitates to a well-defined tonal center, tonal centers in modern music are usually vague and often nonexistent. When tonality vanishes, a primary orienting device for listeners is sacrificed. For this reason the twentieth-century styles in which some semblance of tonality is retained are more accessible. Those in which serial (twelve-tone) procedures or abstract logic is substituted for tonality present problems that can be surmounted only by familiarity with the particular idiom. Atonal (without tonality) music generated by random procedures is equally problematic for totally different reasons.

Orchestration

Most aspects of contemporary music have been the center of controversy at one time or another, but even the critics of modern music have only praise for orchestration in the twentieth century. The exploitation of instrumental color in the present century is unprecedented. Modern instruments and orchestras have reached a pinnacle of perfection, and composers have taken full advantage of newly discovered and developed instrumental resources. In this respect at least, the composers of this century have never been excelled.

All of the elements of music in combination produce musical styles. Prior to the twentieth century, musical styles could be associated with time periods, and within a given time frame a relatively high degree of stylistic consistency could be expected. This situation no longer prevails. At the turn of the century romantic, nationalistic, and impressionistic styles coexisted. The twentieth century has remained a period of stylistic diversity.

Style

Composers of the romantic persuasion updated their musical vocabularies and became *neoromantics.* Others reverted to classic ideals and became *neoclassicists. Gebrauchsmusik,* that is, music intended for practical use (implying that it is suitable for amateurs), is often cited as a phase of neoclassicism, though it could as well be classified as neobaroque. *Primitivism,* from primitive, and *barbarism,* from barbaric, are descriptive stylistic terms applied to individual works. Compositions in contrasting styles were composed concurrently, and some composers changed styles from work to work. A distinctive twentieth-century style that has attracted loyal and dedicated adherents is *expressionism.*

Expressionism is the name for the style of Schoenberg and his school. The term, like impressionism, was borrowed from painting and as in painting, the two styles are antithetical. Where the impressionists used ultrarefined techniques in naturalistic portrayals of the external world as perceived by the senses, the expressionists Pablo Picasso (see colorplate 17) and Vasily Kandinsky (see colorplate 18) expressed the subconscious, inner self in grotesque abstractions with utter disregard for reality and the traditional principles of beauty and design. Expressionism in music is characterized by fragmentation of thematic material, disjunct lines, discordant harmony, and a high degree of abstract organization. Schoenberg, Berg, and Webern were pioneer expressionists in music.

Expressionism

Arnold Schoenberg was born in Vienna in 1874. Following a distinguished if controversial musical career in Europe, he came to this country in 1933. He taught a master class at the Malkin Conservatory in Boston before settling permanently in southern California, where he acquired U.S. citizenship and Americanized the spelling of his name. In 1935 he was appointed professor of music at the University of Southern California in Los Angeles, and the next year he moved across town to a similar position at the University of California. He retired from the university in 1944 at the age of seventy but continued to compose and to teach a select group of private pupils during the remaining seven years of his life.

Schoenberg

Arnold Schoenberg

To Schoenberg must be attributed one of the most profound innovations in the annals of music. He devised a system of "composition with twelve tones related only to one another" in which conventional principles of harmony, counterpoint, and tonality are replaced by new precepts of tonal organization. Schoenberg's method is based on a series of twelve different notes in a prescribed order which establishes a pattern of intervals. This series (and its resulting sequence of intervals) is the total basis for a strict serial composition. Within the limits imposed by the series in its various guises, the composer is free to distribute the pitches and to regulate the rhythm, texture, instrumentation, and form as in nonserial compositions. The freedom is disciplined, however, for every note from beginning to end appears only in relation to its assigned position in the original series. This approach seems like a radical departure from conventional practices, but Schoenberg claimed historical precedents for it and staunchly defended it as a logical and necessary forward step in the evolution of music. In composing his *String Quartet no. 4* (see page 86) Schoenberg stringently observed his own principles of serial organization. Serial procedures prevail in *A Survivor from Warsaw*, but they do not control the pitch inflections in the part of the narrator.

SCHOENBERG: *A Survivor from Warsaw (1947)*   6:15
(1874–1951)

Schoenberg, whose gifts were literary and artistic as well as musical, wrote the text in English for this dramatic cantata for narrator, men's chorus, and orchestra. The narration is a first person recounting of the horrors experienced by a Jew during the occupation of Warsaw by the Nazis. The rhythm of the narration is notated precisely, but in lieu of exact pitches only rising and falling vocal inflections are indicated. At the climax of the narrative the chorus sings a traditional Hebrew prayer in unison while the orchestra provides an elaborate setting.

Berg

Alban Berg

Serial music, being difficult to play and to comprehend, has never attracted a wide audience, but many disciples have been converted to serial composition. Alban Berg (1885–1935) was one of the first and most distinguished composers to come under Schoenberg's influence. His mature works are atonal, but he did not follow serial procedures as consistently or rigidly as Schoenberg. An irrepressible lyricism and romanticism broaden the appeal of his music. The opera *Wozzeck*, and the *Violin Concerto* commissioned and premiered by the American violinist Louis Krasner are recognized masterpieces.

ALBAN BERG: *Violin Concerto (1935)*   23:40
(1885–1935)   1. *Andante—Allegretto*   10:20
                   2. *Allegro—Adagio*   13:20

Berg agreed to write a violin concerto early in 1934 but did not begin work on it until a beautiful young girl to whom he was deeply attached died unexpectedly. His reaction to the tragic event was to compose this monument ''to the memory of an angel'' in three months of feverish creativity. It was a requiem for her and for him. He did not live to hear the first performance the following year.

After an introduction of approximately one minute's duration, the solo violin clearly announces the twelve notes of the series in their original order starting on the lowest pitch and ascending in an unbroken line to the last note of the series in a very high register. The flavor of the series permeates the work and provides an effective if subconscious unifying element. It is not necessary or even desirable to search for evidence of the series when listening to serial music for pleasure.

Anton Webern (1883–1945), a composer closely associated with Schoenberg and Berg in the early development of twelve-tone composition, was the ultimate expressionist. His music is not as accessible as that of Berg, but it has had a greater direct influence on the younger generation of serialists. Composers like Pierre Boulez (1925–   ) and Karlheinz Stockhausen (1928–   ), who have extended serial procedures to parameters of music other than pitch (such as rhythm, dynamics, and tone color), pay particular homage to Webern. Webern's contact with Americans was brief and tragic. His son was killed in a World War II air raid, and he was shot fatally when he violated a curfew imposed by U.S. occupation troops. The University of Washington in Seattle acquired his manuscripts, which are the object of much scholarly study. The ten-minute *Symphony, op. 21* is probably a better example of Webern's mature style, but the *Three Songs, op. 18* provide a more ingratiating introduction to his music.

Anton Webern

ANTON WEBERN: *Three Songs,* op. 18 *(1925)*   3:25   3/9–11
(1883–1945)   *1. Schatzerl klein (Sweetheart, Dear)*   :59
                        2. Erlösung (Redemption)   1:05
                        3. Ave, Regina   1:21

These songs demonstrate Webern's penchant for brevity and economy of means. His music gives the impression of having been distilled to the point where only the essence remains. His texture is sparse and transparent. No masses of sound or multiplicity of lines compete with each other for attention. The problem is to perceive the thread of continuity which forges the disjointed fragments into a unified whole. When Webern conceived these songs, the principles of twelve-tone composition were newly formulated. In this, his second opus using the method, he already handles it with assurance and imagination. Translation of the words page 201.

If the expressionist movement emanating from Vienna exemplifies the break with musical tradition, the prevailing style of Russian music represents its continuation. Listening to a work of Dmitri Shostakovich, born in St. Petersburg, immediately after hearing examples of expressionist music places these contemporaneous styles in sharp relief.

Shostakovich was catapulted to instant fame by his *First Symphony,* written while he was still in his teens. A series of more progressive works aroused the ire of Soviet officialdom and put him in a position of disrepute. His *Fourth Symphony* was rehearsed but denied performance after its modernism was criticized. He quickly repudiated his sporadic ventures into "decadent modernism" and did penance with the production of works strictly in accordance with the dogma of "socialist realism." With his preeminence as a Soviet composer reestablished, he represented his country as a delegate to the Cultural and Scientific Conference for World Peace in New York in 1949. He visited this country again in 1959 as a participant in a cultural exchange program between the Soviet Union and the United States. His *Fifth Symphony,* along with the *First Symphony,* remain as the most successful of his fifteen works in the form.

Dmitri Shostakovich

SHOSTAKOVICH: *Symphony no. 5,* op. *47 (1937)*   47:39
(1906–1975)   *1. Moderato*   17:17
     2. Allegretto   4:45
     3. Largo   15:55
     4. Allegro non troppo   9:32

Upon the premiere of this symphony in Leningrad it was praised as "an example of true Soviet art, classical in formal design, lucid in its melodic and harmonic procedures, and optimistic in its philosophical connotations."

Prokofiev

Serge Prokofiev

Serge Prokofiev (1891–1953), though more progressive and cosmopolitan than Shostakovich, was influential and admired in Soviet musical circles. From 1918 until he established Soviet citizenship in 1933, he lived principally in the United States and France. His reputation was spread by international tours as a pianist, frequently playing his own compositions. His stature as a composer is predicated at least partially upon the breadth of his endeavors. He wrote in all of the conventional forms—symphonies, suites, concertos, ballets, operas, symphonic poems, piano music, and chamber music, and in addition he composed film scores and music for children. One of his most famous works, if not his greatest, is in the latter category.

SERGE PROKOFIEV: *Peter and the Wolf (1936)*   22:15
(1891–1953)

Though intended for children, Prokofiev's basic compositional techniques, somewhat simplified, are embodied in this delightful fable for narrator and orchestra. Its appeal is not limited to children. Like youth, it is almost a shame to waste it on them.

Hindemith

Paul Hindemith

Paul Hindemith (1895–1963) was a complete and practical musician. He played several instruments—the violin, viola, and piano—professionally. He was a composer, conductor, teacher, theorist, and author. His impact on twentieth-century music through his students, his writings, and his personal appearances was enormous. As a composer he would be classified by contemporary standards as a traditionalist, but his music is not old-fashioned by any stretch of the imagination. His youthful works were regarded as radical, as are the works of most young composers, but he is known as the champion of *Gebrauchsmusik* (music for practical use) and *Hausmusik* (music to be played at home). The practicality of his approach can be gathered from the fact that there are seventy-nine entries, some for multiple works, under his name in the current Schwann *Opus* catalog. He regarded composition as a craft, and he was a master craftsman. He was against atonality and serialism but not against dissonance or complexity. Critics detect in his music classic, romantic, baroque, archaic, and modern influences, which is to say that he wrote in the style that suited his purpose at the moment. His friendship with Jewish musicians brought him into conflict with the Nazi regime, and he left his native Germany the year after *Mathis der Maler (Matthias the Painter)* was composed. He concertized in this country during the late 1930s and settled here in 1940, teaching at Yale and Harvard before retiring and moving to Zurich, Switzerland, where he died.

PAUL HINDEMITH: *Mathis der Maler (1934)*   25:38   *3/12
(1895–1963)
1. *Angelic Concert*   8:00
2. *Entombment**   4:08
3. *The Temptation of Saint Anthony*   13:30

The symphony *Mathis der Maler* is taken from the semihistorical opera of the same name. The opera depicts episodes in the life of the painter Mathis Gothart Nithart, known as Mathis Grünewald, and the symphony relates specifically to three facets of the Isenheim altarpiece which he painted. The title of each movement of the symphony is taken from the subject shown in one panel of the painting (see colorplate 6). Themes of *Entombment* page 343.

Bartók

Béla Bartók (1881–1945), one of the titans of twentieth-century music, developed a dynamic, personal style which is not easily categorized. He is connected with no "ism" unless it be that of modernism. He did extensive research and publication in the field of folk music but except for a few articles did not write about art music. He taught piano but not composition. The style of his works was problematical until near the end of his career, when he adopted a more felicitous idiom. These factors contributed to the delay in recognizing the magnitude of his genius. He first toured the United States in 1927 as a concert pianist. In 1940 he came to New York, where he lived in relative poverty and obscurity until his death. Though not unknown during his lifetime, fame and remuneration commensurate with the worth of his music came posthumously. Bartók's output, just short of one hundred works, includes many arrangements of folk songs and dances, and folk influences of his native Hungary abound in the other works. Practically all forms and mediums were included in his production, with piano music and chamber music especially abundant. The one form that he never attempted was a symphony, but his *Concerto for Orchestra* is very close to a symphony in concept.

Béla Bartók

BÉLA BARTÓK: *Concerto for Orchestra* *(1945)*   36:16
(1881–1945)

1. *Introduction: Andante non troppo—*   9:48
   Allegro vivace
2. *Game of Pairs: Allegretto scherzando*   6:17
3. *Elegy: Andante, non troppo*   7:11
4. *Interrupted Intermezzo: Allegretto*   4:08
5. *Finale: Presto*   8:52

This work was written for the Koussevitzky Music Foundation in memory of Mrs. Natalie Koussevitzky, wife of the then conductor of the Boston Symphony Orchestra. It is not a problematic or experimental composition but a solid artistic achievement in the eloquent musical language of our time. Bartók provided the following program notes for the first performance:

The general mood of the work represents, apart from the jesting second movement, a gradual transition from the sternness of the first movement and the lugubrious death-song of the third, to the life-assertion of the last one. . . . The title of this symphony-like orchestral work is explained by its tendency to treat the single orchestral instruments in a *concertant* or soloistic manner. The 'virtuoso' treatment appears, for instance, in the fugato sections of the development of the first movement (brass instruments), or in the *perpetuum mobile*-like passage of the principal theme in the last movement (strings), and especially in the second movement, in which pairs of instruments consecutively appear with brilliant passages. . . .

The "interruption" in the *Interrupted Intermezzo* is a parody of an insipid theme from the Shostakovich *Seventh Symphony*. Written in Leningrad while that city was under siege by the Nazis during World War II, the symphony enjoyed a spectacular if short-lived success. Also LG 3/14.

Stravinsky

Igor Stravinsky

Igor Stravinsky (1882–1971) made his first big splash in the musical world with his ballet *The Firebird* in 1910 when impressionism was still a controversial style. *The Firebird* (see page 185) shows definite traces of impressionist influence, but within three years Stravinsky was blazing new trails. The style of his 1913 ballet *The Rite of Spring* (see pages 61 and 68) is anything but impressionistic. The descriptive labels attached to the music of *The Rite (Le Sacre)* are primitivism and barbarism. The elemental force of its throbbing rhythms and strident harmonies, not to mention its sensual choreography, shocked the staid audience at the Paris premiere and provoked a near riot. Not content to capitalize on the sensation he had created, Stravinsky turned immediately to new modes of expression, exploring unusual small instrumental combinations. These pioneering efforts paved the way for another twentieth-century style, neoclassicism. Where other composers of his generation were caught in the wake of changing styles, he was

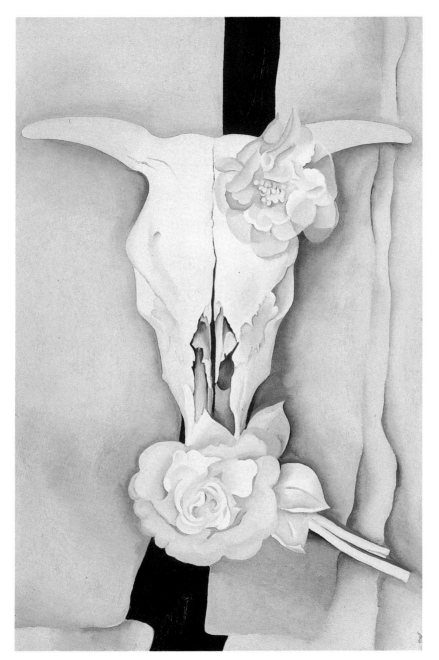

Georgia O'Keeffe:
*Cow's Skull with
Calico Roses*
(1932)
*Oil on canvas,
91.2 × 61 cm.*

Georgia O'Keeffe
(1887–1986), like
Grant Wood, was a
student at the Art
Institute of Chicago
where the paintings
of both are now
exhibited, but unlike
Wood she was
entirely American
trained, having
completed her
studies in New York
City. She was a
recognized artist and
a liberated woman
long before the
feminist movement
was organized and
the barriers to
women painters and
composers were
assailed. Feminine
touches can be
detected in her
paintings—the roses,
for example—as can
her profound
reverence for the
moods and artifacts
of the desert
Southwest where she
spent much of her
maturity and later
years.

*Gift of Georgia O'Keeffe,
1947.712 © 1992 The
Art Institute of Chicago,
All Rights Reserved.*

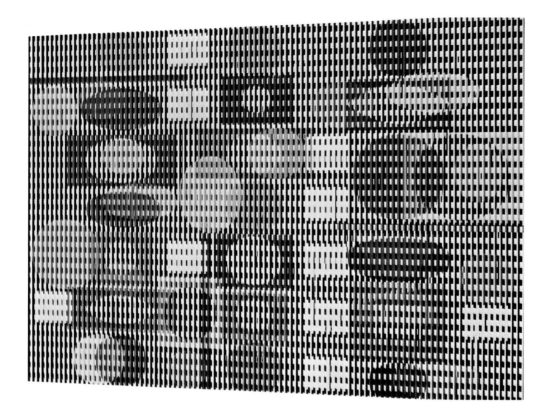

COLORPLATE 22

Agam:
Double Metamorphosis II (1964)
Oil on corrugated aluminum, in eleven parts, 8'10'' × 13'2¼''

Op (optical) art, of which Agam (Yaacov Gipstein, 1928–   ) is an exponent, surfaced as a significant movement in the early 1960s concurrently with major technical advances in electronic music.

Collection, The Museum of Modern Art, New York. Gift of Mr. and Mrs. George M. Jaffin.

COLORPLATE 23

Steve Magada:
Trio (1966)
Oil on canvas, 29" × 36"

Musicians and musical instruments have been favorite subjects for artists of all periods and styles. Steve Magada (1925–1971) was a twentieth-century painter who continued this tradition.

Virginia O. Magada.

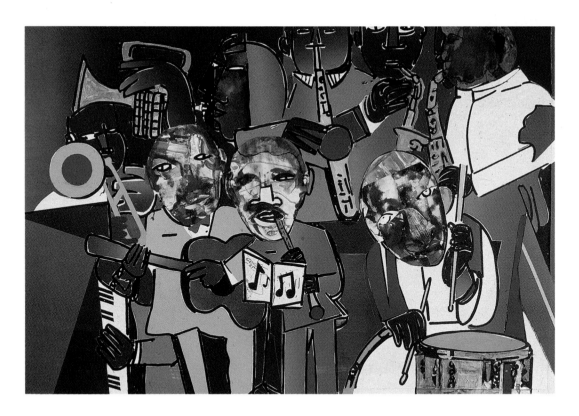

COLORPLATE 24

Romare Bearden:
Opening at the Savoy (1987)

Romare Bearden (1914–1988) began his career as a cartoonist, but he studied painting and developed a very personal cubist style. His subjects were mainly African-Americans with whom he identified and shared life experiences. The Savoy Ballroom in the Harlem section of New York hosted several innovative jazz bands in the 1920s and 1930s and was the site of the famous "battle of the bands" jazzfests.

Estate of Romare Bearden, courtesy of ACA Galleries, New York, New York.

at the forefront spearheading the changes. His creativity did not diminish or stagnate with advancing years. At the age of seventy he turned to a new (for him) style of composition employing serial procedures in a distinctly personal way. During an incredibly active and varied musical career spanning more than six decades he composed for virtually every conventional medium and invented new ones. There is no doubt that his influence on twentieth-century music has been greater than that of any other composer. Each of his many styles has attracted a legion of imitators. Like a prophet, he was without honor only in his own country, Russia, which he left in 1911. His many extended trips took him around the world, but he resided principally in France until 1939, when he moved to Hollywood. His death in 1971 brought to a close not only a spectacular career but a significant epoch in the history of music. No single work by Stravinsky can be regarded as typical or representative, but the *Octet* is a perennial favorite and, after the ballets, one of his most influential works.

IGOR STRAVINSKY: *Octet* (1923, *revised 1952*)   14:40
(1882–1971)   *1. Sinfonia*   :00
                               2. Theme with variations   4:00
                               3. Finale   11:17

The *Octet* for flute, clarinet, two bassoons, two trumpets, and two trombones illustrates Stravinsky's preoccupation with unusual instrumental combinations. The original version in 1923 was one of the first works in this century to revert to classic ideals, a philosophy which subsequently was embraced by many composers. Stravinsky provided the following program notes for a 1952 performance:

Composition, structure, form, here all are in the line of the eighteenth-century masters. Sonority has not been my first concern, and indeed, must be considered only as a result. The introduction is comparable—has an importance in the whole scheme—to the introductions in late Haydn symphonies. The *Allegro* (1) is a typical two-theme *sonata-allegro* (form) in the key of E-flat. The second movement is a theme with variations, a form which has occupied me in many works from *Pulcinella* and the *Concerto for Two Pianos, Jeu de Cartes,* to *Danses Concertantes* and the two-piano *Sonata.* In the *Octet,* however, it is the first variation which recurs rather than the theme in its original state. The final variation is a *fugato* (with added—nonstrictly *fugato*—notes) with, as subject, the intervals of the theme inverted. A measured flute cadenza modulates to the finale in C major, a kind of rondo with coda.

Also LG 3/6.

Unlike the composers discussed in this chapter who were *in* but not *of* the United States, Charles Ives (1874–1954) was a twenty-four-carat American. He traced his lineage back to Captain William Ives who came to Boston on the *Truelove* in 1635. His father, after service in the Civil War as a Union

Ives

Charles Ives

Army bandmaster, became the leading musician in Danbury, Connecticut, where Charles was born. Young Ives learned to play the drums, cornet, piano, violin, and organ and became a member of his father's band. He listened with interest as his father had the band play with sections stationed in various locations around the town and as he dabbled with experimental tunings of a many-stringed contrivance. These effects and the sounds of rural New England were absorbed and reflected in his music. "Virtually every work he wrote," according to Nicolas Slonimsky, "bears relation to American life, not only by literary association, but through actual quotation of American music sources, from church anthems to popular dances and marches." Most of the innovations of twentieth-century music—atonality, polytonality, polymeters, microtones, and tone clusters—were anticipated in his music early in the century when Schoenberg was just severing his ties with romanticism. One can only imagine what his influence would have been if his music had become known as soon as it was written instead of suffering tragic neglect. His music was too far ahead of its time from the beginning, and he was too isolated from the mainstreams of musical activity to promote it. Between 1896 and 1920 he produced a profusion of works, few of which were performed until years later. He was not, however, a starving musician. After graduating from Yale in 1898 he went into business and became a partner in a prosperous insurance agency, which gave him freedom to compose without concern for financial returns. He published his *Concord Sonata* for piano and 114 songs at his own expense and distributed copies gratis. His manuscript scores are now in the Yale library where they are attracting the attention they should have had eighty years ago. The first work of his to be issued by a commercial publisher was *Three Places in New England* in 1935, twenty-one years after it was completed and fifteen years after he had virtually stopped composing.

3/7

CHARLES IVES: *Three Places in New England* (1914)
(1874–1954)   *2. Putnam's Camp, Redding, Connecticut*   5:37

The music of Ives is not suave or sophisticated. He had no opportunity, and perhaps no inclination, to polish and perfect his technique through repeated hearings of his own works and those of his European contemporaries. Music for him was a primordial means of expression. The approach is always simple and direct, even when the means are extremely complex. Like the New England countryside, his music has a peculiar rough-hewn beauty which is sometimes sentimental, sometimes crude, but always filled with vitality. For descriptive information about all three movements of *Three Places in New England,* see page 166.

Elliott Carter

Elliott Carter (1908–   ), born in New York and educated at Harvard,   **Carter**
is generally recognized as one of the most important twentieth-century
American composers. His reputation has grown slowly but steadily over a
long lifetime. Though the bulk of the works for which he is known were
written in the last half of the century, he is not associated with any of the
types of new music covered in the next chapter. He developed a very strong,
pesonal style which is not easily described or imitated, so his influence is
not detected in the works of younger composers, though his ideas are widely
disseminated. A principal preoccupation of his is rhythm (see page 268),
and he uses rhythmic relationships as an integral factor in his structural
designs. The rhythmic devices characteristic of Carter's music are illustrated in the *Fantasy* of his *Eight Etudes and a Fantasy* for woodwind quartet
written at midcentury.

ELLIOTT CARTER: *Eight Etudes and a Fantasy (1950)*
(1908–   )   *Fantasy*   5:30

In each *Etude* a specific aspect of woodwind sound and/or technique is demonstrated. Given this emphasis, they are not representative of Carter's style. However,
elements of the *Etudes* are incorporated in the *Fantasy*, which is typical, so they should
be heard preceding it, time permitting.

In Conclusion   A point in time has now been reached when compositions written during the first half of this century can be viewed with a degree of perspective and objectivity. Some winnowing of the significant and enduring from the trivial and transient has taken place. Among the composers and works that have survived the process are an impressive number with American connections. Where the history of music prior to 1900 could have been written with barely a mention of this country, a high percentage of the important musicians since then have lived, worked, or visited here. The biographical information in this chapter highlights these events. The influx of European musicians during the Nazi/World War II period contributed to the burgeoning American music and elevated the United States to a position of preeminence among the nations of the world.

The composers discussed in this chapter are recognized giants of twentieth-century music. They reached their maturity relatively early in the century. The quantity and quality of their music and innumerable performances have earned them international reputations, and their influence on the mainstreams of recent music has been enormous. The works cited are but an infinitesimal sampling of the brilliantly conceived and executed works by a host of composers writing in these contemporary styles. Care has been exercised to assure that such works are amply represented in preceding chapters. The composers are listed in the chronology on page 266. The styles prevalent prior to 1950, while still current, can no longer be regarded as radical. That distinction has passed to a new generation of composers whose fascinating explorations are considered in the next chapter.

CHRONOLOGY

1883			Varèse	1965		
	1900		Krenek		1991	
	1900		Luening			
	1901		Partch	1974		
		1908	Messiaen		1992	
		1911	Ussachevsky		1990	
		1912	Cage		1992	
		1916	Babbitt			
		1922	Foss			
		1922	Xenakis			
		1923	Kraft			
		1925	Boulez			
		1925	Schuller			
		1928	Stockhausen			
		1930	Coleman			
		1933	Penderecki			
		1933	Subotnick			
		1934	Wolff			
		1935	Riley			
		1937	Verco			
		1937	Glass			
		1938	McLean			
		1939	Zwilich			

24

THE NEW MUSIC

Summarizing the trends in music since 1950 is complicated by the lack of perspective. Inherent in the writing of history while it is still being made is the risk of overlooking something of importance or of glorifying a transient fad, but the time is past when the musical events in the second half of this century can be ignored. The methods and materials of the present and the compositions being created right now constitute the legacy our generation will pass on to posterity. From them will emerge the masterpieces of our time and the foundations of the future. Perhaps some composer currently struggling for recognition will eventually merit a place beside Bach, Mozart, and Beethoven. This composer may come from the ranks of those continuing along the now well-marked paths discussed in the preceding chapter or perhaps from the vanguard exploring new ways and means or carrying old ones to new extremes. What is certain is that today's music is as provocative and unpredictable as tomorrow's headlines.

Certain basic trends in new music are apparent. Pitches are no longer limited to those that can be written in traditional notation and played on conventional instruments. New sound sources are being exploited, and familiar sounds are being modified in new ways. Previous stylistic traits are both revived and rejected. Homage is paid to the past in new works that in one way or another are *retrospective,* whereas romantic and postromantic opulence is sometimes replaced by stark simplicity in a style known as *minimalism.*

In the matter of musical organization two divergent trends can be detected. One is moving toward the systematic organization and absolute control of musical elements according to preconceived rational procedures. The other, striving for spontaneous expression and unlimited freedom, invokes the vagaries of chance, random selection, and improvisation. These contrasting approaches to musical organization are sometimes linked together as *system and chance music.* The new music and its pioneers are surveyed in this chapter. The categories and participants overlap and sometimes, as in system and chance music, start in opposite directions but meet on the other side of the circle.

Total Organization

Total organization in music implies the control of all elements by systematic processes. The concept is an outgrowth of the twelve-tone method of composition, but where only the pitches are governed by serial order in the "classical" twelve-tone system, the new serialism extends to other aspects of music. The variable elements subject to serial control are called *parameters,* borrowing a term from mathematics. They include rhythm (durations), tempo (speed levels), dynamics (degrees of loudness), articulation (modes of attack), density (number of parts), octave distribution (spacing), and form (structural design). As a rule the initial pitch series is transformed by some rational method into an order of values applicable to the other serially controlled parameters. The procedures vary from composer to composer and from work to work, but the possibilities that have been used include deriving the values of the other series from the notes, intervals, versions, and frequencies of the pitch series. The roots of total organization can be traced back to Arnold Schoenberg (1874–1951) and Anton Webern (1883–1945).

Milton Babbitt (1916–   ) was one of the first composers to extend the principles of systematic organization beyond the realm of pitch. In the first of his *Three Compositions for Piano* his point of departure is the usual twelve-tone pitch series, but with special properties. The series, or *set,* is constructed in a way that eliminates pitch duplications between halves (six-note segments) of certain sets, a trademark of Babbitt's music and a device on which he is an authority. He uses all four forms of the set—*prime* (original), *retrograde* (pitches in reverse order), *inversion* (intervals in opposite direction, or mirrored), and *retrograde inversion* (reverse order of inversion pitches), but only eight of the forty-eight possible pitch levels. All eight of the selected set forms are used in each of the six sections of the piece, so the set forms are a structural determinant.

In the first five sections of the work the dynamic levels are associated with the forms of the set as follows:

$$
\begin{aligned}
\text{Prime} &= \textit{mp} \text{ (moderately soft)} \\
\text{Retrograde} &= \textit{mf} \text{ (moderately loud)} \\
\text{Inversion} &= \textit{f} \text{ (loud)} \\
\text{Retrograde inversion} &= \textit{p} \text{ (soft)}
\end{aligned}
$$

In the final section the relative dynamic levels remain the same, but all are softer, leading to a fade-out at the end.

With reference to tempo, the following metronome marks are given for the composition.

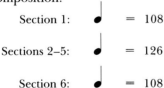

Section 1: ♩ = 108

Sections 2–5: ♩ = 126

Section 6: ♩ = 108

The return of the beginning tempo in section 6, completing an A B A pattern of tempos, corresponds with the return in the right-hand part of the section 1 left-hand line.

Babbitt constructs a rhythm series by partitioning twelve sixteenth-note units. The original form can be represented by the numbers 5 1 4 2 and the retrograde by the numbers 2 4 1 5. The inversion is obtained by subtracting the original numbers from 6, with 1 5 2 4 the result and 4 2 5 1 the retrograde inversion. The scheme is clearer in the rhythmic notation.

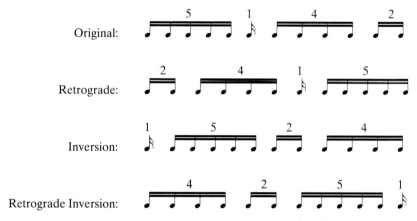

Original:

Retrograde:

Inversion:

Retrograde Inversion:

To reduce the rigidity of strict compliance with the serial rhythm, the duration of the last note of each group may be, and often is, prolonged or shortened.

Analysis of Babbitt's compositional decisions illuminates the logic of his thought processes. The impact of this logic on the aural experience of a performance is left for the listener to decide.

3/16

MILTON BABBITT: *Three Compositions for Piano (1947)*
(1916–   )   *Number 1*   1:25

This work was published by Boelke-Bomart in 1957 and is reprinted in Charles Burkhart's *Anthology for Musical Analysis.* The anthology contains information about the composition, and a detailed analysis is given in George Perle's book *Serial Composition.*

Olivier Messiaen (1908–1992) was another pioneer of total organization. In his 1949 piano composition *Modes de valeurs et d'intensités* each of the twelve notes is associated with a certain fixed duration, degree of intensity, and mode of playing.

Pierre Boulez (1925–   ), who studied composition with Messiaen at the Paris Conservatory, borrowed the pitch series from Messiaen's *Modes* for his *Structures Book I* (1952) for two pianos. The notes of the pitch series are numbered consecutively, and these numbers represent the same notes in all permutations of the series. The duration series is derived from the pitch series by multiplying a thirty-second note value by factors of 1 to 12 in order. Thus, the first note in this series has a duration equivalent to one thirty-second note, the second to two thirty-second notes, and the twelfth to twelve thirty-second notes. There are twelve degrees of intensity, likewise correlated with the numbers of the pitch series, from very, very, very soft to very, very, very loud, though only ten are used. Corresponding with the ten degrees of intensity actually used are ten modes of attack. For these four parameters each number represents a specific note, duration, intensity, and mode of attack, not a position in the series. This system of numbering enables Boulez to represent all serially controlled elements numerically and to arrange the numbers in checkerboard patterns showing all forms of the various series for reference while composing. The rational plan of organization also extends to the ordering of serial forms, determining the overall structure, and to such parameters as density, register distribution, and tempo. Unfortunately, the LP recording of *Structures* (Wergo 60011) is no longer available.

Pierre Boulez

Sestina (1957) by Ernst Krenek (1900–1991) is a perfect example of ultimate serialization. A sestina is a poetic form developed by the troubadours in which six key words at the ends of lines rotate in a prescribed pattern so that no order is repeated and all possibilities are exhausted. Krenek wrote a sestina in German as a text for his composition for voice and instrumental ensemble. His English translation of the text preserves all of the features of the sestina form. The notes by the composer on the LP record jacket (Orion 78295, now out of print) provide authentic insights to the philosophy and techniques of total organization.

According to Krenek the musical setting of his *Sestina* is based on a series of twelve tones divided in two sets of six each. The tones of each set rotate in a pattern identical with that of the key words in the poem. Durations are derived by a formula from the relative magnitude of the intervals between tones of the pitch set and additional factors. Other parameters regulated serially are density, spacing, speed, dynamics, and "other details too complex to be described here." Krenek concludes his analysis with the following statement:

Ernst Krenek

It is obvious that so complete a determination by serial rule of a sufficient number of parameters will make control of the remaining ones impossible. In an exact mathematical sense they already are ordered, as a result of the determination of the other parameters. But what happens in this remaining sector is well-nigh unpredictable (except perhaps by electronic computation), and although intentionally brought about by the composer, it is not consciously planned by him as the sector analyzed above. Therefore these happenings may be considered chance results. The paradox of ultimate necessity's causing unpredictable chance is the topic of the *Sestina*.

When ultimate control in composition is coupled with absolute precision in performance, the end result is predetermined at the moment of conception, but the nature and complexity of the procedures make the outcome and, even more significantly, the effect unpredictable. Unpredictable outcomes can also be produced by the reverse approach—by reducing or eliminating controls and introducing elements of chance, possibilities explored in the following sections.

Indeterminacy/ Aleatory

The antithesis of total organization is *indeterminacy*, a term and concept of composition associated with John Cage (1912–1992). In an indeterminate work the composer relinquishes control over the sonic events and leaves compositional decisions in large measure to performers or to chance. The absence or minimization of controls results in maximum freedom, but at the risk of creating a chaotic jumble of sound that does not qualify as music if music is defined as "organized" sound. Where music ends, noise begins, but consensus is lacking on the placement of the dividing line. The air is always full of sound, but is it music? The following "composition" by Cage suggests that he thinks it is.

JOHN CAGE: *4'33"* (1952)		4:33
(1912–1992)	*I. Tacit*	:33
	II. Tacit	2:40
	III. Tacit	1:20

According to the score this piece may be performed by any instrumentalist or combination of instrumentalists and last any length of time, but it is invariably known by the total duration of its three movements as first performed by pianist David Tudor on August 29, 1952, in Woodstock, New York. No sounds are produced intentionally. The only function of the performer(s) is to indicate in some way the beginnings and endings of the movements. Tudor did it by closing the lid over the keyboard for the beginnings and opening it for the endings. Tudor's activities can be duplicated by anyone with a stopwatch. The sounds of the piece, however, are any that occur spontaneously during the performance, and they are different on every occasion. (On Hungaroton compact disc HCD-12991)

John Cage

Granting the validity of the premise that random sounds are or can be music means that the definition of music must be broadened to include sonic events in which any and all parameters are indeterminate. John Cage is the high priest and leading expounder of this philosophy. A sampling of quotations from the descriptive notes in a catalog of his works (Henmar Press Inc., 1962) will give some idea of his *modus operandi* and provide an introduction to indeterminacy as a trend in new music.

Music for Piano I (1952) is written entirely in whole notes, their duration being indeterminate. Each system is seven seconds. Dynamics are given but piano tone production on the keyboard or strings is free. The notes correspond to imperfections in the paper upon which the piece was written.

TV Koeln (*TV Cologne*) uses noises produced either on the interior of the piano construction or on the exterior, together with auxiliary instruments and keyboard aggregates specified only as to the number of tones in them. (On Wergo compact disc WER 60157-50)

Imaginary Landscape no. 4 (1951) for 12 radios, 24 players and conductor. Kilocycle, amplitude and timbre changes are notated. Two players are required for each radio. (The sounds are those produced by the radios as the players rotate the tuning and volume knobs.)

The *Concert for Piano and Orchestra* (1957–1958) is without a master score, but each part is written in detail in a notation where space is relative to time determined by the performer and later altered by a conductor. Both specific directives and specific freedoms are given to each player including the conductor. Notes are of three sizes referring ambiguously to duration or amplitude. . . . The pianist's part is a "book" containing 84 different kinds of compositions, some, varieties of the same species, others, altogether different. The pianist is free to play any elements of his choice, wholly or in part in any sequence.

Cage suggests combining certain of his indeterminate works, compounding the indeterminacy. His *Atlas Eclipticalis* (1961) for instrumental ensemble and his *Winter Music* (1957) for 1 to 20 pianos were performed simultaneously on a 1983 concert recorded and previously available on 4-Mode 3/6.

In some indeterminate works of Cage compositional decisions are made by tossing coins and similar chance operations. In other works various procedures differing markedly in conception and realization isolate the ensuing events from the conscious control of the composer. The notation is unconventional and rarely provides more than loose guidelines for the executants, who are more than mere performers. The latitude in interpreting the guidelines can result in renditions of the same work that have little in common except the title. A work is less a product than a process renewed with each performance. Compositions in this style assume a definite form only when they are recorded, and there is a certain incongruity in a recording of an indeterminate work.

Aleatory is a term used to signify, particularly in connection with European composers and works, a type of chance music with more circumscribed operations than those associated with indeterminacy and Cage. Karlheinz Stockhausen (1928–   ) is a confirmed experimentalist who has assayed practically every new and controversial approach to composition from electronic to total organization, so it is not surprising that he has also been attracted to aleatory. The procedures employed by Stockhausen in his *Klavierstück* (*Piano Piece*) *XI* typify the salient characteristics of aleatory.

STOCKHAUSEN: *Klavierstück (Piano Piece) XI* (1956)

(1928–)	*First Version*	14:05
	Second Version	12:45

Piano Piece XI, an example of aleatory, consists of nineteen discrete sections all written on one large sheet of music paper. The nineteen sections are unified by a common germ idea—a rhythmic cell structure with fixed time units divided by characteristic note sequences. The sections may be played in any order and repeated or omitted depending on where the pianist's glance falls on the page at each juncture in the performance. The piece begins randomly with whichever section first comes into the pianist's view. At the end of each section there are performance directions regarding the tempo, dynamics, and articulation of the next section, which is also randomly selected by the chance focus of the pianist's vision. A section may be repeated once with notated variants, but not unaltered. The performance ends when the pianist's glance falls on a section for the third time. It is apparent from these performance instructions that an infinite number of dissimilar versions of *Piano Piece XI* are possible. Two are recorded by Bernhard Wambach on Koch Schwann CD 310 009 H1.

Terry Riley (1935–   ) has demonstrated that the principles of aleatory can be applied in works for large and indeterminate groups of performers. His highly publicized *In C* is for any number and kind of instruments, but the more players, the better. All performers read from identical parts consisting of fifty-three fragments, each one played in strict order but repeated *ad infinitum.* The one exception is the constant pulse (C's) played in the top two octaves of a grand piano by a beautiful girl. Once the pulse is established, the performers individually determine when to enter with the first figure and how many times to repeat it and each ensuing figure. When the last figure is reached, it is repeated until the entire ensemble arrives at figure 53 and is playing it together in unison. The players then drop out gradually until only the pulse is left, sounding alone for a few moments after the rest of the ensemble is finished.

TERRY RILEY: *In C* *(1964)*   Duration variable
(1935–   )

Each of the current CD recordings of this work (Argo 430380-2 ZH, CBS MK-7178, and Celestial Harmonies 13026-2) has a different duration, as does every performance. Riley indicates that performances often last over an hour, with each figure repeated for a minute or more, and that performances could last days, months, or a year! A duration much beyond an hour would seem to be more of a philosophical concept than a practical reality. Anyone who has experienced (endured?) a performance will probably agree that an hour of C major is a great sufficiency.

Riley's *In C* is somewhat arbitrarily placed in the aleatory category, but this is not to suggest that is is lacking in other attributes. A risk of considering different aspects of music separately is that overlapping characteristics tend to be overlooked or ignored. For instance, Riley's directions for *In C* permit the rotation of elements in the figures like the rotation of elements in certain totally organized serial works. Its repetitiousness is reminiscent of minimalism (see page 298), and it is retrospective (see page 270) in its tonality—C major—and its incipient canonic form.

To the extent a composer's score, no matter how vague or permissive the notation, determines the musical activities, performers function as interpreters. Projecting their own creativity becomes a primary concern of performers only in improvisation.

Group Improvisation

Improvisation can be defined as the art of performing music spontaneously without the assistance of notation or memory. Solo improvisation has existed in music since its beginnings. Bach, Handel, Mozart, and Beethoven were renowned improvisers, and improvising is the stock-in-trade of every jazz musician. The affinity between indeterminacy and improvisation is obvious, as are the differences. In both, the work materializes at the moment of performance, but performers are guided in the former by external elements or processes. In the latter, performers follow their own creative instincts and utilize their full technical and musical resources in a unified composer-performer role. Predetermined elements may serve as points of departure for improvisation. In jazz the spontaneously improvised melodic lines usually reflect the form and harmonic progressions of a familiar song (except in free jazz). The type of improvisation that attracts avant-garde musicians is that in which preexistent elements are minimal. Improvisation in its purest state has no composer, and there is no composition independent of the performance. Each beginning and ending frames a new work or version which has never existed before and never will again. Permanency is achieved only when an improvised performance is captured on a recording.

The Improvisation Chamber Ensemble founded by Lukas Foss in 1957 practiced a type of improvisation which, as the name implies, was more akin to classical chamber music than to jazz. Their approach was to chart a formal or textural plan from which individual guide-sheets for the four instruments of the ensemble (piano, clarinet, percussion, and cello) were extracted. Any predetermined pitch patterns were notated on the guide-sheets, and at designated points the role of each performer—such as to lead, respond, or support—was assigned. The members rehearsed as a group to improve their improvisational skills and their ability to interact effectively with each other in joint creative ventures. Repeated improvisations from the same chart tended to evolve and stabilize but never to become mere rote repetitions. Serendipitous moments, invented by the players but not planned, were highlights of the performances. The Improvisation Chamber Ensemble is no longer active, but it can still be heard in the interludes of the *Time Cycle* recording.

Lukas Foss

LUKAS FOSS: *Time Cycle* (1960)		30:30
(1922–)	1. *We're Late*	3:50
	Improvised Interlude No. 1	2:20
	2. *When the Bells Justle*	5:00
	Improvised Interlude No. 2	4:50
	3. *Sechzehnter Jänur (January 16)*	5:45
	Improvised Interlude No. 3	3:05
	4. *O Mensch, gib Acht*	5:40
	(O Man! Take Heed!)	

Sections for the improvisation ensemble alternate with sections for soprano and orchestra. The two groups never play together. The improvised interludes contrast with the composed movements in which serial devices are combined with complex contrapuntal procedures in a highly organized but transparent texture. The four composed movements are unified by a common chord (C-sharp, A, B, D-sharp) and by a common literary theme (time, clocks, bells) but otherwise are unrelated. (On CRS-8219)

As previously stated, improvisation is the stock-in-trade of every jazz musician. However, jazz improvisation generally implies extemporaneous elaboration on the melody, harmony, and form of a familiar song. With the harmony and form intact, the improvisations become, in effect, variations on a theme. This analogy does not apply to *free jazz*, a term ascribed to Ornette Coleman (1930–   ) and used by him for an extended composition.

The free jazz approach to improvisation has much in common with that of the Improvisation Chamber Ensemble. There is no fixed form or pattern of chord changes, but there is advance planning and preparation for performances and some notation or memorization of thematic motives. Otherwise, the occasional playing *in unison* (at the same time and pitch) would not be possible. The distinctive jazz features are the rhythm, style, and instrumentation. A high intensity jazz beat is prominent, and the background of the players in traditional jazz styles is evident in their free improvisation. Typical, and some atypical, instruments of jazz are used in small combos. Piano and guitar are sometimes excluded, because their harmonic function does not exist in free jazz. The ensemble for Coleman's *Free Jazz* is unusually large—alto saxophone (Coleman), two trumpets, bass clarinet, two basses (playing plucked and bowed), and two sets of drums.

ORNETTE COLEMAN: *Free Jazz (1960)*   36:00
(1930–   )   *Excerpt*   10:03

The complete recording is on Atlantic 1364-2. The excerpt is included in the *Smithsonian Collection of Classic Jazz,* revised edition.

Coleman continues to explore new directions in jazz and has codified his recent thinking in his "harmolodic theory." This theory guides the improvisation of the melodic lines and the resulting harmonic texture in his 1985 recording (with Pat Metheny) of *Song X.*

Improvisation, one of the older but still viable approaches to music making, is essentially an intuitive and irrational art. One of the newer approaches to composition, conversely, is predicated entirely upon logic and reason.

Formalized Music

Music produced by compositional processes governed by abstract logic is classified by Iannis Xenakis (1922–   ) as *formalized music.* In his book *Formalized Music: Thought and Mathematics in Composition* (Indiana University Press, 1971; revised edition, Pendragon Press, 1992) he describes his revolutionary theories in detail. His investigations have led to a sort of abstraction and formalization of compositional processes. He explains in mathematical terms the logical causes of sound sensations and their uses in wanted constructions and attempts to give the art of music a reasoned support less perishable than the impulse of the moment. For his purposes the qualifications "beautiful" and "ugly" are irrelevant. The quantity of intelligence conveyed by the sounds is the true criterion of their validity. He denounces linear thought (polyphony) and perceives contradictions in serial music. In their place he proposes "a world of sound-masses, vast groups of sound-events, clouds, and galaxies governed by new characteristics such as density, degree of order, and rate of change, which require definitions and realizations using probability theory."

Xenakis is of the opinion that existing concert halls are unsuitable for present-day music and that a new kind of architecture, a field in which he has worked, should be devised. In the meantime he suggests performing works like his symbolic *Terretektorh* in a large ballroom from which all possible aural and visual obstructions have been removed and where the listeners are free to move about or sit on portable stools. According to his directions the ninety members of the orchestra are to be scattered quasi-stochastically throughout the hall, each seated on an individual dais. This distribution of the players brings a radically new kinetic conception to music and, in his opinion, combined with the mobility of the audience enriches the composition in both spatial dimension and movement. Variable speeds and accelerations of sound movement are realized. The composition is thus a "sonotron," to quote Xenakis, "an accelerator of sonorous particles, a disintegrator of sonorous masses, a synthesizer. It puts the sound and the music all around the listener and close up to him. It tears down the psychological and auditive curtain that separates him from the players when positioned far off and on a pedestal, itself frequently enough placed inside a box." It is obvious that the spatial concepts of Xenakis cannot be adequately recorded or reproduced by existing means, but opportunities to hear his orchestral works in live performances that comply with his directions are rare. For the foreseeable future most listeners will experience them only in their recorded versions.

Iannis Xenakis

In his music Xenakis utilizes sounds from all sources or, in his words, all classes of sonic elements—vocal, instrumental, concrète (microphone collected), electronic (synthesized), and digital (computer generated). When writing for conventional instruments, his usual procedure is to represent the mathematical operations graphically and then to transcribe the graphs into staff notation. In his *Formalized Music* Xenakis gives the mathematical formula used to plot the graphs from which the conventional notation was derived for his *Pithoprakta*. Illustrations in the book show a sample graph and its transcription.

IANNIS XENAKIS: *Pithoprakta* (1956)   8:10
(1922–   )

Pithoprakta is scored for forty-six string instruments—twelve first violins, twelve second violins, eight violas, eight cellos, and six basses—each with an individual part. The parts are transcriptions of jagged lines generated by a mathematical formula and drawn on a graph where speed and pitch are represented proportionally. (On Chant du Monde compact disc LDC-278368)

In the revised edition of *Formalized Music,* added material examines recent breakthroughs in music theory and includes original computer programs illustrating newly proposed methods of composition. As an invitation to future exploration, Xenakis provides a summary of the latest developments in sound synthesis employing stochastic procedures (random selection and probability distribution).

The theoretical treatises and compositions of Xenakis exert a profound influence on contemporary musical thought. Their impact would be even greater, no doubt, if more musicians had the necessary command of higher mathematics to comprehend fully his philosophic concepts and to apply his compositional methods. The problems of microtonal music are equally intriguing and vexing, but in a very different way.

Microtonal Music

Microtones, that is, intervals smaller than the semitones accommodated by conventional notation and instruments, have been included in various theoretical systems from the time of the ancient Greeks. Since microtones have been recognized in theory and the ability of the human ear to discern them is unquestioned, their inclusion in practical music would seem to be a logical step in its evolution. The barriers to this seemingly logical development have, until recently, discouraged all but a few hardy individualists.

Existing notation, instruments, and players are ill-suited to the increased complexity of true microtonal music. Devising a new system of notation, designing and constructing new instruments or adapting old ones, and training performers are formidable tasks. Harry Partch (1901–1974) was one of few who accepted the challenge on all counts. After formulating a convincing rationale for a scale of forty-three unequal intervals (in place of twelve equal intervals), he proceeded to develop a notational system, build instruments, and teach performers for the single purpose of playing his music. If recognition was meager and slow in coming, perhaps it was because much of his time and energy were consumed in these peripheral activities without which his music would not have been heard at all. His flair for words and visual effects adds to the impact of his dramatic works, where he is at his best. Regrettably, there is little opportunity to see them on stage. Next best is seeing the film *Windsong* (available through Cinema 16, New York), a modern rendering of the ancient myth of Daphne and Apollo, for which he did the music. Ten Partch instruments are heard on the sound track playing music based, like all he wrote, on the forty-three-tone scale.

HARRY PARTCH: *Windsong (1958)*   11:00
(1901–1974)

The recording of *Windsong* on CRI CD-7000 is an excerpted version of the film sound track.

Harry Partch

Partch's theories and achievements—abstract and applied; creative and constructive—are chronicled in his profusely illustrated book *Genesis of a Music,* second edition (Da Capo Press, 1974). A collection of his journals, essays, introductions, and librettos for his, as he called them, "redemptive, corporeal, theater works" was published posthumously under the title *Bitter Music* (University of Illinois Press, 1991).

A simpler, but more limited and theoretically less valid, type of microtonal music than that of Partch is possible if the only microtonal intervals used are equal quarter tones exactly half as large as the smallest intervals in traditional music. There are twenty-four tones in a quarter-tone scale, half of which coincide with conventional pitches. Quarter-tone music can be notated on a conventional staff with the addition of a few new symbols and can be played on several conventional instruments with relatively minor adaptations in the playing techniques and mechanisms. Penderecki's *Threnody for the Victims of Hiroshima* (see page 82) and Don Ellis's *House in the Country* (see page 312) illustrate this type of microtonal music.

The problems that impede the progress of microtonal music are of no concern to composers making electronic music. They have at their command the full range of audible frequencies, and working directly on computer discs and magnetic tape they have no need for notation or performers.

Any recording or transmission of sound involves electronic equipment, but the designations *electronic music* and *electro-acoustic music* are reserved for sounds generated and/or modified electronically and used artistically. Early experiments with electrical instruments date back to the last century, but the electronic age of music really began with the invention of the magnetic tape recorder in the 1940s.

Electronic Music

The reel-to-reel tape recorder provided not only a highly efficient means of sound recording and reproduction but also several easy and practical ways to modify sounds. For example, by increasing or decreasing the speed at which the tape traveled over the playback head, the pitch could be raised or lowered. When the direction of the tape was reversed, the sounds were heard backwards. A tape loop fashioned by joining the two ends of a piece of tape repeated a sound pattern endlessly. Sounds could be fragmented and rearranged by cutting and splicing the tape on which they were recorded, and any number of sound tracks could be combined. Starting in 1952 Vladimir Ussachevsky (1911–1990) and Otto Luening (1900–   ) produced electronic music using tape manipulations of this sort. Recordings of several of their compositions are still available.

Tape manipulations were used on recorded sounds from various sources. Tape music constructed from nonelectronic sound sources is called *musique concrète*. In musique concrète sounds from natural sources—voices, instruments, or any other vibrating medium—were modified by tape manipulations and, subsequently, electronically.

In addition to natural sounds recorded on tape through a microphone, there were electronic sounds produced by audio oscillators and generators. Oscillators produced a simple waveform with a single frequency (no overtones) and a sound like a test tone or a tuning fork. Generators produced more complex waveforms and various tone qualities. Electronic devices in the circuitry available to modify both concrète and electronic sounds included amplifiers, filters, modulators, equalizers, and reverberation units.

Processed sounds were recorded on one or more tapes. Multiple tapes were synchronized and their signals passed through a mixer where they were balanced and combined for recording on a final composite tape. The tape recording *is* the work. It may be transferred to LPs, cassettes, or compact discs for commercial distribution, and some graphic representation of its content may be prepared for copyright purposes, but the actual composition, in both the general and the specific sense, takes place in the sound studio on the tape. *Poème Electronique* by Edgard Varèse is, to use the composer's words, an example of "organized sound" created directly on magnetic tape. Oscillator, generator, voice, bell, and percussion sounds, though modified and reshaped, are recognizable in this landmark electronic composition.

Edgard Varèse

EDGARD VARÈSE: *Poème Electronique* (1958)   8:05
(1883–1965)

This work was first heard in the Philips Corporation pavilion at the Brussels World's Fair. The interior shape of the building designed by the architect Le Corbusier in collaboration with Iannis Xenakis provided a series of hyperbolic and parabolic curves along which 425 loudspeakers were meticulously placed. Visitors passing through the building were engulfed in continuous arcs of sound while viewing unrelated, diverse images projected on the ceiling. A simple recording gives only a glimpse of the total aural and visual experience conceived by Varèse, Le Corbusier, and Xenakis. Available on *Electro-Acoustic Music: Classics,* Neuma CD 450-74.

In the early days of electronic music makeshift devices intended for other functions were used to generate and modify the sound materials. Widespread interest in electronic music and advances in electronic technology led to the development of music *synthesizers,* integrated systems of electronic components designed expressly for the production and control of musical sounds. By 1965 synthesizers with voltage controls and programmable sequencers, which vastly enhanced their efficiency and flexibility, were available. A synthesizer of this type was used by Morton Subotnick in creating his *Silver Apples of the Moon,* which he views as a work "intended to be experienced by individuals or small groups of people listening in intimate surroundings . . . a kind of chamber music twentieth-century style."

MORTON SUBOTNICK: *Silver Apples of the Moon* (1967)
(1933–   )   *Part I*   16:30
                                     Part II   15:00

According to the composer, "The title *Silver Apples of the Moon,* a line from a poem by Yeats, was chosen because it aptly reflects the unifying idea of the composition, heard in its pure form at the end of Part II." The piece was composed especially for the Elektra/Nonesuch recording N5-71174.

As synthesizers have been standardized and mass produced, their price range has been reduced to affordable levels for individuals and educational institutions. Versatility and simplicity of operation have improved dramatically. A growing number of college music departments have fully equipped electronic music studios and routinely include the study of electronic music in the curriculum. Even in the more adventuresome public schools, students are introduced to electronic music and music making. These developments have taken place in a remarkably brief span of time.

The next great advancement in synthesizer technology came a decade after the advent of voltage controls with the introduction of digital (computer) controls, making real-time synthesis and live performance of sophisticated electronic music a reality. Computer applications to music, which began as soon as musicians gained access to computers, passed in rapid succession through a series of stages. The early stages are of historical interest but do not have much bearing on current practices. Much of the initial thrust was in the development of specialized music programs and eventually languages for mainframe computers. These activities continue in the large electronic music studios.

Modern computers can produce or reproduce any sound with total fidelity, as evidenced by the new digital recordings. All of the audible frequencies are available, but the pitches can be limited to those of a conventional scale, a twelve-tone scale, or any arbitrary set of pitch relationships. Computers can be programmed to produce strict serial music or to make random selections within prescribed limits and in a sense to "compose" in accordance with instructions provided by the programmer. A computer program that defines general extents rather than specific details and allows random selection of unspecified parameters of sound will produce a type of indeterminate music and many variants of the same composition. Some computer systems are designed to assume decision making at the individual tone level, freeing composers to concentrate on decisions at a higher level affecting the broad aspects of sound and structure. Barry Vercoe explores several of these possibilities in his *Synapse*.

An obvious disadvantage of pure electronic music is that there is nothing to watch during a performance, a disadvantage shared by all music heard via recordings. This deficiency is remedied in concert performances when live performers are used in conjunction with electronic tapes. Many of the composers who have worked extensively in the electronic medium have combined prerecorded and live sound. Live performers supply an intrinsic visual element and at the same time provide a desirable link with more conventional music. Obviously, the distinction between live and synthesized sound is lost on recordings, but on the recording of *Synapse* the viola part is readily distinguished from the sounds produced by the computer.

BARRY VERCOE: *Synapse for Viola and Computer* (1976)   5:30
(1937–   )

One of the music languages for large, third-generation computers is Barry Vercoe's MUSIC 360. Since becoming director of the MIT Experimental Music Studio he has concentrated his efforts on the use of smaller computers that are more accessible to composers and on another language, MUSIC 11. *Synapse* is one of the first works produced by the new system, which allows composers to communicate with the computer using traditional musical terms and to see, hear, and modify the musical materials as they compose. This work is in a strict twelve-tone style throughout, but two distinct methods were used. The first and last parts were written by the composer at home and taken to the studio a section at a time for sound synthesis and revision. The computer was more active in the composition of the contrasting middle section starting at 3:25. Only certain procedures for the use of the row were specified by the composer, and the computer organized the details and synthesized the sound. A tape with the computer part and a synthesized version of the viola part on separate channels was given to the viola player as a guide to synchronizing the two parts. Otherwise, learning to synchronize the intricate rhythms of the live and prerecorded elements would have been a formidable task. *Synapse* is included on the recording *Computer Generations* (CRI SD 393).

With the appropriate programs and peripherals, desktop and even the smaller notebook computers are capable of music synthesis. IBM PCs (and compatibles) and Apple Macintoshes are currently the most widely used platforms. The musical uses of computers have been facilitated by the adoption of MIDI, the acronym for Musical Instrument Digital Interface, as the industry standard protocol for communication between musical instruments and computers. The protocol consists of a set of digital messages defining the audio signals and musical events. Numerous programs are available that provide the necessary environment for interactive composing and performing with computers and synthesizers linked by MIDIs.

Computer technology has made it possible to reduce the size and price of synthesizers enormously. The simplest and least expensive models are readily playable by beginners and can be bought for the price of a sophisticated toy. At the other end of the spectrum from the inexpensive electronic instruments are the large, expensive, digital synthesizers with resources that challenge the imagination of experts. In these synthesizers various input, sound-producing, control, and output devices are integrated in a unified system. Several makes are mass-produced and in widespread use.

The Synclavier® 6400 digital audio system (see colorplate 25) is a comprehensive electronic music system. It is capable of synthesizing strikingly realistic instrumental sounds and abstract electronic effects by means of sampling and FM (frequency modulation) synthesis. The system's control features include a customized Macintosh® II graphics workstation, a velocity/pressure sensitive programmable keyboard, a button control panel, and synchronization codes. With a direct-to-disc multitrack recorder, it provides a complete computerized recording environment for music, effects,

FIGURE 24.1

Fairlight Computer
Musical Instrument.

*Photo courtesy of
Fairlight ESP Pty Ltd.,
Sydney, Australia.*

dialogue, and for synchronization with a video monitor or live performers. Christian Wolff (1934–   ) used a Synclavier in realizing his *Mayday Materials* at the Bregman Electronic Music Studio of Dartmouth College.

CHRISTIAN WOLFF: *Mayday Materials* *(1989)*
(1934–   )   *Part 9*   4:56

Part 9 of *Mayday Materials* utilizes sampled flute tones out of *Cindy,* an Appalachian folk song and square dance tune. More information about the *Mayday* music for the Lucinda Childs dance is given on pages 44 and 186.

The Fairlight Computer Musical Instrument (see figure 24.1) is a synthesizer that can digitally synthesize sound and, like other digital synthesizers, can also reproduce accurately acoustic and natural sounds that have been digitally memorized directly from a microphone or tape. Only one note of a sample sound is necessary for it to be played polyphonically through the full pitch range. A computer musical instrument digitizes the sound, turning it into thousands of numbers which define its waveform. The sound can then be played back at any pitch, modified, or combined with other synthesized or sampled sounds. A touch-sensitive keyboard, faders, and foot pedals control expression automatically or manually. The Fairlight can duplicate the sound of any instrument or a whole orchestra. Keyboard performances can be played back at any speed without pitch change, making difficult passages much easier for players with limited keyboard facility. Another method of input for the Fairlight is a typewriter keyboard and the Fairlight Music Composition Language, which uses many standard musical terms, such as letter names for the notes. Numerous functions of the Fairlight can be achieved simply by pointing the *light pen* with which it comes equipped to the relevant part of its video graphics display terminal. The light pen can also be used to draw waveforms that define sound characteristics directly on the video screen. This procedure was used by Barton McLean (1938–   ) in creating his *Etunytude.*

> **BARTON MCLEAN:** *Etunytude (1982)*   5:28
> (1938–   )
>
> The title *Etunytude,* according to the composer, refers to the characteristic aspects
> of the work—its tunefulness and its etudelike character. All of the sound is gen-
> erated internally by a Fairlight Computer Musical Instrument. The input to the
> computer is mainly by means of the light pen, which is used to draw the contour of
> sound waves on the video screen. Musically, the work is unified by recurring motives
> and a modified return of the first theme toward the end. (On *Computer Music from
> the Outside In,* Smithsonian/Folkways 37465)

Rock musicians, who are among the most avid users of electronic instruments of all types, quickly perceived the advantages of digital synthesizers. Stevie Wonder, the Jacksons, and members of the Bee Gees, Fleet-
wood Mac, and Led Zeppelin are among the many performers who have
used Fairlights.

The features of digital synthesizers described with reference to the
Synclavier® and the Fairlight are by no means exhaustive, and they are also
available on other makes. The capabilities of digital synthesizers seem to be
virtually unlimited now, but periodicals devoted to electronic and computer music report a host of new and improved products every issue.

Multimedia

Multimedia and *mixed media* are terms applied to contemporary works in
which two or more distinct art forms are combined. Technically, a composite art form such as opera or ballet qualifies for the category, but in
current usage the terms generally imply a combination of avant-garde music
with spectacular visual effects. The visual elements may be supplied by live
musicians, actors, or dancers; they may be still or moving projected images
or merely a display of lights within the hall, a so-called *light show.* Senses
other than hearing and sight may be involved, and sensory stimulation outside the performance area may be regarded as relevant to the artistic experience. Aleatory is the rule rather than the exception. When significant
elements of the production are left to chance, the result is a *happening.*
Audience participation is often encouraged. More extreme multimedia
concepts lead to *total theater* in which distinctions between composer, performer, and spectator are obscured. Philosophically and aesthetically the
multimedia protagonists are heading in a direction that ultimately leads to
embracing all sensual experience as art and in which distinctions between
art and life approach the vanishing point.

Meaningful illustrations of multimedia works are not practical in a
classroom situation, and therefore none are suggested. The Varèse *Poème
Electronique,* cited as an example of electronic music (see page 294), was an
early multimedia work as initially presented at the Brussels World's Fair.

Minimalism

In late twentieth-century music, extremes and opposites abound. There is
total organization and indeterminacy, mathematical formality and intuitive
improvisation, high tech complexity and simplistic *minimalism.*

Conceptually, minimalism can be categorized as the use of minimal means, presumably to obtain maximum effects. In musical practice minimalism is characterized by prolonged and persistent repetitions of static figures, the absence of developmental procedures, and the lack of goal-oriented movement. The reaction of listeners ranges from boredom to mesmerization, depending somewhat on their susceptibility to the hypnotic effect of seemingly endless uneventful activity.

The chief protagonist for minimalism is Philip Glass (1937–   ). After four years of course work in music, mathematics, and philosophy at the University of Chicago, he continued his studies at the Juilliard School of Music in New York and later in Paris on a Fullbright Fellowship. More decisive in his development as a minimalist composer than his formal studies were his encounters with Ravi Shankar and the music of India (see page 325) and with the music of the North African Arabs in Morocco. He organized the Philip Glass Ensemble in 1968 and has since presented concerts and made recordings with the group, promoting his music throughout the United States and Europe. His commissioned opera, *The Voyage*, commemorating the 1992 quincentenary of Columbus's landing in the New World, was premiered and given six sold-out performances at the Metropolitan Opera in New York.

Glasspiece # 1 is too brief to evoke the saturation response of a full-scale minimalist work, some of which last hours, but it is a valid example of the style.

PHILIP GLASS: *Glasspieces (1983)*      3/17
(1937–   )   *1. Rubric*   6:03

The dance *Glasspieces* with choreography by Jerome Robbins was premiered by the New York City Ballet. The music for the ballet was arranged by Glass for full orchestra. The recording is the original version scored for the Philip Glass Ensemble—electronic keyboards, strings, horns, flute/piccolo, saxophones, and drums.

Feminism

Feminism is not a musical style in the sense that minimalism is, but it is certainly a post–World War II phenomenon. Before then a professional career in music other than as a singer was extraordinary for a woman. Now, the feminist movement is as evident in music as in any area of endeavor. Women are routinely included as members of symphony orchestras playing virtually all of the instruments, not just the harp which was their entrée. They appear regularly as soloists and as members of chamber ensembles. It is becoming increasingly difficult to remember when or why it was ever otherwise.

The feminist doctrine has not been as successful in other musical domains. Excluding vocalists, jazz and popular music are almost a masculine monopoly. The number of recognized feminine conductors and composers falls far short of parity, but harbingers of change are in the air. Women have appointments as conductors and music directors of orchestras with

Ellen Taaffe Zwilich

full concert seasons and make guest appearances with major musical organizations. Sigma Alph Iota, an international music fraternity for women, lists many women composers in the annual contemporary American music issue of their journal *Pan Pipes,* and the works of women composers are increasingly available on recordings.

Ellen Taaffe Zwilich (1939–   ), a Pulitzer Prize winner, is one of the women composers well represented on recordings. The current *Opus* catalog lists eight of her major works recorded on CDs by the Indianapolis Symphony, the Louisville Orchestra, and the New York Philharmonic orchestra and ensembles. The *Concerto Grosso* "to Handel's *Sonata in D* for violin and continuo, first movement" was recorded by the New York Philharmonic, Zubin Mehta conductor.

4/1–2

ELLEN TAAFFE ZWILICH: *Concerto Grosso "after Handel"*
(1939–   )   *(1985)*

1.	*Maestoso*	2:41
2.	*Presto*	2:08

This concerto grosso (see page 157) was commissioned by the Washington Friends of Handel (see page 235) to commemorate the 300th anniversary of his birth. The first performance in 1986 was by Stephen Simon and the Handel Festival Orchestra at the Kennedy Center. The Handel theme given on page 344 is the generating force underlying all five movements of the complete work.

In adopting the archaic concerto grosso form and borrowing a theme from Handel, Zwilich is preserving traditions likely as old as the art of music. Other instances of recalling prior works and practices have been documented in the preceding pages. Period styles from the past have also been revived intermittently in this century. They are usually prefaced by "neo," as in *neoclassic* and *neoromantic.* By such means contemporary composers sometimes maintain direct ties with their roots, but the prevailing trends apparent on the surface are experimentation and the exploration of new paths.

In Conclusion   What will the music of the future be like? No one knows, of course, but one thing is certain—the styles of music will continue to evolve as some innovations are assimilated and others are abandoned. Composers will persist in their quest for new methods and materials, and each succeeding generation will have its own "new music."

25 JAZZ

There are no adequate designations for broad categories of music. Terms like *classical* and *jazz* are used so loosely as to be almost meaningless. Devotees are inclined to develop precise terminology for music in their particular spheres of interest and to label other types with some general or condescending term. In jazz circles the styles of music considered up to this point are regarded as "classical" or, disparagingly, "longhair," whereas to academic musicians "classical" is a specific period in the history of music (1750–1825). The Columbia House advertisements for CDs and cassettes differentiate between styles of rock and popular music—hard rock, soft rock, modern rock, heavy metal, R & B/soul, easy listening, rap, light sounds, and dance pop—but have single categories for country, jazz, and classical. The areas of music listed in the foreword of the ASCAP (American Society of Composers, Authors and Publishers) *Biographical Dictionary* include some of the same classifications and some additional ones: pop, rock, country, gospel, jazz, rhythm and blues, new wave, theater, film, symphonic/concert, and electronic. Though jazz is a single category in both lists, it encompasses a variety of styles that are surveyed in this chapter.

Jazz fans tend to regard jazz more like concert music than popular or dance music. Without becoming totally disassociated from dance elements, jazz is increasingly perceived as an abstract art form intended for concentrated listening independent of overt physical responses. Critical reviews of performances and recordings appear in specialized and general interest periodicals. Jazz musicians are highly proficient instrumentalists, and many are now academically trained.

Jazz, dance, and popular music cannot be completely divorced. In some periods, like the swing era, *jazz* and *popular* were almost synonymous terms, and the music was infinitely danceable. The more durable popular tunes from the past have continued to be played in the current jazz styles and to serve as a basis for jazz improvisation, unlike the pop/rock tunes which are unsuitable for this purpose. In some respects the youth-oriented rock music and its performers have more in common with early jazz and its practitioners than with jazz since the emergence of rock, and the attitudes toward rock are not so different from the attitudes at the time toward early jazz.

Jazz, once regarded by some as a destructive influence whose sudden appearance on the musical scene would be matched by an equally sudden and welcome demise, is now an established and accepted mode of musical

Note: The *Smithsonian Collection of Classic Jazz* is available in LP and CD formats from the Smithsonian Institution Press, Washington, D.C. 20560, phone 1–800–782–4612; in Pennsylvania and Alaska (717) 794–2148.

expression. The classics, regarded by others as remnants of the past out-living their usefulness but refusing to die, continue to flourish if not to prosper. If history repeats itself, different kinds of music will exist side by side in the future as they have since the cults of Apollo and Dionysus cultivated contrasting musical styles in ancient Greece. Classic and jazz styles occupy parallel positions in contemporary culture. The esteemed traditions of the classics are matched by the brief but colorful history of jazz which began around the turn of the century in the Storyville section of New Orleans. The year 1897, when the first piano rag was published, is often used as a point of departure by jazz historians, though the term was not widespread until 1917 when the first jazz recordings were made by the Original Dixieland Jazz Band.

The origins of jazz have been attributed to a wide range of forces and influences. Rags, hymns, spirituals, blues, work songs, quadrilles, marches, waltzes, American minstrels, Spanish and French music—all have been suggested as ancestors of jazz. Whatever its forebears, the miracle that is jazz was synthesized from diverse elements by a people in a foreign environment without any ready-made, adequate, or appropriate means of musical expression. In the beginning jazz was uniquely a product of African-Americans. Residual elements retained from their African heritage and influences absorbed from their New World surroundings were fused into an essentially new musical language.

Some obvious features of earlier music, such as syncopation and the pentatonic (five-tone) scale which exist in primitive African music and several other traditions, were appropriated by jazz for its own use. Outright borrowing of tunes from other styles started at once. Early rag pieces like *High Society* and *I Wish I Could Shimmy Like My Sister Kate* were being played in quite different versions by the brass bands of the town. The still popular *Tiger Rag* was based on the quadrille *Get Out of Here*. In spite of this borrowing, jazz was definitely something new, something more than the sum of its parts. Though its genesis may be earlier, the documented story of jazz commences with the piano rags played in New Orleans during the final decade of the last century.

Ragtime

Ragtime piano playing was mostly improvisatory in a percussive style with little use of pedal. The absence of a text was conducive to nonlyric, instrumental melodies. Harmony was basically the primary chords of conventional music. Rhythm, the most distinctive feature of ragtime, was characterized by elaborate syncopations, sometimes created by short notes in accented portions of the measure (and conversely, longer notes in unaccented portions) and sometimes by cross rhythms between melodic groupings of three and six notes in conjunction with underlying beat patterns of two and four. Other rhythmic devices included placing accents just before and after the normal pulse and using rests where accents normally fall. These rhythmic characteristics are the common denominators of jazz.

Though elements of ragtime had been heard earlier, apparently no example of the style appeared in print before 1897 when *Harlem Rag* by Tom Turpin (1873–1922) was published. That same year a piano method book, *Ragtime Instructor*, by Ben Harney (1871–1938) came out. Harney was a white songwriter and pianist playing in New York. At this early date jazz had already crossed the color line and the boundaries of the South, but it was to remain for some time, essentially if not exclusively, a product of southern black culture.

The ragtime craze reached its zenith around the turn of the century. The most famous rag composer then, as now, was Scott Joplin. The theme music for the Academy Award–winning motion picture *The Sting* was from Joplin's rag *The Entertainer*. The film sparked an instantaneous rag and Joplin revival. His *Maple Leaf Rag* is universally regarded as a classic in the style.

Scott Joplin

SCOTT JOPLIN: *Maple Leaf Rag* (1899)
(1868–1917)

3:01

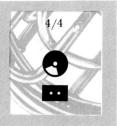

4/4

Maple Leaf Rag takes its name from the Maple Leaf Club in Sedalia, Missouri, where Joplin played. It has a clear sectional structure—AA BB A CC DD—in which each strain, except the return of A, is repeated immediately. The performance by Joplin was taken from a piano roll.

During the ragtime piano era small miscellaneous groups of instrumentalists, many of whom could not read music, collectively improvised for popular entertainments, parades, and dances. The results could not have been other than wildly contrapuntal and shockingly dissonant. Free improvisation, however, was to become a continuing feature of the infant art.

Blues

The publication in 1912 and 1914 respectively of the *Memphis Blues* and the *St. Louis Blues* by W. C. Handy ushered in the next jazz epoch. The blues, stemming more or less directly from spirituals and work songs, introduced several characteristics of subsequent jazz. They were different from rags in several respects. As songs, their melodies are vocal in style rather than instrumental. The texts, usually lamenting the absence or loss of a lover, typically are sung in a declamatory manner over a steady pulsating accompaniment. The tempo generally is slow, though faster blues are not unknown. Whereas ragtime harmonies are mostly triads, blues traditionally are based on a standard chord progression which includes seventh chords. Like most popular music, blues are predominantly major, but notes approximating the third and seventh scale degrees of natural minor are featured melodically, sometimes while the corresponding major note is in the accompaniment. These *blue notes* take their name from the style. Blues singers often slide into notes and hover in the vicinity of but not exactly on the notated pitch.

The words, melody, and harmony in blues generally conform to a standard twelve-bar pattern. The words most often consist of three lines, the second of which is a repetition or slightly altered version of the first. The third line completes the thought and ends with a terminal rhyme. The poetic meter is predominantly iambic pentameter (U—U—U—U—U—) or a rough approximation of it. Each line of the text is set as a musical phrase with a distinctive melodic and harmonic content, which is to say that the repetition in the words is not reflected in the music. Frequently the singer has a long note or a rest at the end of a phrase during which a brief instrumental improvisation, called a *break*, is interpolated. All of these features are illustrated in the first strain of Handy's *St. Louis Blues*.

4/5

W. C. HANDY: *St. Louis Blues* (1914)   3:09
(1873–1958)

The *St. Louis Blues* is not a simple blues but an extended composition of three distinct strains. The first and third strains, each of which is repeated in the printed version, are perfect examples of twelve-bar blues form. The unrepeated middle strain is a less typical sixteen-bar blues. On the 1925 Bessie Smith recording, reproduced in the *Smithsonian Collection of Classic Jazz* and in the *Listeners Guide* recording, the third strain is not repeated. Louis Armstrong, playing cornet, provides the instrumental breaks.

W. C. Handy with Duke Ellington

The styles of ragtime and the blues coalesced in *jazz*. Ferdinand "Jelly Roll" Morton (1885–1941), a first-generation jazzman from New Orleans, listed himself as the originator of jazz on his calling cards, and certainly he contributed significantly to its history. By the second decade of the century when the term first appeared in print, jazz bands had already migrated from New Orleans and were appearing regularly in Chicago, New York, and San Francisco. Chicago was the new mecca.

With the entrance into the field of white and trained musicians, a refining, and in a sense, a corrupting process began. The crude virility of primitive jazz was mellowed by the intrusion of European elements—sentimental melodies of the ballad and Viennese operetta type and impressionist harmonies. The lusty blues singers were largely replaced by crooners. The bands grew to sizes which made improvisation impractical, and written arrangements became the rule. With the addition of strings the bands became so large and the arrangements so pretentious that the anomalous name *symphonic jazz* was coined for the style. What must have appeared to symphonic jazz innovator Paul Whiteman, his admirers, and imitators as a great elevation of jazz style and a popularization of classic values, in retrospect seems to have been a rather unfortunate compromise for both. Before the Roaring Twenties were over, there were three distinct branches of jazz: *symphonic*, *sweet* (popular), and *hot* (Dixieland). Symphonic and sweet popular music retained some of the superficial aspects of jazz and were appropriate for dancing all the varied steps of the fox trot, but only hot was true to the original traditions.

Small groups, mainly black, continued to play hot jazz all through this period, not only preserving its traditions but enhancing them. Vocalists with these groups often improvised in an instrumental style using nonsense syllables, a contribution of hot jazz known as *scat singing*. Louis Armstrong was an illustrious scat singer and hot jazz performer on the cornet. He is heard in both roles on the suggested recording. Jazz pieces are often more closely identified with a performer or group than with a composer. In such instances, like the following, the performers are named in place of the composers.

Louis Armstrong

LOUIS ARMSTRONG'S HOT FIVE: *Hotter Than That*   3:00   4/6
(1927)

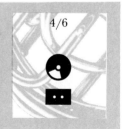

Lillian Hardin Armstrong, who married Louis in 1924, wrote *Hotter Than That* and played piano on the recording. Detailed analyses of the piece are given in Frank Tirro's *Jazz: A History* and in William Austin's *Music in the Twentieth Century* (both W. W. Norton).

Dixieland is a durable style that spans the history of jazz. The first white jazz band, one instrumental in introducing the new style of music north of the Mason-Dixon line, was the Original Dixieland Jazz Band. Early Dixieland was coarse and undisciplined. Vigor and abandon were its trademarks.

*Original Dixieland
Jazz Band*

Studied perfection was foreign to its nature, and a certain crudeness of tone and technique were part of the bargain. Though at times Dixieland style has become somewhat more restrained, refined, and, for purists, tainted by influences of newer jazz styles, its basic traditions have been preserved in their unadulterated form in the French Quarter of New Orleans.

In other parts of the country periods of declining interest in Dixieland have been followed by revivals. Turk Murphy spearheaded one such revival starting in the 1940s in San Francisco. He formed his own New Orleans style band, toured extensively, and played in New York City nightclubs between 1948 and 1960. Then he returned to his home base in San Francisco where he opened his own club and continued to play traditional New Orleans jazz until his death in 1987. The personnel in Murphy's band changed over the years, but the style of playing, illustrated in the following example, remained intact.

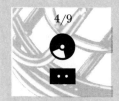

4/9

TURK MURPHY AND HIS BAND: *High Society* (1955)   3:08

High Society is a perennial favorite. This version was recorded during a performance at the New Orleans Jazz Festival before a live audience. The clarinet solo has a ring of authenticity, though the clarinetist (Bill Carter) was only twenty years old and a newcomer in the band at the time.

Boogie-Woogie and Kansas City

Boogie-woogie and *Kansas City* are jazz styles that developed in the twenties and carried over into the thirties. Boogie characteristically is a piano style in blues form with an insistently repeated bass figure played by the left hand while a totally independent improvisation is played by the right hand. Short fragments were sometimes repeated in the right-hand part. When similar repeated fragments—which were always rhythmic and could be either melodic or harmonic—appeared in the instrumental Kansas City style, they were called *riffs*. Kansas City jazz featured a heavy, four-beat rhythm in contrast to the two-beat rhythm prevalent in preceding styles. Bennie Moten's band, which later became Count Basie's, was the most famous in the area. Kansas City style, according to some authorities, led directly into the big band era and the birth of *swing* in the mid-thirties.

The swinging big band of Duke Ellington was one of the best. In conception and performance his *Old King Dooji* has a propulsive four-beat rhythm and the use of riffs in common with Kansas City style plus the subtleties and refinements that make it swing.

Swing

DUKE ELLINGTON: *Old King Dooji* (1938)
(1899–1974)

2:29   4/7

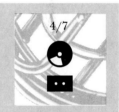

This is a sterling example of post–Kansas City style and of pre–World War II swing. King Dooji must have been a mythical king of a mythical kingdom, because composer Ellington provided no clue to his identity.

Swing was much closer to the spirit of jazz than the sweet and commercial music that was still being played, but the very nature of the big bands required that the emphasis be shifted from individual improvisation to precise group performance of written arrangements. The arrangements, however, incorporated many features of jazz rhythm and made provision on occasion for improvisation in breaks and hot choruses and over riffs and subdued backgrounds. In addition, the tradition of improvising was kept alive by smaller groups consisting of members and associates of the big bands. Benny Goodman had a fifteen-piece orchestra and was called the King of Swing, but there was also a Benny Goodman Trio, Quartet, Quintet, and Sextet. There were some regulars in the Benny Goodman small groups—Teddy Wilson, piano; Gene Krupa, drums; and Lionel Hampton, vibraharp (vibraphone); all of whom became band leaders—but the personnel varied. The following example is played by the four regulars.

Duke Ellington

BENNY GOODMAN QUARTET: *Dizzy Spells* (1938)

5:44   4/8

Benny Goodman and his band made history on January 16, 1938, when they played a jazz concert in New York's prestigious Carnegie Hall. The Trio and the Quartet were represented on the program, and the performance of *Dizzy Spells* that night is the one reproduced in the *Listeners Guide* recordings.

Benny Goodman

Many of the musicians in the swing bands were real jazz enthusiasts, and often after engagements with the band they congregated in small clubs for impromptu *jam sessions.* The jam sessions were completely unwritten, unrehearsed, and unstandardized. Any number could play. For patrons who found inspired, uninhibited improvisation more appealing than the studied perfection of formal performances and listening more enjoyable than dancing, staged jam sessions became a regular form of entertainment.

Evidence that the spirit of big band swing has spread to Europe and is thriving is provided by the 1988 CD recording in Paris of *Jazz Brunch* by the Claude Bolling Big Band. It includes their version of composer George and lyricist Ira Gershwin's hit tune *'S Wonderful* from the 1927 Broadway musical *Funny Face.*

4/13

GERSHWIN/BOLLING: *'S Wonderful (1927/1988)**   3:46

The "Jazz Brunch" was originally served in the plush lounge of the Hotel Méridien in Paris to an enthusiastic crowd of head-wagging, foot-stomping gourmets. Bolling is the featured pianist. The style and song choice are vintage swing.

*(Date of composition/date of recording)

Bebop

With the end of World War II the curtain rang down on the swing era, though the style was far from extinct. The power and discipline of its full-throated sections were muffled and the very foundations of jazz were assailed by a disturbing upheaval known as *bebop* or merely *bop.* Bop shunned time-honored formulas to experiment with exciting new rhythmic, melodic, and harmonic materials. As is often the case with experimenters, their music was sometimes pointlessly eccentric and sometimes just misunderstood. The players still unswervingly committed to swing and Dixie were united in their resistance to the inroads of bop. Its frenzied repetition of trivial melodic tidbits was a threat to the traditions for which they stood. This iconoclastic upstart temporarily split jazzmen into factions and alienated them from their fans, but from the rubble of the conflict arose a rejuvenated art which is contemporary jazz. The older styles survive in modified forms, and new ones have been added. In retrospect, the advent of bop was a momentous turning point in the evolution of jazz music.

Progressive Jazz

Progressive jazz with the late Stan Kenton as its leading exponent was the successor to symphonic jazz and swing. Kenton formerly played for dances, but his ideas were more dramatically embodied in recordings and concert performances of music that was quite undanceable. He often abandoned rigid, conventional rhythmic patterns, prime requisites of dance music, in favor of fluid pulses and asymmetric meters. The instrumentation was large and lavish, including on occasion strings and such unlikely jazz instruments as flutes, oboes, and French horns. Symphonic materials and techniques were borrowed freely—not insipid romantic melodies but the heady harmonies and dissonant counterpoint of the twentieth century. The term *neophonic* was used by Kenton for one phase of his progressive jazz, one that

COLORPLATE 25
Synclavier® 6400 Digital Audio System

Courtesy of New England Digital Corporation, Lebanon, NH.

COLORPLATE 26
Balinese Gamelan

Photograph © George Holton/Photo Researchers, Inc.

he was instrumental in introducing in many educational institutions. Whether or not progressive jazz is really jazz depends upon the point of view, but there is no denying that it is a style with logical antecedents cultivated by a legion of dedicated musicians. Progressive jazz in its various phases has been a remarkably durable style. Kenton's first band was organized in 1941. In 1973 he celebrated his sixty-first birthday playing a concert in London that was recorded live and released as *Birthday in Britain* (Creative World W. 1065).

STAN KENTON AND HIS ORCHESTRA: *Ambivalence*   7:54
(1973)

Ambivalence from the *Birthday in Britain* album was composed and arranged by Hank Levy. The instrumentation of the touring orchestra heard on the recording was not as extravagant as that used in some of Kenton's studio recordings, but the solo instruments for this piece are flute(!) and alto saxophone. The elements of rhythm, harmony, and form receive typical progressive jazz treatment.

An important contribution of the late Stan Kenton was his promotion of big band jazz in schools and colleges. Initially there was intractable resistance to the recognition of *stage bands* or *jazz ensembles,* as jazz bands on campus are often called, as valid performing groups. The enthusiasm of the students and a few hardy pioneers—music teachers with jazz experience, sympathetic administrators, and professional clinicians—overcame all obstacles and gained acceptance of jazz-oriented performing groups in educational institutions at all levels. The early jazz ensembles were direct descendants of the big swing bands, but rock influence is now pervasive and *jazz/rock* a common name for the style of music they play. Opportunities to participate in jazz groups are now available to most instrumental music students (violin, viola, and cello players excepted). Jazz influence is also spreading to singers and vocal groups. Institutions of higher education increasingly are offering credit courses and majors and minors in *commercial music,* the usual academic title for the field.

Modern Jazz

The small combo counterpart of progressive jazz is *modern jazz* under which might be listed such subclassifications as *cool, West Coast, funky,* and *free.* Cool style is characterized by the relaxed understatement and elegant transparency epitomized in the playing of Lester Young (1909–1959) during the last decade of his career. West Coast is the brand of cool cultivated mainly by white musicians in the Los Angeles area. Gerry Mulligan was a charter member of this school. In funky jazz the feeling of bop is revived. It is more direct and rhythmic than cool. Any type of jazz that abandons the traditional restraints of harmony and form can be labeled free jazz. Ornette Coleman's *Free Jazz* (Atlantic SD-1364) is a 36-minute free improvisation by Coleman and seven other musicians.

Modern jazz, in both the general and the specific sense, descends directly from the improvisations of small groups in the thirties and early forties and particularly from Charlie Parker (1920–1955) and bop. The size

and instrumentation of the groups vary. All of the usual instruments of jazz are used, along with some newly converted such as flute and French horn and of recent vintage such as vibes and electric guitar. The players of modern jazz tend to be thoroughly knowledgeable musicians with solid academic training and virtuoso techniques. Versed in both the classics and jazz, they achieve a highly polished style even in spontaneous performances. In their hands the traditional elements of jazz become suave and sophisticated. Modern jazz is not so much something new as it is a new perfection of old methods. It is the type of jazz most generally admired by nonjazz musicians and a type that seems to proffer great potential for future development. It is doubtful that any modern jazz selection can be regarded as typical, but the following are representative. The first is closer to traditional jazz in that it uses a Gershwin popular tune of yesteryear as a point of departure.

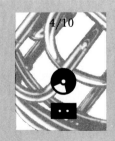

4/10

MODERN JAZZ QUARTET: *But Not for Me* (1930/1965)   3:44

The Benny Goodman Quartet and the Modern Jazz Quartet have three instruments in common—piano, vibraharp, and drums. The use of the bass in the MJQ in place of Goodman's clarinet is only one of the reasons for the great difference in the sound of the two groups. The flavor of the MJQ improvisation is definitely cool, though clearly in the mainstream jazz tradition. Founded by pianist John Lewis in 1952, the MJQ was still appearing as a group forty years later.

In the second example of modern jazz the combination of instruments (trumpet, two saxophones, piano, bass, and drums) is more traditional than in the Modern Jazz Quartet, but the style of playing is farther out. The late

Miles Davis was both the composer and the leader of the group. The piece evolves from a germ motive introduced at the beginning. The motive and crux of the piece is a two-chord progression in a long-short rhythm that sounds like an emphatic musical setting of the title words, "so what!"

MILES DAVIS SEXTET: *So What (1959)*   9:05

This Miles Davis group is remarkable in that both saxophone players, John Coltrane and Julian "Cannonball" Adderly, went on to form their own groups and to make impressive contributions to jazz before their untimely deaths in 1967 and 1975 respectively. The tragedy continued with the death of Miles Davis, who played trumpet, in 1991. *So What* is in the *Smithsonian Collection of Classic Jazz.*

Third Stream Music

Third stream is a term first used circa 1960 by Gunther Schuller (1925–   ) to denote a special kind of modern jazz which is a synthesis of jazz and recent "classical" elements. Creators of third stream music must, of course, be well grounded in jazz and the other contemporary idioms. The synthesis is accomplished in several ways. For example, two performing mediums may be combined as they are in Schuller's *Conversations* for jazz quartet and string quartet, or a twelve-tone row may be used as the basis for jazz improvisation as in *Improvisational Suite No. 1* by Don Ellis (1932–1978). The Modern Jazz Quartet recorded *Third Stream Music* (Atlantic cassette tape 1345-4) in 1960 and was an active force in third stream music. The MJQ disbanded in 1974 but has reunited periodically since then. The group celebrated its thirty-fifth anniversary in 1987 with a concert in the Hollywood Bowl. John Lewis, MJQ musical director and pianist, composed several works for jazz quartet and orchestra and commissioned others. Third stream music, which seemed promising for a while, now seems to be going the way of its predecessor, symphonic jazz, and to be fading from the musical scene.

Crossover/ Fusion

The great diversity of current musical styles seems to have resulted in part from combining traits of otherwise separate styles. The terms *crossover* and *fusion* have been adopted for styles in which this process can be observed. Crossover, more specifically, is applied to artists identified with one style of jazz or popular music who make recordings of a different type, almost inevitably with residual traces of their usual style. Crossover is also applied to recordings that appear in more than one category on the charts and appeal to a broader audience than the one intended. In fusion, as broadly defined, the elements of previous jazz styles have been renovated and combined with features of classic, ethnic, rock, and electronic music. Though the term is applicable to any music in which two or more distinct influences can be detected, such as Latin jazz and pop rock, present usage generally implies some interaction of jazz and rock styles with the effect of popularizing jazz.

Don Ellis

Fusion, now in the broad sense, is amply illustrated in the recordings of the Don Ellis Band, though they were made before the term was fashionable. Ideas from every conceivable source are absorbed and given a jazz interpretation. The massive sound of the big swing bands can be heard in places, sometimes playing rock progressions. Other passages echo the cool style. Some of the rhythms can be traced back to sources in Mexico or Spain, Bulgaria, and India. Riffs of Kansas City origin are much in evidence, as are blues characteristics. A single piece provides only a narrow view of this type of fusion, but the following example embraces several diverse influences.

4/11   **DON ELLIS BAND:** *House in the Country* (1969)   2:46

The instrumentation of the Don Ellis Band is as eclectic as its performance style. It includes all of the usual jazz instruments in profusion plus voices, but that is only the beginning. The saxophone players double on flute, oboe, and bass clarinet. The trumpet players double on quarter-tone trumpets and fluegel horns, which are like oversized cornets. The piano player doubles on the harpsichord and the clavinet, the latter an electronic keyboard instrument. The most striking feature of the instrumentation, however, is the use of electronics to generate and modify the sounds. The late Don Ellis plays an electrophonic trumpet, and Pete Robinson plays an electronic Fender-Rhodes piano. A ring modulator specially built for the band and a Conn Multivider, both electronic devices used to modify tones, are also listed in the instrumentation.

In Conclusion

By the time these words reach print, some of the suggested recordings will be out of print. New ones will have taken their place, and they should be substituted. What will the new jazz be like? As of now the future course of jazz is an enigma, but perhaps from today's multiplicity of styles a new style will emerge and dominate the field for a time. Since its inception jazz has demonstrated a pronounced tendency to restyle itself almost every decade. Advances in electronic technology have added a new dimension to jazz since the sixties. Amplification through conventional and contact microphones facilitates balancing otherwise impractical instrumental combinations. Electronic devices are now in use that drastically modify the range and quality of conventional instruments and provide reverberation and echo effects in live performances. Synthesizers are used extensively. Despite all the changes in styles over the years a thread of continuity runs through the history of jazz, and consistent elements preserve its identity as a coherent body of music.

Though jazz is a newcomer in the field of the arts, it is the logical inheritor of honorable traditions. Some of the most venerable musical practices are preserved only in jazz and popular music. Playing keyboard instruments from symbols other than notation was an indispensable accomplishment for musicians of the baroque period. This practice, a lost art as far as other musicians are concerned, flourishes with the players of jazz and popular music. The symbols have changed from numbers below the staff to letters and numbers above the staff, but the principles are the same. Improvisation, another lost art for academic musicians, is revived in jazz. Bach, whose prowess in playing from symbols and in improvising was legendary, probably would be disenchanted with colleagues less ably endowed and delighted with the fresh new turn these ancient arts have taken in the hands of jazz musicians.

Jazz, traditional and all its variants, continues to survive and evolve in a milieu of richly varied musics. With the proliferation of AM and FM radio music stations; network, independent, public, and cable television stations; and CD (compact disc), cassette, and DAT (digital audio tape) recordings, a safe assumption is that more music is being made and heard than ever before in human history. During the last year for which statistics were available from the Recording Industry Association of America, sales of recordings totaled more than 619 million units.

There is no real competition between the various types of music, because the approaches, aims, and audiences are different. The singers and players of popular music strive to produce songs so attuned to the times and so appealing to the younger generations that they soar to the top of the charts, however briefly. The performers of the standard concert literature cultivate faithful renditions of precisely notated compositions presumably of enduring value and worthy to pass on to posterity. Jazz musicians occupy an intermediate niche, aspiring to both popularity and artistic integrity. Jazz, though transitory by nature, has been rescued by the magic of recordings and has prevailed for almost a century as the vernacular idiom of American music.

With jazz styles in a constant state of flux, there perhaps is no better way to end this chapter than with two works from opposite poles of the current jazz scene. Both are by young performer-composers born in New Orleans, the cradle of jazz, who have already achieved stardom.

By the time Harry Connick, Jr., had celebrated his twenty-fourth birthday, his recordings as a vocalist, pianist, and composer had sold in the millions and won two Grammy awards, including one for the album from the motion picture sound track of *When Harry Met Sally*. He had also recorded *Blue Light, Red Light,* by which he hoped "to make jazz and (big band) swing music loved by the whole world."

Harry Connick, Jr.

HARRY CONNICK, JR.: *Blue Light, Red Light* (1991)
(1967–   )   *1. Someone's There*   3:28

4/14

In its reincarnation of big band swing, the title song of the album is retrospective, but not without new twists. The "hardest swinging musicians in the world," as Connick describes them, are more restrained on this track than on some of the others in the album. Connick's performance and compositional style as a whole is eclectic rather than innovative.

Wynton Marsalis

The second example of current jazz is by Wynton Marsalis. Marsalis and Connick have points in common. Both have New Orleans origins and precocious talents, and both studied with Wynton's father, Ellis Marsalis, a prominent New Orleans musician. Despite these common roots, their styles at this stage in their development are miles apart. Connick is quoted as saying, "I've always been an entertainer," which is not to detract from his stature as a musician, but it does reflect his attitude. The image Marsalis projects is that of an instrumentalist totally dedicated to the art of music and particularly to expanding the frontiers of jazz. His models include trumpeters from Louis Armstrong to "Dizzy" Gillespie and jazz masters of every persuasion.

Marsalis's style of trumpet playing and composing traces its ancestry to blues, swing, and popular songs, but all of the elements—melody, harmony, rhythm, and texture—are liberated and adventuresome. His concept of rhythm is especially inventive. The number of beats in phrases is traditional, but implications of bar lines and regular groupings are often replaced by shifting accents creating irregular beat patterns and divisions. Seemingly free improvisation is unified by thematic material and form. No single selection illustrates the many facets of Marsalis's music, but *Much Later* provides a sample.

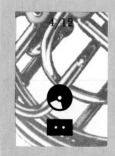

WYNTON MARSALIS: *Much Later* (1986)   4:35
(1961–   )

Wynton Marsalis, trumpet, is joined in the recording of the album *J Mood,* which concludes with *Much Later,* by Marcus Roberts ("J Master"), piano; Robert Leslie Hurst III, bass; and Jeff "Tain" Watts, drums. Each member of the quartet makes a unique and personal contribution to the ensemble while retaining a highly individual identity. These young musicians recently embarked on careers in jazz promise to make their mark as the sum of their work increases.

The big band of Harry Connick, Jr., and the quartet of Wynton Marsalis represent contrasting aspects of current jazz, and possibly one or the other, or both, of them will set the course for the future.

26 FOLK AND POPULAR MUSIC

Folk music and popular music are alike in that they are both the music of the people rather than of the connoisseurs, and both are relatively unsophisticated in comparison with concert music and the more esoteric styles of jazz. From another perspective, folk music is the popular music of the past, and popular music is the music of the folk (people) now. Covering folk and popular music in the same chapter facilitates discussing their similarities and differences, and their familiarity makes extended consideration unnecessary.

Folk Music

Folk music is the expression of a group of kindred people bound together by ties of race, language, religion, or custom. It has existed since the first spontaneous stamping of rhythm and chanting of melody. It includes all the songs and dances originated or used among the common people. The words of the songs generally are artless poems dealing with mundane phases of everyday life, but texts of genuine charm, wit, and pathos are not foreign to the genre. The mores and folkways of the people are reflected in the lines. Tales of romantic and tragic love, patriotism, moral lessons, legendary figures, bits of philosophy and history, all are suitable subjects. Any thought or emotion which touches the lives and fancies of an ethnic group may find expression in song and dance.

The songs, requiring only the voice for performance, greatly exceed the number of dance tunes. The latter are inconsequential by comparison but make a fascinating study, partially because of their association with distinctive instruments such as bagpipes, zithers, guitars, and fiddles and with distinctive manners of playing. The folk instruments and playing styles are also used in song accompaniments.

A traditional view that folk songs develop anonymously as the result of concerted action and that folk dance music springs from unpremeditated accompaniments for rustic entertainments is valid only for aboriginal peoples in primitive societies. The folk music of Europe and the Americas is too sophisticated to have originated in deliberate joint ventures. The initial spark in folk music, as in art music, must come from an individual intellect. The will of the people is manifest in the selection and modification of its folk art. Acceptance is a more cogent reason for the classification than origin. Applying this criterion, the songs of Stephen Foster (1826–1864) and Irving Berlin's *White Christmas* (1942) are as much a part of our folk

315

heritage as the songs of anonymous origin handed down through generations. Anonymity of authorship, often cited as a characteristic of folk music, is increasingly rare in these days of copyrights and publication. Most of the songs whose composers are unknown date from earlier times.

Few folk songs, if any, however, date back to ancient times. If any do, they have been so transformed through the years it has been impossible to trace them. Of course it is difficult to verify the lineage of a song which has been sung for generations in innumerable variations before it assumed definitive, written form. Modifications occur even after a song is notated and published. Community sings always turn up slightly discrepant versions of familiar songs. Tracing a folk song back to its origin is complicated by the fact that the text is as prone to change as the music. Not only do folk melodies exist in several versions (a traditional song learned by word of mouth is almost never sung in exactly the same way by two singers), but each locale may have a different set of words. The earliest authenticated secular folk songs date from the thirteenth century. Several are preserved from the fifteenth and sixteenth centuries, but living folk songs are mostly of more recent origin, predominantly from the eighteenth and nineteenth centuries.

Everyone agrees that folk music possesses certain national traits, but objective descriptions of these traits are not easily formulated. Short notes occurring on the beat *(Scotch snaps)* sometimes are pointed out as characteristics of Scotch music. Certain cadence formulas (approaching the tonic note from a third above or below) are mentioned as characteristics of American music. While it is true that these features appear in the literatures indicated, they also appear elsewhere. Obvious similarities are observable in the folk music of widely separated cultures. It is possible for a person attuned to the dialects of folk music to identify the sources of melodies in familiar styles almost instinctively, just as one recognizes dialects in one's native tongue without being able to describe the differences precisely. It can only be deduced that the composite sound somehow reflects the national personality. The locality from which a folk song comes can be pinpointed more accurately by its text and the manner of performance than by its musical traits.

Folk melodies have a proven ability to attract and to communicate with listeners. In the folk song literature composers have a tested treasury of thematic material. As early as the fifteenth century they started taking advantage of it. A French folk song, *L'homme armé,* was used in at least thirty polyphonic Masses between the fifteenth and seventeenth centuries. The practice of using thematic elements of folk origin in art music continues unabated. It was and is particularly prevalent in the music of nationalistic composers.

Borrowing between folk music and art music is not a one-way street. Individually composed and published songs are assimilated directly into the folk song literature. Dozens of Stephen Foster songs have acquired folk song status during the last century. In addition to outright adoption of composed songs in the folk repertory, songs of anonymous origin show evidence of art music's rational procedures in their forms and melodic contours. Continuous interaction between folk and art music is an established practice.

The United States has one of the largest and most varied folk song literatures. Immigrants from all over the world brought the songs and dances of their native lands with them. The ethnic groups that contributed to this musical melting pot have tended, with some exceptions, to lose their identity. In the process of Americanization, their native tongues and customs have been forgotten and their musical traditions transformed and assimilated. Each has made a contribution to the total body of American folk music and then adopted it as its own. The music of the Latin Americans in California and the Southwest is a special case, having been widely disseminated and adopted but not assimilated. To these imported influences, styles of essentially indigenous origin were added: Native American and African-American music, patriotic songs, cowboy songs, revivalist hymns, and spirituals. An incomparable treasury of recorded folk music is deposited in the Library of Congress, and recordings of authentic folk music are being issued commercially in increasing numbers.

Until World War II folk music was not much in evidence in urban America, but the situation changed in the years following the war. Some TV stars made careers specializing in folk and folklike music. A network television studio may seem to be a strange place to practice folk art, but folk music and performers readily adapted to the changing times and tastes. The social movements of the sixties inspired a whole new body of music in the folk tradition. Gospel songs are heard by millions of noncommunicants, and some radio stations program country and western music exclusively.

Without disparaging broadcasts or recordings, it should be noted that folk music ideally is a participation activity. To really experience the joy of folk music, get together with a few friends, a collection of folk songs if necessary, and a guitar. It will not be difficult to find a guitarist. There are more than 10 million nonprofessional guitar players in this country.

The distinctions between folk music and popular music are by no means as clear as they once were, and popular music cannot be entirely disassociated from jazz. The blurring of the dividing lines between musical styles was dramatized in a Newport Jazz Festival when types characterized as gospel, ragtime, blues, swing, Afro-Latin, soul, pop-rock, Dixieland, bebop, cool, and electronic jazz-rock were all heard in the same series of concerts.

The critical difference between folk music and popular music is longevity. A song becomes a true folk song only after it has survived for a generation or more and has become a part of a folk tradition. A popular song, almost by definition, is one with broad, immediate, and implicitly transient appeal. A pop tune rarely remains in the Top 40 for more than a season. Even so, the two categories are not mutually exclusive. Genuine folk songs have become popular hits, and some popular songs of past eras have acquired folk status.

The degree of sophistication distinguishes popular music from jazz, more so now than when jazz was in its infancy. Popular music tends to be simple, direct, and uncomplicated. Jazz styles all exhibit some degree of complexity, at least in their rhythms. The nature of the differences between popular music and jazz makes it possible for the same piece to be a simple popular song and also the basis for highly sophisticated jazz improvisation.

Country Music

Loretta Lynn

The type of popular music most akin to folk music is *country*. Country music is not far from its bluegrass and hillbilly roots. It could quite logically be regarded as a kind of folk music if it were not for its phenomenal popular and commercial success. Commercial exploitation of country music began on November 28, 1925, when the first WSM Barn Dance program was broadcast over radio station WSM in Nashville. The early programs, by all accounts, were not too different from the rustic entertainments that could be heard in real barns around the countryside. When the show followed a Metropolitan Opera broadcast, the announcer's introduction was, "Well, folks, you've been up in the clouds with grand opera; now get down to earth with us in a four-hour shindig of Grand Ole Opry." The name caught on; Grand Ole Opry became a national institution; and Nashville became the mecca of country music.

Practically every country music personality has been associated with the Grand Ole Opry at one time or another, and it has made stars of many of them. Loretta Lynn is one. Without it, she might still be singing folk songs for a few friends in Van Lear, Kentucky, where she grew up as a coal miner's daughter. Instead, she has found fame and fortune as an award-winning country singer.

> ## LORETTA LYNN: *Just a Woman* (1985)   2:59
>
> *Just a Woman* is a song from the Loretta Lynn album of the same name. Conceivably, the song could survive the test of time and achieve folk status, but that is unlikely considering the large and growing number of popular songs in country style. The name of the performer is given in lieu of the name of the composer, which is customary in popular music identifications and catalogs.

The popularity of country music is cresting as fans of the folk-tinged rock of the sixties and seventies find country music more congenial than rap and the other extreme rock styles. These listeners can tune their radios to one of the 2,400 stations that play country exclusively, making it the top radio format in number of outlets, or to a station that incidentally programs crossover country hits. The growth of country has led to splintering. Subcategories include traditional, rock-country, alternative, redneck, bluegrass, and country folk. Country music has drawn listeners from those disenchanted with the elitism of current jazz and the youth orientation of recent rock, but rock and pop music still account for more than half of all record purchases.

Rock/Pop

Rock is the popular music of our time. *Rock 'n' roll,* as it was called initially, emerged as a distinct musical type in the fifties. The song *Rock Around the Clock* by Bill Haley and the Comets, released in 1955 and used in the motion picture *Blackboard Jungle,* is credited with being the first rock single. Rock's immediate predecessors were race music and what was then called country and western, which were themselves products of composite influences. Rock is now divided by critics and reviewers into several classifications. The Columbia House advertisements for CD and cassette recordings list six with representative artists: hard rock (Van Halen and ZZ Top), soft rock (Michael Bolton and Mariah Carey), modern rock (R.E.M. and Red Hot Chili Peppers), heavy metal (Skid Row and Ozzy Osbourne), R & B/soul (Luther Vandross and Boyz II Men), and rap (L. L. Cool J. and Public Enemy). The categories and performers on the list change frequently.

Rock music is not easily described, but its sound is unmistakable. It is essentially vocal music, but the instruments—typically electric guitars and basses, synthesizers, and percussion—impart a distinctive flavor. An obvious characteristic is the consistently high dynamic level. In live performances the instruments and voices are amplified to the point where the music can almost be felt as well as heard, and listeners are inclined to adjust the volume controls to achieve the same effect from radios and from record, tape, and compact disc players. The impact of the music apparently is dependent to some extent on a sound intensity approaching the threshold of pain, though there is evidence that overexposure to such sounds permanently impairs hearing. Rock rhythm has fast, heavy, even divisions of the beat. The melodies are declamatory rather than lyric. They typically have many repeated notes and figures within a narrow range. The harmonic vocabulary of rock is limited but not stereotyped. Since rock is in revolt against the musical conventions of the establishment, the standard progressions of jazz and classical music are shunned. In both the melodies and the harmonies strong folk and modal influences can be detected. The forms are extended by multiple verses and irregular repetitions of choruses. Some songs begin with an introduction and have instrumental interludes. To avoid the formulas associated with traditional endings, cadences have been replaced in large measure by fade-outs. With age, rock is showing signs of mellowing and also of reverting to its raucous origins.

Rock music reached a new pinnacle of popularity with the movie *Dirty Dancing.* Within a year of its release the film grossed over $100 million in theaters, more than 360,000 copies of the videocassette were sold, and sales of the soundtrack album exceeded 6 million. Some of the songs on the record are new, but others date back to the beginnings of rock, providing a panoramic view of popular music since that time. Dates are given for the initial release of the songs on the sound track.

MOTION PICTURE: *Dirty Dancing* (1987)

	(I've Had) The Time of My Life (1987)	4:47
	Be My Baby (1963)	2:37
	She's Like the Wind (1987)	3:51
	Hungry Eyes (1987)	4:06
	Stay (1960)	1:34
	Yes (1987)	3:15
	You Don't Own Me (1963)	3:00
	Hey Baby (1961)	2:21
	Overload (1987)	3:39
	Love Is Strange (1956)	2:52
	Where Are You Tonight (1987)	3:59
	In the Still of the Night (1956)	3:03

(I've Had) The Time of My Life won the Academy Award and the Golden Globe Award for the best song and the Grammy Award for the best pop duet for the year 1988.

The latest wrinkle in the story of popular music is the rock video. MTV—Music Television—fostered the video concept from its inauspicious beginnings to its sensational overnight success. The visual aspects of these productions are obviously inspired by the antics of rock performers on stage, but the video medium expands to infinity the possibilities for combining sound with movement, shape, and color. State-of-the-art digital recorders are used in recording, processing, and editing everything that is seen and heard. Videos are not without critics, but their impact on the music industry and the listening and viewing public has been nothing short of revolutionary.

The diversity and vitality of rock music, now approaching its fifth decade, proves that it is no passing fancy. Whether it will continue to develop within a basic rock framework, gradually evolve into a new style, or be replaced by an essentially different kind of popular music is, at this time, anybody's guess. Trends in popular music are as changeable and unpredictable as the weather.

Other Popular Styles

Though rock is the prevailing popular style, it is by no means the only one. Composers are still writing songs for movies and musicals in the styles of Hollywood and Tin Pan Alley. The following song from a Broadway musical is representative.

JERRY HERMAN: *La Cage aux Folles* (1983)
(1933–   )   *Song on the Sand (La da da da)*   3:55

Jerry Herman's Broadway successes include, in addition to *La Cage, Hello Dolly!* and *Mame.* The title song of *Hello Dolly!* was a big hit, but in the present musical climate songs from musicals are found less frequently on the rating charts. *Song on the Sand* receives hit treatment in *La Cage.* The melody is first heard in the prelude. The song is featured in the first act and returns in the second act and finale.

A newspaper in the Los Angeles area lists local radio stations according to programming speciality, and it is informative to observe the designations for the stations that feature music. The number of stations is given in parentheses for each classification. They are: pop/rock (15), pop/rock oldies (5), easy listening (5), black/urban (3), country (3), nostalgia (2), jazz (2), and classical (2). In addition, there are ten Spanish language stations, three Asian language stations, and eight religious stations that include some music. The categories are not well defined, and stations under different headings probably play some of the same music.

One way to survey the current styles and hits is to listen to one or two selections broadcast on the various AM and FM radio bands. Considering the prevalence of TV, the number of radio stations is amazing. Another way to scan the current music scene is to look through the bins of a store with a large stock of compact discs and cassettes, where all of the styles and stars of popular music are certain to be abundantly represented.

27 THE MUSIC OF OTHER CULTURES

The body of music discussed in the preceding chapters, though vast and varied, is representative of a miniscule portion of the world's music. Each geographic region and ethnic group has its own distinctive music, instruments, and traditions. Ethnomusicology is a thriving branch of music scholarship devoted to the study of regional and non-Western music. Recordings and films made by ethnomusicologists have made it possible to become familiar with music from the far corners of the earth, and worldwide travel has exposed millions of people to the music of foreign lands. Some music of other cultures has meaning only for the members of the community which created it and for the scholars who examine it scientifically, but some has universal appeal. A sampling of the latter type of ethnic music is presented in this chapter. The purpose is neither scholarly nor scientific but to expand the range of listening experiences and to entertain. Since recordings of the music of other cultures are not always readily available, all of the suggested examples are included in the *Listeners Guide* recordings.

Africa

A special affinity exists between the music of black Africa and the American people. Large numbers of the population are of African descent, and African influences were decisive in the formulation of the jazz idiom. The music of the black tribes and nations of Africa is remarkably homogeneous considering the diversity of their languages, physical features, cultural traits, and life-styles. Throughout central Africa a strong predilection for percussion-type instruments sounded by striking or shaking and its corollary, a preoccupation with the rhythmic aspect of music, are evident. An acute sense of rhythm seems to be innate. In African music multiple rhythms are combined in such complex relationships that the high degree of organization in the patterns may not be perceived by the uninitiated, but the catchy polyrhythms rarely fail to evoke an emotional response. Africans, whether participating or observing, become emotionally involved in their music, and it is an inherent part of their daily lives from birth to death.

The first example of African music is from Senegal, the westernmost country in Africa. The inhabitants are principally Wolofs and Mandingos. Their dress and dietary customs reflect their Moslem religion, but their intricate drumming is distinctly West African in style. In a favorite form of entertainment, drummers and spectators gather in a circle. An individual from among the spectators moves to the center of the group where he or she dances impromptu, alone or with a partner, until exhausted or displaced by another dancer. Meanwhile, the complex rhythms of the drums continue without interruption. Drum sounds predominate in *Greetings from Podor,* but individual voices, group singing, and handclapping can also be heard.

AFRICA/SENEGAL: *Greetings from Podor*   1:30

This recording was made during a 1969 trans-Africa expedition by Hovercraft. Podor is a town of some four thousand inhabitants on the Senegal River, which marks the border between Senegal and Mauritania to the north.

From Dakar, the capial of Senegal, it is about thirteen hundred miles southeast as the crow flies to Accra, the capital of Ghana. The distance between the two countries must have been a formidable barrier to cultural exchanges in the time before modern means of transportation and communication, but the music of both countries belongs to the same West African tradition. The people and music of Ghana are better known in the United States. Probable reasons are that Ghana is more populous, Christian missionaries were active there, and many Ghanaians speak, read, and write English.

The Ashanti (also spelled Asante) people inhabit the inland plateau region of Ghana. The ceremonial drums of the Asantehene, paramount chief of the Ashanti, heard in the next example are used in pairs, one tuned to a relatively low pitch, the other to a higher pitch. One is regarded as male, the other as female. A piece of metal attached to the head of the male drum sounds when it is played. The drums are made of wood and shaped like a bowl on top of a cylinder. The drum head, which goes on the bowl end, traditionally was made from the skin of elephant ears.

AFRICA/GHANA: *Ceremonial Drums of the Asantehene*   1:02

This is another example of authentic African music recorded in the field. It is important to record and preserve the ceremonial music of the paramount hereditary chief (Asantehene) while it is still possible, because his authority and the reasons for the music's existence are diminishing since Ghana gained its independence and formed a central government.

Japan

Japanese music throughout its history has been closely associated with drama and dance. Kabuki, more spectacle than drama, incorporates traditional themes, acting, and dancing in theatrical performances designed for the tastes of the common people. It emerged as a distinct dramatic type before the beginning of the sixteenth century. It is not the most venerable Japanese dramatic genre, but since the eighteenth century it has been the most popular.

In 1954 the Azuma Kabuki Musicians toured this country and gave American audiences their initial exposure to the music and dance traditions of the Orient. The following example is from a recording of the troupe made at that time. The high-pitched, nasal voice quality which characterizes Japanese singing can be heard in the part of the narrators. The string instruments included in the ensemble are shamisens (samisens). The shamisen has a long neck, three silk strings, and a square sound box made of wood and covered top and bottom with skin. It is played with a fan-shaped ivory pick and is the popular instrument used in Japan by street singers and geishas.

4/17   JAPAN/KABUKI: *O-Matsuribayashi (Festival Music)*   1:54

In addition to the singing narrators, the ensemble includes shamisens, drum and bass drum, bell, flute, and gong. The music is a modern arrangement of older classics.

Strangely, it is not the traditional music of Japan that is taught in the Japanese public schools, but mainly Western music. This practice was instituted by Emperor Mutsuhito (reigned 1868–1912) and continues to the present time. As a result modern Japan has excellent symphony orchestras and opera companies that perform occidental music and composers who write in European styles.

Indonesia

Western music has made no inroads in Bali, one of some three thousand islands included in the Southeast Asian Republic of Indonesia. Though the island is small (93 miles long and at most 50 miles wide) and has a population under 2 million, it is justly world famous for its indigenous music and dance, which are inseparable. Music is an integral part of the Balinese way of life. No temple ceremony or village festival, and there are many, is complete without a program of dances and plays. Many villagers spend their nights practicing the intricate movements of the ritual dances and rehearsing the musical accompaniments. Except in certain plays and temple ceremonies, the music of Bali and Java, its larger neighbor to the west, is almost purely instrumental. In both countries the instrumental ensembles are known as *gamelans,* orchestras consisting principally of gongs, metallophones, drums, and cymbals (see colorplate 26).

The twenty-five-piece gamelan heard on the recorded example is reputed to be the foremost in Bali. It is from the village of Pliatan, where it plays ceremonial temple music and accompanies both traditional and modern forms of the dance. The *Kapi Radja* serves as an overture to a recorded dance program, *Dancers of Bali.*

*Ravi Shankar with
Chatur Lal and
Nodu C. Mullick.*

BALI/GAMELAN: *Overture—Kapi Radja*   2:59    4/18

Kapi Radja is a composition in modern style based on a melody from North Bali.
The musicians of that region have introduced bold innovations within the framework of native musical idioms.

India

The music of Bali is community centered. The gamelans are large ensembles that produce a composite sound, and there are no individual star performers. In contrast, the music of India is performed exclusively by small
groups and individuals who have dedicated their lives to perfecting their
art. The procedures of Indian music, which have their foundation in religion and philosophy, are fantastically complicated. To master them requires intense and prolonged mental and physical discipline. The nature of
the complexity lies in the requirement that the performers must create
seemingly free and spontaneous improvisations that conform strictly to interrelated melodic, rhythmic, and structural patterns.

Ravi Shankar, the *sitar* player on the recorded example, is the greatest
and most renowned of India's musicians. The sitar is a plucked string instrument with a long neck and six tone-producing strings. The sound is
resonated by nineteen sympathetic strings and two seasoned gourds, one
at the base of the instrument and the other at the upper end of the neck.
Twenty frets on the neck are moved to adjust the tuning, which varies from
piece to piece. Smaller (microtonal) pitch deviations are made by pulling
the strings sideways on the fingerboard. The sitar is accompanied by *tabla*

and *tamboura*. The tabla is a pair of hand drums tuned to the main tones of the pitch pattern upon which the improvised melody is based. The tamboura is another plucked string instrument with four or five strings, each tuned to a tone of the melodic pitch pattern, which are always played open, providing a continuous drone accompaniment.

4/19 · **INDIA/RAVI SHANKAR:** *Thumri* · 5:26

Thumri denotes a type of Indian music which is less orthodox in style than most of the music played by Ravi Shankar. In Thumri style the inclusion of folk themes and changing from one underlying pitch pattern to another are permissible. The melodies are lyrical but highly ornamented. The mood is light and capricious.

Bulgaria

The ancient Bulgars began their westward migration from the Far East and by the eighth century had occupied the territory at the junction between East and West which is now Bulgaria. Traces of oriental influence which some detect in Bulgarian music can be ascribed to the Eastern origin of the people or to the Turkish occupation of the country which began in the fourteenth century and lasted until 1878. It was during the period of subjugation and comparative isolation that the music traditions, which thrive to the present time, developed among the common people. Bulgarian folk music is functional. There are songs and dances for every occasion—Sundays, feast days, fairs, weddings, work, and worship.

It can be generalized that Bulgarian tunes have a limited range and that the songs are mostly homophonic, but these features are not distinguishing. The striking feature of Bulgarian music is its rhythm. A high percentage of the meters in Bulgarian music are asymmetric (see page 67), many involving unequal divisions of seven-beat measures. Similar metric patterns occur in the folk music of Rumania, Greece, Yugoslavia, Albania, and Turkey. One view is that the meters which divide $3 + 2 + 2$ and $2 + 2 + 3$ are triple meters that have the first or third beat elongated. Curiously, the pattern with an elongated second beat ($2 + 3 + 2$) is unknown in the folk music of Eastern and Southern Europe. The following round-and-chain dance is a brilliant example of $2 + 2 + 3$ Bulgarian rhythm.

4/20 · **BULGARIA:** *Tsone Mile Chedo/Eleno Mome* · 2:02

The performers on the recording are peasant virtuosos recruited from various parts of Bulgaria by the State Folk Dance Ensemble. They are heard playing, in addition to a drum, four pairs of native instruments: two gaidas—medium-sized bagpipes with one drone and a chanter with eight holes; two gudulkas—string instruments played in an upright position with a primitive bow; two tamburas—plucked string instruments with a long, fretted neck (compare the tamboura of India); and two kavals—shepherd pipes about 30 inches long with seven holes and no mouthpiece. As is customary, this dance piece has two distinct tunes, the second in this instance introduced by the kavals near midpoint in the performance.

Spain

The essence of Spanish music is captured in *flamenco,* the songs and dances of the Andalusian Gypsies. Flamenco is not a single, well-defined style, but a group of related styles that belong to a common tradition. Arabic, Moorish, Byzantine, and Jewish influences are detected in flamenco, but it is invariably associated with the Gypsies of southern Spain.

In an audio recording of flamenco the movements of the dancers must be imagined, but the sounds of the *zapateados* (foot stamping), castanets, and clapping can be clearly heard. The emotional intensity of the singing matches the rhythmic intensity of the guitar playing. Flamenco encompasses all modes of playing the guitar, but its trademark is the rapid, rhythmic strumming of full-bodied chords. The spirit of flamenco in its natural setting, the cantinas of the region, and its varied elements are vividly displayed in *Sevillanas.*

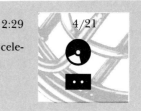

SPAIN/FLAMENCO: *Sevillanas*   2:29   4/21

Sevillanas is a popular flamenco song and dance performed at the feasts and celebrations of Seville.

Latin America

The Spanish conquest engulfed but did not obliterate the rich cultures of pre-Columbian Latin America. The varied surviving and assimilated influences make valid generalizations impossible regarding the music of the vast area and ethnically diverse populations. For an isolated example, one from Mexico, the most populous nation of the region and the one in closest proximity, seems a logical choice.

In western Mexico with the state of Jalisco at its center, the traditional ensembles are *mariachis.* They have spread throughout the country and now typify Mexican music on both sides of our common border. The mariachi instrumentation has a nucleus of guitars (one bass) to which are added violins and/or trumpets, often in pairs to play the melodic line in thirds, and sometimes marimbas and other percussion instruments. The Jose Ortega Mariachi Ensemble heard on the recording includes all of the above, but the total ensemble is not always utilized. The instrumentalists frequently double as vocalists, singing solos and harmony parts, but the following selection is an instrumental dance.

LATIN AMERICA/MARIACHI: *Jarabe Mexicano*   3:14   4/22
(Mexican Hat Dance)

The *jarabe* is a traditional Mexican courting dance in which a couple performs intricate steps around the brim of a sombrero. The man's elegant costume features the tight pants of a charro (cowboy); the woman's a white blouse and a long, full skirt. The music characteristically has multiple parts in contrasting meters and tempos, as in this example. The percussive sounds produced by the feet of the dancers are reminiscent of the foot stamping heard in the Spanish flamenco recording.

West Indies

Folk music with the potential for mass appeal is apt to be cultivated, refined, commercialized, and transported to the concert stage, recording studio, and television screen. This phenomenon was observed in the evolution of jazz and country music. The following example from the West Indies reverses the process and shows a typical American popular song converted to a folk idiom. The popular song *Fire Down Below* (not to be confused with the chantey of the same name) was the title song of a 1957 Columbia motion picture starring Rita Hayworth, Jack Lemmon, and Robert Mitchum. The song was created especially for the motion picture by Ned Washington and Lester Lee and was released independently on two major record labels, but the Native Steel Drum Band of the West Indies treats it like an anonymous folk tune.

Steel drums are true folk instruments of recent origin. In the late 1930s "Spree" Simon discovered that different pitches could be produced by striking the head of an oil barrel in different places, and the concept of the steel drum was born. Steel drums are made by hand out of discarded oil barrels of various sizes which became plentiful in and around Trinidad, a former West Indies British colony, during World War II. Designs and shapes are hammered into the heads of the barrels so that each area produces a definite pitch when it is struck. The steel drums are played with large mallets producing a powerful dynamic sound. A steel drum band consists of about eighteen drums plus an assortment of untuned percussion instruments such as maracas, claves, and bells.

4/23   **WEST INDIES/STEEL DRUM BAND:** *Fire Down Below*   3:27

This performance by the Native Steel Drum Band was recorded on location in the West Indies by a recording crew for Everest Records. The performers, who are black, possess the same rhythmic drive and predilection for percussion instruments as their African ancestors.

In Conclusion

This brief and highly selective survey of the music of other cultures provides only a glimpse into the treasury of the world's music. It does, however, confirm the fact that not just Western art music but all of the modes of human expression using rhythm and pitch—ethnic, folk, popular, jazz, modern, and ultramodern music included—are essential ingredients in the tonal universe. Each makes its own special contribution to the glorious art of music.

APPENDIX: MUSIC EXAMPLES

Examples in chronological order.

SEIKILOS: *Epitaph*   91, 221*

Ho - son zes phai - nou, me - den ho - lo - os sy ly - pou - ou.

Pros o - li - gon e - es - ti to ze - en, to te - los ho chro - nos a - pai - tei - ei.

GREGORIAN CHANT: *Mass IV—Kyrie*   84, 91, 223*

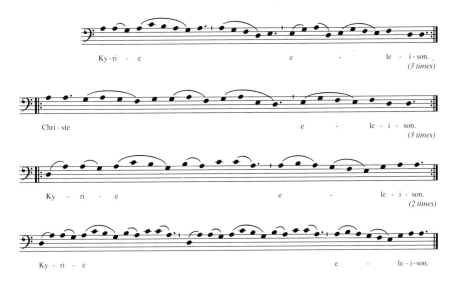

Ky - ri - e   e - le - i - son.
                              (3 times)

Chri - ste   e - le - i - son.
                              (3 times)

Ky - ri - e   e - le - i - son.
                              (2 times)

Ky - ri - e   e - le - i - son.

*Page(s) of the text where the example is cited.

76, 98, 142, 168   PURCELL: *Dido and Aeneas—When I am laid in earth*

Ground

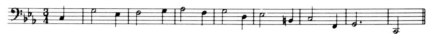

143   BACH: *Passacaglia and Fugue*

Theme

157, 234   VIVALDI: *Violin Concerto in A minor—III*

Ritornello theme

Presto

BACH: *Two-Part Invention no. 3*

41, 66, 108   BACH: *French Suite no. 4—VI*

*Identifying letters and numbers above the themes correspond with those in the listening guides for the examples given in Part Two of the text.

19, 122   BACH: *Partita no. 3 for Violin—III*

96, 136   BACH: *Well-Tempered Clavier vol. 1, no. 16*

210   BACH: *Wie schön leuchtet der Morgenstern*

HANDEL: *Messiah—He was despised*   120

BACH: *Schübler Chorale Prelude no. 1*   40, 42, 155

BACH: *Musical Offering*   134

71, 118, 243

MOZART: *Symphony no. 35—III*

126

BEETHOVEN: *Piano Sonata no. 2—IV*

HAYDN: *String Quartet, "Emperor"—II* 50, 139

BEETHOVEN: *Piano Sonata no. 8—I* 80, 128

119

BEETHOVEN: *Violin Sonata no. 5—III*

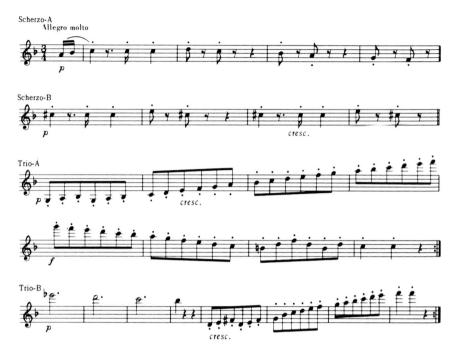

139

BEETHOVEN: *Piano Sonata no. 12—I*

BEETHOVEN: *Symphony no. 5—I*   103

SCHUBERT: *Who Is Sylvia*   17, 74, 194

BERLIOZ: *Symphonie Fantastique—I*   164

114

SCHUMANN: *Scenes from Childhood no. 1*

111

SCHUMANN: *Scenes from Childhood no. 7*

47, 108, 261

CHOPIN: *Mazurka no. 24*

20, 65, 141

PAGANINI: *Caprice no. 24*

17, 98, 109

MENDELSSOHN: *Elijah, no. 4*

MENDELSSOHN: *Elijah, no. 15*   98

13, 60, 115, 153   WAGNER: *Lohengrin–Prelude to Act III*

WAGNER: *Die Meistersinger—Prelude*

BRAHMS: *Variations on a Theme of Haydn*

162

MUSSORGSKY: *Pictures at an Exhibition*

124, 253

BRAHMS: *Symphony no. 2—III*

63, 112, 148

TCHAIKOVSKY: *Nutcracker Suite—Russian Dance*

DVOŘÁK: *Symphony no. 9 (5)—I*   147

Motto theme

SOUSA: *Hands Across the Sea*   54, 62, 116

HINDEMITH: *Mathis der Maler—II*   60, 113, 275

60   BARBER: *Symphony no. 1*

300   ZWILICH: *Concerto Grosso* "after Handel"

CREDITS

PHOTOGRAPHS

Chapter 3

Figures 3.1, 3.2: Courtesy of Scherl & Roth, Inc. Elkhart, IN; **3.3:** Courtesy of F. E. Olds & Sons, Elkhart, IN; **3.5:** Courtesy of G. Leblanc Corporation, Kenosha, WI; **3.8:** Courtesy of Yamaha International Corporation; **3.9:** Conn French horn photo courtesy of United Musical Instruments U.S.A., Inc.; **3.10:** Courtesy of G. Leblanc Corporation, Elkhart, IN; **3.11:** Conn Trombone and Bass Trombone photo courtesy of United Musical Instruments U.S.A., Inc.; **3.12:** Courtesy of Selmer Company, L. P., Elkhart, IN; **3.13:** Courtesy of Lyon & Healy Harps, Chicago, IL; **3.14:** Courtesy of Gibson Guitar Corp., Nashville, TN; **3.15:** © The Bettmann Archive; **3.16a,b:** Courtesy of Mark of the Unicorn, Inc., Cambridge, MA; **3.17:** Courtesy of New England Digital Corporation, Lebanon, NH; **p. 45:** © The Bettmann Archive.

Chapter 4

Figure 4.1: Eastman School Of Music, Rochester, NY © Evan Wilcox, Photographer; **p. 61:** © 1992 Chris Lee. All rights reserved.

Chapter 5

Page 64: Artex Prints, Westport, CT; **p. 89:** Artex Prints, Westport, CT.

Chapter 11

Page 147: Historical Pictures Stock Montage, Chicago, IL.

Chapter 14

Page 170: Print & Picture Department, Free Library of Philadelphia; **p. 171:** Artex Prints, Westport, CT; **14.1:** Historical Pictures Stock Montage, Chicago, IL; **p. 173:** Print & Picture Department, Free Library of Philadelphia; **14.2:** Courtesy of Opera News; **p. 176:** Library Of Congress; **p. 179:** © The Bettmann Archive; **p. 181:** © AP/Wide World Photos; **p. 182:** © AP/Wide World Photos.

Chapter 15

Page 186: Historical Pictures Stock Montage, Chicago, IL.

Chapter 18

Figures 18.1, 18.2: From The Music of the Sumerians, Babylonians and Assyrians by Francis W. Galpin. Used by permission of Cambridge University Press.; **18.3:** From Sounds from Silence by Kilmer, Crocker and Brown. Used by permission of Bit Enki Publications, Berkeley, California; **pp. 227, 228:** Brown Brothers Stock Photos.

Chapter 19

Page 232: © The Bettmann Archive; **p. 233:** Print & Picture Department, Free Library of Philadelphia; **p. 234:** Print & Picture Department, Free Library of Philadelphia; **p. 236:** Print & Picture Department, Free Library of Philadelphia.

Chapter 20

Pages 240, 241, 243: Print & Picture Department, Free Library of Philadelphia.

Chapter 21

Pages 247, 248, 249, 250, 251: Print & Picture Department, Free Library of Philadelphia; **p. 252:** Brown Brothers Stock Photos; **pp. 253, 254, 255:** Print & Picture Department, Free Library of Philadelphia; **p. 256:** Brown Brothers Stock Photos.

Chapter 22

Page 262: Historical Pictures Stock Montage, Chicago, IL; **p. 263:** Print & Picture Department, Free Library of Philadelphia.

Chapter 23

Page 271: Historical Pictures Stock Montage, Chicago, IL; **p. 272:** Historical Pictures Stock Montage, Chicago, IL; **p. 273:** © The Bettmann Archive; **p. 273:** © AP/Wide World Photos; **p. 274:** Historical Pictures Stock Montage, Chicago, IL; **p. 275:** Print & Picture Department, Free Library of Philadelphia; **p. 276:** Historical Pictures Stock Montage, Chicago, IL; **p. 278:** © The Bettmann Archive.

Chapter 24

Page 285: © AP/Wide World Photos; **pp. 285, 286, 289:** Historical Pictures Stock Montage, Chicago, IL; **p. 291:** Indiana University School Of Music; **p. 292:** Historical Pictures Stock Montage, Chicago, IL; **p. 294:** BMI Archives, Broadcast Music, Inc.; **24.1:** Photo courtesy of Fairlight ESP Pty Ltd., Sydney, Australia.

Chapter 25

Pages 303, 304: Frank Driggs Collection; **p. 305:** © UPI/ Bettmann Newsphotos; **p. 306:** Frank Driggs Collection; **p. 307:** © Bob Coyle; **pp. 308, 311:** Frank Driggs Collection; **p. 313:** © Dan Golden/Shooting Star; **p. 313:** © Yoram Kahana/ Shooting Star.

Chapter 26

Page 318: © AP/Wide World Photos.

Chapter 27

Page 325: © Silverstone/ Magnum Photos, Inc.

COLOR PLATES

1: Courtesy of the French Government Tourist Office; **2, 3, 4, 5:** Scala/Art Resource, New York; **6A–C:** (top left) Scala/Art Resource, New York; (top right) Giraudon/Art Resource, New York; (bottom) Scala/Art Resource, New York; **7:** Widener Collection, © 1992, National Gallery of Art, Washington, 1597/1599, oil on canvas, 1.935 × 1.030 (76 1/8″ × 40 1/2″); **8:** Scala/Art Resource, New York; **9:** Scala/Art Resource, New York; **10:** The Metopolitan Museum of Art, Munsey Fund, 1934; **11:** The Metropolitan Museum of Art, Wolfe Fund, 1931. Catharine Lorillard Wolfe Collection; **12:** Scala/Art Resource, New York; **13:** Chester Dale Fund, © 1992, National Gallery of Art, Washington, oil on linen, .925 × .746 (36 3/8″ × 29 3/8″); **14:** Gift of the W. L. & May T. Mellon Foundation, © 1992, National Gallery of Art, Washington, canvas, .615 × .970 (24 1/8″ × 38 1/8″); **15:** Chester Dale Collection, © 1992, National Gallery of Art Washington, oil on linen, .734 × 1.005 (28 7/8″ × 39 5/8″); **16:** Chester Dale Collection, © 1992, National Gallery of Art Washington, oil on canvas, 1.511 × 1.802 (59 1/2″ × 71″); **17:** Chester Dale Collection, © 1992, National Gallery of Art Washington, wood, 1.054 x .690 (41 1/2″ × 27 1/8″); **18:** 1914. Oil on canvas, 64 × 36 1/4″. Collection, The Museum of Modern Art, New York, Mrs. Simon Guggenheim Fund; **19:** Friends of American Art Collection, 1930.934, ©1992 The Art Institute of Chicago. All Rights Reserved; **20:** 1931. Oil on canvas, 45 × 55″. Collection, The Museum of Modern Art, New York. Given anonymously; **21:** Gift of Georgia O'Keeffe, 1947.712, © 1992, The Art Institute of Chicago. All Rights Reserved; **22:** 1964. Oil on corrugated aluminum, in eleven parts, 8′10″ × 13′2 1/4″. Collection, The Museum of Modern Art, New York. Gift of Mr. & Mrs. George M. Jaffin.; **23:** Virginia O. Magada; **24:** Estate of Romare Bearden, courtesy of ACA Galleries, New York, New York; **25:** Courtesy of New England Digital Corporation, Lebanon, NH; **26:** © George Holton/Photo Researchers, Inc.

LINE ART

A-R Editions, Inc.: p. 72, p. 283, p. 284, p. 329, p. 338, p. 340, p. 344.

GLOSSARY AND INDEX OF TERMS

Bourrée a dance of French origin frequently included in suites.

Bow 18

Bow form 130

Brass instruments 28

Break 304

Bridge 18, 112

Brillante brilliant.

Brio spirit.

Buffo comic.

BWV, Bach-Werke-Verzeichnis (Catalog of Bach Works) source of the identifying numbers for Bach works.

Cadence a closing effect associated with the ends of phrases. 103

Cadenza an improvisatory passage typically found in concertos. 130

Camerata, Florentine 167

Canon 132

Cantabile singing style.

Cantata 127, 209

Cantus planus 223

Capriccioso capricious.

Caprice, capriccio an instrumental composition in a free or whimsical style.

Cassation 150

Castanets a palm-size percussion instrument in the shape of a scallop shell played by flamenco dancers.

CD compact disc.

Celesta 40

Cello 18, 20, 21

Cembalo harpsichord.

Chaconne 142

Chamber music 48

Chance music 282

Chant monophonic, liturgical music.

Chimes 33

Choir a group that sings sacred music; a section of related instruments. 52

Choral pertaining to a chorus or choir.

Chorale a Protestant congregational hymn.

Chorale prelude a type of organ composition based on a chorale. 154

Chord three or more tones sounding together.

Chords 79
    eleventh 81
    ninth 81
    seventh 80
    thirteenth 81
    triad 79

Choreography the composition and arrangement of dance movements, as for a ballet.

Chorus a body of singers; in vocal music the unchanging words and music that alternate with the verses.

Chromatic denoting a note or chord foreign to the tonality.

Chromatic scale 83

Church (ecclesiastical) modes 83

Clarinet 25

Classicism 239

Clavecin harpsichord.

Claves a pair of cylindrical hardwood sticks; Latin-American percussion instruments.

Clavier keyboard.

Clef a sign indicating the pitch of the notes on a staff.

Clicktrack 189

Coda a concluding section added to a musical form. 113

Codetta a small coda added to a principal part within a form. 113

Coloratura colorful, florid; applied to highly ornamented passages in vocal music and to the voices that sing them.

Combo a small jazz ensemble.

Compound binary form 115

Compound ternary form 117

Computer music electronic music produced by digitally controlled synthesizers.

Con with.

Concertino a small concerto; the solo group in a concerto grosso.

Concertmaster 59

Concerto a composition for a solo instrument with orchestra.

Concerto grosso 157

Conductor's beat 69

Continuo the figured bass part or its realization. 231

Contrabass 18, 21, 22

Contrabassoon 28

Contralto alto voice.

Contrapuntal employing counterpoint; polyphonic.

Cornet 29

Countermelody a secondary melody associated with a principal melody.

Counterpoint the art of combining melodies and the melodies thus combined. 94, 269

Countersubject a thematic counterpoint, especially to the subject of a fugue. 136

Country music 318

Courante 147

Credo a part of the Mass. 203

Crescendo   gradually louder.

Crossover   311

Cyclic form   146

Cymbals   33

Da capo (D.C.)   repeat from the beginning.   119

Da capo aria form   119

Damper   a mechanism that stops the vibration of a sound source, such as a piano string.

Dance
  modern   185
  theatrical   187

Dance band   56

DAT   digital audio tape.

DDD   digitally recorded, edited, and mastered.

Decay   10

Decibel   the smallest unit of perceived loudness.   8

Deciso   with decision.

Decrescendo   gradually softer.

Development   a section, particularly in sonata form, in which the themes are worked out.   127

Di   of.

Dies irae   day of wrath; a section of the Requiem Mass and the plainsong melody associated with it.

Digital synthesizer   a computer controlled synthesizer.

Diminuendo   gradually softer.

Diminution   decreased rhythmic values, usually halved.

Disco   a style of pop music especially appropriate for dancing.

Divertimento   a multimovement instrumental form.   150

Dixieland   305

Dominant   the fifth degree of the scale and the chord and key associated with it.

Double bass   22

Doux   sweet.

Downbeat   69

Drums   33
  bass   33
  side   33
  snare   33
  tenor   33

Duet, duo   a composition for, or a group of, two performers.   49

Duration   9

Dynamics   11, 87

E, ed   and.

Eastman Wind Ensemble   55

Electronic instruments   42, 293

Electronic music   293

Elegy   a composition in the mood of a lament.

Embouchure   the formation of the lips and tongue in relation to the mouthpiece of a wind instrument.   23

Encore   a composition played or sung in response to applause at the end of a concert.

Energico   energetic.

English horn   27

Ensemble   a small group of performers; the art of playing together.

Episode   a passage between themes or statements of the subject, especially in a fugue.   136, 156

Eroica   heroic.

Espagnol(e)   Spanish.

Espressivo   expressively.

Ethnomusicology   the study of regional and non-Western music.   322

Etude   a study piece.

Euphonium   31

Exposition   the section of a composition in which the themes are stated.   127
  double   130

Expressionism   271

Expressive/sensitive style   239

Fairlight CMI   a computer musical instrument.   297

Fandango   a Spanish dance, possibly of South American origin.

Fantasia   155

Feminism   299

Figured bass   a bass line with number and symbol notation for chords.   231

Finale   a final movement or section.

Fine   end.   119

Flageolet   a simple wind instrument of the flute family.

Flamenco   327

Flute   23, 24

FM (frequency modulation)   a method of generating sound digitally; also a form of radio transmission.

Folk music   315

Follower   132

Foreign keys   keys with fewer than five tones in common.   86

Formalized music   290

Forte   loud.

Fortissimo   very loud.

Free part form   114

French horn   29, 30

Frequency the number of sound-producing vibrations per second.

Frets thin strips of material fixed across the fingerboard of certain string instruments where the strings are stopped.

Fugato a fugal passage in a more extended form. 136

Fugue 95, 135

Funèbre funereal.

Fuoco fire.

Fusion 311

Gallant style 239

Gamelan 324

Gavotte a dance of French origin frequently included in suites.

Gebrauchsmusik music for practical use.

Genre a general classification for artistic works that have features in common.

Gigue 148

Giocoso playful.

Giojoso joyful.

Giusto just, strict, proper.

Glissando sliding between tones sounding the intervening pitches.

Glockenspiel 33

Gloria a part of the Mass. 203

Gong a broad, slightly convex metal disc; an oriental percussion instrument.

Grand Ole Opry 318

Grave slow, solemn.

Grazia, grazioso grace, graceful.

Greek music 221

Gregorian chant the monophonic liturgical music of the Roman Catholic Church. 91, 223

Ground, ground bass a bass theme which is repeated continuously. 142

Guitar 37

Habanera a dance of Cuban origin popular in Spain.

Half step a minor second; a semitone.

Happening 298

Harmony the sounding together of different tones, especially in chord progressions. 77, 269

Harp 36

Harpsichord 40, 41

Hausmusik music to be played at home.

Heterophonic texture, heterophony 90, 92

Homophonic texture, homophony 90, 97, 231

Horn, French 29, 30

Hydraulis 221, 222

Hz, hertz cycles per second.

Imitation repetition in another part after a short time lapse. 94

Impresario an agent, manager, or producer.

Impressionism 262

Impromptu a casual character piece, usually for piano. 158

Improvisation 288

Incidental music 187

Indeterminacy 285

Instrumentation the writing of music for particular instruments or the instruments written for.

Intensity the physical characteristic of sound that produces loudness.

Intermezzo a digression interposed between parts of a more profound work.

Interval the difference in pitch between two tones.

Intervals 77

Introduction a passage or section preceding the main body of a form. 115

Invention a term used by Bach for two-part contrapuntal compositions.

Inversion contrary motion, ascending intervals becoming equivalent descending intervals and vice versa, or the reversal of the above-below relationship between two melodic lines.

Isorhythm a principle of organization involving repetitions of a rhythmic pattern. 226

Jam session a spontaneous jazz performance.

Jazz 301

Jazz ensemble 309

Jazz styles 302
   bebop, bop 308
   boogie-woogie 306
   cool 309
   crossover 311
   Dixieland 305
   free 309
   funky 309
   fusion 311
   hot 305
   jazz/rock 309
   Kansas City 306
   modern 309
   neophonic 308
   progressive 308
   sweet 305

K., Köchel catalog   source of the identifying numbers for Mozart works.

Key   the tonal center of a work or passage, identified by a letter name.   82

Keynote   the central note of the key; the first degree of the scale in tonal music; the tonic note.

Konzertstück   concert piece.

Kyrie   a part of the Mass.   203

Larghetto   not quite as slow as largo.

Largo   broad, large; a very slow tempo.

Lent, lento   slow.

Libretto   the story and words of a dramatic musical work.

Lied   song.

Lieder   songs; plural of lied. 47

Linear   pertaining to lines, emphasizing the horizontal (contrapuntal) aspect of music as opposed to the vertical (harmonic).

Lyre, lyra   an ancient instrument with plucked strings attached to a crossbar between two curved arms.   221

Lyric   songlike, expressing intimate rather than epic or heroic ideas.

M.M., Maelzel metronome   69

Ma   but.

Maestoso   majestically.

Magnificat   canticle of the Virgin Mary.   213

Major   a term denoting a quality of interval, scale, chord, key, tonality, or mode.

Manual   one of the keyboards of an organ or harpsichord.

Maraca   a Latin-American percussion instrument made of a gourd or gourdlike shell containing seeds or pebbles.

Marcato   marked.

Marcia, marciale   march, marchlike.

Mass   the solemn rite of the Roman Catholic Church commemorating the sacrifice of Christ.   203

Mazurka   a dance of Polish origin in triple time (meter).

Measure   a metric unit in music consisting of a specific number of beats and pattern of accents. 63, 65

Mediant   the third degree of the scale and the chord and key associated with it; the relative major of a minor key.

Medley   a hodgepodge of loosely connected tunes.

Menuet, menuett, menuetto, minuetto   minuet.

Meter   the number and pattern of beats in a measure of music. 62

Meter signature   the numerical representation of the meter.   68

Metronome   a device used to establish tempos in music.   69

Mezzo forte   moderately loud.

Mezzo piano   moderately soft.

Mezzo-soprano   the female voice range between soprano and alto.   14, 15

Microtones   intervals smaller than a semitone.   292

MIDI (musical instrument digital interface)   43, 296

Mikrokosmos   microcosm (Bartók).

Minor   a term denoting a quality of interval, scale, chord, key, tonality, or mode.

Minuet   a French dance of rustic origin but courtly style in a moderately fast triple meter.

Miserere   Vulgate Psalm 50. 242

Mode   pertaining to major or minor or to one of the scale patterns of early church music. 82

Moderato, modéré   moderate.

Modulation   change of key. 86

Molto   very, much.

Monophonic texture, monophony   music consisting of a single unaccompanied line. 90

Time   meter.

Time signature   the numerical representation of the meter.   68

Timpani   32

Tin Pan Alley   originally the area on West 28th Street in New York City where popular music publishers were concentrated and, by extension, the source of popular music in general.

Toccata   a brilliant, freely constructed composition.   158

Tonality   82, 270

Tone color   8, 87

Tone painting   161

Tone poem   163

Tone quality   8

Tone row   85

Tonic   the first degree of the scale and the chord and key associated with it; the keynote.

Top 40   the forty most popular songs as established by various surveys.

Tosto   nearly.

Total organization   282

Total theater   298

Transition   a connecting passage between structural elements of a musical form. 112

Transpose   to change to another pitch level.

Traps   the percussion instruments, collectively, used in jazz and popular music.

Très   very.

Triads   79

Triangle   33

Trio   a composition for, or a group of, three performers; the contrasting section in marches, minuets, and scherzos.   49, 115, 116, 117

Trombone   31, 32
    bass   31, 32

Troubadours   224

Trouvères   225

Trumpet   28, 29

Tuba   30, 31

Tuba mirum   a section of the Dies irae.

Tubular bells   33

Tune   (noun) a melody; (verb) to adjust the pitch.

Tutti   all; the full ensemble.

Twelve-tone system   a technique of composition based on a series of twelve different tones.   85, 271

Two-part form   107

Un   a, an.

Unison   at the same pitch.

Upbeat   69

Valse   waltz.

Variation form   138
    continuous   141
    sectional   138

Variazioni   variations.

Verse(s)   in vocal music the words and music preceding or alternating with the chorus.

Vibraphone, vibraharp, vibes   33

Vibrato   slight, rapid fluctuation in pitch or intensity used to augment the emotional quality of sustained tones.

Vielle   224

Vif   lively.

Viola   19, 20

Violin   19

Violoncello (cello)   18, 20, 21

Virtuoso   a performer who excels in technical ability.   19

Vivace   lively, quick.

Voices   14

Vorspiel   prelude.   153

Waltz   a perennially popular dance in triple meter that originated about 1800.

Whole step   a major second.

Whole tone scale   84

Wind ensemble   54

Wind instruments   22, 24

Woodwind instruments   23

Xylophone   33

Zapateados   327

INDEX OF COMPOSERS, PERFORMERS, AND WORKS